AF267428

The
Returning
Backslider

The Returning Backslider

Richard Sibbes

Sovereign Grace Publishers, Inc.
P.O. Box 4998
Lafayette, IN 47903

*Printed In the United States of America
By Lightning Source, Inc.*

PREFACE

Beloved reader, lest thou art twice dead, plucked up by the roots, there is joy divine ahead of you in these pages. Not for nought was Richard Sibbes called the "Sweet Dropper of England," for he, like the Sweet Singer of Israel, lets fall heavenly dew from his spiritual pen unto the sweet edification of his hearers. Thomas Manton wrote of him, "sweet and heavenly distillations usually dropping from him with such a native elegance as is not easily to be imitated."

In this book, as the title has suggested to you, he deals with the blessed gift of repentance sent unto backsliders. Beware lest you divorce yourself wholly from such company at the outset, lest you proceed as if you were a disinterested observer peering into the closets of others. For, dear friend, if you think yourself not to be intended among those who either have lately fallen back from the way of holiness, or else are apt to do so at any given moment, then surely you are dodging the plain import of this fourteenth chapter of Hosea, as well as a major portion of the writings of the prophets.

Neither count yourself so far enveloped in personal holiness as to be beyond the need for repentance. But you may say, I am a child of God, I need no longer listen to the message, "Turn! or burn!" It is true that if you are a new man in Christ Jesus you cannot have reverted to being an old man again. The fact that you shall not ever revert does not mean that you never need convert, however. For we read of the Lord saying to Peter, "When thou art converted" etc. Yea, and what a season of repentance was heralded for Peter at that time!

The incomparable Thomas Goodwin well states that this repentance which is so freely counted to be our daily need, as well as an occasional road to recovery from more serious seasons of backsliding, is described in Scripture in terms as if it were a new conversion. He instances in the case of David, Psalm 51, as he repents of his shocking fall. "Recovery after great falls has in it all the transactions and workings that is in a new conversion, and is indeed the same work acted over anew in a man's spirit..."

"Here," he continues, "is the same humiliation or conviction of sin...together with a renewed sight and view of the original corruption..." etc. "Here is a fresh and vehement going out, and longing for washings by Christ's blood, 'Wash me throughly from mine iniquity, and cleanse me from my sin.' and 'Purge me with hyssop, and I shall be clean; wash me, and I shall be whiter than snow' etc...

"For sanctification and holiness (too). He having seen the

bottom corruption of his nature, verse 6, he seeks for a sanctification of his nature of the right kind; even the contrary
frame of heart to his natural uncleanness, 'Create in me a
clean heart,'....And so gives up his heart in acknowledgment of
his utter and total dependence upon God's grace and power to
work it: 'Create in me, O God.' Do thou it, for I am no more
able to work it than to create a world..."
    'Except ye be converted,' says Christ unto His disciples
that were already converted, 'ye cannot enter into the kingdom
of God.' And these kind of workings you have now heard of in
David's heart, which may both help us to judge of ourselves
whether we have been converted, or rightly recovered after our
relapses....For David was a grown Christian before, and yet
this second work upon him (is) greater than his first."

REPENTANCE ALWAYS PRECEDES FAITH AND IS INSEPARABLE FROM IT
    Many who shuck off the call for repentance apparently
assume that they are wearing faith in Christ like a glove all
the while. Such is not the import of Scripture. For there we
see repentance and faith as inseparable as the head and tail of
a penny: they are not graces welded together, but smelted together in the Divine mold, and there is no acting of faith in
any true sense without the concomitant turning away from sin
and unbelief, which IS repentance. So much the more we ought
to court this grace without which we may not have that faith
by which we see the glories of God so clearly as to transform
and transport us into that "joy unspeakable, full of glory."
    In this marvelous book before you, Richard Sibbes will
lead you by the hand through the manifold considerations which
will mayhap be needed to convince you of the need for personal
repentance. When you have gone from prayer to praise to
reformation with him, then will you begin to think straight
regarding your present state. It is remarkable how little we,
whose minds have been transformed by daily renewing, are able
to think straight. It calls to mind a searching address by
that venerable old patriarch of France, Robert Dubarry, wherein he said a few things about straight thinking:
    "this world," said he, "resembles a huge asylum for
half-insane people, no one ever escaping that degrading mis-
fortune, though everyone is boasting that he thinks straight,
whilst proudly and stubbornly sticking to his evident folly....
In the course of such general deception, real facts have become a matter of unconcern, practically everything being taken
for granted or being systematically denied....To that wrong use
of truth, of facts, of words, and of logic, we add, for a complete picture, the harboring of wrong ideas, and a mule-like
refusal to change, evidence being ever repulsed with great

loss....Is not man's intellect hopelessly ensnared?....Was not
Renan right when he said that what gave him the truest notion
of infinitude was human stupidity? A stupidity which prevents
him "seeing the kingdom of heaven": a stupidity which has made
of "the wisdom which God ordained before the world unto our
glory, a mystery which none of the princes of this world knew,
for had they known it, they would not have crucified the Lord
of glory"—A stupidity which causes "the natural man to refuse to receive the things of the Spirit of God; for they are
foolishness unto him."

      The clear-thinking doctor went on to remind his hearers
that though they were the vessels of honor upon whom God had
bestowed His Spirit, they were still but men; and as men, they
were blind, mad, and dead to the things of God. "There is," he
said, "no possible exception, not even among us, dear friends."

      So we must say unto you, dearly beloved reader, there is
no exception to the need for repentance, not even among us. We
who desire the sincere milk of the word may also be found often
with ungodly and worldly lusts which war against our souls. If
this book is not a help to you in this soul-conflict, then do
we miss our guess. Not only does the saintly Sibbes give you
instructions as to your state, whether backslidden or no; as to
what to do if you are a backslider; but also how to avoid backsliding (see page 148). Is that not worth something? Does it
not fit your condition?

      For you may be wedged miserably between the horns of
two dilemmas; like the lady Dubarry mentioned, who came as a
customer into the shoe store, saying, "I want shoes in which I
shall feel quite at ease, though not too bulky in their appearance." "I see what you are looking for, Madam," replied the
alert sales girl: "Shoes large inside, and small outside. I'm
so sorry, but we do not carry that line here."

      So do we not carry the line here, nor can we promise it
of Richard Sibbes either, which will be comfortable for you in
all cases, and which will at the same time allow you to preen
your feathers among your fellow-saints. There is heart-work
to be done, and that is the merchandise which we come to sell
you this good day. REPENTANCE! R E P E N T A N C E! WHO WILL
BUY THIS GOOD BOOK ON REPENTANCE? Will you Sir? May God bless
you with that holy grace!

By His Unspeakable Mercy,

Jay Green, Publisher

CONTENTS

THE RETURNING BACKSLIDER

SERMON I.

*O Israel, return unto the Lord thy God; for thou hast fallen by thine iniquity.
Take with you words, and turn to the Lord; say unto him, Take away all iniquity, &c.*—Hos. XIV. 1, 2.

The whole frame of godliness is a mystery, Col. i. 26. The apostle called
it 'a great mystery,' comprehending all under these particulars: 'God was
manifested in the flesh, justified in the Spirit, seen of angels, preached unto
the Gentiles, believed on in the world, received up into glory,' 1 Tim. iii.
16. Amongst which mysteries, this may well be the 'mystery of mysteries.'
'God was manifest in the flesh,' which includeth also another mystery,
the graciousness and abundant tender mercy of God towards miserable,
wretched, and sinful creatures; even in the height of their rebellion,
appointing such a remedy to heal them. Which is the subject of this
chapter, and last part of this prophecy: which, as it thunders out terrible
judgments against hard-hearted impenitent sinners (such as were the most
part of Israel), so is it mingled full of many and sweet consolations to the
faithful, in those times, scattered amongst the wicked troop of idolaters
then living.

The time when Hosea prophesied was under the reign of Uzziah, Jotham,
Ahaz, and Hezekiah, kings of Judah; and in the days of Jeroboam, the son
of Joash, king of Israel, in whose days idolatry was first universally set up,
and countenanced by regal power. This Jeroboam, 'who caused Israel to sin,'
1 Kings xv. 34, that he might strengthen himself, made use of religion,
and profanely mixed it with his civil affairs in carnal policy, and so leavened
the whole lump of Israel with idolatry, that shortly after, the whole ten
tribes, for their sin, and their injustice, cruelty, lust, security, and such
other sins as accompanied and sprang from this brutish idolatry, were led
away captive by the king of Assyria, and the Lord's righteous judgment
made manifest upon them.

There being, notwithstanding, amongst these some faithful ones, though
thinly scattered, who mourned for, and by their good examples, reproved
these abominable courses: there being also a seed of the elect unconverted;
and of the converted, some that were carried down too far in the strength
of this stream of wickedness: in this chapter, therefore, being the con-

clusion of this prophecy, there are many excellent and heavenly encouragements ; also many earnest incitements to repentance and returning to the Lord, with free and gracious promises, not only of pardon and acceptance, but of great rewards in things spiritual and temporal to such as should thus return.

' O Israel, return unto the Lord thy God, for thou hast fallen by thine iniquity.'

' Take with you words, and turn to the Lord; say unto him, Take away all iniquity,' &c.

In this chapter we have,

1. *An exhortation to repentance, with the motives enforcing the same :* ' O Israel, return unto the Lord thy God,' ver. 1.

2. *The form :* ' Take with you words, and say unto the Lord,' &c., ver. 2.

3. *A restipulation, what they should do : and return back again, having their prayers granted.* 1. *Thanksgiving :* ' So will we render the calves of our lips.' 2. *Sound reformation of their beloved sin :* ' Ashur shall not save us,' &c.; *with the reason thereof :* 'For in thee the fatherless findeth mercy,' ver. 3.

4. *God's answer to their petitions.* 1. *In what he will do for them :* ' Heal their backsliding, love them freely, and be as the dew unto Israel;' *with the reason thereof :* 'For mine anger is turned away from him,' ver. 4. 2. *What he will work in them, a proportionable speedy growth in height, breadth, and depth :* ' He shall grow as the lily, and cast forth his roots as Lebanon,' &c.; which mercy is further amplified *by a blessing poured out also upon their families :* ' They that dwell under his shadow shall return,' ver. 5-7.

5. There is set down a further effect of this repentance and gracious work in them, *a sound and strong well-rooted indignation against their former darling sins ;* ' Ephraim shall say, What have I any more to do with idols?' backed with a *strong consolation :* 'I have heard him and observed him,' &c., ver. 8.

6. *The diverse event and issue* of this God's so gracious dealing, is shewed both in the godly and wicked. 1. The wise and prudent understand and know that the ways of the Lord are right, and shall walk in them; but, 2. ' The transgressors shall fall therein,' ver. 9.

' O Israel, return unto the Lord thy God, for thou hast fallen by thine iniquity.'

Every word hath his weight, and, in a manner, is an argument to enforce this returning.

' O Israel!' Israel, we know, 1, is a word *of covenant.* Jacob was Israel, a prince and wrestler with God, as they also ought to be. Therefore he enforceth, You also ought to return, because you are Israel. And, 2, It was also an *encouragement* for them to return, because God so acknowledgeth them to be Israel, and will be gracious unto them, though they were such hideous sinners.

' Return,' saith he, ' unto the Lord Jehovah,' who is the chief good. For when a man returneth to the creature, which is a particular, changeable good, unsatisfying [to] the soul, he is restless still until he come unto Jehovah, who is the all-sufficient, universal good, who fills and fills the soul abundantly. Therefore, ' return ' to him who is the fountain of all good, and giveth a being unto all things, and not to ' broken cisterns,' Jer. ii. 13. He is Jehovah, like himself, and ' changeth not.' And then he is *thy* God. Therefore, return to him who is thy God in covenant, who will make good his gracious covenant unto thee, and did choose thee to be ' his people before all the nations of the world.' This, therefore, is also an encouragement to return. And then,

' Thou hast fallen by thine iniquity.' Therefore, because thou art fallen by thy iniquities, and thine own inventions have brought these miseries upon thee, and none but God can help thee out of these miseries, seeing he only can, and is willing to forgive thy sins and revive thee, therefore,

' O Israel, return unto the Lord thy God, for thou hast fallen by thine iniquity.'

Now, in that he forewarneth them of the fearful judgments to come, which were to fall upon them unless they were prevented by true repentance, hence in general it is to be observed,

That *God comes not as a sudden storm upon his people, but gives them warning before he smites them.*

This is verified in Scripture. When the cry of Sodom and Gomorrah was great, the Lord said, ' Because the cry of Sodom and Gomorrah is great, and because their sin is very grievous, I will go down now and see whether they have done altogether according to the cry of it which is come unto me; and if not, I will know,' Gen. xviii. 20, 21. And wherefore was the ark of Noah so long in building, but to give warning to that sinful age, which were nothing bettered by it. The like we have of Pharaoh and all the Egyptians, who had so many warnings and miracles shewed before their destruction came, Exod. xi. 1, *seq.* Thus God dealt in Amos : ' Therefore, thus will I do unto thee; and because I will do this unto thee, prepare to meet thy God, O Israel,' Amos iv. 12. ' O Jerusalem, Jerusalem,' saith Christ, ' thou that killest the prophets, and stonest them which are sent unto thee, how often would I have gathered thy children together, even as a hen gathereth the chickens under her wings, and ye would not,' Mat. xxiii. 37. What need we stand upon proofs? Are not all the threatenings of Scripture as so many warning-pieces of approaching judgments?

1. The reason hereof is, *his own nature.* ' He is a God of long-suffering,' Exod. xxxiv. 6. He made the world in six days, yet hath continued it six thousand years, notwithstanding the many sins and provocations thereof, ' his mercies being over all his works,' Ps. cxlv. 9.

2. And partly *from a special regard to his own dear children*, these terrible threatenings not being killing and wounding, but, like Jonathan's warning arrows, who, though he shot, yet meant no other harm to David save to forewarn him of harm, 1 Sam. xx. 20.

Use. Let us, therefore, observe God's gracious and mild dealing in so much mercy, who giveth us so many warnings by his servants, and lesser judgments which we have had amongst us; let us take notice and believe, so as belief may stir up fear, and fear may provoke care, and care stir up endeavours to provide us an ark, even a hiding-place betimes, before winter and worse times come upon us.

Hence issueth another general point, that

The best provision for preventing of destruction is spiritual means.

God himself is a spirit, and spiritual means reach unto him who is the first mover of the great wheel of all the affairs of this world. It is preposterous to begin at the second cause. We trouble ourselves in vain there, when we neglect the first. We should therefore begin the work in heaven, and first of all take up that quarrel which is between God and our souls. If this be done first, we need not fear the carriage of second things, all which God, out of his good providence and gracious care, will frame to work for good to his, Rom. viii. 28, for whose sakes, rather than help should fail, he will create new helps, Isa. iv. 5. Wherefore, in all things it is best to begin with God.

The third general point is this, that

Of all spiritual means, the best is to return to the Lord.

In this returning, 1. *There must be a stop.* Those who have run on in evil ways must first stop their lewd courses. For naturally from our birth and childhood we are posting on to hell; and yet such is our madness (unless the Spirit of God shew us ourselves) to be angry with those who stand in our way.

To make this stop, then (which is always before returning).

(1.) There must be *examination and consideration whither our ways tend.* There be stopping considerations, which both waken a man and likewise put rubs in his way; if a man, upon examination, find his ways displeasing unto God, disagreeing from the rule, and consider what will be the end and issue of them (nothing but death and damnation), and withal consider of the day of judgment, the hour of death, the all-seeing eye of God, and the like. So the consideration of a man's own ways, and of God's ways towards him, partly when God meets him with goodness ;—I have hitherto been a vile wretch, and God hath been good to me, and spared me ;—and partly when God stops a wicked man's ways with thorns, meets him with crosses and afflictions. These will work upon an ingenious* spirit, to make him have better thoughts and deeper considerations of true happiness, and the way unto it. God puts into the heart of a man, whom he intends to save, serious and sad considerations, what estate he is in, whither his course leads; and withal he lets them feel some displeasure of his, towards them, in those ways, by his ways towards them; whereupon they make a stop.

(2.) There must be *humiliation, with displeasure against ourselves,* judging and taking revenge of ourselves, working and reflecting on our hearts, taking shame to ourselves for our ways and courses; and withal, there must concur some hope of mercy. For so long as there is hue and cry, as we say, after a traitor, he returns not, but flies still and hastes away; but offer a pardon, and he returneth. So, unless there be hope of pardon, to draw a man again to God, as the prodigal was moved to return by hope of mercy and favour from his father, Luke xv. 18, we will not, we dare not else return.

(3.) There must be a *resolution to overcome impediments.* For when a man thinks or resolves to turn to God, Satan will stir up all his instruments, and labour to kill Christ in his infancy, and to quench good while it is in the purpose only. The dragon stood watching for the birth of the child, Rev. xii. 4 ; so doth Satan observe the birth of every good resolution and purpose, so far as he can know them, to destroy them.

Use: Let it be thought of by us in all our distresses, and in whatsoever other evidences of God's anger, whether this means have been taken up by us. It will be thus known.

[1.] Turning is a change of the posture of the body; so is this *of the frame of the mind.* By this we know a man is in a state of turning. The look of his intentions, purposes, the whole bent of his soul is set another way, even upon God; and his word is the star of direction towards which he bends all his thoughts.

[2.] *His present actions, also, be contrary to his former.* There is not only a change of the disposition of his soul, ' Behold all things are become new;' not some things, but all ; not only ' new,' but with a ' behold ' new, 2 Cor.

* That is, 'ingenuous.'—G.

v. 17. This change undoubtedly sheweth that there is a true conversion and unfeigned.

[3.] *By our association.* He that turns to God, turns presently to the company of God's people. Together with the change of his nature and course of life, there is a change of company; that is, of such as we make choice of for amity and friendship, Isa. xi. 10, *seq.* Other company, by reason of our callings, and occasionally, may be frequented.

[4.] It is a sign that one is not only turned, but hath gone backwards from sin a great way, *when the things of heaven only are great things in his eyes.* For, as the further a man goeth from a place, the lesser the things behind him seem, so the greater the things before, he being nearer to them. The more sublime and high thoughts a man hath of the ways of God, and the meaner thoughts of the world and worldly matters he esteemed so highly of in the days of his vanity, the more he is turned unto God.

This returning is further enforced, saying, 'Return unto the Lord thy God.'

It is very emphatical and significant in the original (*a*). Return, *usque ad Jehovam,* even to Jehovah, as though he should say, Do not only begin to return towards Jehovah, but so return as you never cease coming till you come to Jehovah.

'Even unto the Lord thy God.'

It is not enough to make a stop, and forbear the practising of our former sins; but we must come home, even unto the Lord our God, to be pardoned and healed of him.

The prodigal son had been never a whit the better to see his sin and misery, and to be grieved for his wicked life past, unless he had come unto his father for pardon and comfort, Luke xv. 20. And when those were pricked in their hearts at Peter's sermon, asking Peter ' what they should do ?' he exhorted them, ' To repent, every one to be baptized in the name of Jesus Christ, for the remission of sins, and so they should receive the Holy Ghost,' Acts ii. 38. And when Christ invites all those who ' are weary and heavy laden to come unto him,' Mat. xi. 28, he bids them not now be further humbled and grieved for their sins, but by faith to come unto him to be healed, and so they should find rest and peace to their souls. It is not sufficient for a wounded man to be sorry for his brawling and fighting, and to say, he will fight no more ; but he must come to the surgeon to have his wounds stopped, dressed, and healed, or else it may cost him his life. So it is not enough to be humbled and grieved for sin, and to resolve against it. We shall relapse again, do what we can, unless we come under the wing of Christ, to be healed by his blood.

Use. Many think they have repented, and are deceived upon this false ground. They are and have been grieved for their sins and offences ; are determined to leave and forsake them, and that is all they do. They never lay hold on Christ, and come home to God.

' For thou hast fallen by thine iniquity.'

Here divers points might be insisted on.

1. *That where there is a falling into sin, there will be a falling into misery and judgment.*

This is made good in the experience of all times, ages, persons, and states. Still the more sinful any were, the more fearful judgments fell upon them ; and as soon as any man came into a sinful state, he entered into a declining state ; as Jacob said of his son Reuben, who had defiled his bed, ' Unstable as water, thou shalt not excel ; because thou wentest up to thy father's bed,' Gen. xlix. 4. So sin still debaseth a man. So much sin, so much loss of excellency.

The use hereof is, *first*, against those that complain of their troubles and miseries, as though God and men had dealt hardly with them; whereas their own ways, indeed, have brought all these evils upon them, Lam. iii. 39. God is a sufficient, wise, and holy disposer and orderer of all the ways of men, and rewarder of good and evil doings. God being wise and just in his disposing of all things, it must needs follow, that it shall go well with those that are good; as the prophet speaks, 'Say unto the just, that it shall be well with them, for the reward of their works shall be given them,' Isa. iii. 10. And if it fall out otherwise than well with men, the blame must be laid on their own sin. As the church confesseth, and therefore resolveth, 'I will bear the indignation of the Lord, because I have sinned against him, until he plead my cause, and execute judgment for me; he will bring me forth in the light, and I shall see his righteousness,' Micah vii. 9. If Adam sin, he shall find a hell in a paradise. If Paul return, and return to God, he shall find a heaven in a dungeon.

Secondly, It should move us therefore to seek unto God by unfeigned repentance, to have our sins taken away and pardoned; or else, however we may change our plagues, yet they shall not be taken away; nay, we shall still, like Pharoah, change for the worst; who, though he had his judgments changed, yet sin, the cause, remaining, he was never a whit the better, but the worse, for changing, until his final ruin came.

'The wages of sin is death,' Rom. vi. 23. Sin will cry till it hath its wages. Where iniquity is, there cannot but be falling into judgment. Therefore they are cruel to their own souls that walk in evil ways; for undoubtedly God will turn their own ways upon their own heads. We should not therefore envy any man, be he what he will, who goeth on in ill courses, seeing some judgment is owing him first or last, unless he stop the current of God's wrath by repentance. God, in much mercy, hath set up a court in our hearts to this end, that, if we judge ourselves in this inferior court, we may escape, and not be brought up into the higher. If first they be judged rightly in the inferior court, then there needs no review. But otherwise, if we by repentance take not up the matter, sin must be judged somewhere, either in the tribunal of the heart and conscience, or else afterwards there must be a reckoning for it.

Thirdly, Hence we learn, since the cause of every man's misery is his own sin, *that therefore all the power of the world, and of hell, cannot keep a man in misery, nor hinder him from comfort and happiness, if he will part with his sins by true and unfeigned repentance.* As we know, Manasseh, as soon as he put away sin, the Lord had mercy upon him, and turned his captivity, 2 Chron. xxxiii. 12, 13. So the people of Israel, in the Judges. Look how often they were humbled and returned to God, still he forgave them all their sins. As soon as they put away sin, God and they met again. So that, if we come to Christ by true repentance, neither sin nor punishment can cleave to us, Ps. cvi. 43, 44; cvii. 1, 9.

'Thou hast fallen,' &c. Fallen blindly, as it were. Thou couldst not see which way thou wentest, or to what end thy courses did tend. Therefore thou art come into misery before thou knowest where thou art. A sinner is blind, 'The god of this world hath put out his eyes,' 2 Cor. iv. 4. They see not their way, nor foresee their success. The devil is ever for our falling. That we fall into sin, and then fall into misery, and so fall into despair, and into hell, this pleaseth him. 'Cast thyself down,' saith he to Christ, Mat. iv. 6. 'Down with it, down with it,' saith Edom, Ps. cxxxvii. 7. Hell is beneath. The devil drives all that way.

Use. Take heed of sin! take heed of blindness! Ponder the path of your feet! keep your thoughts heavenward! stop the beginnings, the first stumblings! pray to God to make our way plain before us, and not to lead us into temptation!

'Take with you words, and turn to the Lord: say unto him,' &c., ver. 2.

These Israelites were but a rude people, and had not so good means to thrive in grace as Judah had. Therefore he prompts them here with such words as they might use to God in their returning. 'Take with you words,' whereby we see how gracious God is unto us in using such helps for our recovery, and pitying us more than we pity ourselves. Is not this a sufficient warrant and invitation to return, when the party offended, who is the superior, desires, entreats, and sues unto the offending, guilty inferior, to be reconciled?' 2 Cor. v. 5.

But this is not all. He further sheweth his willingness in teaching us, who are ignorant of the way, in what manner and with what expressions we should return to the Lord. He giveth us not only words, and tells us what we shall say, but also giveth his Spirit so effectually therewith, as that they shall not be lifeless and dead words, but 'with unexpressible sighs and groans unto God,' Rom. viii. 26, who heareth the requests of his own Spirit. Christ likewise teacheth us how to pray. We have words dictated, and a spirit of prayer poured upon us; as if a great person should dictate and frame a petition for one who were afraid to speak unto him. Such is God's graciousness; and so ready is he in Jesus Christ to receive sinners unto mercy.

'Take unto you words.' None were to appear empty before the Lord at Jerusalem, but were to bring something. So it is with us. We must not appear empty before our God. If we can bring nothing else, let us bring words; yea, though broken words, yet if out of a broken and contrite heart, it will be a sacrifice acceptable.

This same taking of words or petitions, in all our troubles and afflictions, must needs be a special remedy, it being of God's own prescription, who is so infinite in knowledge and skill. Whence we observe, that

They who would have help and comfort against all sins and sorrows, must come to God with words of prayer.

As we see in Jonah's case, in a matchless distress, words were inforcive,* and did him more good than all the world besides could. For after that he had been humbled, and prayed out of the whale's belly, the whale was forced to cast him out again, Jonah ii. 10. So the prodigal son being undone, having neither credit nor coin, but all in a manner against him, yet he had words left him: 'Father, I have sinned against heaven and before thee, and am no more worthy to be called thy son: make me as one of thy hired servants,' Luke xv. 18, *seq.* After which, his father had compassion on him. And good Hezekiah, being desperately sick of a desperate disease, yet when he set his faith a-work, and took with him words, which comfort only now was left unto him, we know how after he had turned his face towards the wall, and prayed with words, God not only healed him of that dangerous disease, but also wrought a great miracle for his sake, causing the sun to come back ten degrees, Isa. xxxviii. 2, 8. Thus, when life seemed impossible, yet words, prayers, and tears prevailed with God. Jehoshaphat, also, going to war with Ahab, against God's commandment,

* That is, 'prevailing, or invested with a power of enforcing.'—ED.

and in the battle, being encompassed with enemies, yet had words with him ready, and after prayer found deliverance, 1 Kings xxii. 32. Elijah, likewise, after a great drowth and famine, when rain had been three years wanting, and all in a manner out of frame for a long time, ' took with him words,' James v. 18 ; and God sent rain abundantly upon the earth again.

The reason is, because prayer sets God on work ; and God, who is able and willing to go through with his works, sets all the creatures on work, Hos. ii. 21, 22. As we heard of Elijah, when he prayed for rain, the creatures were set a-work to effect it, 1 Kings xviii. 45, *seq.*

Obj. Where it may be objected, Oh, but rain might come too late in that hot country, where all the roots and herbs might be withered and dried up in three years' space.

Ans. Yet all was well again. The land brought forth her increase as formerly. For faithful prayer never comes too late, because God can never come too late. If our prayers come to him, we shall find him come to us. Jehoshaphat, we read, was in great distress when three kings came against him ; yet when he went to God by unfeigned and hearty fasting and prayer, God heard him, fought for him, and destroyed all his enemies, 2 Chron. xx. 3. *seq.* The Scripture sheweth, also, how after Hezekiah's prayer against Sennacherib's blasphemies and threatenings, the Lord sent forth his angel, and destroyed in one night a hundred fourscore and five thousand of the Assyrians, 2 Chron. xxxii. 21, *seq.*

Use 1. This is, first, *for reproof* of those who, in their distresses, set their wit, wealth, friends, and all a-work, but never set God a-work, as Hezekiah did in Sennacherib's case. The first time he turned him off to his cost, with enduring a heavy taxation, and yet was never a whit the better for it, 2 Kings xviii. 15, *seq.;* for Sennacherib came shortly after and besieged Jerusalem, until Hezekiah had humbled himself and prayed ; and then God chased all away and destroyed them. He had better have done so at first, and so saved his money and pains, too. The like weakness we have a proof of in Asa, who, when a greater army came against him of ten hundred thousand men, laid about him, prayed and trusted in God, and so was delivered, with the destruction of his enemies, 2 Chron. xiv. 11, yet in a lesser danger, 2 Chron. xvi. 2, against Baasha, king of Israel, distrusted God, and sent out the treasures of the house of God and of his own house unto Benhadad, king of Syria, to have help of him, by a diverting* war against Baasha, king of Israel, which his plot, though it prospered, yet was he reproved by the prophet Hanani, and wars thenceforth denounced against him, 2 Chron. xvi. 7. This Asa, notwithstanding this experiment, afterwards sought unto the physician, before he sought unto God, 2 Chron. xvi. 12.

Use 2. Secondly. *This blameth that barrenness and want of words to go unto God,* which, for want of hearts, we often find in ourselves. It were a strange thing to see a wife have words enough for her maids and servants, and yet not to be able to speak to her husband. We all profess to be the spouse of Christ. What a strange thing, then, is it to be full when we speak to men, yet be so empty and want words to speak to him ! A beggar, we know, wants no words, nay, he aboundeth with variety of expressions ; and what makes him thus fruitful in words ? His necessity, and, in part, his hope of obtaining.

These two make beggars so earnest. So would it be with us. If we found sufficiently our great need of Christ, and therewith had hope, it

* That is, ' diverging or dividing.—G.

would embolden us so to go to God in Christ, that we should not want words. But we want this hope, and the feeling of our necessities, which makes us so barren in prayer.

Prepare thyself, therefore, to prayer, by getting unto thee a true sense of thy need, acquaintance with God, and hope to obtain, and it will make thee fervent in prayer, and copious in thy requests.

Use 3. Thirdly, this is for *consolation*. Though one should want all other means, yet whatsoever their misery be, if they can take words, and can pray well, they shall speed well, Isa. xxxviii. 3. If the misery be for sin, confess it, and ask pardon for it, and they shall have it, ‘and be cleansed from all unrighteousness,’ 1 John i. 9. Words fetch the comfort to us, though it be the ‘blood of Christ only that hath paid the debt,’ Isa. liii. 5.

THE SECOND SERMON.

Take with you words, and turn to the Lord; say unto him, Take away all iniquity, and receive us graciously: so will we render the calves of our lips. —Hos. XIV. 2.

As we lost ourselves in the first Adam, so the mercy of God, in the covenant of grace, found out a way to restore us again by the ‘second Adam,’ 1 Cor. xv. 47, Jesus Christ, in whom all the promises are ‘yea and amen; yesterday and to-day, and the same for ever,’ Heb. xiii. 8. And as the wisdom of God did freely find out this way at first, comforting our first parents with it in paradise; so this bowels of incomprehensible love of his hath so gone on from time,* in all ages of the church, comforting and raising up the dejected spirits of his church, from time to time, and awakening them out of their drowsiness and sleepy condition. And many times, the greater sinners he dealt with, the greater mercies and tender bowels of compassion were opened unto them, in many sweet and gracious promises tendering forgiveness, and inviting to repentance; as here in this chapter, and whole prophecy, is shewed. What tribe so wicked, so full of idolatry and rebellion, as Ephraim? and yet here Ephraim and Israel are taught a lesson of repentance. As the tender nurse feeds her child, and puts meat in its mouth, so here the Lord puts words in the mouth of this rebellious people.

‘Take with you words, and turn unto the Lord.’

Obj. What need God words, he knows our hearts before we speak unto him?

Ans. It is true: God needs no words, but we do, to stir up our hearts and affections; and because he will have us take shame unto ourselves, having given us our tongues as an instrument of glorifying him, he will have our ‘glory,’ Ps. xvi. 9; lvii. 8, used in our petitions and thanksgivings. And therefore, in regard of ourselves, he will, as was said, have us take words unto ourselves, for exciting of the graces of God in us by words, blowing up of the affections, and for manifestation of the hidden man of the heart. God will be glorified by the outward, as well as by the inward man.

‘And turn to the Lord.’ He repeats the exhortation of returning, to

* That is, ‘from time to time,’ or ‘through all time.’—ED.

shew that *words must not be empty, but such as are joined with a purpose of turning to God.* For otherwise, to turn to him with a purpose to live in any sin, is the extremity of profane impudence. To come to ask a pardon of the king, with a resolution to live still in rebellion against him, what is this but mockery, as if one should come with a dagg* to shoot him? Such is our case, when we come to ask forgiveness, with a purpose to offend. It is the extremity of profaneness, to come to ask a pardon, to the intent that we may sin still. Therefore he repeats it again, ' Take unto you words, and turn to the Lord.' The form is—

' Take away all iniquity, and receive us graciously,' or ' do good to us :' ' so will we render the calves of our lips ;' wherein we have,

1. A *petition:* (1.) *To take away all iniquity;* (2.) *To receive them graciously.*

2. A *re-stipulation,* or promise of thankfulness back again to the Lord, ' So will we render the calves of our lips.' So that we may observe, hence—

What God will grant us. He will have us ask of him. ' Yet for all these things I will be sought unto of the house of Israel,' Ezek. xx. 31, saith God ; because he will have us acknowledge our homage and dependence upon him. Therefore we must ask what he hath purposed to give. ' Take away all iniquity,' &c., where there is an implication of a confession of their sins and great iniquities. ' Take away iniquity,' and ' Take away all iniquity,' that is, our manifold guilt. So, before petition, there must ·be a free and full confession, as was shewed before.

Now, this confession here is made to God, and to God only, saith Austin in this case. Because it is a point in controversy, it is good to hear what the ancients say. There are a curious sort of men, who are busy to search into other men's lives, and are careless in amending their own. Saith he, ' What have I to do with men to hear me confess, when I have offended God ? We must confess to God, and to God only.' † But in some cases there may be public and private confession to men. Public, in public offences, for the satisfaction of the church, and the glory of God ; for preventing of scandal. Private, to ministers, for the quieting of conscience. But this is only in some cases. Men go not to the chirurgeon, as the papists would have it, for every little prick of their finger. No ; but yet in some cases it is good to open the matter to a minister, ' who hath the tongue of the learned,' Isa. l. 4. But the sin is toward God, against him, he only being able to forgive sins, as the Pharisees confessed : ' None can forgive sins but God,' Mark ii. 7. The papists, therefore, herein are worse than the Pharisees.

The petition is, ' Take away iniquity,' and ' all iniquity.' Why all ?

First. Because where there is any true goodness in the heart, that hatred which carries the bent of the soul against one sin, is alike against all, as I shewed ; and the devil carries thousands to hell by this partial obedience, because he knows at any time where to have such. God and a purpose to sin will not stand together, nor dwell in a heart that allows itself in any sin, be it never so small. He saith, Take away all, because the Spirit of God works in a man renewed, such a disposition of sincerity to hate all alike.

Secondly, he saith, ' Take away all iniquity,' because the heart, which desires to be at peace with God, desires also to be like God, who hates all sin. Therefore, saith the sanctified soul, forgive all sin. Take all away, that I may have nothing in me displeasing unto thee. I desire to join

* That is, ' small pistol.'—G.   † Augustine, Conf. Introd., *et alibi.*—G.

with the Lord; to hate what he hateth, and as he hateth; to carry a perfect hatred to the whole kind. 'Take away all iniquity.' Hatred is not satisfied, but with the utter abolishing of the thing hated. Therefore it hath this extent here. 'Take away all sin,' both the guilt and the reign of every sin, that none may rule in me; nay, by little and little, purge out all. 'Take away iniquity,' and the train of all which it draws after it—judgments. 'Take away iniquity,' that is, forgive the sin, and overcome the power of it by sanctifying grace, and remit the judgments attending it.

'Take it away.' That is, take away the guilt of it utterly by pardon, and the remainders thereof by sanctifying grace, so as the Spirit may rule, and be all in all in us. They see sin is an offensive thing, and therefore they say, 'Take it away,' as an offensive, odious thing, and as a burden. For howsoever it be sweet as honey in the committing it, afterwards, when the conscience is thoroughly awaked, it is most offensive and bitter. So as in this case, a sinner would gladly run from his own conscience, and from himself; run anywhere from the tormenting and racking thoughts of conscience awaked, and withal hates the place where it was committed, and the company with whom, yea, the thoughts of them. As Absalom hated Tamar after he had lien with her, so a sinner awaked from sin hates what he formerly loved. As good men love the circumstances of anything which puts them in mind of any good they have done, loving both place and person. So it is with a sinner. When his conscience is awaked, he hates all things which puts him in mind of his sins. Therefore, 'Take it away,' forgive it, cast it into the bottom of the sea, blot it out of thy remembrance, cover it, impute it not; all which phrases shew a taking away.

Therefore, I beseech you, let us examine ourselves hereby, whether our desire of forgiveness be sound or not. If we desire sin should be taken away, we cannot think of it with comfort. For in that many think with delight of their old sins, what do they else, but repeat them over again and again? But where the heart is soundly touched with a saving sense of sin, O then he cries, 'Take it away;' take it out of my conscience, that it cause not despair there; and out of thy remembrance, that no advantage be taken against me for it. 'Take it away.' But it is no otherwise taken away than by satisfying of divine justice. How much are we beholden to Christ, therefore, who hath borne and taken away our sins, and as the scape-goat, gone away with the burden of all into the wilderness of oblivion. Blessed be God, and the Lamb of God, that taketh away the sins of the world! We can never bless God too much, nor sufficiently, for Christ. 'Blessed be God, the Father of our Lord Jesus Christ,' Eph. i. 3. Now we may think of sin without shame and despair. O blessed state, when a man can think of his former odious, and filthy, loathsome sins, and yet not despair! Because, when he believes in Christ, the blood of Christ purgeth all away, takes away all sin. He hath taken them away.

You see here, in the first place, they pray for the taking away of their iniquity. For, take away this, and all other mercies follow after, because this only is it which stops the current of God's favours, which removed, the current of his mercies run amain. As when the clouds are gone, the sun shines out; so let our sins be removed, and God's favour immediately shines upon us. Therefore, first 'Take away all iniquity,' and then we shall see nothing but thy fatherly face in Christ. You see what the care of God's children is, to seek mercy and favour in the first place; as David, 'Have mercy on me, O Lord!' Ps. li. 1. This he begs first of all. Whereas God had threatened other terrible judgments, as that the sword should never depart from his house, &c., yet he neglects all, as it were, and begs only for mercy, ' to take away iniquity.' For a sinner is never in such a blessed condition as he should be in, until he prize and desire mercy above all ; because, though we be in misery, until then, with sinful Ephraim, Hos. vii. 14, we howl upon our beds for corn and wine, preferring earthly, sensual things before all. But that soul and conscience which is acquainted with God, and the odiousness of sin, that soul God intends to speak peace unto in the end, desires pardon of sin and mercy above all. For it knows that God is goodness itself, and that, when the interposing clouds are vanished, God cannot shew himself otherwise than in goodness, grace, and mercy. ' Take away all iniquity.'

Quest. Before I go further, let me answer one question. Ought we not to think of our former sins ? Shall God take them away altogether out of the soul ?

Ans. Oh no ! Take them away out of the conscience, O Lord, that it do not accuse for them ; but not out of the memory. It is good that sin be remembered, to humble us, to make us more thankful, pitiful, and tender-hearted unto others, to abase us and keep us low all the days of our life, and to make us deal gently and mercifully with others, being sensible of our own frailties. As they are naught in the conscience, so they are good to the memory. Therefore, let us think often of this, what the chief desire of our souls to God should be for—mercy, to have sin taken away. In all the articles of our creed, that of chiefest comfort is, that of ' remission of sins.' * Wherefore are all the other articles of Christ, his birth, death, and crucifying, but that he might get the church ? and that the privileges thereof might be, ' forgiveness of sins, resurrection of the body, and life everlasting ; ' but forgiveness of sins is in the first place.

Quest. But may some say, How shall I know whether or no my sins be forgiven ?

1. By something that goes before.
2. By something which follows after.

Ans. There is somewhat which goes before, viz.:—

First, an humble and hearty confession, as, ' If we confess our sins, he is faithful and just to forgive us our sins, and to cleanse us from all unrighteousness,' 1 John i. 9. Therefore, whether I feel it or not, if I have heartily, fully, and freely confessed, my sins are forgiven. God in wisdom and mercy may suspend the feeling thereof, for our humiliation, and for being over-bold with Satan's baits ; yet I ought to believe it. For I make God a liar else, if I confess heartily, and acknowledge my debt, to think that he hath not cancelled the bond.

Secondly, sin is certainly pardoned, *when a man finds strength against it ;* for where God forgives, he gives strength withal : as to the man whom he healed of the palsy, ' Thy sins are forgiven thee ; take up thy bed and walk,' Mat. ix. 2, 6. When a man hath strength to return to God, to run the way of his commandments, and to go on in a Christian course, his sins are forgiven, because he hath a spirit of faith to go on and lead him forward still. Those who find no strength of grace, may question forgiveness of sins. For God, where he takes away sin, and pardons it, as we see here in this text, after prayer made to take away iniquity, he ' doth good to us.'

The *third* evidence is, *some peace of conscience ;* though not much, perhaps, yet so much as supports us from despair, as, ' Therefore, being justified by faith, we have peace with God through our Lord Jesus Christ,' Rom. v. 1 ;

* Creed, Article X.—G.

that is, being acquitted from our sins by faith, we have peace with God ; so much peace, as makes us go boldly to him.   So that one may know his bonds are cancelled, and his sins forgiven, when with some boldness he dare look God in the face in Jesus Christ.   A Judas, an Ahithophel, a Saul, because they are in the guilt of their sins, cannot confess comfortably, and go to God, which, when with some boldness we can do, it is a sign that peace is made for us.

Fourth. Again, where sin is pardoned, *our hearts will be much enlarged with love to God;* as Christ said to the woman, ' Her sins, which are many, are forgiven her, because she loved much,' Luke vii. 47.   Therefore, when we find our hearts inflamed with love to God, we may know that God hath shined upon our souls in the pardon of sin ; and proportionably to our measure of love is our assurance of pardon.   Therefore we should labour for a greater measure thereof, that our hearts may be the more inflamed in the love of God.   It is impossible that the soul should at all love God angry, offended, and unappeased ; nay, such a soul wisheth that there were no God at all, for the very thoughts thereof terrify him.

Fifthly. Again, where sin is forgiven, *it frames the soul suitably*, to be gentle, merciful, and to pardon others.   For, usually, those who have peaceable consciences themselves are peaceable unto others ; and those who have forgiveness of sins, can also forgive others.   Those who have found mercy have merciful hearts, shewing that they have found mercy with God.   And, on the contrary, he that is a cruel, merciless man, it is a sign that his heart was never warmed nor melted with the sense of God's mercy in Christ.   Therefore, ' as the elect of God,' saith the apostle, ' put on bowels of compassion,' 1 Peter iii. 8, as you will make it good that you are the elect of God, members of Christ, and God's children.

Therefore, let us labour for the forgiveness of our sins, that God would remove and subdue the power of them, take them away, and the judgments due to them, or else we are but miserable men, though we enjoyed all the pleasures of the world, which to a worldly man are but like the liberty of the tower* to a condemned traitor, who though he have all wants supplied with all possible attendance, yet when he thinks of his estate, it makes his heart cold, damps his courage, and makes him think the poorest car-man or tankard-bearer, at liberty, happier than he, who would not change estates with him.   So it is with a man that hath not sued out his pardon, nor is at peace with God.   He hath no comfort, so long as he knows his sins are on the file,† that God in heaven is not at peace with him, who can arm all the creatures against him to be revenged of him.   In which case, who shall be umpire betwixt God and us, if we take not up the controversy betwixt him and our souls ?   Therefore, it being so miserable a case to want assurance of the forgiveness of sins, it should make us be never an hour quiet till we have gotten it, seeing the uncertainty of this life, wherein there is but a step betwixt hell, damnation, and us.   Therefore sue unto God, ply him with broken and humble hearts, that he would pardon all the sins of our youth and after-age, known and unknown, that he would pardon all whatsoever.   ' Take away all iniquity.'

' And do good to us.'   For so it is in the original,‡ but it is all one, ' Receive us graciously, and do good to us.'   All the goodness we have from God, it is out of his grace, from his free grace and goodness.   All grace, every little thing from God is grace.   As we say of favours received of

---

* That is, the state-prison.—G.   † See note *b*, vol. I. p. 289.— .

‡ See note *a*.—G.

great persons, this is his grace, his favour ; so this is a respect which is put upon all things which we receive from God, when we are in covenant, all is gracious. Take we the words as they are, the more plain, in the original. ' Take good, and do good to us :' take good out of thy treasure of goodness, and do good to us, bestow upon us thy own good. First, ' take away our iniquities,' and then take good out of thy bounty, ' and do good to us.' Whence we see—

Doct. *That God's mercy to his children is complete and full.*

For he takes away ill, and doth good. Men may pardon, but withal they think that they have done wondrous bountifully when they have pardoned. But God goes further. He takes away ill, and doth good ; takes good out of his fountain, and doth good to us.

Use. Therefore, let us make this use of it, to be encouraged, when we have the first blessing of all, forgiveness of sins, to go to him for more and more, and gather upon God further and further still. For because he is a fountain of goodness that can never be drawn dry, he is wondrously pleased with this. We cannot honour him more than by making use of his mercy in the forgiveness of sins ; and of his goodness, in going to him for it ; and having interested ourselves in his goodness, go to him for more. Lord, thou hast begun : make an end ; thou hast forgiven my sins ; I want this and that good ; together with the pardon of my sins, do me good. ' Receive us graciously,' or, ' do us good.' Now, good is the loadstone of the soul, the attractive that draws it. Therefore, after forgiveness of sins, he saith, ' do good.' The petition is easy, God will soon grant it. For nothing else interposeth betwixt God and us, and makes two, but sin, which being removed, he is all goodness and mercy. ' All his ways are mercy and truth,' Ps. xxv. 10. Yea, even his sharpest ways are mercy, all mercy. When sin is forgiven, there is goodness in all, in the greatest cross and affliction. ' Do good to us.'

The soul, we see, desires good, and needs good. It is a transcendent word here, and must be understood according to the taste of God's people, of a sanctified soul. ' Do good.' Especially do spiritual good to us. Together with the forgiveness of sins, give us the righteousness of Jesus Christ, sanctifying grace, such good as may make us good first. For the desire must be such as the person is, who makes it. Wicked men, as it is said of Balaam, have good gifts, without the good God ; but we must not be so pleased with gifts, unless we be good ourselves, and see God making us good. ' Can an evil tree bring forth good fruit ?' Mat. vii. 18. Therefore, the apostle calls the regenerate person ' God's workmanship,' &c., Eph. ii. 10. We are God's good work, and then we do good works ; being made good, good comes from us. ' Do good to us.'

It is an acknowledgment of their own emptiness, ' Do good to us.' We are blind in our own understandings, enlighten us. We are perplexed, set us right. We are dull, quicken us. We are empty, fill us. We are dark, shine upon us. We are ready to go out of the way, establish us. Every way do good to us suitable to our wants. The best that we can bring to thee is emptiness. Therefore do thou good to us ; fill us with thy fulness. Do good to us every way, whereby thou usest to convey spiritual things to thy servants' souls. Give us first thy grace, thy Spirit, which is the spring of all good things ; for the Spirit of God is a Spirit of direction, of strength, of comfort, and all. Therefore he who hath the Spirit of God hath the spring of all. That is begged in the first place. And then give us good magistrates, to rule us well, and good ministers, who are the dispensers of grace, instruments of our salvation, the conduit pipes whereby thou derivest and conveyest good to us. When thou hast made us good, continue the means of salvation for our good every way. The church, when she saith, 'Do good to us,' hath a large desire. Here be seeds of wondrous large things in these two short petitions, 'Take away all iniquity,' and 'do good to us.' *A bono Deo*, &c. From the good God nothing can come but what is good. Therefore do good to us in all spiritual things. The prophet David aims at this excellent good, saying that other men are for corn, wine, and oil, and say, 'Who will shew us any good? But, Lord, lift thou up the light of thy countenance upon us,' Ps. iv. 6, 7. Thy lovingkindness is better than life, therefore do good to us. When thou hast forgiven our sins, shine graciously upon us in Jesus Christ.

And it extends its limits likewise to outward prosperity, this desire of doing good. Let us have happy days! Sweeten our pilgrimage here! Let our profession of religion be comfortable! Do not lay more crosses upon us than thou wilt give us strength to bear! Do good to us every way! But mark the wisdom of the Holy Ghost in dictating of this prayer to them. He speaks in general, 'Do good to us;' not to do this or that good, but he leaves it to the wisdom of God, as they here frame their hearts unto the will of God. 'Do good to us,' spiritual. That needs no limitation, because we cannot more honour God than to depend upon him for all spiritual good things. Thou art wiser, and knowest what is good for us better than we ourselves. Beggars ought to be no choosers. Therefore 'do good to us,' for the particulars we leave them to thy wisdom. Oh, beloved, it is a happy and blessed privilege to be under the conduct of so wise and all-sufficient a God, who is good, and as he is good, knows best what is good for us. We would have riches, liberty, and health; aye, but it may be it is not good for us. 'Do good to us.' Thou, Lord, knowest what is best. Do in thine own wisdom what is best.

Use. Which should teach us not to limit the Holy One of Israel in our desires of any outward thing whatsoever. Especially desire forgiveness and spiritual good things, leaving the rest to his wise disposing. Yet notwithstanding, out of the sense of pain and grief, we may pray either for the mitigation or removing of a cross, if God be so pleased. Because he hath put in us self-love, not sinful, but love of preserving our nature, therefore he permits us, if it may stand with his good pleasure, to desire the good of our outward man, as, Lord, give us bodily health, for we cannot else be instruments of serving thee. With reservation of God's good pleasure, we may desire such and such things, conditionally, that when we see God will have it otherwise, we rest contented, sit down quietly, knowing that whatsoever health, sickness, or crosses he sends, it comes from his goodness and love, and shall turn to our good at length. If we love God, all shall work for good.

'Take away our iniquity, and do us good.' We should make this petition for the church and ourselves. Pardon our sins, and do good to us, to our persons, to the state, to the times wherein we live, to the church at home and abroad, do good to all.

And we may observe this from the order, and know what good we have. It comes from God in love, when it comes after forgiveness of sins. How then, may we take comfort of all the good things we have enjoyed, having seen many good days, enjoyed many good blessings, in health, wealth, good magistracy, ministry, peace, plenty, and the like! If all this goodness of God lead us to God, and draw us nearer to him, 'after forgiveness of sins,' grounded on the former evidences I spake of, then they come in love. But never let us think to have true comfort with a blessing, or any good thing we enjoy, till we have assurance of God's love and mercy in the forgiveness of sins, lest God strip us naked of all the good things we have, and make us as naked as Dives in hell, who had not anything that was good to refresh his body or soul. So that all good things we enjoy here without this, will only aggravate our condemnation. Let us observe, therefore, how all our good things are joined with spiritual good (whether we ourselves are made better by them or not), having our sins pardoned. I beseech you, let us renew our requests for forgiveness of sins every day, making our accounts even with God, desiring grace to set our souls in a holy and sanctified frame with God, that ourselves may be good, our conversation good, and that then he would 'do good to us' all other ways, and sanctify all other things. This is the method of God's Spirit in setting us right onwards in our heavenly journey, first to have forgiveness of sins, then sanctification, to be better ourselves, and then to look for peaceable and comfortable days in this world, if God see it good. What can be more? 'Take away all iniquity, and do us good,' all manner of good.

Therefore, since all good comes from God, the first and chief good, let us labour to have communion with him by all sanctified means, that so he may take away our ill, and do us every way good to our souls, bodies, conditions. Oh, what a blessed thing is it for a Christian to keep a strict and near communion with the fountain of goodness, who can do more for us than all the world besides! When we are sick on our deathbeds, or when conscience is thoroughly awaked, then to speak peace comfortably to us in this great extremity, is more worth than all this world. Therefore let us labour to keep communion with God, that he may speak peace to our souls when nothing else can.

I beseech you, therefore, let us take heed how we break or walk loosely with God, seeing we can have no further comfort of any good thing we enjoy, than we are careful to keep and maintain our peace and communion with him at all times. And when we run into arrearages with God, then be sure we lie not in sin, but say, 'Take away all iniquity, and do good to us,' labouring to be in such an estate as God may give us his Holy Spirit, both to make us good and to sanctify unto us all other good. There be good things which are good of themselves, and which make all other things good. Thus, by communion with God, we ourselves are made good, and all other things likewise are made good to us, all his ways being mercy and truth unto those who fear him. Therefore resign we ourselves and all that we have unto his wisdom and disposing, because ofttimes there is good where we imagine the worst of evils to be, as it is sometimes good to have a vein opened to be purged. The physician thinks so, when yet the patient, impatient of reason's issue, thinks not so. But as the physician is wiser than the patient, to know what is best for him, so God is wiser than man, to know what is good for him, who intends us no hurt when he purgeth us by affliction.

All our care, therefore, should be to annihilate ourselves, to come with empty, poor souls to God, 'Do good to us.' In which case it is no matter what our ill be, if he do us good, who hath both pardon and rich grace to remove the evil of sin, and convey all grace unto us out of his rich treasury.

'So will we render the calves of our lips.'

Here is the re-stipulation or promise. They return back again to God, for there is no friendship maintained without rendering. When God hath entered into covenant with us, then there is a kind of friendship knit up betwixt him and us, he becoming our friend. We must not, therefore, be like graves, to swallow up all, and return nothing, for then the intercourse betwixt God and us is cut off. Therefore the same Spirit which teacheth them to pray, and to ' take to them words,' teacheth them likewise to take unto them words of praise, that there may be a rendering according to receiving, without which we are worse than the poorest creature that is, which rendereth according to its receipt. The earth, when it is ploughed and sowed, it yields us fruit. Trees being set, yield increase. Beasts being fed, render in their kind. Yea, the fiercest, untamed beasts, as we read of the lion, have been thankful in their kind. The heavens, saith the psalmist, declare the glory of God, and the firmament shews forth his praise, Ps. xix. 1. So there must be a return, if we be not worse than beasts. Therefore the church here promiseth a return by the same Spirit which stirred her up to pray. ' So will we render the calves of our lips.'

Now, this promise which the church makes here of praise, is a kind of vow, ' So will we render,' &c. To bind one's-self is a kind of vow. The church therefore binds herself, that she may bind God; for binding herself by vow to thankfulness, she thereby binds God; who is moved with nothing we can do so much as with setting forth of his praise, which was his end in all the creation, the setting forth of his glory. The end of the new creature is the end of all things both in nature and grace; the end whereof is God's glory, from whence all things come and wherein all things end: as we say of a circle, all things begin and end in it. All other things are for man, and man for God's glory. When the soul can say, ' Lord, this shall be for thy honour, to set forth thy praise,' it binds God. Hence, that they might move God to yield to their prayers, they bind themselves by a kind of vow. Do thus, O Lord, and thou shalt not lose by it, thou shalt have praise; ' so will we render thee the calves of our lips.'

So promises and vows of praise are alleged as an argument to prevail with God, for the obtaining of that the church begs for: ' So will we render,' &c. Not to enter into the commonplace of vows, only thus much I say, that there is a good use of them, to vow and promise thankfulness when we would obtain blessings from God. That which a promise is to men, that a vow is to God; and usually they go together in Scripture, as it is said of David, that ' he vowed unto God, and sware unto the mighty God of Jacob,' Ps. cxxxii. 2. So we have all in baptism vowed a vow. So that it is good to renew our vows often, especially that of new obedience; and in this particular to vow unto him that we will praise him, and strive that his glory be no loser by us.

1. It is good thus to vow, if it were but *to excite and quicken our dulness and forgetfulness of our general vow;* to put us in mind of our duty, the more to oblige us to God and refresh our memories. This bond, that having promised, now I must do it, provokes the soul to it. As it helps the memory, so it quickens the affections.

2. Besides, as by nature we are forgetful, *so we are inconstant;* in which respect it is a tie to our inconstant and unsteady natures. For there are none who have the Spirit of God at all, with any tenderness of heart, but will thus think: I have vowed to God. If it be a heinous thing to break with men, what is it wittingly and willingly to break with the great God? A vow is a kind of oath. This is the sacrifice of fools, to come to God, and yet neither to make good our vows, nor endeavour to do it.

Let us consider therefore what we have done in this case. By permission of authority, there was a fast lately, when we all renewed our vows (we mocked God else); [and] received the communion. Will God be mocked, think you ? No ; but howsoever man may forget, God will not, but will come upon us for non-payment of our vows and covenants. Lay we it to heart therefore what covenants we have made with God of late. And then, for the time to come, be not discouraged if you have been faulty in it. There is a general vow, wherein, though we have failed (if we be his children, and break not with God in the main, cleaving·to him in purpose of heart, occasionally renewing our purposes and covenants), yet let not Satan discourage us for our unfaithfulness therein. But be ashamed of it, watch more, look better to it for the time to come, and make use of the gracious covenant ; and, upon recovery, say with the church, ' So will we render the calves of our lips.'

It was the custom under the Jewish policy, you know, to offer sacrifices of all sorts. But the Spirit of God speaks here of the church of the Jews under the New Testament ; especially what they should be after their conversion, having reference to the Jews in Christ's time, and to the believing Jews in all times, implying thus much ; howsoever, not legal sacrifices of calves, bullocks, sheep, and lambs, yet the ' calves of the lips,' which God likes better, are acceptable to him. And it likewise implies some humiliation of the church. Lord, whatsoever else we could offer unto thee, it is thine own, though it were the beasts upon a thousand mountains ; but this, by thy grace, we can do, to ' praise thee,' Ps. l. 23. For God must open and circumcise our lips and hearts before we can offer him the ' calves of our lips.' Thus much the poorest creature in the world may say to God, Lord, ' I will render thee the calves of my lips.' Other things I have not. This I have by thy gracious Spirit, a heart somewhat touched by the sense of thy favour. Therefore ' I will render thee the calves of my lips ;' that is, praise, as the apostle hath it, ' By him therefore let us offer the sacrifice of praise to God continually ; that is, the fruit of our lips, giving thanks to his name,' Heb. xiii. 15. ' So will we render thee the calves of our lips.' Whence the point is,

Doct. That God's children at all times have their sacrifices.

There is indeed one kind of sacrificing determined* and finished by the coming of Christ, who was the last sacrifice of propitiation for our sins. The more to blame those who yet maintain a daily sacrifice, not of laud and praise, but of cozening and deluding the world, in saying mass for the sins of the quick and the dead ; all such sacrifices being finished and closed up in him, our blessed Saviour ; who, ' by one sacrifice,' as the apostle speaks, ' hath perfected them that are sanctified,' Heb. x. 14, vii. 27 ; and that, ' by one sacrifice, when he offered up himself,' Heb. x. 12 ; when all the Jewish sacrifices ended. Since which, all ours are but a commemoration of Christ's last sacrifice, as the fathers say : the Lord's supper, with the rest, which remain still ; and the sacrifice of praise, with a few others, I desire to name.

1. First, The sacrifice of a broken heart, whereof David speaks, Ps. li. 17 ; which sacrifice of a wounded, broken heart, by the knife of repentance, pleaseth God wondrously well.

2. And then, a broken heart that offers Christ to God every day ; who, though he were offered once for all, yet our believing in him, and daily presenting his atonement made for us, is a new offering of him. Christ is

* That is, ' abolished ' = fulfilled.—G.

crucified and sacrificed for thee as oft as thou believest in Christ crucified. Now, upon all occasions we manifest our belief in Christ, to wash and bathe ourselves in his blood, who justifieth the ungodly. So that, upon a fresh sight of sin, with contrition for it, he continually justifieth us. Thus, when we believe, we offer him to God daily; a broken heart first, and then Christ with a broken heart.

3. And then when we believe in Christ, we offer and sacrifice ourselves to God; in which respect we must, as it were, be killed ere we be offered. For we may not offer ourselves as we are in our lusts, but as mortified and killed by repentance. Then we offer ourselves to God as a reasonable and living sacrifice, when we offer ourselves wholly unto him, wit, understanding, judgment, affections, and endeavour; as Paul saith of the Macedonians, 'they gave themselves to God first, and then their goods,' 2 Cor. viii. 5. In sum, it is that sacrifice Paul speaks of, 'to present our bodies a living sacrifice, holy, acceptable unto God,' &c., Rom. xii. 1. For a Christian who believeth in the Lord Jesus is not his own, but sacrificeth himself to him that was sacrificed for him. As Christ is given to us, so he that believes in Christ gives himself back again to Christ. Hereby a man may know if he be a true Christian, and that Christ is his, if he yields up himself to God. For 'Christ died and rose again,' saith the apostle, 'that he might be Lord both of quick and dead,' Rom. xiv. 9. 'Therefore,' saith he, 'whether we live or die, we are not our own,' Rom. xiv. 8. What we do or suffer in the world, in all we are sacrificed. So saith a sanctified soul, My wit, my will, my life, my good, my affections are thine; of thee I received them, and I resign all to thee as a sacrifice. Thus the martyrs, to seal the truth, as a sacrifice, yielded up their blood. He that hath not obtained of himself so much as to yield himself to God, he knows not what the gospel means. For Christian religion is not only to believe in Christ for forgiveness of sin; but the same faith which takes this great benefit, renders back ourselves in lieu of thankfulness.

So that, whatsoever we have, after we believe, we give all back again. Lord, I have my life, my will, my wit, and all from thee; and to thee I return all back again. For when I gave myself to believe in thy dear Son, I yielded myself and all I have to thee; and now, having nothing but by thy gift, if thou wilt have all I will return all unto thee again; if thou wilt have my life, my goods, my liberty, thou shalt have them. This is the state of a Christian who hath denied himself. For we cannot believe as we should unless we deny ourselves. Christianity is not altogether in believing this and that; but the faith which moves me to believe forgiveness of sins, carries us also unto God to yield all back again to him.

4. More especially, among the sacrifices of the New Testament are alms, as, 'To do good and to communicate forget not, for with such sacrifices God is well pleased,' Heb. xiii. 16.

5. And among the rest, the sacrifice of praise, which is in the same chapter, verse 15. First, he saith, By him, that is, by Christ, let us offer the sacrifice of praise to God continually, that is, the fruit of our lips: which is but an exposition of this place, which, because it is especially here intended, I will a little enlarge myself in.

The 'calves of our lips' implies two things:

Not only thankfulness to God, but glorifying of God, in setting out his praise. Otherwise to thank God for his goodness to us, or for what we hope to receive, without glorifying of him, is nothing at all worth. For in glorifying there are two things.

1. *A supposition of excellency.* For that cannot be glorified, which hath no excellency in it. Glory in sublimity hath alway excellency attending it. And

2. *The manifestation of this glory.*

Now, when all the excellencies of God, as they are, are discovered and set out, his wisdom, mercy, power, goodness, all-sufficiency, &c., then we glorify him. To praise God for his favours to us, and accordingly to glorify him, is ' the calves of our lips ; ' but especially to praise him. Whence the point is—

That the yielding of praise to God is a wondrous acceptable sacrifice.

Which is instead of all the sacrifices of the Old Testament, than which the greatest can do no more, nor the least less ; for it is the sacrifice and fruit of the lips. But to open it. It is not merely the sacrifice of our lips ; for the praise we yield to God, it must be begotten in the heart. Hereupon the word, λογός, speech, signifieth both reason and speech, there being one word in the learned language for both.* Because speech is nothing but that stream which issues from the spring of reason and understanding : therefore, in thanksgiving there must not be a lip-labour only, but a thanksgiving from the lips, first begotten in the heart, coming from the inward man, as the prophet saith, 'Bless the Lord, O my soul ; and all that is within me, bless his holy name,' Ps. ciii. 1. Praise must come from a sound judgment of the worth of the thing we praise for. It must come from an affection which desires that God may have the glory, by the powers of the whole inward man, which is a hard matter, to rouse up ourselves to praise God with all the powers of our soul, ' all that is within me, praise his holy name,' Ps. ciii. 1. There goeth judgment, resolution of the will, strength of affections, and all with it.

And then again, besides this, ' the calves of our lips ' carries us to work. The oral thanksgiving must be justified by our works and deeds ; or else our actions will give our tongue the lie, that we praise him with the one, but deny him in the other. This is a solecism, as if one should look to the earth, and cry, O ye heavens ! So when we say, God be praised, when yet our life speaks the contrary, it is a dishonouring of God. So the praise of our lips must be made good and justified by our life, actions, and conversation. This we must suppose for the full understanding of the words, ' We will render,' from our hearts, ' the calves of our lips ; ' which we must make good in our lives and conversations, ever to set forth thy praise in our whole life.

Quest. But why doth the prophet especially mention lips, ' the calves of our lips,' which are our words ?

Ans. 1. Partly, because Christ, who is the Word, delights in our words.

2. Because our tongue is our glory, and that whereby we glorify God.

3. And especially because our tongue is that which excites others, being a trumpet of praise, ordained of God for this purpose. Therefore, ' the calves of our lips ; ' partly, because it stirs up ourselves and others, and partly, because God delights in words, especially of his own dictating. To come then to speak more fully of praise and thanksgiving, let us consider what a sweet, excellent, and prevailing duty this is, which the church, to bind God, promiseth unto him, ' the calves of our lips.' I will not be long in the point, but only come to some helps how we may come to do it.

First, this praising of God must be *from an humble, broken heart.* The

* Cf. p. 153 and note *o*, p. 195.—G.

humble soul that sees itself not worthy of any favour, and confesseth sin before God, is alway a thankful soul. 'Take away our iniquity, and then do good to us.' We are empty ourselves. Then will 'we render thee the calves of our lips.' What made David so thankful a man? He was an humble man; and so Jacob, what abased him so in his own eyes? His humility: 'Lord, I am less than the least of thy mercies,' Gen. xxxii. 10. He that thinks himself unworthy of anything, will be thankful for everything; and he who thinks himself unworthy of any blessing, will be contented with the least. Therefore, let us work our hearts to humility, in consideration of our sinfulness, vileness, and unworthiness, which will make us thankful: especially of the best blessings, when we consider their greatness, and our unworthiness of them. A proud man can never be thankful. Therefore, that religion which teacheth pride, cannot be a thankful religion. Popery is compounded of spiritual pride: merit of congruity, before conversion; merit of condignity, and desert of heaven, after; free will, and the like, to puff up nature. What a religion is this! Must we light a candle before the devil? Is not nature proud enough, but we must light a candle to it? To be spiritually proud is worst of all.

2. And with our own unworthiness, add this: *a consideration of the greatness of the thing we bless God for;* setting as high a price upon it as we can, by considering what and how miserable we were without it. He will bless God joyfully for pardon of sin, who sees how miserable he were without it, in misery next to devils, ready to drop into hell every moment. And the more excellent we are, so much the more accursed, without the forgiveness of sins. For the soul, by reason of the largeness thereof, is so much the more capable and comprehensible of misery; as the devils are more capable than we, therefore are most accursed. Oh, this will make us bless God for the pardon of sin! And likewise, let us set a price upon all God's blessings, considering what we were without our senses, speech, meat, drink, rest, &c. O beloved! we forget to praise God sufficiently for our senses. This little spark of reason in us is an excellent thing; grace is founded upon it. If we were without reason, what were we? If we wanted sight, hearing, speech, rest, and other daily blessings, how uncomfortable were our lives! This consideration will add and set a price to their worth, and make us thankful, to consider our misery without them. But, such is our corruption, that favours are more known by the want, than by the enjoying of them. When too late, we many times find how dark and uncomfortable we are without them; then smarting the more soundly, because in time we did not sufficiently prize, and were thankful for them.

3. And then, *labour to get further and further assurance that we are God's children, beloved of him.* This will make us thankful both for what we have and hope for. It lets out the life-blood of thankfulness, to teach doubting or falling from grace. What is the end, I beseech you, why the glory to come is revealed before the time? That we shall be sons and daughters, kings and queens, heirs and co-heirs with Christ, and [that] 'all that he hath is ours?' Rom. viii. 17. Is not this knowledge revealed beforehand, that our praise and thanksgiving should beforehand be suitable to this revelation, being set with Christ in heavenly places already. Whence comes those strong phrases? 'We are raised with Christ; sit with him in heavenly places,' Eph. ii. 6; 'are translated from death to life,' Col. i. 13; 'transformed into his image;' 'partakers of the divine nature,' &c., 2 Pet. i. 4. If anything that can come betwixt our believing,

and our sitting there, could disappoint us thereof, or unsettle us, it may as well put Christ out of heaven, for we sit with him. If we yield to the uncomfortable popish doctrine of doubting, we cannot be heartily thankful for blessings ; for still there will rise in the soul surmises, I know not whether God favour me or not : it may be, I am only fatted for the day of slaughter ; God gives me outward things to damn me, and make me the more inexcusable. What a cooler of praise is this, to be ever doubting, and to have no assurance of God's favour ! But when upon good evidence, which cannot deceive, we have somewhat wrought in us, distinct from the greater number of worldlings, God's stamp set upon us ; having evidences of the state of grace, by conformity to Christ, and walking humbly by the rule of the word in all God's ways : then we may heartily be thankful, yea, and we shall break forth in thanksgiving ; this being an estate of peace, and 'joy unspeakable and glorious,' 1 Pet. i. 8, wherein we take everything as an evidence of God's love.

Thus the assurance of our being in the state of grace makes us thankful for everything. So by the contrary, being not in some measure assured of God's love in Christ, we cannot be thankful for everything. For it will always come in our mind, I know not how I have these things, and what account I shall give for them. Therefore, even for the honour of God, and that we may praise him the more cheerfully, let us labour to have further and further evidences of the state of grace, to make us thankful both for things present and to come, seeing faith takes to trust things to come, as if it had them in possession. Whereby we are assured of this, that we shall come to heaven, as sure as if we were there already. This makes us praise God beforehand for all favours ; as blessed Peter begins his epistle, ' Blessed be the God and Father of our Lord Jesus Christ, which, according to his abundant mercy, hath begotten us again unto a lively hope, by the resurrection of Jesus Christ from the dead, to an inheritance incorruptible and undefiled, and that fadeth not away, reserved in heaven for you,' &c., 1 Pet. i. 3, 4. As soon as we are newborn, we are begotten to a kingdom and an inheritance. Therefore, assurance that we are God's children will make us thankful for grace present, and that to come, as if we were in heaven already. We begin then the employment of heaven in thanksgiving here, to praise God beforehand with cherubims and angels. Let us, then, be stirred up to give God his due beforehand, to begin heaven upon earth ; for we are so much in heaven already, as we abound and are conversant in thanksgiving upon earth.

THE THIRD SERMON.

So will we render the calves of our lips. Asshur shall not save us ; we will not ride upon horses · neither will we say any more to the works of our hands, Ye are our gods : for in thee the fatherless findeth mercy.—Hos. XIV. 2, 3.

The words, as we heard heretofore, contain a most sweet and excellent form of returning unto God, for miserable, lost, and forlorn sinners ; wherein so far God discovers his willingness to have his people return unto him, that he dictates unto them a **form of** prayer, ' Take with you words, and turn to the Lord ; say unto him, Take away iniquity.' Wherein we see how detestation of sin must be as general as the desire of pardon, and that none heartily pray to God to 'take away all iniquity' who have not grace truly to hate all iniquity. 'And do good to us,' or do graciously to us ; for there is no good to us till sin be removed. Though God be goodness itself, there is no provoking or meriting cause of mercy in us. But he finds cause from his own gracious nature and bowels of mercy to pity his poor people and servants. It is his nature to shew mercy, as the fire to burn, a spring to run, the sun to shine. Therefore, it is easily done. As the prophet speaks, 'Who is a God like unto thee ?' Micah vii. 18.

Where we come to speak of the re-stipulation, 'So will we render the calves of our lips.' Where God's favour shines, there will be a reflection. Love is not idle, but a working thing. It must render or die. And what doth it render ? Divers sacrifices of the New Testament, which I spake of ; that of a broken heart ; of Christ offered to the Father, to stand betwixt God's wrath and us ; ourselves as a living sacrifice ; alms-deeds and praise, which must be with the whole inward powers of the soul.

'Praise is not comely in the mouth of a fool,' saith the wise man, nor of a wicked man. Saith God to such, 'What hast thou to do to take my words in thy mouth, since thou hatest to be reformed, and hast cast my words behind thee ?' Ps. l. 16, 17. There are a company who are ordinary swearers and filthy speakers. For them to praise God, James tells them that these contrary streams cannot flow out of a good heart, James iii. 10, 11. Oh, no ; God requires not the praise of such fools.

I gave you also some directions how to praise God, and to stir up yourselves to this most excellent duty, which I will not insist on now, but add a little unto that I then delivered, which is, *that we must watch all advantages of praising God from our dispositions.* 'Is any merry ? let him sing,' saith James, v. 13. Oh ! it is a great point of wisdom to take advantages with the stream of our temper to praise God. When he doth encourage us by his favours and blessings, and enlarge our spirits, then we are in a right temper to bless him. Let us not lose the occasion. This is one branch of redeeming of time, to observe what state and temper of soul we are in, and to take advantage from thence. Is any man in heaviness ? he is fit to mourn for sin. Let him take the opportunity of that temper. Is any disposed to cheerfulness ? Let him sacrifice that marrow, oil, and sweetness of spirit to God. We see the poor birds in the spring-time, when those little spirits they have are cherished with the sunbeams, how they express it in singing. So when God warms us with his favours, let him have the praise of all.

And here I cannot but take up a lamentation of the horrible ingratitude of men, who are so far from taking advantage by God's blessings to praise him, that they fight like rebels against him with his own favours. Those tongues which he hath given them for his glory, they abuse to pierce him with blasphemy ; and those other benefits of his, lent them to honour him with, they turn to his dishonour ; like children who importunately ask for divers things, which, when they have, they throw them to the dog. So favours they will have, which, when they have obtained, they give them to the devil ; unto whom they sacrifice their strength and cheerfulness, and cannot be merry, unless they be mad and sinful. Are these things to be tolerated in these days of light ? How few shall we find, who, in a temper of mirth, turn it the right way ?

1. But to add some encouragements to incite us to praise God unto the former, I beseech you let this be one, that *we honour God by it.* It is a

well-pleasing sacrifice to him.　If we would study to please him, we cannot do it better than by praising him.

2. And *it is a gainful trading with God.*　For in bestowing his seed, where he finds there is improvement in a good soil, with such a sanctified disposition as to bless him upon all occasions, that there comes not a good thought, a good motion in the mind, but we bless God who hath injected such a good thought in our heart; there, I say, God delights to shower down more and more blessings, making us fruitful in every good work to the praise of his name.　Sometimes we shall have holy and gracious persons make a law that no good or holy motion shall come into their hearts, which they will not be thankful for.　Oh! when God seeth a heart so excellently disposed, how doth it enrich the soul!　It is a gainful trade. As we delight to bestow our seed in soils of great increase, which yield sixty and an hundredfold, if possible, so God delights in a disposition inclined to bless him upon all occasions, on whom he multiplies his favours.

3. And then, in itself, *it is a most noble act of religion*, it being a more base thing to be always begging of God; but it argueth a more noble, raised, and elevated spirit, to be disposed to praise God.　And it is an argument of less self-love and respect, being therefore more gainful to us. Yea, it is a more noble and royal disposition, fit for spiritual kings and priests thus to sacrifice.

4. Again, indeed, *we have more cause to praise God than to pray;* having many things to praise him for, which we never prayed for.　Who ever prayed for his election, care of parents in our infancy, their affection to us, care to breed and train us to years of discretion, besides those many favours daily heaped upon us, above all that we are able to think or speak? Therefore, praise being a more large sacrifice than prayer, we ought to be abundant in it.　For those that begin not heaven upon earth, of which this praise is a main function, they shall never come to heaven, after they are taken from the earth; for there is no heavenly action, but it is begun upon earth, especially this main one, of joining with angels, seraphim, and cherubim, in lauding God.　Shall they praise him on our behalf, and shall not we for our own?　We see the choir of angels, when Christ was born, sang, ' Glory be to God on high, on earth peace, and goodwill towards men,' Luke ii. 14.　What was this for?　Because Christ the Saviour of the world was born; whereby they shew that we have more benefit by it than they.　Therefore, if we would ever join with them in heaven, let us join with them upon earth.　For this is one of the great privileges mentioned by the author to the Hebrews, unto which we be come to, ' communion with the spirits of just men made perfect, and to the company of innumerable angels,' Heb. xii. 22, 23.　We cannot better shew that we are come to that blessed estate and society spoken of, than by praising God.

5. And lastly, if we be much in praising God, *we shall be much in joy,* which easeth misery.　For a man can never be miserable that can be joyful; and a man is always joyful when he is thankful.　When one is joyful and cheerful, what misery can lie upon him?　Therefore, it is a wondrous help in misery to stir up the heart to this spiritual sacrifice of thanksgiving by all arguments, means, and occasions.　Our hearts are temples, and we are priests.　We should alway, therefore, have this light and incense burning in our hearts, as the fire did alway burn on the altar in Moses's time, that we may have these spiritual sacrifices to offer continually.　Where this is not, the heart of that man or woman is like ' the abomination of desolation,'

Dan. xii. 11, which, when the daily sacrifice was taken away, was set up in the temple. And certainly where there is not praising of God, the heart is ' an abomination of desolation,' having nothing in it save monsters of base lusts and earthly affections.

Ques. But how shall we know that God accepts these sacrifices of praise ?

Ans. How did he witness the acceptation of those sacrifices under the old law ? ' By fire from heaven,' Judges vi. 21 ; 1 Kings xviii. 24, *et seq.* This was ordinary with them. So, if we find our hearts warm, cheered and encouraged with joy, peace, and comfort in praising God ; this is as it were a witness by fire from heaven that our sacrifices are accepted. Let this now said be effectual to stir you up to this excellent and useful duty of thanksgiving, without multiplying of more arguments, save to put you in mind of this, that as we are exhorted to ' delight ourselves in the Lord,' Ps. xxxvii. 4, one way, among the rest, to do it, is to ' serve him with cheerfulness.' It is an excellent thing to make us delight in God, who loves a cheerful giver and thanksgiver. ' So will we render the calves of our lips.' But to proceed.

After this their solemn covenant and promise of yielding praise to God, that if he would forgive all their sins, and do good to them, then he should have the best they could do to him again : praise here is a promise of new obedience, which hath two branches,

1. *A renunciation of the ill courses they took before.*

' Asshur shall not save us ; we will not ride upon horses ; neither will we say any more to the works of our hands, Ye are our gods.'

2. Then there is *a positive duty implied* in these words, ' For in thee the fatherless findeth mercy.'

Whereof, the one springs from the other ; ' Asshur shall not save us, we will not ride upon horses ; neither will we say any more to the works of our hands, Ye are our gods.' Whence comes all these ? ' For in thee the fatherless findeth mercy.' Thou shalt be our rock, our trust, our confidence for ever. What will follow upon this ? ' Asshur shall not save us any longer ; we will not ride upon horses,' &c. For we have pitched and placed our confidence better ; on him in whom ' the fatherless findeth mercy.'

' Asshur shall not save us.' The confidence which this people had placed partly in Asshur, their friends and associates, and partly in their own strength at home, now promising repentance, they renounce all such confidence in Asshur, horses and idols. ' Asshur shall not save us,' &c.

First, for this, ' Asshur shall not save us,' that is, the Assyrians, whom they had on the one side, and the Egyptians on the other : it being, as we see in the prophecies of Isaiah and Jeremiah, ordinary with God's people, in any distress, to have recourse to the Assyrians, or Egyptians, as if God had not been sufficient to be their rock and their shield. We see how often the Lord complains of this manner of dealing. ' Woe unto them that go down into Egypt for help, and stay on horses, and trust in chariots, because they are many,' &c., Isa. xxx. 2, and xxxi. 1. The prophets, and so this prophet, are very full of such complaints : it being one of the chief arguments he presseth, their falseness in this, that in any fear or peril, they ran to the shelter of other nations, especially these two, Egypt and Assyria, as you have it, ' Ephraim feedeth on wind, and followeth after the east wind ; he daily increaseth lies and desolation, and they do make a covenant with the Assyrians, and oil is carried into Egypt,' Hosea xii. 1, that is, balm, who had this privilege above all other nations, to abound in precious balms; which balm and oil they carried into Egypt, to win their favour against the Assyrians. Sometimes they relied on the one, and sometimes on the other, the story and causes whereof were too tedious to relate. Wherefore I come to the useful points arising hence. ' Asshur shall not save us.'

1. That man, naturally, is prone to put confidence in the creature.

2. That the creature is insufficient and unable to yield us this prop to uphold our confidence.

3. That God's people, when they are endowed with light supernatural to discern and be convinced hereof, are of that mind to say, ' Asshur shall not save us.'

But, to make way to these things, we must first observe two things for a preparative.

Doct. First, That reformation of life must be joined with prayer and praise. There was prayer before, and a promise of praise; but, as here, there must be joined reformation of their sin. That it must be so, it appears, first, for *prayer*. It is said, ' If I regard iniquity in my heart, the Lord will not hear my prayer,' Ps. lxvi. 18. And for *praise*, ' The very sacrifice of the wicked (who reforms not his ways) is abominable,' Prov. xv. 8. So that, without reformation, prayer and praise is to no purpose. Therefore it is brought here after a promise of praise. Lord, as we mean to praise thee, so we intend a thorough reformation of former sins, whereof we were guilty. We will renounce Asshur, and confidence in horses, idols, and the like. Therefore let us, when we come to God with prayer and praise, think also of reforming what is amiss. Out with Achan, Josh. vii. 19. If there be any dead fly, Eccles. x. 1, or Achan uncast out, prayer and praise is in vain. ' Will you steal, lie, commit adultery, swear falsely, and come and stand before me,' saith the Lord, by the prophet Jeremiah, Jer. vii. 9. Will you offer to pray to me, and praise me, living in these and these sins? No; God will abhor both that prayer and praise, where there is no reformation. ' What hast thou to do to take my name in thy mouth, since thou hatest to be reformed, and hast cast my words behind thee, saith God,' Ps. l. 16, where he pleads with the hypocrite for this audacious boldness in severing things conjoined by God. Therefore, as we would not have our prayers turned back from heaven, which should bring a blessing upon all other things else: as we would not have our sacrifices abominable to God, labour to reform what is amiss, amend all, or else never think our lip-labour will prove anything but a lost labour without this reformation.

A *second* thing, which I observe in general, before I come to the particulars, is,

Doct. That true repentance is, of the particular sin which we are most addicted to, and most guilty of.

The particular sin of this people, whom God so instructs here, was their confidence in Assyria, horses, and idols. Now therefore repenting, they repent of the particular, main sins they were most guilty of; which being stricken down, all the lesser will be easy to conquer. As when Goliath himself was stricken down, all the host of the Philistines ran away, 1 Sam. xvii. 51. So when Goliath shall be slain in us, the reigning, ruling, domineering sin, the rest will easily be conquered.

Use. Therefore let us make an use of *examination* and trial of our repentance. If it be sound, it draws with it a reformation; as in general, so especially of our particular sins. As those confess and say, ' Above all other things we have sinned in this, in asking a king,' 1 Sam. xii. 8. We were naught, and had offended God many ways before ; but herein we have been exceeding sinful, in seeking another governor, being weary of God's gracious government over us. So a gracious heart will say, I have been a wretch in all other things, but in this and that sin above all other. Thus it was with the woman of Samaria, when she was put in mind by Christ of her particular grand sin, that she had been a light woman, and had had many husbands, he whom she lived with now not being her husband, John iv. 18. This discovery, when Christ touched the galled part, did so work upon her conscience that it occasioned a general repentance of all her other sins whatsoever. And, indeed, sound repentance of one main sin will draw with it all the rest. And, for the most part, when God brings any man home to him, he so carries our repentance, that, discovering unto us our sinfulness, he especially shews us our Delilah, Isaac, Herodias, our particular sin ; which being cast out, we prevail easily against the rest. As the charge was given by the king of Aram against Ahab, 'Fight neither against great nor small, but only against the king of Israel,' 2 Chron. xviii. 30 ; kill him, and then there will be an end of the battle. So let us not stand striking at this and that sin (which we are not so much tempted to), if we will indeed prove our repentance to be sound ; but at that main sin which by nature, calling, or custom we are most prone unto. Repentance for this causes repentance for all the rest ; as here the church saith, ' Asshur shall not save us ; we will not ride upon horses,' &c.

It is a grand imposture, which carries many to hell ; they will cherish themselves in some gross main sin, which pleases corrupt nature, and is advantageous to them ; and by way of compensation with God, they will do many other things well, but leave a dead fly to mar all ; whereas they should begin here especially. Thus much in general, which things premised, I come to the forenamed particulars. First,

Doct. That naturally we are apt and prone to confidence in outward helps and present things.

This came to our nature from the first fall. What was our fall at first ? A turning from the all-sufficient, unchangeable God, to the creature. If I should describe sin, it is nothing but a turning from God to one creature or other. When we find not contentment and sufficiency in one creature, we run to another. As the bird flies from one tree and bough to another, so we seek variety of contentments from one thing to another. Such is the pravity of our nature since the fall. This is a fundamental conclusion. Man naturally will, and must, have somewhat to rely on. The soul must have a bottom, a foundation to rest on, either such as the world affords, or a better. Weak things must have their supports. As we see, the vine being a weak thing, is commonly supported by the elm, or the like supply. So is it with the soul since the fall. Because it is weak, and cannot uphold nor satisfy itself with itself, therefore it looks out of itself. Look to God it cannot, till it be in the state of grace ; for being his enemy, it loves not to look to him or his ways, or have dealing with him. Therefore it looks unto the creature, that next hand unto itself. This being naturally since the fall, that what we had in God before when we stood, we now labour to have in the creature.

Reason 1. Because, as was said, having lost communion with God, somewhat we must have to stay the soul.

2. *Secondly,* Because Satan joins with our sense and fancy, by which we are naturally prone to live, esteeming of things not by faith and by deeper

grounds, but by fancy. Now, fancy having communion with sense, what it discovers and presents for good and great, fancy makes it greater. And the devil, above all, having communion with that faculty of fancy, and so a spirit of error being mixed therewith, to make our fancy think the riches of the world to be the only riches; the greatness and goodness of the creature to be the only greatness and goodness; and the strength thereof the only strength. This spirit of error joining with our own spirits, and with the deceit of our natures, makes us set a higher value on the creature, enlargeth and enrageth the fancy, making it spiritually drunk, so as to conceive amiss of things.

Use. Briefly for use hereof, it being but a directing point to others. Let us take notice of our corruption herein, and be humbled for it ; taking in good part those afflictions and crosses which God sends us, to convince and let us see that there is no such thing in the creature as we imagined ; because naturally, we are desperately given to think that there is somewhat more therein than there is. Now affliction helps this sickness of fancy, embittering unto us all confidence in the creature. Therefore it is a happy and a blessed thing to be crossed in that which we over-value, as these Israelites here did the Assyrians and the Egyptians : for being enemies, they trusted in a 'broken reed,' 2 Kings xviii. 21, as we shall see further in the second point.

Doct. How these outward things cannot help us.

How prone soever we are to rely upon them, they are in effect nothing. They cannot help us, and so are not to be relied upon. 'Asshur shall not save us.' Indeed it will not, it cannot. These things cannot aid us at our most need. So that that which we most pitch upon, fails us when we should especially have help. Some present vanishing supply they yield, but little to purpose. They have not that in them which should support the soul at a strait, or great pinch, as we say.

Reason. The reason is largely given by Solomon in the whole book of Ecclesiastes, 'All is vanity and vexation of spirit,' Eccles. i. 14. There is a vanity in all the creatures, being empty and not able to support the soul. They are vain in their continuance, and empty in regard of their strength. They are gone when we have need of them. Riches, as the wise man saith, are gone, and have wings to fly away, in our most need, Prov. xxiii. 5. So friends are fugitive good things, being like to the brooks mentioned in Job, vi. 15 : which when in summer there is need of, then they are dried up, and yet run amain in winter, when there is no need of them. So, earthly supports, when there is no need of them, then they are at hand ; but when we have most need of them, are gone. 'They are broken cisterns,' as the prophet calls them, Jer. ii. 13. Cisterns, that is, they have a limited capacity. A cistern is not a spring. So all their support, at the best, is but a bounded and a mixed sufficiency ; and that also which will quickly fail : like water in a cistern, which if it be not fed with a continual spring, fails or putrefies presently. Likewise these outward things are not sufficient for the grievance ; for being limited and bounded, the grievance will be above the strength of the creature ; which though sometime it be present and do not fail, yet the trouble is such, that it is above the strength of the creature to help. So that for these and the like respects, there is no sufficiency, nor help to be expected from the creature. 'Asshur shall not save us.' He is not a sufficient ground of trust. Why ?

1. He is but a creature.
2. He is an enemy.

3. He is an idolater.

So that, take him in all these three relations, he is not to be trusted.

1. *He is a creature.* What is a creature? Nothing, as it were. Saith the prophet, ' All creatures before him are as nothing, and as a very little thing.' And what it is, when he pleaseth, he can dissolve it into nothing, turn it into dust. Man's breath is in his nostrils, Isa. ii. 22. ' All flesh is grass, and all his glory as the flower of grass,' Ps. ciii. 15. If a man trust the creature, he may outlive his trust. His prop may be taken from him, and down he falls. Asshur must not be trusted, therefore, as a creature, nor as a man, for that brings us within the curse. Thus saith the Lord, ' Cursed be the man that trusteth in man, and maketh flesh his arm,' &c., Jer. xvii. 5. So trusting in the creature not only deceives us, but brings us within the curse. In that respect, Asshur must not be trusted.

2. But Asshur likewise was an *enemy*, and a secret enemy. For howsoever the ten tribes unto whom Hosea prophesied were great idolaters, yet they were somewhat better than Asshur, who was without the pale of the church, and a wholly corrupted church. Therefore, they were enemies to the ten tribes, and, amongst other reasons, because they were not so bad as they, nor deeply enough dyed with idolatry.

Many think they may comply with popery in some few things, to gain their love, and that there may be joining with them in this and that ; but do we think that they will ever trust us for all this ? No ; they will alway hate us, till we be as bad as they, and then they will despise us, and secure themselves of us. Therefore, there is no trusting of papists, as papists ; not only creatures, but as false, and as enemies. For this is the nature of wicked men. They will never trust better than themselves, till they become as bad as they are, after which they despise them. Say they, Now we may trust such and such a one ; he is as bad as we, becom'd * one of us. Which is the reason why some of a naughty dispositson take away the chastity and virginity of men's consciences, making them take this and that evil course, and then they think they have such safe, being as bad as themselves. Wherein they deal as Ahithophel's politic, devilish counsel was, that Absalom should do that which was naught, and then he should be sure that David and he should never agree after that, 2 Sam. xvi. 21 ; and that then by this discovery the wicked Jews, set on mischief, might secure themselves of Absalom. So they, now that they join with us, God will forsake them ; we shall have them our instruments for anything. First, they would have the ten tribes as bad as they, and then give them the slip whensoever they trusted them.

3. Again, neither were they to be trusted *as idolaters*, to have league and society with them. There may be some commerce and traffic with them, but amity and trust, none. Asshur and Egypt were horrible idolaters, and therefore not to be trusted in that respect. As we see the prophet in this case reproved good Jehoshaphat, when he had joined with wicked Ahab, king of the ten tribes, ' Shouldst thou help the ungodly, and love them that hate the Lord ? therefore wrath is upon thee from before the Lord,' 2 Chron. xix. 2. So we see it is a dangerous thing to be in league with idolaters, even such as the ten tribes were, who had some religion amongst them. This good king was chidden for it.

' We will not ride upon horses.'

What kind of creature a horse is, it is worth the seeing. What a description God gives of him, that we may see what reason the Spirit of God hath

* That is, ' become.'—G.

to instance in the horse.   Saith God to Job, 'Hast thou given the horse strength? hast thou clothed his neck with thunder? canst thou make him afraid as a grasshopper? the glory of his nostrils is terrible.   He paweth in the valley, and rejoiceth in his strength: he goeth on to meet the armed men.   He mocketh at fear, and is not affrighted; neither turneth he back from the sword.   The quiver rattleth against him, the glittering spear and the shield.   He swalloweth the ground with fierceness and rage: neither believeth he that it is the sound of the trumpet.   He saith among the trumpets, Ha, ha; and he smelleth the battle afar off, the thunder of the captains, and the shouting,' Job xxxix. 19–21.   A notable and excellent description of this warlike creature.   And yet for all this excellency, so described by the Spirit of God, in another place the psalmist saith, 'A horse is a vain thing for safety, neither shall he deliver any by his great strength,' Ps. xxxiii. 17.   ' Some trust in chariots, and some in horses; but we will remember the name of the Lord our God,' Ps. xx. 7.   So in another place, ' The horse is prepared against the day of battle, but victory is of the Lord,' Prov. xxi. 31.

How oft have you in the Psalms that proud warlike creature disparaged, because naturally men are more bewitched with that than with any other creature.   If they have store of horses, then they think they are strong. Therefore God forbids the king ' to multiply horses to himself, nor cause the people to return to Egypt, to the end he should multiply horses,' &c., Deut. xvii. 16, because God is the strength of his church, when there is no multitude of horses.   You see it is a bewitching creature, and yet a vain help.   A place like this we have, Isa. ii. 7, complaining there of the naughty people which were among the Jews, at that time as bad as the Israelites. Saith he, ' Their land also is full of silver and gold; neither is there any end of their treasures; their land is also full of horses, neither is there any end of their chariots.'   What, is there a fault in that?   No. Luther saith, ' Good works are good, but the confidence in them is damnable.'   So gold and silver, horses and chariots, are good creatures of God. But this was their sin, confidence in these things.   ' There is no end of their treasures.'   If they had treasure enough, they should do well enough. ' Their land also was full of horses.'   Was this a fault?   No; but their confidence in them.   They thought they were a wise people to have such furniture and provision of munition for war.   But God was their king, and the chief governor of his people; and for them to heap up these things, to trust over-much in them, it was a matter of complaint.   ' Their land also is full of idols.'

Thus you see there is no confidence to be put neither in the one nor the other, neither in the association of foreign friends, who will prove deceitful, ' reeds of Egypt,' that not only deceive, but the splinters thereof fly about, and may run up into the hand.   Such are idolaters and false friends, deceitful and hurtful.   Nor in home.   There is no trust in horses, munition, or such like.   What doth this imply?   That to war and have provision in that kind is unlawful and unnecessary, because he finds fault here with horses and the like?   No; take heed of that; for John Baptist, if the soldier's profession had been unlawful, he would have bid them cast away their weapons; but he bids them ' do violence to no man, neither accuse any falsely,' &c., Luke iii. 14.   And God would never style himself ' the Lord of hosts, and a man of war,' Isa. xlii. 13, and ' he that teacheth our hands to war, and our fingers to fight,' Ps. xviii. 34, unless it were good in the season. Therefore war is lawful, seeing in the way to heaven we live in the midst of enemies.

Therefore it is but an anabaptistical fancy to judge war to be unlawful. No, no; it is clean another thing which the Holy Ghost aims at: to beat back carnal confidence. For it is an equal fault to multiply help and to neglect them. Either of both are fatal many times: to multiply horses, trusting in them, or to spoil horses and other helps vainly, so to weaken a kingdom. Therefore there is a middle way for all outward things, a fit care to serve God's providence, and when we have done, trust in God without tempting of him; for to neglect these helps is to tempt him, and to trust in them, when we have them, is to commit idolatry with them. Beware of both these extremes, for God will have his providence served in the use of lawful means. When there is this great care in a Christian commonwealth, there is a promise of good success, because God is with us. Otherwise, what is all, if he be our enemy? So we see the second point made good, *that these outward things of themselves cannot help.* Therefore comes this in the third place:—

Obs. That when God alters and changes and mouldeth anew the heart of a man to repentance, he altereth his confidence in the creature.

A Christian State will not trust in Asshur, nor in horses. It is true both of State and persons. The reason will follow after in the end of the verse, 'For in thee the fatherless findeth mercy.' Because, when a man hath once repented, there is a closing between God and him, and he seeth an all-sufficiency in God to satisfy all his desires. Therefore he will use all other things as helps, and as far as it may stand with his favour. For he hath Moses's eye put in him, a new eye to see him that is invisible, Heb. xi. 27, to see God in his greatness, and other things in their right estimate as vain things. What is repentance but a change of the mind, when a man comes to be wise and judicious, as indeed repentant men are the only wise men? Then a man hath an esteem of God to be *El-shadai,* all-sufficient, and all other things to be as they are, uncertain; that is, they are so to-day, as that they may be otherwise to-morrow, for that is the nature of the creatures. They are *in potentia,* in a possibility to be other things than they are. God is alway 'I AM,' alway the same. There is not so much as a shadow of changing in him. Wherefore, when the soul hath attained unto this spiritual eyesight and wisdom, if it be a sinful association with Egypt or Asshur, with this idolater or that, he will not meddle; and as for other helps, he will not use them further than as subordinate means. When a man is converted, he hath not a double, not a divided heart, to trust partly to God and partly to the creature. If God fail him,* he hath Asshur and horses enough, and association with all round about. But a Christian he will use all helps, as they may stand with the favour of God, and are subordinate under him. Now for trial.

Quest. How shall we know whether we exceed in this confidence in the creature or not?

Sol. 1. We may know it by *adventuring on ill courses and causes,* thinking to bear them out with Asshur and with horses. But all the mercenary soldiers in the world, and all the horses at home and abroad, what can they do when God is angry? Now, when there is such confidence in these things as for to out-dare God, then there is too much trust in them. That trust will end in confusion, if it be not repented of, for that lifts up the heart in the creature. And as the heathen man observes, 'God delights

* That is, the 'double-minded' man.—G.

to make great little, and little great.' It is his daily work to ' cast down mountains, and exalt the valleys,' Isa. xl. 4. Those that are great, and boast in their greatness, as if they would command heaven and earth, God delights to make their greatness little, and at length nothing, and to raise up the day of small things. Therefore the apostle saith, ' If I rejoice, it shall be in my infirmities,' 2 Cor. xii. 9, in nothing else ; for God delights to shew strength in weakness.

2. *By security and resting of the soul in meaner things*, never seeking to divine and religious helps when we are supplied with those that are outward. For these people, when they trusted to Assyria and Egypt, those false supports and sandy foundations, they were careless of God, and therefore must trust in somewhat else. Wherefore, if we see a man secure and careless, certainly he trusts too much to uncertain riches, to Asshur, to Egypt, to friends, or to outward helps. His security bewrays that. If a man trust God in the use of the means, his care will be to keep God his friend by repentance and daily exercises of religion, by making conscience of his duty. But if he trust the means and not God, he will be careless and weak in good duties, dull and slow, and, out of the atheism of his heart, cry, Tush ! if God do not help me, I shall have help from friends abroad, and be supported with this and that at home, horses and the like, and shall be well.

Use 1. Let us therefore enter into our own souls, and examine ourselves, how far forth we are guilty of this sin, and think we come so far short of repentance. For the ten tribes here, the people of God, when they repented, say, 'Asshur shall not save us ; we will not ride upon horses.' He speaks comparatively, as trusted in. Therefore, let us take heed of that boasting, vain-glorious disposition, arising from the supply of the creature. Saith God, ' Let not the wise man glory in his wisdom ; neither let the mighty man glory in his might: let not the rich man glory in his riches ; but let him that glorieth glory in this, that he understandeth and knoweth this, that I am the Lord, which exercise lovingkindness, judgment, and righteousness in the earth,' &c., Jer. ix. 23, 24. Let a man glory that he knows God in Christ to be his God in the covenant of grace ; that he hath the God of all strength, the King of kings and Lord of lords to be his : who hath all other things at his command, who is independent and all-sufficient. If a man will boast, let him go out of himself to God, and plant himself there ; and for other things, take heed the heart be not lift up with them.

1. Consider what kind of thing boasting is. It is idolatry, for it sets the creature in the place and room of God.

2. And it is also spiritual adultery, whereby we fix our affections upon the creature, which should be placed on God ; as it is in James, ' Ye adulterers and adulteresses, know ye not that the friendship of the world is enmity with God ?' &c., James iv. 4.

3. Habakkuk calls it drunkennness, Hab. ii. 4, 5, for it makes the soul drunk with sottishness and conceitedness, so as a man in this case is never sober, until God strip him of all.

4. And then again, it puts forth the eye of the soul. It is a kind of white, that mars the sight. When a man looks to Asshur, horses, and to outward strength, where is God all this while ? These are so many clouds, that they cannot see God, but altogether pore upon the creature. He sees so much greatness there, that God seems nothing. But when a man sees God in his greatness and almightiness, then the creature is

nothing, Job xlii. 6. But until this be, there is a mist and blindness in the eye of the soul.

And when we have seen our guiltiness this way (as who of us in this case may not be confounded and ashamed of relying too much on outward helps ?), then let us labour to take off our souls from these outward things, whether it be strength abroad or at home. Which that we may do, we must labour for that obedience which our Saviour Christ exhorts us unto in self-denial, Mat. xvi. 24, not to trust to our own devices, policy, or strength, wit, will, or conceits, that this or that may help us, nor anything. Make it general ; for when conversion is wrought, and the heart is turned to God, it turns from the creature, only using it as subordinate to God. We see, usually, men that exalt themselves in confidence, either of strength, of wit, or whatsoever, they are successless in their issue. For God delights to confound them, and go beyond their wit, as we have it, Isa. xxx. 3. They thought to go beyond God with their policy, they would have help out of Egypt, this and that way. Oh, saith the prophet, but for all this, God is wise to see through all your devices ; secretly hereby touching them to the quick, as sottish persons, who thought by their shallow brains to go beyond God. You think religious courses, and the obedience God prescribeth to you, to be idle, needless courses ; but, notwithstanding, God is wise. He will go beyond you, and catch you in your own craft. ' Therefore, the strength of Pharaoh shall be your shame, and the trust in the shadow of Egypt your confusion,' Isa. xxx. 3. Thus God loves to scatter Babels fabrics, Gen. xi. 8, and holds that are erected in confidence of human strength against him. He delights to catch the wise in their own craft, to beat all down, lay all high imaginations and things flat before him, that no flesh may glory in his sight. There is to this purpose a notable place in Isaiah : ' Behold, all ye that kindle a fire, that compass yourselves about with sparks,' Isa. l. 11. For they kindled a fire, and had a light of their own, and would not borrow light from God : ' Walk in the light of your fire, and in the sparks that ye have kindled.' But what is the conclusion of all ? ' This shall ye have of mine hand.' I dare assure you of this, saith the prophet. ' You shall lie down in sorrow.' Those that walk by the light and spark of their own fire, this they shall have at God's hands : ' they shall lie down in sorrow.'

Let us therefore take heed of carnal confidence. You have a number who love to sleep in a whole skin, and will be sure to take the safest courses, as they think, not consulting with God, but with ' flesh and blood.' It might be instanced in stories of former times, how God hath crossed emperors, and great men in this kind, were it not too tedious. But for present instance, you have many who will be of no settled religion. Oh, they cannot tell, there may be a change. Therefore they will be sure to offend neither part. This is their policy, and if they be in place, they will reform nothing. Oh, I shall lay myself open to advantages, and stir up enemies against me. And so they will not trust God, but have carnal devices to turn off all duty whatsoever. It is an ordinary speech, but very true, policy overthrows policy. It is true of carnal policy. When a man goes by carnal rules to be governed by God's enemy and his own, with his own wit and understanding, which leads him to outward things, this kind of policy overthrows all policy, and outward government at length. Those that walk religiously and by rule, they walk most confidently and securely, as the issue will shew. Therefore, consider that, set God aside, all is but vanity. And that,

First, In regard they do not yield that which we expect they should yield. There is a falsehood in the things. They promise this and that in shows, but when we possess them, they yield it not. As they have no strength indeed, so they deceive.

2. Then, also, there is a mutability in them ; for there is nothing in the world but changes. There is a vanity of corruption in them. All things at last come to an end, save God, who is unchangeable.

3. Then again, besides the intrinsical vanity in all outward things, and whatsoever carnal reason leads unto, they are snares and baits unto us, to draw us away from God, by reason of the vanity of our nature, vainer than the things themselves. Therefore take heed of confidence in anything, or else this will be the issue : we shall be worse than the things we trust. 'Vanity of vanities, all things are vanity,' Eccles. i. 1 ; and man himself is lighter than vanity, saith the psalmist, Ps. lxii. 9. He that trusts to vanity, is worse than vanity. A man cannot stand on a thing that cannot stand itself,—*stare non stante*. A man cannot stand on a thing that is mutable and changeable. If he doth, he is vain with the thing. Even as a picture drawn upon ice, as the ice dissolves, so the picture vanisheth away. So it is with all confidence in the creature whatsoever. It is like a picture upon ice, which vanisheth with the things themselves. He that stands upon a slippery thing, slips with the thing he stands on. If there were no word of God against it, yet thus much may be sufficient out of the principles of reason, to shew the folly of trusting to Asshur, and horses, and the like.

Let this be the end of all, then, touching this carnal confidence : to beware that we do not fasten our affections too much upon any earthly thing, at home or abroad, within or without ourselves. For 'God will destroy the wisdom of the wise,' 1 Cor. i. 19. Let us take heed, therefore, of all false confidence whatsoever. Let us use all outward helps, yet so as to rely upon God for his blessing in the use of all. And when they all fail, be of Jehoshaphat's mind : 'Lord, we know not what to do,' 2 Chron. xx. 12. The creature fails us, our helps fail us ; 'but our eyes are upon thee.' So when all outward Asshurs, and horses, and helps fail, despair not ; for the less help there is in the creature, the more there is in God. As Gideon with his army, when he thought to carry it away with multitudes, God told him there were too many of them to get the victory by, lest Israel should vaunt themselves of their number, and so lessened the army to three hundred, Jud. vii. 2 ; so it is not the means, but the blessing on the means which helps us. If we be never so low, despair not. Let us make God ours, who is all-sufficient and almighty, and then if we were brought a hundred times lower than we are, God will help and raise us. Those who labour not to have God, the Lord of hosts, to go out with their armies, if they had all the Asshurs and horses in the world, all were in vain. It was therefore a good resolution of Moses. Saith he to God, 'If thy presence go not with us, carry us not hence,' Exod. xxxiii. 15. He would not go one step forward without God. So, if we cannot make God our friend to go out before us, in vain it is to go one step forward. Let us therefore double our care in holy duties, renewing our covenant with God, before the decree come out against us. The more religious, the more secure we shall be. If we had all the creatures in the world to help us, what are they but vanity and nothing, if God be our enemy ! These things we know well enough for notion ; but let us labour to bring them home for use, in these dangerous times abroad. Let us begin where we should, that our work may be especially in heaven. Let us reform our lives, being moderately careful, as Christians should, without tempting God's providence, using rightly all civil supports and helps seasonably, and to the best advantage ; for, as was said, the carelessness herein for defence may prove as dangerous and fatal to a State, as the too much confidence and trust in them.

THE FOURTH SERMON.

Asshur shall not save us ; we will not ride upon horses ; neither will we say any more to the works of our hands, Ye are our gods : for in thee the fatherless findeth mercy.—HOS. xiv. 3.

WE shewed you heretofore at large, how the Spirit of God, by the prophet, doth here dictate a form of turning unto these Israelites, ' Take unto you words ;' and then teacheth them what they should return back again, thanks. ' So will we render the calves of our lips.' Wherein they shew two things. 1. They that have no great matters to render, oxen or sheep, &c. 2. They shew what is most pleasing unto God, the calves of our lips ; that is, thanksgiving from a broken heart, which, as the Psalmist speaks, pleaseth God better than ' a bullock that hath horns and hoofs,' Ps. lxix. 31. But this is not enough. The Holy Ghost therefore doth prescribe them, together with prayer and thanksgiving, reformation. ' Asshur shall not save us ; we will not ride upon horses ; neither will we say any more to the works of our hands, Ye are our gods : for in thee the fatherless findeth mercy.' So that here you have reformation joined with prayer and praise. Whence we observed divers things : that without reformation our prayers are abominable ; that in repentance there must be reformation of our special sin ; which here they do. Take this one thing more in the third place, which shall be added to the former.

Obs. In reformation, we must go not only to the outward delinquencies, but to the spring of them, which is some breach of the first table.

The root of all sin, is the deficiency of obedience to some command of the first table. When confidence is not pitched aright in God, or when it is misapplied, and misfastened to the creature : when the soul sets up somewhat for a stay and prop unto it, which it should not do, this is a spiritual and subtle sin, and must be repented of, as here, ' Asshur shall not save us,' &c. It were good therefore for all those who seriously intend the work of repentance, to take this course. If the gross fault be of the second table, take occasion of sorrow and mourning thence. But when you have begun there, resolve and bring all to the breeding sin of all, which is the fastening of the soul falsely, when it is not well fastened and bottomed in the root. And therefore it was well done by Luther, who, in a Catechism of his, brings in the first commandment into all the commandments of the first and second table, ' Thou shalt have no other gods but me.' Therefore thou shalt sanctify the Sabbath, honour thy father and mother, shalt not take my name in vain, shalt not commit adultery, shalt not steal, &c., (b). Because he that hath no God but that God in his heart, will be sure to sanctify the Sabbath, honour his father and mother, not commit adultery, nor steal. And whence come all the breaches of the second table ? Hence, that there is not the true fear and love of God in our hearts ; and it is just with God, for their spiritual sins, to give them up to carnal and gross sins. Therefore, though the Israelites here had many gross sins to repent of, yet they go to the spring-head, the breeding sin of all, false confidence. This is to deal thoroughly, to go to the core. ' Asshur shall not save us ; we will not ride upon horses.' From whence, in the third place, may descend to the next branch of their sin, idolatry.

'Neither will we say any more to the works of our hands, Ye are our gods.'
All false confidence hath two objects : for it is always either,

1. Out of religion ; or,
2. In religion.

For the first, all ill confidence and trust, if it be out of religion, it is in the creature ; either,

1. Out of us ; or,
2. In ourselves.

Secondly, if it be in religion, it is in a false god, as here, ' Neither will we say any more to the works of our hands, Ye are our gods.' Observe hence in the first place.

Obs. Man naturally is prone to idolatry.

The story of the Bible, and of all ages, sheweth how prone men are to idolatry and will-worship, and what miseries ensued thereupon. Amongst other instances, we see how presently after that breach in the kingdom of David and Solomon, by Jeroboam's setting up of two calves, how suddenly they fell to idolatry, 1 Kings xiii. 33, *seq.;* 2 Chron. xiii. 8. So that after that, there was not one good king amongst them all, until the nation was destroyed. And so in the story of their antiquities, see how prone they were to idolatry in the wilderness. Moses doth but go up to the mount, and they fall to idolatry. cause Aaron to make a calf, and dance round about it, Exod. xxxii. 4, *seq.* ; Ps. cvi. 19. The thing is so palpable, that it need not be stood upon, that man's nature is prone to idolatry which will not raise itself up to God, but fetch God to itself, and conceive of him according to its false imaginations.

Now idolatry is two ways committed, in the false, hollow, and deceitful heart of man : either,

1. By attributing to the creature that which is proper to God only, investing it with God's properties ; or,
2. By worshipping the true God in a false manner.

1. So that, in the *first* place, idolatry *is to invest the creature with God's properties.* Go to the highest creature, Christ's human nature. We have some bitter spirits (Lutherans they call them) Protestants, who attribute to the human nature of Christ, that which only is proper to God, to be every where, and therefore to be in the sacrament, (c). You have some come near them, both in their opinion and in their bitterness. They will have a *nescio quomodo.* Christ is there though they know not how. But this is to make Christ's human nature a god, to make an idol of it. So prayers to saints and angels, this makes idols of them, because it invests them with properties to know our hearts, which he must know unto whom we pray. And then, it gives unto them that which is proper to God, worship and prayer. But, we must call upon none but whom we must believe in, and we must believe in none but God. Therefore, worshipping of saints or angels is idolatry.

Secondly, idolatry *is to worship the true God in a false manner ;* to fix his presence to that we should not fix it to ; to annex it to statues, images, crucifixes, the picture of the Virgin Mary and the like. Not to run into the common place of idolatry, but to come home unto ourselves.

Quest. Whether are the papists idolaters or not, like unto these Israelites, who say (being converted), 'Neither will we say unto the works of our hands, Ye are our gods?'

Ans. I answer, Yes; as gross as ever the heathens were, and worse. The very Egyptians, they worshipped none for gods but those who were alive; as a papist himself saith (though he were an honest papist), the Egyptians worshipped living creatures, but we are worse than they; for we worship stocks and stones, and a piece of bread in the sacrament. And to this purpose, one of their Jesuits confesseth this, and yielded the question for granted, that if there be not a transubstantiation of the bread turned into the body and blood of Christ, we are worse idolaters than these and these nations; because we worship a piece of bread, which is a dead thing. But we assume (according to the Scriptures, the judgment of the church, and of the truth itself), the bread is not transubstantiated, at least it is a doubtful matter, for if it be not the intention of the priest, it is not. See here upon what hazard they put the souls of people!

Obj. But they have many shifts for themselves; as, among the rest, this is one, that *they do not worship the image, but God or Christ before the image.*

Ans. To which the answer is, that the fathers who wrote against the heathens meet with this pretence. The Pagans had this excuse. We worship not this statue of Jupiter, but Jupiter himself. Thus they have no allegation for themselves, but the heathen had the same, which the ancient Fathers confuted. They are guilty of idolatry in both the forenamed kinds. For, first, they worship things that they should not, as appears by their invocation of saints, vows to them; their temples, altars, and the like, full of their images, giving them honour due unto God. And then, they worship the true God in a false manner before their images. There is no kind of idolatry but they are grossly guilty of it. Whereof let this be the use.

Use 1. *First* of all, of *thankfulness,* that God hath brought us into Goshen, into a kingdom of light; that we are born in a time and place of knowledge of the true God, wherein is the true worship of the true God. It is a matter that we cannot be too thankful to God for.

Quest. How shall we shew ourselves thankful?

Ans. In keeping fast the true worship of God we have, and keeping out idolatry; in reviving laws in that kind, if not making new. What if there were liberty given for men to go about the country to poison people! Would we endure such persons, and not lay hold of them? So in that we are freed from Jesuits who go about to poison the souls of God's people, let us shew our thankfulness for this, and shun idolatry of all sorts whatsoever.

Use 2. *Secondly,* See from hence that there can be *no toleration of that religion,* no more, as was said, than to suffer and tolerate poisoners. As they said of coloquintida in their pottage, 2 Kings iv. 40, so 'there is death in the pot' of Romish religion. Therefore it were good to compel them to come in and serve the Lord their God. As it is said, good Josiah compelled those in his time to serve the Lord, 2 Chron, xxxiv. 33, so it were good such courses were taken to reform and reclaim them. As Saint Augustine said of himself in his time, being a Donatist, he altered his judgment by force. In which case it would be with them as with children, who, when they are young, must be forced to school, but afterwards they thank them who forced them. So it is in religion, though it cannot be forced, yet such might afterwards bless God for them who brought them to the means; who, instead of their blindness, trained them up in more knowledge, by forcing them to use the means for which, when God should open their eyes, they might bless God another day. But this point of gross idolatry, so largely handled in books, is only touched by the way, that we may hate idolatry the more; which could not be left out, the words leading to say somewhat of it, seeing how these converts here hate it, and out of that hatred make this profession, ' Neither will we say any more to the works of our hands, Ye are our gods,' &c.

But this is not all; we must know that there be other idols than the idols which we make with our hands. Besides these religious idols, there be secular idols in the world, such as men set up to themselves in their own hearts. Whatsoever takes up the heart most, which they attribute more to than to God, that is their idol, their god. A man's love, a man's fear, is his god. If a man fear greatness rather than God, that he had rather displease God than any great person, they are his idols for the time. ' The fear of a man brings a snare,' Prov. xxix. 25, saith the wise man. And those who get the favour of any in place, sacrifice therefore their credit, profession, religion, and souls, it is gross idolatry; dangerous to the party, and dangerous to themselves. It was the ruin of Herod to have that applause given to him, and taken by him, ' The voice of God, and not of man,' Acts xii. 22. So for any to be blown up with flatterers, that lift them up above their due measure, it is an exceeding wrong to them, prejudiceth their comfort, and will prove ill in the conclusion; indeed, treason against their souls.

So there is a baser sort of idolaters, who sacrifice their credit and state, whatsoever is good within them, their whole powers, to their base and filthy pleasures. Thus man is degenerate since his fall, that he makes that his god which is meaner than himself. Man, that was ordained for everlasting happiness and communion with God, is now brought to place his happiness and contentment in base pleasures. Whereas it is with the soul of man for good or ill, as it applies itself to that which is greater or meaner than itself. If it apply itself to confidence and affiance in God, then it is better. For it is the happiness of the soul to have communion with the Spring of goodness, as David speaks, ' It is good for me to draw near to God,' &c., Ps. lxxiii. 28. When we suffer the soul to cleave in affiance to earthly things, it grows in some measure to the nature of the things adhered to. When we love the world and earthly things, we are earthly. Till the Spirit of God touch the soul, as the loadstone doth the heavy iron, drawing it up, as it were, it will cleave to the creature, to baser things than itself, and so makes the creature an idol, which is the common idolatry of these times. Some make favour, as the ambitious person; some their pleasures, as baser persons of meaner condition; and some riches. Every man as their temper and as their temptations are.

Now, it is not enough to be sound in religion one way in the main; but we must be sound every way, without any touch of idolatry. In a special manner the apostle calls the 'covetous man an idolater,' Eph. v. 5, because he makes riches his castle, thinking to carry anything with his wealth. But his riches oftentimes prove his ruin; for whatsoever a man loves more than God, God will make it his bane and ruin; at least, be sure to take it away, if God mean to save the party. Therefore here they say, ' Asshur shall not save us; we will not ride upon horses; neither will we say any more to the works of our hands, Ye are our gods.'

' For in thee the fatherless findeth mercy.'

Here he shews the reason of their rejecting of all false confidence in

Asshur, in horses, in idols ; because they had planted their confidence in the true God. They said so when they had smarted by Asshur, and by idolatry. Then 'Asshur shall not save us,' &c. They knew it by rule before ; but till God plagued them, as he did oft by Asshur and by Egypt, when he broke the reed that it did not only not uphold them, but run into their hands, they made no such acknowledgment. Hence observe,

Obs. Usually it is thus with man, he never repents till sin be embittered to him.

He never alters his confidence till his trusts be taken away. When God overthrows the mould of his devices, or brings them upon his own head, setting him to reap the fruit of his own ways, embittering sinful courses to him, then he returns. Instruction without correction doth for the most part little good. When Asshur had dealt falsely with them, and idolatry would do them no good, then they begin to alter their judgment. What makes men, after too much confidence in their wit, when they have, by their plots and devices, gone beyond what they should do, and wrapped and entangled themselves in a net of their own weaving, as we say, alter their judgment ? They are then become sick of their own devices. This makes the change. For till then the brain hath a kind of net to wrap our devices in. So, many have nets in their brains, wherewith they entangle themselves and others with their idle devices ; which, when they have done, and so woven the web of their own misery, then they begin to say, as the heathen saith when he was deceived, 'O fool am I, I was never a wise man !' Then they begin to say, I was a fool to trust such and such. I have tried such and such policies, and they have deceived me. I will now alter my course. And surely men of great parts are seldom converted till God confound their plots, and lays flat all their false confidence. When Asshur disappoints them, then 'Asshur shall not save us,' &c.

Use. Therefore make this use of it, *not to be discouraged when God doth confound any carnal plot or policy of ours,* as to think that God hates either a nation or a person when they have ill success in plots and projects which are not good. Nay, it is a sign rather that God intends good, if they make a right use it. God intends conversion, to translate false confidence from the creature to himself, and to learn us to make God wise for us. It is a happy thing when in this world God will disappoint a man's courses and counsels, and bring him to shame, rather than he should go on and thrive in an evil and carnal course, and so end his days. There is no evidence at all which can be given of a reprobate, because there may be final repentance, repentance at the last. But this is one and as fearful a sign as may be, to thrive and go on in an evil course to the end. When God shall disappoint and bring a man to shame in that he prided in and built upon, it is a good sign. If thereupon we take advantage to turn to God, and lay a better bottom and foundation, as we see here, 'Asshur shall not save us ; we will not ride upon horses,' &c.

'For in thee the fatherless findeth mercy.'

As if he should say, We have that supply of strength and comfort from thee that Asshur, horses, and idols cannot give. Therefore we will alter our confidence, to fix and pitch it upon thee, and trust thee ; because 'in thee the fatherless findeth mercy.' We shall not need to say, In thee will we trust ; for, if God be apprehended thus, as one in whom 'the fatherless findeth mercy,' affiance will follow. For the object is the attractive and loadstone of the soul ; so that if a fit object be presented unto it, affiance, confidence, and trust will of itself follow. Therefore the Spirit of God forbears multiplication of words, and sets down this, 'For in thee the fatherless findeth mercy;' and doth not say, In thee will I trust, for that is implied. Whatsoever conceives that God is so gracious and merciful to despicable, miserable persons, such as are set down in this one particular, 'fatherless,' they cannot but trust in God. Therefore the one is put for the other, 'for in thee the fatherless findeth mercy.' Whence, from the dependence of the words, observe,

Obs. That it is not sufficient to disclaim affiance in the creature, but we must pitch that affiance aright upon God.

We must not only take it off where it should not be placed, but set it where it should be. 'Cease from evil, and learn to do well,' Isa. i. 16, 17. Trust not in the creature. 'Cease from man,' as the prophet saith, 'whose breath is in his nostrils,' Isa. ii. 22; 'Commit thy ways to God, trust in him,' Ps. xxxvii. 5. The heathen, by the light of nature, knew this, that for the *negative* there is no trusting in the creature, which is a vain thing. They could speak wonderful wittily* and to purpose of these things, especially the Stoics. They could see the vanity of the creature. But for the *positive* part, where to place their confidence, that they were ignorant in. And so for the other part here, 'Neither will we say any more to the works of our hands, Ye are our gods.' Idolaters can see the vanity of false gods well enough. In Italy you have thousands of the wittier and learneder sort, who see the folly and madness of their religion. And among ourselves, how many witty men can disclaim† against popery, who yet in their lives and conversations are not the better for it; because they think it enough to see the error that misleads them, though they never pitch their confidence as they should do. It is not enough therefore to rest in the negative part. A negative Christian is no Christian; not to be an idolater, not to be a papist; no, there must be somewhat else. We must bring forth good fruit, Mat. iii. 10, or else we are for the fire, and are near to cursing and burning, Heb. vi. 8. This is spoken, the rather because many think themselves well when they can disclaim against the errors of popery; and that they are good Christians, because they can argue well. Oh! such make religion nothing but a matter of opinion, of canvassing an argument, &c. But it is another manner of matter, a divine power exercised upon the soul, whereby it is transformed into the obedience of divine truth, and moulded into it. So that there must be a positive as well as a negative religion; a cleaving to God as well as a forsaking of idols.

Again, in the severing of these idols from God, we must know and observe hence,

Obs. That there is no communion between God and idols.

'Neither will we say any more to the works of our hands, Ye are our gods: for in thee the fatherless findeth mercy.' There must be a renouncing of false worship, religion, and confidence, before we can trust in God. 'Ye cannot serve God and Mammon,' saith Christ, Mat. vi. 24. We cannot serve Christ and Antichrist together. We may as well bring north and south, east and west together, and mingle light and darkness, as mix two opposite religions. You see here, one of them is disclaimed ere affiance be placed in the other. Therefore the halters betwixt two religions are here condemned. It was excellent well said by Joshua. They had there some mixture of false worship, and thought therewith to serve also Jevovah. 'No,' saith he, 'you cannot serve Jehovah,' Josh. xxiv. 19. What is Joshua's meaning when he saith they could not? Not only that they had no power of themselves; but, you are a naughty, false

* That is, 'with wit' == wisdom.—G.   † That is, 'declaim.'—G.

people, you think to jumble God's worship and that of heathens together; 'you cannot serve God' thus. So a man may say to those who look Romewards, for worldly ends, and yet will be Protestants, You cannot serve God; you cannot be sound Christians, halting thus betwixt both. These are not compatible, they cannot stand together; you must disclaim the one if you will cleave to the other. We see the ground here, 'Neither will we say any more to the works of our hands, Ye are our gods: for in thee the fatherless findeth mercy.'

Again, whereas upon disclaiming of false confidence in the creatures and idols, they name this as a ground, 'For in thee the fatherless findeth mercy,' observe,

In what measure and degree we apprehend God aright to be the all-sufficient true God, in that measure we cast away all false confidence whatsoever.

The more or less we conceive of God as we should do, so the more or less we disclaim confidence in the creature. Those who in their affections of joy, love, affiance, and delight, are taken up too much with the creature, say what they will, profess to all the world by their practice that they know not God. By the contrary, those who know and apprehend him in his greatness and goodness as he should be apprehended, in that proportion they withdraw their affections from the creature and all things else. It is with the soul in this case as with a balance. If the one scale be drawn down by a weight put in it, the other is lifted up. So where God weighs down in the soul, all other things are light; and where other things prevail, there God is set light. 'Asshur shall not save us,' for he can do us no good; nor 'horses,' because they are vain helps. How attained they to this light esteem of Asshur and horses? 'For in thee the fatherless findeth mercy.' That which is taken from the creature, they find in God. And this is the reason why the world so malign good and sound Christians. They think, when God gets, that they lose a feather, as we say, some of their strength. Surely so it is; for when a Christian turns to God and becomes sound, he comes to have a mean esteem of that which formerly was great in his sight. His judgment is otherwise, as we see here, Asshur, horses, idols, and all, they esteem nothing of them. Horses and the like are good, useful, and necessary to serve God's providence in the use of means; not to trust in, or make co-ordinate with God. In the world especially, great persons would be gods in the hearts of people; therefore, when they see any make conscience of their ways, they think they lose them; because now they will do nothing but what may stand with the favour of God. Thus far from the connection. Now to the words themselves.

'For in thee the fatherless findeth mercy.'

Wherein we have set forth unto us for our consideration of God's rich goodness towards poor miserable sinners—

1. The attribute of God, *mercy.*

2. The fit object thereof, *the fatherless.*

Mercy is God's sweetest attribute, which sweeteneth all his other attributes; for, but for mercy, whatsoever else is in God were matter of terror to us. His justice would affright us. His holiness likewise (considering our impurity) would drive us from him. 'Depart from me,' saith Peter to our Saviour, 'for I am a sinful man,' Luke v. 8. And when the prophet Isaiah saw God in his excellency a little, then he said, 'Woe is me, for I am undone, because I am a man of unclean lips,' &c.. Isa. vi. 5. His ower is terrible; it would confound us; his majesty astonish us. Oh !

but mercy mitigates all. He that is great in majesty, is abounding in mercy ; he that hath beams of majesty, hath bowels of mercy. Oh ! this draweth especially miserable persons. ' In thee the fatherless findeth mercy.' And now, in the covenant of grace, this mercy sets all awork. For it is the mercy of God by which we triumph now in the covenant of grace ; in that mercy which stirred up his wisdom to find out a way for mercy by satisfying his justice. So that the first moving attribute of God that set him awork about that great work of our salvation by Jesus Christ, in the covenant of grace, was mercy, his tender mercy, his bowels of mercy. Therefore, of all others, that attribute is here named. ' For in thee the fatherless findeth mercy.'

Mercy in God, supposeth misery in the creature, either present or possible ; for there is, 1. A preventing ; 2. A rescuing mercy.

A *preventing mercy*, whereby the creature is freed from possible misery that it might fall into ; as it is his mercy that we are not such sinners in that degree as others are. And every man that hath understanding is beholden to God for their preventing, as well as for their rescuing mercy. We think God is merciful only to those unto whom he forgives great sins. Oh ! he is merciful to thee that standeth. Thou mightst have fallen foully else. Mercy supposeth misery, either that we are in, or may fall into. So that mercy in God may admit of a threefold consideration.

1. It supposeth *sin*. So there is a *pardoning mercy* for that. Or,
2. *Misery;* that is, a *delivering mercy.* Or,
3. *Defect or want in the creature*, which is, *supplying mercy.*

Wheresoever mercy is conversant, it is usually about one of these three, either sin, or misery, or defects and wants ; that is, to persons in misery. For, indeed, the word is more general than fatherless. Deserted persons, that are forsaken of others, and have no strength of their own, they are here meant by the fatherless, who have no means, wisdom, power, or ability of their own, but are deserted and forsaken of others. Whence the chief truth that offers itself to be considered of us is this,

That God is especially merciful to those persons who stand most in need of mercy.

First, Because *these do relish mercy most*, and give him the glory of it, applying themselves most to his mercy, being beaten out of the creature ; and the more we have communion with God, being driven out of the creature and other comforts, the more he discovers himself to us. As the nearer we are to the fire, the hotter it is ; so the nearer we are to God, the more good and gracious he every way shews himself unto us. Now, what makes us near him, but extremity of misery, whereby we are beaten from all other holds whatsoever ? It is acknowledged to be his work, when he doth it for those that are deserted of all others, Hosea v. 15. Then he hath the chief glory of it. This is one end why God suffers his children to fall into extremity of great sorrows and perplexities, to fall very low in depths of miseries (as the Scripture speaks), Ps. cxxx. 1, that he might discover a depth of his mercy beyond the depth of their misery, to shew that there is a depth deeper than that depth, for their misery is finite. Oh ! but the bowels of his compassions are infinite, both in measure and time. ' His mercy endureth for ever,' Ps. cxxxvi. 1, *seq.*

Again, *God is jealous of their affiance and confidence*, knowing that naturally, unless we fall into some straits and weaning extremities, we shall place our affiance upon the creature. Therefore, he deals thus with us. He knows our sickness well enough, that we are desperately addicted to present things. Therefore, to cure this sickness in us, he draws us by extremities from the creature to himself, which, when it fails, we go to him. 'Help, Lord!' Why? 'For vain is the help of man,' Ps. lx. 11. It is time then to help. 'Help, Lord, for the godly are perished from the earth,' Ps. xii. 1. It is time to help, Lord, for if thou do not, none will; whereby they come to have their confidence upon the rock, which is worth all. Other men, they run from creature to creature, from help to help, as sick bodies do to this and to that drug, and to this and that potion. They seek to many things to beg comfort from; but a Christian hath a sure foundation that he may stay upon. 'In thee the fatherless findeth mercy.'

To come now to speak of the words as they lie in the whole. They carry another instruction,

That God is very gracious and merciful to fatherless and distressed persons.

As we have it, Ps. x. 18, 'that God will judge the fatherless and oppressed; that the man of the earth may no more oppress;' so Ps. cxlvi. 9, it is said, 'The Lord preserveth the strangers, he relieveth the fatherless and widow,' &c. And for the general we have it, 'The Lord relieveth all that fall, and raiseth up all that be bowed down,' Ps. cxlv. 14. God he opens his ear to hear their cry, to judge the fatherless and the oppressed. The like we have in Exodus, 'Also thou shalt not oppress a stranger,' for ye know the heart of a stranger, seeing ye were strangers in the land of Egypt,' Exod. xxiii. 9. And saith he, 'Thou shalt not afflict any widow or fatherless child. If thou afflict them in any wise, and they cry at all unto me, I will surely hear their cry,' Exod. xxii. 21. These, among many, are direct places to shew the truth of this, that God is merciful, not only in general, but to those persons set down by a *synecdoche*, a figure where one is set down for all of the same kind. God is merciful to all persons, in any kind of misery or distress whatsoever. As the apostle speaks, God is he 'who comforteth the abject person,' 2 Cor. vii. 6, the forlorn, the castaway persons of the world; and he is 'a very present help in trouble,' Ps. xlvi. 1. So as when there are none to help, then he awaketh and rouseth up himself to lay hold for us. 'His own arm brings salvation for his own sake.'* So when there is misery, and none to help, God will find cause and ground from his own bowels to shew mercy, to take pity and compassion upon his poor church and children. Which should teach us,

Use 1. First of all, *to take notice of this most excellent attribute of God*, and to make use of it upon all occasions at our most need, then to present to our souls God thus described and set out by his own Spirit, to be 'he that comforteth the abject,' and sheweth mercy to the fatherless and oppressed. This we should make use of for the church in general, and for every one of ourselves in particular. The church hath been a long time like a forlorn widow, as it were. God hath promised that he will have a care of the 'widow and the fatherless,' and so he will of his poor church.

We see in the parable, the widow, with her importunity, prevailed with an unrighteous judge, Luke xviii. 5. The church now being like a widow, what is wanting but a spirit of supplication and prayer? Which spirit, if the church had to wrestle with God, and lay hold upon him as Jacob did, Hos. xii. 4, and not suffer God to rest till he had mercy on his poor church, certainly it would be better with it than it is, for God comforteth the widow, Isa. lxii. 7. If one, what will he do for the whole spouse, which hath so long been a despicable and forlorn widow? And for the time to come it ought to minister matter of comfort for the church. Certainly, God that

* Isa. xli. 17, lix. 16, lxiii. 5, xlviii. 9.

is merciful to the fatherless, he will be merciful to the poor church. We see in the Revelation, though the woman was persecuted by the dragon, yet there were given two wings of a great eagle to her, that she might fly unto the wilderness, where she had a place provided of God, Rev. xii. 14. It alludes to the story of the Israelites when they came out of Egypt. God provided for them in the wilderness. They had manna from heaven, and water out of the rock; and till they came to Canaan, God provided every way for them in a marvellous manner. So God will be sure to provide for his in the wilderness of this world. He will have a harbour still for the church, and a hiding-place from the stormy tempests of her adversaries, Isa. iv. 5, 6. Therefore let us not despair, but stir up a spirit of prayer for the church, that he who shews mercy to the fatherless, and commands mercy to be shewed to the widow, that he would shew that himself which he requires of us. And why may not we hope and trust for it. The church in this world is, as it were, a fatherless person, a pupil, an orphan, a sheep in the midst of wolves, as Daniel in the lions' den, as a ship tossed in the waves, as a lily among thorns. It is environed with enemies, and of itself, like the poor sheep, is shiftless.* What is the church but a company of weak persons? Not so witty† for the world as worldly-wise men are, not so strong in the arm of flesh, nor so defenced, but a company of persons who have a hidden dependence upon God we know not how, and hang, as it were, by a thread, as the church in this land, and abroad in other places. The true church is maintained, we know not how. God keeps up religion, the church, and all, because he is merciful to the fatherless, who have no shifting wits, as the worldly Ahithophels have. God is wise for them that are not wise for themselves, and powerful for them that have little strength of their own. Therefore let us not be discouraged though we be weak creatures, a little flock, like a company of sheep, yet notwithstanding we have a strong shepherd, Ps. xxiii 1. The church is like a vine, a poor, despicable, withered, crooked, weak plant, which winds about, and must be supported, or else it sinks to the ground; yet it is a fruitful plant, Isa. v. 1, 7. So the church of God, a number of weak Christians professing religion, they want many helps, yet God supports them, and hath ordained this and that haven for them, as this magistrate and that person. God hath one support or other for them. While they are fruitful and true vines, God will have a care of them, though they be never so weak and despised in the eye of the world, Isa. liv. 11.

Use 2. Again, this should teach us *to make God our all-sufficiency in all estates whatsoever*, and not to go one hair's breadth from a good conscience, for fear of after-claps.‡ I may be cast into prison, I may lose my goods. What of all this? Is not God all-sufficient? And is not he especially seen in comforting of those who stand in most need of comfort, who want other helps? And will he be indebted to any man who stands out in a good quarrel for his cause? Isa. xli. 17. Will he not give needful supply, if not in this world, yet in a better, of all comforts whatsoever? It is a good supply when the loss is in outward things, and the supply in inward peace, grace, and strength. It is a happy loss that is lost to the advantage, Isa. lx. 17; lxiv. 5. There was never any man yet, from the beginning of the world, who lost by cleaving to religion and good causes. God ever made it up one way or other. Therefore this is a ground of courage to cast ourselves upon doing good when God offers the occasion, relying upon

---

* That is, 'without expedients.'—G.　　　　† That is, 'wise.'—G.
‡ That is, 'judgments, trials.'—G.

God, as Esther did, ' If I perish, I perish,' Esther iv. 16. She meant, ' If I perish, I shall not perish.' Such have a better condition in the love and favour of God than they had before, or should have had, if they had not perished. It is the way not to perish, so to perish. It is as clear and true as the sunshine, but we want faith to believe it.

Use 3. And then, again, let us make use of it in another kind, to resist another temptation. What will become of my poor children, if I do thus and thus, stand thus and thus, and go on in my innocency? What will become of thy children? It was well spoken by Lactantius, ' Because God would have men stand out and die in a good cause willingly, therefore he hath promised in a special manner to be a father to the fatherless, and a husband to the widow' (*d*). Are we the chief fathers of our children? No; we are but under God, to bring those who are his children into the world. We are but instruments. God is the chief father, best and last father, ' The everlasting father,' Isa. ix. 6, who takes upon him to be a father to the fatherless, whom he chargeth all not to hurt. Experience shews how he blesseth the posterity of the righteous, who have stood in defence of the truth. Therefore let us make no pretences either for baseness, dejection of spirit, or covetousness, to keep us from well doing, for God will reward all.

Quest. Oh, say some, I could be content not to be so worldly, but it is for my children.

Ans. What saith the apostle? ' Let those who are married be as if they were not married,' 1 Cor. vii. 29, meaning in regard of this scraping of wealth together by unlawful means of covetousness, or in regard of readiness to do works of mercy. What, doth God appoint one ordinance of marriage, to take a man off of all duties? No; notwithstanding this we must do fitting works of mercy. God will be the father of the fatherless. Many use oppression, and go to hell themselves to make their children rich. Who commands us to make our children, in show, a while happy here, to make our souls and bodies miserable for ever? There is a moderate care, as the apostle speaks, so that ' he who cares not for his own, is worse than an infidel,' 1 Tim. v. 8; but we must not make this pretence to excuse injurious and extortive courses. But let God alone. He will do all things well; trust him. Or, if anything should befall us otherwise than well, what if it do? God is the God of the fatherless. Whatsoever he takes away, he supplies it better another way. For whence have the creatures that infusion to help? Is it not from God? And when the creature is taken away, is not God where he was?

Use 4. And let us also learn hence that we answer God's dealing, in shewing mercy to the fatherless and such as stand in need, as the apostle exhorts, ' Put on, therefore, as the elect of God, holy and beloved, bowels of mercy,' &c., Col. iii. 12, as if he should say, as you would prove yourselves to be elect members of Christ and children of God, so shew your likeness in this particular, ' The bowels of mercy and compassion.' This hath ever been, and yet is at all times, a character of God's children, and shall be to the end of the world. It is a sign such a one hath found bowels of mercy, that is ready upon all occasions to pour forth those bowels of compassion upon others, as hard-heartedness this way shews a disposition which yet hath not rightly tasted of mercy. As we say in another case, those that are appeased in their consciences, in the sense of the forgiveness of sins, they are peaceable to others, because they feel peace. So here, those that feel mercy will be merciful, those that have felt love will be loving to others,

'A good man is merciful to his beast, but the mercies of the wicked are cruel,' Prov. xii. 10. Those, therefore, that are hard-hearted and unmerciful, hardening themselves against the complaints of the miserable, there is, for the present, no comfort for them, that the Spirit of God hath wrought any change in their hearts; for then it would stamp the image of God upon them, they would be merciful to the fatherless, widow, and distressed persons. What shall we think, then, of a generation of men who, by gripping usury and the like courses, have made many widows miserable? Let such profess what they will, whilst they are thus hard-hearted they have not the bowels of Christ. God is so merciful that you see, as the Jews call them (*e*), he hath hedges of the commandments, that is, he hath some remote commands which are not of the main, and all to hedge from cruelty, as, 'Thou shalt not kill the dam upon the nest,' Deut. xxii. 6; 'Thou shalt not seethe a kid in his mother's milk,' Exod. xxiii. 19. What tends this to? Nothing but to shew the mercy and bowels of God, and that he would have us to abstain from cruelty. He that would not have us murder, would have us keep aloof off, and not be merciless to the very dumb creatures, birds and beasts. Therefore let us labour to express the image of our heavenly father in this.

Use 5. Again, we should use this *as a plea against dejectedness at the hour of death*, in regard of those we leave behind us, not to be troubled what shall become of them, when we are to yield up our souls to God; but know that he hath undertaken to be 'the Father of the fatherless, and of the widow.' Therefore, for shame, for shame! learn, as to live, so to die by faith; and as to die by faith in other things, so to die in this faith; that God, as he will receive thy soul, so he will receive the care of thy posterity. Canst thou with affiance yield up thy soul unto God, and wilt thou not with the same confidence yield thy posterity? Thou art an hypocrite, if this distract and vex thee, when yet thou pretendest to die in the faith of Christ. Canst thou yield thy soul, and yet art grieved for thy posterity? No; leave it to God. He is all-sufficient. 'The earth is the Lord's, and the fulness thereof,' Ps. xxiv. 1. We need not fear to put our portion in his hands. He is rich enough. 'The earth and all is his.' Therefore, when we are in any extremity whatsoever, rely on this mercy of so rich and powerful a God; improve it, for it is our portion, especially in a distressed condition. Were it not for faith, wrought by the blessed Spirit of God, he would lose the glory of this attribute of mercy. Now, faith is a wise power of the soul, that sees in God what is fit for it, singling out in God what is fit for the present occasion of distress. Is a man in any extremity of misery? let him look to mercy. Is a man oppressed? let him look to mercy, to be revenged of his enemies. Is a man in any perplexity? let him look to mercy, joined with wisdom, which is able to deliver him. Religion is nothing else but an application of the soul to God, and a fetching out of him somewhat (as he hath discovered himself in the covenant) fit for all our exigents; as there is somewhat in God, and in the promises, for all estates of the soul. Faith, therefore, is witty to look to that in God which is fit for its turn. Let us therefore take heed of Satan's policy herein, who in our extremity, useth this as a weapon to shake our faith. 'Tush,' as it is in the psalm, 'God hath forsaken and forgotten him,' Ps. x. 11. Hath he so? Nay; because I am in extremity, and deserted above others, rather God now regards me more than before; because, 'he scourgeth every son whom he receiveth,' Heb. xii. 6. So retort Satan's fiery darts back again. For indeed, that is the time wherein God exalts and shews himself most glorious and triumphant in mercy, where misery is greatest. ' Where sin abounds, there grace abounds much more,' Rom. v. 20. So where misery abounds, mercy superabounds much more. Therefore let us be as wise for our souls, as Satan can be malicious against them. What he useth for a weapon to wound the soul, use the same as a weapon against him.

To end all, *let faith in God's mercy answer this his description;* and let it be a description ingrafted into us at such a time. Doth God care for the fatherless, and mean persons, who are cast down and afflicted? Why, then, I will trust that God who doth so, being in this case myself. If he will help in extremity, trust him in extremity; if he will help in distress, trust him in distress; if he will help when all forsake, trust him when we are forsaken of all, Hab. iii. 17. What if a stream be taken away? yet none can take away God from thee. What if a beam be taken away? thou hast the sun itself. What if a particular comfort be taken away? So long as God, ' who comforteth the abject,' and is merciful to the distressed, fatherless, and widows, continues with thee, thou needst not fear. A man cannot want comfort and mercy, so long as the Father of mercies is in covenant with him. If he sin, he hath pardoning mercy for him; if weak, he hath strengthening mercy; if in darkness, he hath quickening mercy; if we be dull, dead, and in danger, there is rescuing mercy; and if subject to dangers we may fall in, there is for that preventing mercy, Ps. xxxii. 10. Therefore there is mercy ready to compass God's children about in all conditions. When they are environed with dangers, yet God is nearer to guard their souls, than the danger is to hurt them.

Therefore let us take the counsel of the blessed apostle. ' Be careful for nothing; but in everything, by prayer and supplication, with thanksgiving, let your requests be known to God.' And what then? Will God grant that I pray for? Perhaps he will not; but yet, ' the peace of God, which passeth all understanding, shall guard your hearts and minds through Christ Jesus,' Philip. iv. 6, 7. As if he should say, in nothing be over-careful. Let your care be, when ye have used the means, to depend upon God for support in the event and issue of all. If God deny you what you pray for, he will grant you that which is better. He will set up an excellent inward peace there, whereby he will stablish the soul in assurance of his love, pardon of sins, and reconciliation: whereby their souls shall be guarded, and their hearts and minds preserved in Christ. So they become impregnable in all miseries whatsoever, when they have ' the peace of God, which passeth all understanding,' to guard them within. Therefore let us not betray and lose our comforts for want of making use of them, or for fear some should call us hypocrites. And, on the other side, let us not flatter ourselves in an evil course; but make the conscience good, which will bear us out in all miseries, dangers, and difficulties whatsoever. Nothing makes losses, crosses, banishment, imprisonment, and death so terrible and out of measure dreadful unto us, but the inward guilt and sting in the inside, the tumults of conscience, Gen. xlii. 21. Clear this well once, make all whole within, let conscience be right and straight, let it have its just use and measure of truth and uprightness, and go thy way in peace; I warrant thee, thou shalt hold up thy head, and wind thyself out of all dangers well enough: nothing shall daunt or appal thy courage. For, saith Solomon, ' The righteous is bold as a lion,' Prov. xxviii. 1. What can, what should he fear, who is heir of all things,' Rev. xxi. 7, whose all things are, and who is reconciled to God in Christ, having all the angels and creatures for his servants, Heb. i. 14, for whose sake ' all things must needs work together for good ?' Rom. viii. 28.

THE FIFTH SERMON.

I will heal their backsliding, I will love them freely: for mine anger is turned away from them.—Hos. XIV. 4.

THE superabounding mercies and marvellous lovingkindnesses of a gracious and loving God to wretched and miserable sinners, as we have heard, is the substance and sum of this short, sweet chapter, wherein their ignorance is taught, their bashfulness is encouraged, their deadness is quickened, their untowardness is pardoned, their wounds are cured, all their objections and petitions answered; so as a large and open passage is made unto them, and all other miserable penitent sinners, for access unto the throne of grace. If they want words, they are taught what to say; if discouraged for sins past, they are encouraged that sin may be taken away; yea, all iniquity may be taken away. ' Take away all iniquity.' If their unworthiness hinder them, they are taught for this, that God is gracious. ' Receive us graciously.' If their by-past unthankfulness be any bar of hindrance unto them, they are taught to promise thankfulness. ' So will we render the calves of our lips.' And that their repentance may appear to be sound and unfeigned, they are brought in, making profession of their detestation of their bosom sins, of false confidence and idolatry. ' Asshur shall not save us; we will not ride upon horses; neither will we say any more to the works of our hands, Ye are our gods.' And not only do they reject their false confidence, to cease from evil, but they do good, and pitch their affiance where it should be. For ' in thee the fatherless findeth mercy.'

None must therefore be discouraged, or run away from God, for what they have been, for there may be a returning. God may have a time for them, who, in his wise dispensation, doth bring his children to distress, that their delivery may be so much the more admired by themselves and others, to his glory and their good. He knows us better than we ourselves. How prone we are to lean upon the creature. Therefore he is fain to take from us all our props and supports, whereupon we are forced to rely upon him. If we could do this of ourselves, it were an excellent work, and an undoubted evidence of the child of God, that hath a weaned soul in the midst of outward supports, to enjoy them, as if he possessed them not; not to be puffed up with present greatness, not to swell with riches, nor be high-minded; to consider of things to be as they are, weak things, subordinate to God, which can help no further than as he blesseth them. But to come to the words now read.

' I will heal their backsliding, and love them freely,' &c.

After that the church had shewed her repentance and truth of returning to God: now in these words, and the other verses, unto the end of the chapter (saving the last verse, which is a kind of acclamation issuing from all the rest of the foregoing verses, ' Who is wise, and he shall understand these things ?' &c.), is set down an answer unto that prayer, repentance, and reformation which the church made; all the branches of which their former suit the Lord doth punctually * answer. For they had formerly

* That is, ' point by point.'—ED.

prayed, 'Take away all iniquity, and receive us graciously; do good unto us.' Unto which he answers here, 'I will heal their backsliding,' &c.

Which is thus much: I will pardon their iniquities, I will accept graciously of them, I will love them freely, and so of the rest, as will appear afterwards; and, in sum, God answers all those desires which formerly he had stirred up in his people. Whence, ere we come to the particulars, observe in general,

Obs. Where God doth give a spirit of prayer, he will answer.

It needs no proof, the point is so clear and experimental. All the saints can say thus much from their experience of God's gracious dealing with them; and the Scriptures are full of such instances and promises, which we all know. To name a place or two for all the rest, 'Call upon me in the day of trouble, I will deliver thee, and thou shalt glorify me,' Ps. l. 15. So in another place, 'And it shall come to pass that before they call, I will answer; and whilst they speak, I will hear,' Isa. lxv. 24. It hath been made good to persons, as Daniel, Elijah, Solomon, Jacob, and others; and it hath been, and is, made good unto all ages of the church, from time to time, and shall be unto the end of the world. And therefore the prophet sets down this as a conclusion undeniable from the premises, 'O thou that hearest prayer, unto thee shall all flesh come,' Ps. lxv. 2. Whence he draws this excellent consolation, 'Iniquities prevail against me; as for our transgressions, thou shalt purge them away.'

Reason. The reason is strong, because they are the motions of his own Spirit, which he stirs up in us. For he dictates this prayer unto them, 'Take with you words,' &c., 'and say unto the Lord, Take away all iniquity, and receive us graciously.' So that, where God stirs up holy desires by his Spirit, he will answer exactly; there shall not a sigh be lost. 'Likewise,' saith the apostle, 'the Spirit also helps our infirmities: for we know not what we should pray for as we ought: but the Spirit itself makes intercession for us, with groanings which cannot be uttered,' Rom. viii. 26. Therefore there cannot a groan be lost, nor a darting of a sigh. Whatsoever is spiritual must be effectual, though it cannot be vented in words. For God hath an ear, not only near a man's tongue, to know what he saith; but also in a man's heart, to know what he desires, or would have. As the observing, careful, tender mother many times knows what the child would have though it cannot speak; so God, he knows the desires, sighs, and groans of the heart when we cannot speak. For sometimes there may be such a confusion upon the soul, by reason of divers disturbances, that it cannot express nor vent itself in words. Therefore the Spirit vents itself then in sighs and groans, which are heard and accepted, because they are the desires of his own Spirit. Thus much the prophet David excellently sheweth, 'Lord, thou hast heard the desire of the humble: thou wilt prepare their heart, thou wilt cause thine ear to hear,' Ps. x. 17. God, he first prepares the heart to pray, then his ear to hear their prayers and desires. If this will not encourage us to be much in suit to God, and put up our petitions to him, to labour for a spirit of prayer, I know not what will prevail; when we know that no petition shall be turned back again unanswered. When we are to deal with princes upon earth, they oftentimes regard neither the persons nor their petitions, but turn their backs upon both. Oh! but a Christian hath the ear of God and heaven open upon him; such credit in heaven, that his desires and groans are respected and heard. And undoubtedly a man may know that he shall be heard when he hath a spirit of prayer; in one kind or other, though not in the particulars or kinds we ask, hear he will for our good.

God will not lose the incense of his own Spirit, of a spirit of prayer which he stirs up, it is so precious. Therefore let us labour to have a spirit of prayer, which God regards so much; seeing for a certain, wheresoever he gives a spirit of prayer, he means to give that we pray for; but according to his heavenly wisdom, as here his answer is,

' I will heal their backsliding, I will love them freely,' &c.

God answers them exactly unto all they prayed for, beginning first with the ground of all our comfort, 'forgiveness of sins.' According to their petition, 'Take away all iniquity,' he answers, 'I will heal their backsliding,' or their rebellion. Backsliding is an aggravation of sin. Every sin is not a rebellion, apostasy, or backsliding · for there be also sins of infirmities. We usually rank sins thus, in

1. Sins of ignorance.
2. Sins of infirmity.
3. Sins against knowledge, with a higher hand; and
4. The sins against the Holy Ghost.

Now, this is more than to cure sins of ignorance and of infirmity when he saith, ' I will heal their backsliding.'

Quest. But why doth he answer the higher pitch of an aggravation, when their petition was in a lower strain only, ' Take away all mine iniquity' ?

Ans. To shew that he would answer them fully; that is, that he would heal all sins whatsoever, not only of ignorance and of infirmity, but also sins willingly committed, their rebellions and backslidings. For, indeed, they were backsliding. From the time of Jeroboam, that made the rent, the ten tribes grew worse and worse continually, so that they had been utterly extinguished, but that God was wondrous gracious to send them prophets to preserve many that they should not bow the knee to Baal, being merciful to them to bear with their backsliding so long. For besides their calves, they had false gods. They did not only worship the true God in a false manner by the calves, but they had Baals also. So that we see, God, when he will comfort, will comfort to purpose, and take away all objections that the soul can make, a guilty soul being full of objections. Oh ! my sins are many, great, rebellions and apostasies. But, be they what they will, God's mercy in Christ is greater and more. ' I will heal their backsliding,' or their rebellion. God is above conscience. Let Satan terrify the conscience as he will, and let conscience speak the worst it can against itself, yet God is greater. Therefore, let the sin be what it will, God will pardon all manner of sins. As they pray to pardon all, so he will ' take away all iniquity, heal their backsliding.' But to come nearer the words.

' I will heal,' &c. The healing meant here is especially in the pardon of their sins, answerable to their desires in justification. And there is a healing also in sanctification by the Spirit. When God takes away the venom from the wound, then God cures in sanctification. Both are meant, but especially the first. In a wound we know there is,

1. The malignity and venom of it; and then,
2. The wound itself, so festered and rankled.

Now, pardoning grace in justification takes away the anguish and malice of the wound, so that it ceaseth to be so malignant and deadly as to kill or infect. And then sanctification purgeth and cleanseth the wound and heals it up. Now, God through Christ doth both. The blood of Christ doth heal the guilt of sin, which is the anger and malignity of it ; and by the Spirit of Christ he heals the wound itself, and purgeth out the sick and peccant humour by little and little through sanctification. God is a perfect healer. 'I will heal their backsliding.' See here the state of the church and children of God. They are prone to backsliding and turning away. We are naturally prone to decline further and further from God. So the church of God, planted in a family in the beginning of the world, how soon was it prone to backsliding. This is one weakness since the fall. It is incident to our nature to be unsettled and unsteady in our holy resolutions. And whilst we live in the midst of temptations, the world, together with the fickleness of our own nature, evil examples, and Satan's perpetual malice against God and the poor church, are ill pilots to lead us out of the way. This is spoken to make us careful how to shun backsliding. For we see how many opinions are foisted in amongst us, and have got some head, that durst not before once be named amongst us. Popery spreads itself amain. Even churches are prone to backsliding. Therefore, St Paul's advice is, 'Be not high-minded, but fear; for if God spared not the natural branches, take heed lest he also spare not thee,' Rom. xi. 20, 21. What is become of Rome ? So the same will become of us if we stop not our backslidings.

Now, in that God's promise is, 'I will heal their backslidings,' observe, in the first place,

That sin is a wound and a disease.

Now, as in sickness there is, 1, grief troubling and vexing the party who feels it; and, 2, deformity of the place affected, which comes by wounds and weaknesses; so in all sin, when we are sensible of it, there is first grief, vexation, and torment of conscience, and then, again, deformity. For it takes away the beauty and vigour of the soul, and dejects the countenance. It debaseth a man, and takes away his excellency. As Jacob saith of Reuben, 'Unstable as water, thou shalt not excel, because thou wentest up to thy father's bed,' Gen. xlix. 4. Saith God to Cain, 'Why art thou wroth, and why is thy countenance fallen?' Gen. iv. 6. And the prophet David, he confesseth, 'When I kept silence, my bones waxed old through my roaring all the day long,' Ps. xxxii. 3, 4. So again, 'There is no soundness in my flesh, because of thine anger; neither is there any rest in my bones, because of my sin,' Ps. xxxviii. 3. So that sin is a wound and a disease, whether we consider the miseries it brings on soul and body, or both. Therefore, howsoever a sinful person think himself a goodly person, and wear his sins as ornaments about him, pride, lust, and the like, yet he is a deformed, loathsome person in the eyes and presence of God; and when conscience is awakened, sin will be loathsome, irksome, and odious unto himself, fill him full of grief and shame, so that he cannot endure the sight of his own soul.

Now, all sins whatsoever are diseases. The first sin of all sins, which we call hereditary, original sin, what was * it but an hereditary disease ? A leprosy, which we drew from our first parents, spread over all the soul, having the seeds and spawn of all sin in it. The church of Rome makes it less than other sins, as indeed popery is ignorant both of the height of grace and of the depth of corruption, for if they knew the one, they would be more capable of the other. Why do they not conceive aright of grace and of the height of it ? Because they know not the depth of original sin. And, indeed, the true knowledge of this disease is proper only to the child of God in the true church. None but he knows what original sin is. Others can dispute and talk of it, but none feels it but the child of God. Now, all other particular, actual sins be diseases flowing from hence. So that all diseases in this kind arise either, 1, from ourselves, as we have a

* Qu. 'is it?'—G.

seminary of them in our own hearts; or else, 2, from the infection and contagion of others; or, 3, from Satan, who hath society with our spirits, as men have with the outward man, coming in by his suggestions, and our entertaining of them. So that in that respect sin is like unto a wound and a disease, in regard of the cause of them.

And, in regard of the effects, sin is like a disease. Diseases, if they be neglected, breed death itself, and become incurable. So it is with the diseases and sins of the soul. Neglect them, and the best end of them will be despair in this world. Whereupon we may have advantage to fly unto the mercy of God in Christ. This is the end of sin, either to end in a good despair or in a fruitless barren despair, at the hour of death leading to hell, when they have no grace to repent. 'The wages of sin is death,' &c., Rom. vi. 23. Sin itself is a wound, and that which riseth from sin is a wound too, doubting and despair; for this disease and wound of sin breeds that other disease, a despair of mercy, which is the beginning of hell, the second death. These things might be further enlarged. But for the present only in general know that sin is *a disease and a wound of the soul;* so much worse than the diseases of the body, by how much the soul is more precious than it, and the death of the soul more terrible than the death of the body. Sin is a disease and a wound; for what is pride but a swelling? What is anger but an intemperate heat of the soul, like an ague, as it were? What is revenge but a wildfire in the soul? What is lust but a spreading canker in the soul, tending to a consumption? What is covetousness but a sword, a perpetual wounder of the soul, piercing it through with many sorrows? What is security but, as it were, the lethargy and apoplexy of the soul? And so we might go on in other resemblances (*f*).

Quest. But, it may be demanded, how shall we know that we are sick of this sickness and disease you speak of?

Ans. How do we know that we are sick in body? If the body be extreme cold we know there is a distemper, or if it be extreme hot. So if the soul be so extreme cold that no heavenly motives or sweet promises can work upon it, stir it up, then certainly there is a disease upon the soul.

If the soul be inflamed with revenge and anger, that soul is certainly diseased. The temper of the soul is according to the passions thereof. A man may know by his passions when he hath a sick soul.

If a man cannot relish good diet, then we count him a sick man; so when a man cannot relish holy discourse nor the ordinances of God. You have some men that can relish nothing but profits and pleasures, and such vanities, but no divine thing. Such have sick souls undoubtedly.

So, again, a man may know there is a deadly sickness and soreness upon the soul, 1, when it is senseless of its wounds; and, 2, is senseless of that which passeth from it. As men, we say, are ready to die when excremental things pass from them without any sense, so a man may know that he is desperately soul-sick when oaths, lies, and deceitful speeches pass from him, and yet he is senseless of them. They think not of them. They mean no harm. Doth that argue a sound state of body, when a man is so desperately ill that he feels not his bodily hurts? And is this a good state of soul, when these filthy things come out from it insensibly? It is an argument of extreme deadness of spirit and irreverence, and of a desperate sin-sick soul, when there is no dread or awe of the majesty of God. Let such look about them. It is an aggravation of the danger of the soul this kind of temper. We usually say, when the stomach is so weak that it can hold no nourishment without casting it up again as fast as it receives it, certainly such an one is sick, and in a dangerous state of body. So when a man hears and hears, and reads and reads, and digests nothing into nourishment, but all is left where he heard it, it is a sign they have sick souls when their retentive power is so weak. And there is certainly some sickness, some dangerous obstruction in that soul that cannot digest the wholesome word of God, to make use of it; some noisome lust then certainly obstructs the soul, which must be purged out.

It is a pitiful thing to see the desperate condition of many now, who, though they live under the tyranny of sin, yet flatter their own disease, and account them their greatest enemies who any way oppose their sick humour. What do they most cordially hate? The sound preaching of the word. The very sight of such an one whose calling hath been to put us in mind of our sins, evil courses, and vanities of the world, is loathsome and offensive to carnal men, in whom corruption is grown up to such a tyranny that it sways the whole soul to devise how to satisfy it. Man is so diseased that those lusts in him, which he should labour to subdue and mortify by the power of the Spirit, do so oversway him that all his life is nothing else but a disease and backsliding into sin. And as if we were not corrupt enough ourselves, how many are there who feed their corruptions when they frequent ill places and company, whom they cannot do without, and are as fish in the water, feeding the old man in them. So that such are not only sick, but defend, maintain, and feed their sickness, their whole life being spent this way, which they laugh at, and make ' pride their chain and ornament,' Ps. lxxiii. 6, as the prophet speaks. This is spoken that we may take up a lamentation for the vileness of man's nature, and to teach us how to judge aright of men when they devise how to have their liberty strengthened to go to hell, as it were, with an high hand, having their will so fortified that no man is able to deal with them, thwart them, or teach them anything. If it were offered to most men to have what estate they would in this world, what are their wishes and desires? O that I might live as I list, that I might have what would content my pleasures without control, that I might have no crosses, but go smoothly on! Yet this, which is the desire of most men, is the most cursed estate of all, and most to be lamented. Thus it appeareth sin is a wound and a disease. What use may we make of it?

Use 1. If this be so, then, in the first place, let us know and consider, *that no man who lives in sins unrepented of and uncured, is to be envied, be they never so great.* Who will envy a man that hath a rotten body, covered over with glorious attire? when every man knows that he carries a rotten disease about him; either some disease in the vital parts, or from the rottenness of sin, which puts a kind of shame and scorn. Can we pity a man thus in glorious attire, having a filthy body under it? thus covering their nakedness, in whose case we would not for anything be. And are they not much more to be pitied, who have ulcerous souls, galled and pierced through with many sins? When we see men that are blasphemers, swearers, men guilty of much blood and filthiness, and of many sins hanging upon them, to envy such a man's greatness is extreme folly. Oh, he carries his death's wound about him, as we say. He is stricken already in his side with a deadly dart. Without the healing mercy of God, there is but a step betwixt him and eternal death; wherefore no man is to be envied for his sinful greatness.

Use 2. Again, if this be so, that sin is a disease and wound of the soul, *let us therefore labour to cure it presently.* It is desperate folly in men to neglect their bodies, when they know that they are prone to such and such diseases, which are growing upon them every day. How careful are men, perceiving thus much, to prevent diseases by timely physic ! All sins are diseases, and growing like diseases, run from ill to worse, worse and worse. ' Wicked men,' saith the apostle, ' grow worse and worse,' 2 Tim. iii. 13. Therefore, if sin be a disease, prevent it presently. For as we see, heretics and other the like are hardly sound but at the first, and then are hardly cured. So, if we neglect the diseases of our souls, they will breed a consumption of grace, or such an ill temper of soul, as that it cannot well desire to repent. Nay, when a man lives in wicked, rebellious courses long, God will give him up to such terrors of conscience, that it will not be pacified, but upbraid itself. I have been a sinful, wretched creature; mercy hath been offered me again and again, but now it is too late, having outstood all the means of grace, and rejected them. When they have considered that their lives have for a long time been a mere rebellion, and that they have put off the checks of conscience, the admonitions of the word and Spirit, with the motions thereof. It is long in this case before a man can have peace. For answerable to the continuance in sin, is the hardness of the cure, if it be cured at all.

Therefore there is no dallying with sin. I shall repent at length, but not now. Yet a while I will continue these and these courses, I shall do well enough, &c.; as if a man who were sick, or desperately wounded, should say, I shall do well, and yet neglect to send for the physician. None are so desperately foolish in case of the body, why should we for our souls? Is not that in much more hazard than the body, if we had spiritual eyes to consider of it ? The truth is, people are not convinced of this, that sin is such a sickness, which is the reason they are so careless of it. But when the conscience is awaked, as it will be one day, here or in hell, then they will be of another mind. Nay, in this world, when friends, nor riches, nor anything can comfort, then they cry out, O that they had not been so foolish ! They would give a world, if they had it, for peace of conscience ! This will be the best of it, for men that go on in sin. Therefore, before hardness of heart grow upon us, that disease following the disease of sin, let us take heed, and labour to have our souls healed in time. Thus we have found that sin is a sickness ; for so much is implied, when he saith, ' I will heal their backsliding.' Whence the direct observation is,

That God is the great physician of the soul.

For he saith here, ' I will heal their backsliding ;' so that healing implies the taking away of—

1. The guilt of sin, which is the venom of it, by justification.
2. The rage of sin, which is the spreading of it, by sanctification.
3. The removing the judgment upon our estate.

For, unless God be the more merciful, these things follow. Where there is sin, and breaking of his law, there is a state binding over to damnation and guilt. When there is a sinful disposition raging, and bringing us from one degree of sin to another, then there is God's judgment and wrath revealed from heaven against this. Now, when God heals, he heals perfectly, but in some regards slowly, as we shall see hereafter. In regard of forgiveness of sins, he healeth perfectly. But by little and little in regard of the other, of sanctification. He stops up the issues of our corruption by little and little. For other things, and judgments in this world, he removes the malice, and takes away the sting of them, which is the venom ; as he saith afterward, ' For mine anger is turned away,' which being removed and turned from things, then they are no more judgments. What cared Paul for imprisonment, when he knew God's wrath accompanied not the stocks? Acts xvi. 19, *seq.* Let wrath be taken from the suffering, that the soul be sound, then it is no matter what condition a man be in, he carries heaven and paradise with him. Therefore, so far God removes those diseases and sicknesses of condition, as they carry venom in them; so changing the condition, that whatsoever we suffer, it hath the nature of an exercise, medicine, or correction only. But that which envenoms all, and makes the least cross a curse, and sinks deep, is the anger of God joined with things, Ps. lxxxix. 46. The least cross, when it carrieth with it the anger and vengeance of God, and reports that to the soul, I have offended God, and it is just with him thus to inflict wrath upon me: this is terrible, and it puts a sting to the cross. Now, God here promiseth to remove that, ' I will heal their backsliding.' This principally, in the first place, is meant of healing in regard of justification; taking away that guilt from the soul which enthrals it, and binds it over to condemnation and judgment. God will set the soul at a spiritual liberty, and so heal it. Thus you see the point clear, that God is the great physician of the soul.

Reason 1. For God who made the soul, *knows all the diseases, windings, and turnings of it.* He is an excellent anatomist: 'all things are naked and open before his eyes,' Heb. iv. 13. He knows the inward part of the soul, the seat of all sin. We know not ourselves as he knows us. There is a mystery of self-deceit in the heart, which he knows who can search all the hidden corners of the heart, which is the reason why he is so good a physician, and so excellent. Because he is a discerner and searcher of the heart, who can see all, and so can cure all, being above the sting of conscience, he hath a remedy above the malady. He is greater than our conscience. Therefore he can cure our conscience.

Reason 2. And in the next place, *as he can heal our souls, so he is willing to do it,* which his willingness we may know by the medicine he doth it by, his own dear Son. He hath provided a plaster of his Son's blood to heal us. And besides his own inward willingness, being now a gracious father to us in Christ Jesus, he sends his ambassadors to heal and cure us in his name, 2 Cor. v. 20, to apply his medicines, and to beseech and entreat us to be reconciled. God, by them, entreats us to entreat him for pardon and mercy, and is so willing to be entreated, that ere we shall set out he teacheth us words, as we heard, ' Take unto you words,' &c. As he is an able, so he is a willing physician. Christ, the great physician, together with his Father, expects not that we should first come to him, but he comes first, and sends to us. The physician came to the sick, though for the most part the sick, if able, go to the physician, 1 John iv. 9, 10. But here is the contrary. He came from heaven, took our nature upon him, and therein died, by which his blood-shedding, he satisfied the wrath of God, justly offended with us, Isa. liii. 10. So he heals our souls that way, having undergone the anger and wrath of God, that his blood might quench and appease that anger by a plaster thereof made, and applied to our souls, Isa. liii. 11, 12.

Do we doubt of his willingness, when he comes to us and calls us, ' Come unto me, all ye that labour and are heavy laden, and I will give you rest'? Mat. xi. 28. It is his office which he hath assumed to heal our soul. The many cures he hath done sheweth the ability and willingness of the physician; cures whereof we are incapable, by reason of our mean condition. A king, as his place is greater, so sometimes his sins are greater than others are ; yet he cured Manasseh, that sinful king, 2 Chron. xxxiii. 23, together with Mary Magdalen, Paul, Peter, and the rest, who were a company healed by this physician. Therefore all this is for the glory of our physician. We may see what he can do by what he hath done ; as amongst us physicians are sought after according to their skill and cures done. Consider in the sacrament how ready God is to cure and to heal us, how gracious he is in the sacrament of baptism, wherein he engageth us to believe, admitting us into the covenant, and preventing us with mercy, before we knew what a covenant or seal was, Ezek. xvi. 6, *seq.* And so to persuade us of his willingness to forgive our sins and heal our rebellions, he hath ordained the sacrament, not for his sake, but to strengthen our weak faith, and help us. The point is easy for matter of our understanding, but hard in regard of use and application, especially when it should be made use of, in time of temptation. Then let us lay it up as a comfortable point, this gracious promise of God, ' I will heal their backsliding, I will love them freely,' &c. Lay this up against the hour of temptation, make use of it then, alleging unto God his own promise and nature, as David did, ' Lord, remember the promise wherein thou hast caused me to trust,' Ps. cxix. 49. Thou hast promised pardoning and healing [of] all our trangressions, &c. Remember thy free promises made in Jesus Christ. God cannot deny himself nor his word, but loves to have his bonds sued. Remember this. And when conscience is surprised with any sin, though it be never so great, look not on the disease so much as who is the physician, and what his plaster and medicine is. God is the physician, and the blood of Christ is the plaster. What if our sins be mountains ! There is an ocean and a sea of mercy to swell above and cover these mountains of our sins, Mic. vii. 18, 19. Our sins in this case are like fire, which, falling into the sea, is by and by quenched. What if our sins be of never so long standing (as these their backslidings here had continued hundreds of years, wherein they were a backsliding generation), yet it is no matter of what standing or continuance the disease is, so long as God hath promised to be the physician, and the blood of Christ is the plaster that healeth us, Isa. i. 18, 19. The question is not, What ? How many ? How great ? and of what continuance our sins ? but how we stand affected towards them, hate them, and resolve against them ? That sin cannot hurt us which we fight against, mourn for, complain of, resolve to leave, and truly hate. Let us never stand, then, in comparisons with our sins, which bear no proportion to the infinite skill and power of our great physician, and to the infinite work of Christ's all-sufficient satisfaction. What canst thou object, O man ? ' It is Christ that justifieth the ungodly, who art thou that condemneth ? It is he that died, yea, rather, who is risen again, who is also at the right hand of God, and also maketh intercession for us,' Rom. viii. 33, 34. Thou canst not satisfy for the least sin. God hath laid upon him the iniquities of us all, Lev. xvi. 21. ' The chastisements of our peace was upon him, and with his stripes we are healed,' Isa. liii. 5.

Let us, therefore, be wise for afterwards, hear, read, lay up, and meditate for the time to come. For times will come, if we belong to God, that nothing will content or pacify the soul but the infinite worth and merit of an infinite and free mercy apprehended in the face of Jesus Christ. When our sins are set in order before us, the sins of our youth, middle, and old age, our sins against conscience, against the law and gospel, against examples, vows, promises, resolutions, and admonitions of the Spirit and servants of God; when there shall be such a terrible accuser, and God shall perhaps let the wounds of conscience fly open and join against us; when wrath shall appear, be in some sort felt, and God presented to the soul as ' a consuming fire,' Heb. xii. 29, no comfort in heaven or earth appearing, hell beneath seeming ready to revenge against us the quarrel of God's covenant, Oh then for faith to look through all these clouds! to see mercy in wrath! love in correction! Heb. xii. 6, life in death! the sweetness of the promises! the virtue and merit of Christ's sufferings, death, resurrection, and intercession at the right hand! the sting of death removed, 1 Cor. xv. 55, sin pardoned and done away, and glory at hand! In sum, this promise made good, which leads unto all this happiness, as we shall by and by hear, ' I will heal their backsliding, I will love them freely, for mine anger is turned away.' Oh, this is a marvellous matter, then, to be persuaded of! Therefore let us make a right use of these words in due season, for they are ' like apples of gold, with pictures of silver,' Prov. xxv. 11, like balm to a green wound, like delivery in a ship-wreck. But, indeed, all comparisons come far short of this illustration, as the terror of incensed wrath in the fearful apprehension of eternal, unspeakable misery, is beyond any other fear, apprehension, or joy.

But lest this grace be abused by others (for we must not withhold the children's bread, for fear others partake with them unto whom it belongs not), let them know thus much: that those who turn this grace into wantonness, and will be evil, because God is thus gracious—that there is no word of comfort in the whole Scripture for, them, who stand resolved to go on in their sins, presuming of mercy. See what God saith in this case, ' Lest there should be among you a root that beareth gall and wormwood; and it come to pass when he heareth the words of this curse, that he bless himself in his heart, saying, I shall have peace, though I walk in the imagination of mine heart, to add drunkenness to thirst: the Lord will not spare him, but then the anger of the Lord and his jealousy shall smoke against that man, and all the curses that are written in this book shall lie upon him, and the Lord shall blot out his name from under heaven,' Deut. xxix. 18–20. ' God will wound the hairy scalp of such an one,' Ps. lxviii. 21, who goes on in his wickedness, and means to be so. And in the New Testament those who thus make a progress in sin, what do they? They are said ' to treasure up unto themselves wrath against the day of wrath, and revelation of the righteous judgment of God,' Rom. ii. 5. Therefore God's word speaks no comfort to those who purpose to live in any sin. All the comfort that can be spoken to such is, that yet they are not in hell; that yet they have time to return to this great Physician of the soul. But take such an one in his present condition, he can have no comfort in this estate, wherein there is but a step between him and hell. So as when the rotten thread of this uncertain life shall fail, or is cut asunder, down they fall. We have no comfort here for them, till they return. This precious balm belongs to the wounded conscience. Briefly for use then.

Use. Seeing that our God is a healing God, as we can admire the wisdom, skill, and excellency of our physician, so let us much more make use of him upon all occasions. Trust and cleave to him, not like good Asa (but not good in this), who forgot himself, and sent first to the physicians, 2 Chron. xvi. 12. But let us especially rely upon God, and look to him, who can ' create help,' Isa. iv. 5, and must bless all means whatsoever. He is a healing God, who will heal all rebellions, and the most grievous sicknesses. He is a physician that is good for all turns. There are some diseases which are called the scorn of physicians, as the gout, the ague, and the like; wherein, in some cases, they are put to a stand, and know not what to do. But God is never at a loss. His skill cannot be set down. He is good at all diseases, to pardon all manner of sins. Therefore let us go to him for cure, seeing there is neither sin, nor grief, nor terror of conscience arising thereupon, which can be so great but God can cure both the sin and the terror, if we take a right course, and speak peace to the soul. God is a healing God, arising when he comes 'with healing in his wings,' Mal. iv. 2. As he saith, 'I will heal their rebellion,' &c. And as he is a healing physician, so he puts his patients to no charge. For as he saith, 'I will heal their backslidings;' so he saith, 'I will love them freely.'

Therefore let us the more build upon this truth, which is indeed the sum of all godliness. For what is the gospel but the triumph of mercy? Do but consider the scope of God in the new covenant, whereof the sacrament is a seal, which is only to shew forth the exaltation of the grace and mercy of God in Jesus Christ, above all unworthiness whatsoever. For all there is for the glory of his mercy. For in the covenant of grace, mercy doth triumph against judgment and justice; which mercy of God in Christ is said by the apostle 'to reign unto life everlasting, by Jesus Christ our Lord,' Rom. v. 21. It reigns, and hath a regiment* above, and over all. For mercy in God stirred up his wisdom to devise a way, by shedding of the blood of Christ Jesus, God-man, to satisfy divine justice, and rejoice against it. But whence comes this, that justice should be so satisfied? Because a way is found out, how none of God's attributes are losers by mercy. Wherefore in any temptation, when we are prone to doubt of God's love, say, What! shall we wrong God more, by calling in question his mercy, and the excellency of his lovingkindness, which is more than any other sin we have committed? This is a sin superadded against his mercy, power, goodness, graciousness, and love in healing of sin; which takes away the glory of God in that attribute, wherein he labours to triumph, reign, and glorify himself most, and 'which is over all his works,' Ps. cxlv. 9. Therefore he that offends herein, in denying God the glory of his great, tender, unspeakable mercy, whereby he would glorify himself most in the covenant of grace, he offends God most.

Therefore let us, at such times as God awakens conscience, be so far from thinking that God is unwilling to cure and help us, as to think that hereby we shall honour God more by believing than we dishonoured him by our sin. For the faith of an humble, contrite sinner, it glorifies God more than our better obedience in other things doth; because it gives him the glory of that wherein he delights, and will be most glorified, the glory of his mercy and truth, of his rich, abundant mercy that hath no bounds. There is no comparison between the mercy of God in the covenant of grace, and that to Adam in the state of nature. For in the first he did good to a good man; first he made him good, and then did him good. But when man did degenerate, and was fallen into such a cursed estate as we are, for God then to be good to a sinner, and freely to do good, here is goodness indeed, triumphant goodness. Cain was a cursed person, who said, 'My punishment is greater than can be borne,' Gen. iv. 13. We know who spake it. No; God is a physician for all diseases. If they be 'crimson sins,' he can make them 'white as wool,' Isa. i. 18.

That is, ' government.'—G.

Who would not be careful therefore to search his wounds, his sins to the bottom ? Let the search be as deep as we can, considering that there is more mercy in God, than there can be sin in us. Who would favour his soul ? especially considering, if he neglect searching of it, sins will grow deadly and incurable upon that neglect. Let this therefore encourage us not to spare ourselves, in opening the wounds of our souls to God, that he may spare all. Thus we saw formerly, the church here is brought in dealing plainly with God, and confessing all (for she had an excellent teacher), and God answers all ; beginning with this, ' I will heal their backsliding.' They were idolaters, and guilty of the sins of the second table in a high measure (no petty sins), yet God saith, ' I will heal their backsliding,' &c. Which being healed, then an open highway is made for all other mercies whatsoever, which is the next point we observe hence :

Obs. That the chief mercy of all, which leads unto all the rest, is the pardon and forgiveness of sins.

Healing of the guilt of sin, we see, is set in the front of these petitions formerly shewed ; which as it is the first thing in the church's desire, ' Take away all iniquity,' &c, so it is the first thing yielded to in God's promise, ' I will heal their backsliding,' &c. Pardon of sin, and cure of sin, whereby the conscience ceaseth to be bound over to condemnation, is the first and chiefest blessing of God, and is that for which the church falls out in a triumph. ' Who is a God like unto thee, that pardoneth iniquity, and passeth by the transgression of the remnant of his heritage, because he delighteth in mercy,' &c., Micah vii. 18, 19, 20. And this is that excellent and sweet conclusion of the new covenant also, whereupon all the rest of those former foregoing mercies there are grounded. For, ' I will forgive their iniquity, and I will remember their sin no more,' Jer. xxxi. 34. Yea, this is the effect of that grand promise made to his church after the return of their captivity. ' In those days, and at that time, saith the Lord, the iniquity of Israel shall be sought for, and there shall be none ; and the sins of Judah, and they shall not be found ; for I will pardon them whom I reserve,' Jer. l. 20. The point is plain and clear enough ; it needs no following. The reason is,

Because it takes away the interposing cloud. God is gracious in himself. Pardon of sin removes the cloud betwixt God's gracious face and the soul. Naturally, God is a spring of mercy ; but our sins stop the spring. But when sin is pardoned, the stop is taken away, and the spring runs amain. God is not merciful as a flint yields fire, by force ; but as a spring, whence water naturally issues.

Quest. Seeing forgiveness of sins unstops this spring, why do we not feel this mercy ?

Ans. Surely, because some sin or other is upon the file uncancelled,* perhaps unconfessed ; or because we are stuffed with pride, that we believe not ; or are so troubled, or trouble ourselves, that we apprehend not, or believe not the pardon of sins confessed and hated. But sure it is, forgiveness of sins unstops the spring of mercy, and unveils God's gracious face in Jesus Christ unto us. Sin being not pardoned, this stops, as the prophet speaks. Our iniquity is that which keeps good things from us. Therefore the chief mercy is that which removes, that which unstops the current of all mercy. ' I will heal their backsliding,' &c. Look at a condemned prisoner in the tower ! Let him have all contentment ; as long as he is in the displeasure of the prince, stands condemned, and the sentence

* See note *b*, vol. I., p. 289.—G.

unreversed, what true contentment can he have ? None at all. So it is with a sinner, that hath not his pardon and *quietus est* from heaven. Yield him all contentment which the world can afford ; all the satisfaction that can issue from the creature ; yet what is this to him, as long as he hath not mercy, and that his conscience is not pacified, because it is not cleansed and washed with the blood of Christ?

Sin is like Jonah : whilst he was in the ship, there was nothing but tempest, Jonah i. 4 ; like Achan in the army, Joshua vii. 11, 12 : whilst he was not found out, God's judgment followed the camp. Sin is that which troubleth all. Therefore it must be taken away first ; and therewith all evil is taken away. Therefore, the first mercy is a forgiving, pardoning, and quieting mercy. When the blood of Jesus Christ, by the hand of faith, is sprinkled upon the soul, God creating a hand of faith to sprinkle and shed it upon the soul, ' Christ loved me, and gave himself for me,' then the soul saith, Though my sins be great, yet the satisfaction of Christ is greater. God hath loved me, and gave his own Son for me ; and I apply this to myself, as it is offered to me, and take the offer. This pacifieth the soul, as it is written, ' The blood of Christ, who through the eternal Spirit offered himself without spot to God, is that which purgeth our conscience from dead works to serve the living God,' Heb. ix. 14. To a repentant sinner, this ' blood of sprinkling speaks better things than the blood of Abel,' Heb. xii. 24 : not as his blood cried for vengeance, but mercy, mercy. When the soul is thus pacified, there is the foundation of all other mercy whatsoever. The order is this : when God is reconciled, all is reconciled ; when God is at peace with us in the forgiveness of sins, then all is peaceable at home and abroad. Conscience is in peace within, and all the creatures at peace without ; all which, with all that befalls us, have a command to do us no hurt ; as David gave charge to the people, of Absalom. When God is reconciled and at peace, all things are at peace with us. For is not he Lord of hosts, who hath the command of all the creatures ? Therefore this grace of forgiveness is the chief grace.

To shew it in one instance more. David was a king and a prophet, a comely and a valorous person. But what esteemed he most ? Did he say, Blessed is the man who is a king, or a prophet, or a valiant warrior, or hath dominion, obedience, or great possessions, as I have ? Oh, no. ' Blessed is the man whose sins are forgiven, and whose iniquities are covered,' Ps. xxxii. 1. You see wherein this holy man David sets and pitcheth happiness, in the forgiveness of sins. Blessed is such a man. Though he were a king, he knew well enough that if his sins were not pardoned and covered he had been a wretched man.

Use 1. Therefore, this should teach us to desire of God continually *the pardon of our sins ;* and we should make it the chief desire of our souls that God would shine upon them in Jesus Christ, pardon and accept us in his beloved. They go together.

Use 2. And *bless him for this above all other blessings,* as it is Ps. ciii. 1, 3, ' Bless the Lord, O my soul ; and all that is within me, bless his holy name,' &c. Why ? ' Who forgiveth all thy iniquities, and healeth all thy diseases.' We should bless God most of all for this, that he hath devised a way by Christ to receive satisfaction for sin, to pardon it, and say unto our souls, ' I am thy salvation,' Ps. xxxv. 3. This is the greatest favour of all.

Quest. But you ask, How shall I know that God hath healed my soul in regard of the forgiveness of sins ?

Ans. The answer is, *If, together with pardon of sin, he heal sin.* For God, when he takes away the venom of a wound that endangers death, the deadly disease, he takes away also the swelling of the wound and glowing of it. When he ceaseth to make it deadly, he heals the soul withal, and *subdues our iniquities,* as his promise is, Micah vii. 19. So there is, together with pardoning mercy, curing mercy in regard of sanctification. Where God is a Father to make us sons, he is a Father to beget us anew. So where Christ comes by blood to wash away our sins, he comes by water also and the Holy Ghost; where he is a Comforter in the forgiveness of sins, he is a sanctifier. And the soul of a distressed sinner looks to the one as well as the other. Ask the soul of any man who is truly humbled, What do you chiefly desire? Oh, that God would pardon my sins! But is that all? No; that he would also heal my sins and subdue my rebellions, that I may not any longer be under the government and tyranny of my lusts, but under God's gracious government, who will guide me better than before, Hos. ii. 7. This we see to be the order in the Lord's prayer. After we are taught to say, ' Forgive us our trespasses,' it follows, ' And lead us not into temptation, but deliver us from evil,' which is for the time to come, Mat. vi. 12, 13. So David, ' Cleanse me from my secret sins, and keep me, that presumptuous sins have not dominion over me,' &c., Ps. xix. 12, 13. So that this is the desire of an afflicted conscience truly humbled, curing as well as covering of sin. This is a sure evidence that our sins are pardoned.

2. Then again, *when there is peace:* when the soul feels this, it is a sign that God hath healed the soul. ' For,' saith the apostle, ' being justified by faith, we have peace with God through our Lord Jesus Christ,' Rom. v. 1. The blood of Christ hath a pacifying power in forgiveness of sins. When Jonah was cast out, there was a calm, Jonah i. 12; so when sin is cast out and pardoned, there is a calm in the soul, which comes from the forgiveness of sins.

3. Again, healing is known by this, *if we have hearts willing to be searched,* for then our will is cured, which in the state of grace is more than our obedience. When we would be better than we are, then certainly our will is not in league with corruptions. Now, where the will is so much sanctified, I resolve to be better, I would be better, and I use all means, being glad when any joins with me against my corruptions, I am glad of all such advantages, here is a good sign. As now, when a man goes to church, and desires, ' O that my corruptions might be met withal! O that I might be laid open to myself, and know myself better than I have formerly done!' this is the desire of an ingenuous soul. Where there is no guile of soul, a man is glad to have himself and his corruptions discovered, whereas another frets and kicks, and rageth against the word of God, which is a sign that there is some league betwixt him and his sin. You have some that, above all things in the world, they would not have such and such downright ministers. O take heed; this is a sign of a hollow heart, and that a man is in love with his disease. Can there be a cure where there is a love of the disease?

4. Not to name many, the last, which is a high pitch, shall be, *by our estimation of things here and above.* What hath this healing wrought in thee? What estimation of things? How is thy heart weaned from the world? How are thy affections set on things which are above? Col. iii. 1. When a sick man is soundly recovered, though his distempered palate could not relish the best meats in his sickness, yet now he relishes and

loves the best most of all. Look, then, to ourselves. How forget we, with blessed St Paul, ' the things which are behind, pressing hard to the mark which is before, for the high prize of that calling' ? Philip. iii. 13. How stand we affected, to long for our country ? this world being only the place of our pilgrimage. Surely a soul that is soundly healed is an under-valuing soul, to use this world and all things therein as though we used them not; and it is also a valuing soul, to covet spiritual things above all, 1 Cor. vii. 29, 31. ' O,' saith David, ' how I love thy law, it is my meditation all the day ; I love thy commandments above gold, yea, above fine gold,' Ps. cxix. 97, 127. The joy of this estate ' is a joy unspeakable and glorious,' 1 Pet. i. 8, of which it is said ' the stranger shall not meddle with,' Pro. xiv. 10. Thus much concerning the disease. Before we come to the cure a question ariseth.

Quest. Whence, then, comes a calm in a carnal person ?

Ans. From ignorance and deadness of conscience, or from diversion. As a sick man, when he talks with another man that is his friend, his mind is diverted that he feeleth not his sickness all the while, so wicked men, either their consciences are seared, and they go on in sin, or else they have diversions. Great persons are loath to hear, and are usually full of diversions from the time they rise till they sleep again. All diversions busy conscience about other things ; so they keep themselves, that it may not trouble them. But the peace of a true Christian comes from another ground, from sound knowledge of his disease, and from sound satisfaction, by faith knowing Christ, the Spirit of God sealing this knowledge to the soul. If peace be thus settled, it is a sign of a sound cure.

Quest. But you will say, How shall I know that my sins are pardoned when I am subject to those sins still ?

Ans. Not to speak of transient actual sins, that are past and pardoned, when we have repented of them ; but of the root of all sin, which is weakness and corruption in us, fortified, and, as it were, intrenched by nature, occasions and custom. Of this the question is, How to discern of pardon, the root of sin remaining, and now and then foiling us ? The answer is affirmative. We may have that sin pardoned, which yet occasionally may foil us still. For a man is in the state of health, though he have the dregs of a disease hanging upon him, whereby a man ofttimes hath some little fit of the disease. When nature and physic hath prevailed over the disease, yet after that, there may be grudgings. So when God hath cured the soul by pardon, and hath begun to cure in sanctification, the cure is wrought, though some dregs remain, because those dregs are carried away with daily physic, and daily flying to God, ' Lord, forgive our debts ; Lord, heal us.' Every prayer and renewing of repentance carries some debt away, till death comes, that excellent physician, which once for all perfectly cures both soul and body, bringing both there where both shall have perfection.

Quest. But you will say, Is God's grace weak, that it cannot carry away all dregs of corruption as well as pardon ? Why is pardon in the forgiveness of sins absolute, when yet God suffers the dregs to remain, so as we still are subject to the disease of sin ?

Ans. God is wise. Let us not quarrel with our physician, for he is wiser than we ourselves. For he makes these relics medicinal to us, as thus : naturally we are prone to security and spiritual pride, therefore he makes a medicine of our infirmities, to cure spiritual pride and security, and to set us a-work. Therefore the Jebusites, and the residue of that kind, were left uncast out from among Israel, that thereby he might prove Israel, and lest they should be a prey unto wild beasts to devour them, Judges iii. 1. So some remainders of the flesh are left still in the best, that these wild beasts might not prey upon their souls. Spiritual pride, which is a detestable sin, robbing and denying God of his prerogative, and security, the grave of the soul, to cure these two especially, God makes the relics and remainders of sin a medicine unto us.

Quest. Why doth God suffer these infirmities and diseases to remain in us ?

Ans. Diseases are suffered, to put us in mind of infirmities in the root, which we knew not before. For if these should not sometimes break forth into a disease, we would think our nature were pure. Therefore God suffers them to break forth into diseases. Who would have thought that Moses had been passionate ? Certainly, himself did not know himself, at the waters of strife, that the seeds of anger should be in the meekest man in the world ! Num. xx. 2. Who would have thought that David, whose heart smote him for cutting off the lap of Saul's garment, 1 Sam. xxiv. 4, that so mild a man should have cruelty in him, and yet after that he committed murder ? Who would have thought that Peter, who made such protestations of love to Christ, that though all men forsook him, yet he would not ; yet after that should deny his Master, and forswear him ? Matt. xxiii. 88, 69, &c. All which was to shew us, that it is useful for us sometimes to have our corruptions break out, to put us in mind what inward weaknesses we have unknown and unsearched in us, and that we may know the depth of our corruption. God's children are gainers by all their infirmities and weaknesses, whereby they learn to stand stronger. Here is a main difference betwixt the slips of God's children, and the ordinary evil courses of others. They grow worse and worse. The oftener they fall into sin, the more they are settled upon their dregs. But God's child hath the remainders of corruption in him, from whence he hath infirmities, and whence he breaks into diseases. But notwithstanding, corruption is a loser hereby. For the oftener he falls into sin, it is the weaker and weaker. For the more he sees the root of it, the more he hates it, resolves and strives against it, till it be consummated by repentance and sanctifying grace. Let no man therefore be too much cast down for infirmities, though ofttimes they break out, if thereupon we find a renewed hatred, repentance, and strength against them. For God looks not so much, how much corruption there is in us, as how we stand affected to it, and what good there is, whether we be in league with it, and resist it. It is not sin that damns men, but sin with the ill qualities, sin unconfessed, not grieved for, and unresisted, else God hath holy ends in leaving corruption in us, to exercise, try us, and keep us from other sins. Therefore sin is left uncured.

Now the way to have it cured, both in the pardon and likewise in sanctification, we have it in the context. What doth God say ? ' I will heal their backsliding,' &c. After they had searched their hearts, and thereupon found iniquity, and then prayed, ' Take away all iniquity ;' after they had desired a divorce from their sins, ' Asshur shall not save us ;' and when they had some faith that God would cure them, and accordingly put confidence in God, ' the Father of the fatherless ;' then saith God, ' I will heal their backsliding.' So that sense of pardon in the forgiveness of sins, and sense of grace, comes after sight, sense, weariness, and confession of sin. God doth not pardon sin, when it is not seen, sorrowed for, nor confessed, and where there is not some degree of faith, to come to God, ' the

Father of the fatherless,' and the great Physician of souls. When we do this, as it is said in the context, then we find the forgiveness of sins, with the gracious power of God's Spirit healing of our diseases, ' I will heal their backsliding.'

Let us therefore remember this, lest we deceive our souls, for it is not so easy a thing to attain unto forgiveness of sins as we think.

And then again, though forgiveness of sins be free, yet notwithstanding there is a way whereby we come to forgiveness of sins that costs us some-what. God humbles the soul first, brings a man to himself, to think of his course, to lay open his sins and spread them before God in confession, and working upon the soul hearty repentance; so to come to God, and wait for forgiveness of sins, perhaps a good while before there be a report of it. There are none who have sins forgiven, but they know how they come by it. For there is a predisposition wrought in man's soul by the Spirit, which teacheth him what estate he is in, and what his danger is, whereupon follows confession; and upon that, peace. God keeps his children many times a long while upon the rack before he speaks peace unto them in the forgiveness of sins, because he would not have them think slightly of the riches of his mercy. It is no easy matter to attain unto the sense of the forgiveness of sins, though indeed we should strive to attain it, that so we may walk in the comforts of the Holy Ghost. The difficulty of obtaining or recovering the sense of forgiveness, may be seen in David after his fall. Did he easily obtain sense of pardon? Oh no! God held him on the rack a long time, ' He roared all the day long, his moisture was turned into the drought of summer,' Ps. xxxii. 3, 4. But when he had resolved a thorough, and no slight, confession; when he had resolved to shame himself and glorify God; then saith he, ' And thou for-gavest my sin.' But till he dealt thoroughly with his soul without all guile, he felt no comfort. So it is with the children of God. When in the state of grace they fall into sin, it is no slight ' Lord, have mercy upon me' that will serve the turn; but a thorough shaming of themselves before God, and a thorough confession, resolving and determining to be under another government; to have Christ to govern them as well as to pardon them. God will no otherwise do it. Because he would glorify his rich mercy herein; for who would give mercy its due glory, if forgiveness were easily attained, without shaming of ourselves? If it came easily, without protestation and waiting upon God, as the church here, we should never be thoroughly humbled for our sins, and God would never have the glory of his mercy, nor known to be so just in hating of sin in his dear children, who long ago upon such terms have attained sense of forgiveness of sins. It is worth our trouble to search our souls and to wait at Christ's feet, never to give over until we have attained the sense of forgiveness of sin. It is heaven upon earth to have our consciences enlarged with God's favour in the pardon of sin.

What is the reason that many profess that God is merciful, and Christ hath pardoned their sins, &c.? If the ground be right, it is a high conceit of mercy; and such have been soundly humbled for their sins. But dost thou profess so, who livest carelessly in thy sins, and licentiously still? Surely * thy ground is naught, for hadst thou been upon the rack, in God's scalding-house, and smarted soundly for sin, wouldst thou take pleasure still to live in sin? Oh no! Those that go on carelessly in their actions and speeches, not caring what they are, did they ever smart for sin,

* That is, ' assuredly.'—G.

who carry themselves thus? Surely these were never soundly humbled for sin, nor confessed them with loathing and detestation. Therefore let us mark the context here inferred. After they had confessed, prayed, and waited, resolving reformation in their false confidence, then God promiseth, ' I will heal their backsliding.' It is a fundamental error in a Christian course, the slighting of true humiliation, which goes along in all the fabric and frame of a Christian course. Let a man not be soundly humbled with the sight of his sins, his faith is weaker, and his sanctification and comfort the slighter. Whereas, if a man would deal truly with his own heart, set up a court there, and arraign, judge, and condemn himself (which is God's end in all his dealings, afflictions, and judgments inflicted upon us), the deeper we went in this course, the more would our comfort be, and the report of God's mercy, in the sense of that which follows, ' I will love them freely : for mine anger is turned away.'

THE SIXTH SERMON.

I will love them freely: for mine anger is turned away. I will be as the dew unto Israel; he shall grow as the lily, and cast forth his root as Lebanon. —Hos. XIV. 4, 5.

IT was a good speech of St Austin, ' Those that are to petition great persons, they will obtain some who are skilful, to frame their petitions ; lest by their unskilfulness they provoke anger, instead of carrying away the benefit desired.' So it is here with God's people, being to deal with the great God, and not being able to frame their own petitions, God, as we heard before, doth it for them, and answers them graciously with the same mercies which he had suggested them to ask ; his answer being exact to their petitions, ' I will heal their backsliding, I will love them freely,' &c., wherein God exceeds all physicians in the world whatsoever. For they have nature to help them. Physic is the midwife of nature, helping it to do that which it cannot do itself. Physic can do nothing to a dead man. But God is so great a physician, that he first gives life, and after that spiritual life is in some degrees begun ; by little and little he heals more and more. ' I will heal their backslidings.'

We have an error crept in amongst some of the meaner, ignorant sort of people, who think that God sees no sin when he hath once pardoned men in justification ; who falsely smooth themselves in this wicked, sensual conceit, think they can commit no sin offensive to God ; as though God should frame such a justification for men, to blindfold him, and cast dust, as it were, in his eyes ; or justify men, to make them loose and idle. No ; it is false, as appeareth by this place ; for how can God heal that he sees not ? He sees it not to be revenged on them for it ; but he sees sin, to correct it and to heal it. He sees it not after a revengeful, wrathful justice, to cast us into hell and damn us for it ; but he sees it after a sort, to make us smart and lament for it, and to have many times a bitter sense of his wrath and forsaking, as men undone without a new supply of comfort and peace from heaven. Let a man neglect sanctification, daily sorrow and confession of sin, and now and then even craving new pardon for sins past, casting all upon a fantastic conceit of faith in their justification : what follows but pride, hardness of heart, contempt of others, and neglect of better than themselves, and proneness out of God's judgment, to fall from ill to worse, from one error to another? In this case the heart is false and deceitful. For whilst it pretends a glorious faith to look back to Christ, to live by faith, and lay all on him by justification, it winds itself out of all tasks of religion, sets the heart at liberty, neglects sanctification and mortification of lusts, and beautifying the image of God in them, giving too much way to the flesh. Therefore, away with this false and self-conceited opinion, which draws poison out of that which God speaks to confirm and stablish us, ' That he sees no iniquity in Jacob,' &c., Num. xxiii. 21. Whence from these hyperbolical speeches, they think that God seeth not that which we ourselves see. But, ' He heals our backslidings,' therefore he sees them. For how can he heal a wound, if he see it not? He sees it, but not to their destruction who are freely justified by his grace. But we will leave this point, it being too much honour to them to spend time in confutation of it, and will rather say unto it, as Isaiah speaks of a menstruous cloth, ' Get thee hence,' Isa. xxx. 22.

Now as God is a most gracious God, never weary of well-doing and comforting his people, because it is his nature to be merciful, so he hath suitable expressions of it; he goes on with mercy upon mercy, lovingkindness upon lovingkindness. He had promised before, ' I will heal their backslidings,' take in sum all their apostasy, all shall be healed. But this is not all. He answers all the accusations and doubts of Satan, who is still objecting against us our unworthiness, misery, wretchedness to have such favours conferred on such filthy creatures. Therefore, he takes off all with this which followeth. As they had prayed, ' Receive us graciously;' so the answer is full, and suitable to their request, ' I will love them freely.'

Put case, they out of conscience of their own guilt should see no worth in themselves, or cause why they should be respected, yet I see reason in mine own love. ' I will love them freely.'

Quest. But may some say, How can God love freely?

Ans. Ask thyself. Doth not a father and mother love their child freely? What doth the child deserve of the father and mother a great while? Nothing. But the mother hath many a weary night and foul hand with it. Hath God planted an affection in us to love our children freely; and shall not God much more, who gives this love and plants it in us, be admitted to love freely? But indeed there is absurdity and infidelity in distrust. For it is against reason, to deny the mighty God that which we have in ourselves. If he did not love freely, how could he love us at all? What could he foresee in us to love for beforehand? The very manhood of Christ deserved not the grace of union, it was freely given.

' I will love them freely.' That which, first of all, we observe hence is thus much, *that God loves his people freely.* So saith the apostle, ' God commendeth his love towards us, in that while we were yet sinners, Christ died for us; much more being justified by his blood, we shall be saved from wrath through him,' Rom. v. 8, 9. The like we have in Ezekiel. Saith God, ' Therefore, say unto the house of Israel, Thus saith the Lord God, I do not this for your sakes, O house of Israel, but for mine holy name's sake, which ye have profaned among the heathen whither ye went,' Ezek. xxxvi. 22. Adam when he had sinned that main, great sin, what did he? Fly from God, run away; and when God called to him, and debated the matter with him, he accused God, and excused himself, Gen.

iii. 12, 13. Yet for all this God pitied him, and clothed him, and made him that promise of the blessed seed. What desert was there here in Adam! nay, rather the quite contrary; yet God loved him freely. The same may be said of St Paul, for the time past a persecutor, what deserving was there in him? None at all; yet he found God's free love in his conversion; for, saith God to Ananias, 'He is a chosen vessel unto me, to bear my name before the Gentiles,' Acts ix. 15. Here was no deserving in St Paul, but God's free election, which in time took place, Acts ix. 5. And so we may say of the prodigal, having spent all, his father pardoned all, and loved him freely, Luke xv. 20.

Reason 1. The reason hereof is, *because it is his name and nature to be gracious*, and to love freely; and whatsoever is God's nature, that hath a freedom in the working.

Reason 2. *Because no creature can deserve anything at God's hands.* (1.) Because by nature we are all God's enemies; and therefore what can enemies deserve? Nothing but wrath and vengeance. (2.) If we have any graces, they are the gift of God; and therefore we deserve nothing by them, they being of his own gift. So St James speaks, 'Every good gift, and every perfect gift, is from above, and cometh down from the Father of lights, with whom is no variableness, nor shadow of turning,' James i. 17. And St Paul saith, 'That of him, and through him, and to him, are all things,' Rom. xi. 36. What should follow hereupon? 'To him be glory for ever.'

Use 1. This, in the *first place*, serves for *reproof of our adversaries of the Romish Church*, who say that God loves us for something foreseen in us, which is good, or for somewhat which in time we would do to deserve favour at his hands. But both are false. The cause of love is free from himself; for, 'when we have done our best,' yet, saith the Holy Ghost, 'we are unprofitable servants.' Luke xvii. 10.

Use 2. *Secondly*, It is for reproof of *God's own dear children*, who, because they find no deserving in themselves, are therefore discouraged at the sight of their own unworthiness; whereas, quite contrary, the sight of our own unworthiness should make us the more fit subjects for Christ's free love, which hath nothing to do with them that stand upon deserving. Many of God's dear children are troubled with temptations, doubts, and fears of God's love and favour towards them, because they expect to find it in the fruits of grace, and not in free grace itself. If we would have any sound peace, let us look for it in free grace. Therefore the blessed apostle, in the entrance of his salutations in his epistles, still joineth grace, and then peace, to shew us that if we look for sound peace, we can nowhere find it but in grace. We would find peace in the grace that is in us, but it is labour in vain, for we shall never find it but in free grace.

Use 3. Hence we may also be *comforted in the certainty of our salvation;* for that grace, and love, and favour, whereby we are saved, is in God, not in us. Now, whatsoever is in him is immutable and sure. So saith the apostle, 'Nevertheless, the foundation of God standeth sure, having this seal, the Lord knoweth them that are his; and let every one that nameth the name of Christ depart from iniquity,' 2 Tim. ii. 19. Where speaking of election, which comes from the free love of God, he makes that a sure foundation to build on. If there be a reformation 'to depart from iniquity,' we may be comfortably assured of our salvation. And as it is with election, so is it with all the other fruits of God's love: vocation, adoption, justification, and perseverance. The foundation of God, fastly sealed in the way of holiness, stands good and sure in all, Rom. iii. 24 ; John xiii. 1.

Use 4. This further teacheth us *thankfulness unto God*, who hath so freely loved us ; for if there were deserving on our part, what place were left for thankfulness ? We know, one who deserves nothing, and hath small matters bestowed upon him, at least will be thankful for such favours. But when one is so far from deserving anything, that by the contrary he deserveth all plagues and punishments, hath yet many and abundant mercies bestowed freely upon him, this doth exceedingly provoke (especially a generous spirit) to a suitable thankfulness, as much as may be.

Use 5. And let it likewise breed *confidence in us to God, in all our miseries*, both for pardon of sin, help in distress, and comfort in sorrows, because he 'loves us freely,' and did love us whilst we were enemies. Make, therefore, upon all occasions, the apostle's use of it. 'For if, when we were enemies, we were reconciled to God by the death of his Son, much more, being reconciled, we shall be saved by his life,' Rom. v. 10.

'I will love them freely.'

In the next place, from hence we observe another point, which necessarily followeth upon the former,—*that God did not then begin to love them, when he said, ' I will love them freely ;' but to discover that love unto them, which he carried unto them from all eternity.* For instance hereof, St Paul was beloved of God, ere God manifested his love unto him ; as he testifieth to himself, that the discovery of this free love was, 'when it pleased God, who separated me from my mother's womb, and called me by his grace, to reveal his son in me,' &c., Gal. i. 15, 16. So the apostle blesseth God, in his salutation unto them, 'who had blessed them with all spiritual blessings in heavenly places in Christ,' Eph. i. 3. But whence fetcheth he the ground hereof ? 'According as he hath chosen us in him, before the foundatiom of the world, that we should be holy and unblameable before him in love,' verse 4. We need not multiply places more to prove it. Our adversaries would fain seem to clear God only in all,* and so shroud their arguments under such needless pretences, shift off all places, name we never so many, with their strong heads, distinctions, and sophisms. But God will one day give them no thanks for their labour : the will of God (how unequal soever in our eyes, who cannot with our shallow conceits sound the depth of such mysteries) being ground enough to justify all his actions whatsoever. We will therefore come to some reasons of the point.

Reason 1. Because *whatsoever is in God*, manifested in time, *is eternal and everlasting in him, without beginning and ending ;* for whatsoever is in God is God. God is not loving, but love, 1 John iv. 8 ; and he is not only true, but truth itself, John xiv. 6. He is not wise only, but wisdom itself, 1 Cor. i. 24. And therefore his love, discovered in time, must needs be from all eternity.

Secondly, If God did then first begin to love us, when he manifested his love unto us, *then there should be a change in God,* because he should love them now that he did not formerly love. As we see, those who loved Paul after his conversion loved him not before. There was then a change in the church. In which case, if God should so love, he should be changeable, and so be like unto man.

Thirdly, And then, again, *Christ's prayer,* John xvii., *makes it clear* that the love of God beginneth not with the manifestation thereof ; for Christ there, knowing all the Father's secrets, as coming out of the bosom of the

---

* That is, ' would fain seem only to clear God in all.'—G.

Father, intimates the contrary, where he makes one end of his prayer for them to be, 'That the world may know that thou hast loved them, as thou hast loved me,' John xvii. 23. Now, how he loved Christ is also shewed a little after, 'For thou lovedst me before the foundation of the world,' verse 24. Therefore the saints and children of God are loved with an everlasting former love, not beginning at that instant discovery thereof.

Use 1. The use hereof is, first of all, against those *who measure God's love and favour by their own feeling*, because, as God loved them before, so he loves them as well and as dearly still; when he hideth his face from them, as when he suffered his lovingkindness to shine most comfortably upon them. He loved Christ as dearly when he hanged on the tree, in torment of soul and body, as he did when he said,' This is my beloved son, in whom I am well pleased,' Mat. iii. 17; yea, and when he received him up into glory. The sun shineth as clearly in the darkest day as it doth in the brightest. The difference is not in the sun, but in some clouds which hinder the manifestation of the light thereof. So God loveth us as well when he shineth not in the brightness of his countenance upon us as when he doth. Job was as much beloved of God in the midst of his miseries as he was afterwards when he came to enjoy the abundance of his mercies, Job xlii. 7.

' I will love them freely,' &c.

The last point which we gather from hence, as a special ground of comfort, is this,

That this free love and favour of God is the cause of all other mercies and free favours, whereby he discovereth his love unto us.

(1.) It is the cause of election, 'Even so, then, at this present time also there is a remnant, according to the election of grace,' Rom. xi. 5. So (2.), For *vocation*. When the apostle had shewed that the Ephesians were saved by grace, he adds, 'That in the ages to come he might shew the exceeding riches of his grace, in his kindness towards us through Christ Jesus,' Eph. ii. 7. He afterwards sheweth, when this grace began first to have being, 'For we are his workmanship, created unto good works, which God hath before ordained that we should walk therein,' Eph. ii. 10. (3.) *Forgiveness of sins.* 'In whom we have a redemption through his blood, even the forgiveness of sins, according to the riches of his grace.' Eph. i. 7. So (4.), For the *grace of love.* 'We love him because he loved us first,' 1 John iv. 19. (5.) For *justification and sanctification.* It is said 'that Christ hath loved us.' Why? 'For he hath washed us from our sins in his own blood,' Rev. i. 5; and St John saith, 'He hath made us kings and priests unto God and his Father.' [1.] Kings to fight against the world, the flesh, and the devil. [2.] Priests to teach, instruct, reprove, and comfort ourselves and others by the word of God, and then to offer up the sacrifice of a broken heart, in prayers and praises. All comes from freedom of love. (6.) So *every good inclination* comes hence, 'for it is God which worketh in us, both to will and to do of his good pleasure,' Phil. ii. 13. So (7.) *Every good work.* 'For we are his workmanship, created in Christ Jesus unto good works, which he had before ordained that we should walk therein,' 'for by grace ye are saved,' saith he, 'through faith,' Eph. ii. 8, 10. So (8.) For *eternal life.* The apostle sheweth, 'It is the gift of God, through Jesus Christ our Lord,' Rom. vi. 23.

Use 1. This should teach us, in the first place, *to be humbled*, in that we are so miserable, naughty servants, doing so little work, nay, nothing as we should, yet should have so good wages. But 'God loves us freely,' &c. It should rather humble us the more than puff us up in pride, in regard that there was nothing in us which might deserve anything at God's hand, 1 Cor. iv. 7; Eph. ii. 9.

Use 2. And hence also it followeth that if he loved us from everlasting with a free love, John xvii. 23, 24, in a sort as he loved Christ, that therefore the *effects of his love towards us shall never fail*, as the apostle sheweth, ' The gifts and calling of God are without repentance,' Rom. xi. 29. Faith and repentance, being fruits of his love wrought in us, shall hold out. Therefore the weakness of these graces, as they shall not hinder our salvation, no more should they discourage us, or hinder the comfort of our profession; because that faith and repentance which we have is not any work of ours, but the work of God's free love in us. Therefore they shall be continued and accepted. For our perseverance doth not stand in this, that we have strength in ourselves to continue faithful to God, but because he, out of his free love, continueth faithful to us, and will never fail nor forsake them whom he hath once taken into his everlasting favour, on whom he hath set his everlasting free love, as the apostle speaks of Christ, ' Who also shall confirm you unto the end, that ye may be blameless in the day of our Lord Jesus Christ.' But upon what ground? ' God is faithful, by whom we were called unto the fellowship of his Son, Jesus Christ our Lord,' 1 Cor. i. 8, 9. So that if any of the elect should fall away, God should be unfaithful. The case in perseverance is not how faithful we are, but how faithful God is, who ' guides us here with his counsel in all things, and afterwards receiveth us into glory,' Ps. lxxiii. 24. So in another place, after the apostle had prayed, ' Now the very God of peace sanctify you wholly; and I pray God your whole spirit and soul and body be preserved blameless unto the coming of the Lord Jesus Christ.' What maketh the ground of this his prayer? ' Faithful is he that calleth you, who also will do it,' 1 Thess. v. 23, 24.

Use 3. If, then, we would have God to manifest his free love to us, let us strive to be *obedient to his commandments*, and stir up our hearts by all means to love him who hath so freely loved us.

Quest. Now, how should we manifest our love toward God?

Ans. First, in *loving his word*, as Ps. xix. and Ps. cxix. Secondly, in *loving his people*, 1 John v. 1, 2. Thirdly, in *longing for* and loving his *second coming*, Rev. xxii. 20.

Now followeth the reason of the discovery of this free love shewed now in time to them.

' For mine anger is turned away from him.'

Here is the third branch of God's answer to their petition, ' Mine anger is turned away from him,' which is included and implied in the former, ' I will heal their backsliding.' How could he do this if he were angry? No; he saith, ' I will love them freely,' which argues that his anger was appeased. God knoweth that variety of words and expressions are all little enough to raise up and comfort a doubting, wounded, galled soul, which, when it is touched with a sense of sin and of his displeasure, cannot hear words enough of comfort. This God knows well enough, and therefore he adds expression upon expression, ' I will heal their backsliding, I will love them freely, for mine anger is turned away from him.' The soul which is touched with the sense of wrath, and defiled with the stains of sin's dreadful impressions, receives all this cheerfully, and more too. Therefore, in such cases we must take in good part the largeness of God's expressions,

'For mine anger is turned away from him.' To unfold the words, therefore,

Anger is the inward displeasure which God hath against sin, and his purpose to punish it, accompanied with threatenings upon his purpose, and execution upon his threatenings. The point to be observed in the first place is,

That there is anger in God against sin.

We need not stand to prove the point, it is so manifest to every man. The Scripture is copious in it. If we consider either judgments executed upon sinners, threatenings against sin, or the saint's complaining of it, as Ps. lxxiv. 1, Job xlii. 7, Ps. vi. 1, Ps. xc. 11, Ps. xxxviii. 1, 3, Isa. lxiii. 6, with many the like places, prove that there is anger in God against sin. We will rather see the reason of it.

Because there is an antipathy betwixt him and sin, which is contrary to his pure nature. Sin, as it opposeth God, so it is contrary unto him ; and, indeed, sin would turn him out of his sovereignty. For what doth a man, when he sins wittingly and willingly, but turn God out of his government, and causes the devil to take up God's room in the heart? When a man gives way to sin, then the devil rules, and he thinks his own lusts better than God's will, and his own carnal reason in contriving of sin above God's wisdom in his word ; therefore, he is a proud rebel. Sin is such a kind of thing, that it labours to take away God ; for it not only puts him out of that part of his throne, man's heart, but for the time a man sins, he could wish there were no God to take vengeance of him. Can you wonder, therefore, that God is so opposite to that which is so opposite to his prerogative royal as sin is?

The truth is, God is angry with nothing else but with sin, which is the only object of his anger. That which foolish persons make a trifle and sport of, swearing, filthy speaking, and lying, is the object of God's anger, Ps. xiv. 1. For this offence of sin he did not spare the angels of heaven, 2 Pet. ii. 4, but tumbled them thence, never to return again. Sin also thrust Adam out of paradise, Gen. iii. 23, and made God angry with him and the whole world, so as to destroy it with a flood of water, Gen. vi. 13, and will at last make him burn and consume all with a deluge of fire, 2 Pet. iii. 12. Yea, it made him in a sort angry with his own dear Son, when he underwent the punishment of sin as our surety, so that he cried out, 'My God, my God, why hast thou forsaken me?' Mat. xxvii. 46. If God thus shewed his anger against sin, in punishing it in Christ our surety, who was made sin for us, and yet had no sin in himself, how will he punish it much more in those who are not in Christ? Those who stand in their own sin and guilt, what will become of them? So that God is angry with sin, and with nothing else.

The second thing we gather from this, where he saith, 'My anger is turned away from him,' God's anger being taken especially for judgments, is,

That God's anger is the special thing in afflictions.

They come from his anger, as hath been shewed. Therefore he saith, 'I will take mine anger from you,' whereby he means judgments, the effect of his anger. For in the Scriptures anger is ordinarily taken for the fruits and effects of God's anger, which are terrible judgments, as we may see, Deut. xxix. 20, and so in many other places.

Quest. [Why are] judgments, then, called God's anger?

Ans. 1. Because they issue from his anger and displeasure ; for it is not the judgments, but the anger in them, which lies heavy upon the soul.

When they come from God's anger, they are intolerable to the conscience : else, when we suffer ill, knowing that it is not from God's anger, but for trial of our graces, or for exercise, we bear it patiently. Therefore God saith, ' Mine anger is turned away from him :' for this, unremoved, embittereth every cross, though it be never so small. Let God's anger be upon a man, and he will make a conceit, a very light thing, to be as a heavy cross upon him, and vex him both in body and state more than mightier crosses at some other time shall. Will you see this in one instance, where God threatened his own dear people thus : ' And the Lord will smite thee with the botch of Egypt, and with the emrods, and with the scab, and with the itch, whereof thou canst not be healed,' Deut. xxviii. 27. What ! is a scab, and an itch, and the like, such a terrible judgment, which in these days is set so light by? O yes ! When it comes with God's displeasure ; when the least scratch is set on fire by God's anger, it shall consume us, it proves uncurable, as there it is threatened : ' whereof thou canst not be healed.' When the vermin came in God's anger upon that hardhearted king, all Pharaoh's skill, and his magicians' skill, could not beat them out, because, as they confessed, ' this was the finger of God,' Exod. viii. 19. Let any thing come as a messenger of God's anger, it comes with vengeance, and sticks to the soul, like a ' fretting leprosy,' Lev. xiv. 45, 46, which, when it entered into a house, many times could not be gotten out again with pulling out stones, or scraping them, till the house were demolished. So, when God's anger is raised and kindled against a person, you may remove this and that, change place and company, and use of helps ; yet it will never leave fretting till it have consumed him, unless it be removed by repentance. If it be never so small a scratch or itch, all the physic in the world shall not cure it. For as the love of God makes all other things in God comfortable unto us, so it is his anger which makes all his attributes terrible. As, for his power, the more he loves me, the more he is able to do me good. But otherwise, the more he is angry and displeased, the more his other attributes are terrible. If he be wise, the more he will find out my sins : if he be powerful and angry, the more he can revenge himself on me. Is he angry and just ? the more woe to me. So there is nothing in God when he is angry, but it is so much the more terrible. For this puts a sting in everything : which, when it is removed out of malignant creatures armed with a sting, then they are no more hurtful. The sting of every evil and cross, is God's anger and wrath. This being removed, nothing hurts. All crosses then are gentle, mild, tractable, and medicinal, when God hath once said, ' For mine anger is turned away from him.' After that's gone, whatsoever remaineth is good for us, when we feel no anger in it. What is that which blows the coals of hell, and makes hell hell, but the anger of God, seizing upon the conscience ? This kindles Tophet, and sets it a-fire like a river of brimstone, Isa. xxx. 33. Therefore this is a wondrous sweet comfort and encouragement when he saith, ' For mine anger is turned away from him.' Whence, in the next place, we may observe,

That God will turn away his anger upon repentance.

When there is this course taken, formerly mentioned, to turn unto the Lord and to sue for pardon, to vow reformation, ' Asshur shall not save us,' and a thorough reformation of the particular sin ; and when there is wrought in the heart faith to rely on God's mercy, as the ' Father of the fatherless,' in whom they ' find mercy,' then God's anger is turned away. God, upon repentance, will turn away his anger. The point is clear. We see, when the Lord hath threatened many grievous judgments and plagues for sin, one upon the neck of another, denounced with all variety of expressions in the most terrible manner; yet, after all that thundering, Deut. xxviii. and xxix., it follows, ' And it shall come to pass, when all these things are come upon thee, the blessings and the curses, which I have set before thee, and thou shalt call them to mind among all the nations whither the Lord thy God hath driven thee, and shalt return unto the Lord thy God, &c.; that then the Lord thy God will turn thy captivity, and have compassion upon thee,' &c., Deut. xxx. 1, 2, 3. After repentance, you see the promise comes presently after; not that the one is the meritorious cause of the other; but there is an order of things. God will have the one come with the other. Where there is not sense of sin and humiliation, and thence prayer to God for pardon, with reformation and trusting in his mercy, there the anger of God abides still. But where these are, ' his anger is turned away.' God hath established his order, that the one of these must still follow the other.

Another excellent place to the forenamed, we have in the Chronicles, ' If my people that are called by my name shall humble themselves and pray,' (as they did here in this chapter, ' take words unto yourselves') ' and seek my face and turn from their wicked ways,' 2 Chron. vii. 14 ; as they did here, ' Asshur shall not save us, we will not ride upon horses,' &c. We will no more rely on the barren false helps of foreign strength. What then ? ' I will hear from heaven, and will forgive their sin, and will heal their land,' 2 Chron. vii. 14. Here is the promise, whereof this text is a proof. So in all the prophets there is a multiplication of the like instances and promises; which we will not stand upon now, as not being controversial. It is God's name so to do, as we may see in that well known place of Exodus. ' Jehovah, Jehovah, God, merciful and gracious, longsuffering, and abundant in goodness and truth ; keeping mercy for thousands, forgiving iniquity, and transgression, and sin,' &c., Exod. xxxiv. 6, 7. And so it is said, ' At what time soever a sinner repents himself of his sins from the bottom of his heart, I will put all his sins out of my remembrance, saith the Lord God,' Hebrews viii. 12. The Scripture is plentiful in nothing more ; especially it is the burden of Ezek. xviii. and xxxiii., forgiveness of sins, and removal of wrath upon repentance.

And for example. See one for all the rest. Let the greater include the lesser. Manasseh was a greater sinner than any of us all can be ; because he was enabled* with a greater authority to do mischief, (all which no private man, nor ordinary great man, is capable of, not having the like power) ; which he exercised to the full in all manner of cruelty, joined with other gross and deadly sins; and yet the Scripture shews that, upon his humiliation and praying, he found mercy. God turned away his anger, 2 Chron. xxxiii. 12, 13.

That of the prodigal is a parable also fitted for this purpose, who had no sooner a resolution to return to his father, Luke xv. 23. *Filius timet convitium, &c.* The son fears chiding; the father provides a banquet. So God doth transcend our thoughts in that kind. We can no sooner humble ourselves to pray to him heartily, resolving to amend our ways and come to him, but he lays his anger aside to entertain terms of love and friendship with us. As we see in David, who was a good man, though he slubbered over the matter of repentance, all which while God's hand was so heavy upon him, that his moisture was turned into the drought of summer, he

* That is, ' endued.'—G.

roaring all the day long, Ps. xxxii. 3, 4. But when once he dealt throughly in the business, and resolved, 'I will confess my transgression unto the Lord ; and thou forgavest the iniquity of my sin.' Let our humiliation be real and thorough, with prayer for pardon, and purpose to reform, and presently God will shew mercy.

The reason is clear, because it is his nature so to do. His nature is more inclined to mercy than anger. For him to be angry, it is still upon supposition of our sins. But to be merciful and gracious, it always proceeds from his own bowels, whether we be sinners or not. Without all supposition, God is still merciful unto whom he will shew mercy. 'Who is a God like unto thee,' saith the prophet, 'that pardoneth iniquity? he passeth by the transgression of the remnant of his heritage, and retaineth not his anger for ever ; because he delighteth in mercy.' Things naturally come easily, without pain ; as beams from the sun, water from the spring, and as heat from fire ; all which come easily, because they are natural. So mercy and love from God come easily and willingly. It is his nature to be gracious and merciful. Though we be sinners, if we take this course here, as the church doth, to pray and be humbled, then it will follow, 'Mine anger is turned away from him.' The use is,

First, to observe *God's truth in the performance of his gracious promises,* who, as he makes gracious promises to us, so he makes them good. His promise is, 'If we confess our sins, he will forgive them and be merciful,' Prov. xxviii. 13. So here he says, 'Mine anger is turned away.' As they confess, so he is merciful to forgive them. It is good to observe the experiments* of God's truth. Every word of God is a shield, that is, we may take it as a shield. It is an experimental truth, whereby we may arm our souls. This is an experimental truth, that when we are humbled for our sins, God, he will be merciful unto our sins, and allay his anger, as it is in this text. Therefore it is said, 'Those that know thy name will trust in thee, for thou never failest those who put their trust in thee,' Ps. ix. 10. Let us then open our hearts unto God, and confess our sins unto him ; and if we resolve amendment, we shall find the truth of his gracious promises. He will turn aside his anger, and will never fail us, if we put trust in him. 'The name of the Lord is a strong tower, and the righteous fly to it and are safe,' Prov. xviii. 10. This name of mercy, grace, and favour, is a strong tower to distressed consciences. Let us therefore remember to fly unto it, when our consciences are awaked and distressed with sin, and sense of God's displeasure. Seeing these kinds of promises are as a city of refuge, let us run unto them, and we shall not be pulled from the horns of this altar, as Joab once was from his, 1 Kings ii. 28 ; but shall at all times find grace and mercy to help us at the time of need. It is a comfortable point, 'Mine anger is turned away from him.'

Quest. But it may be said, How is God's anger turned away from his children, when they feel it ofttimes after in the course of their lives ?

Ans. The answer is, that there is a double anger of God, whereby we must judge of things, for either it is,

1. Vindicative ; or, 2. Fatherly anger.

God, after our first conversion, he removeth his vindicative anger, after which, though sometimes he threaten and frown upon us, yet it is with a fatherly anger, which God also removes, with the shame and correction attending it, when we reform and amend our wicked ways.

There is, 1. A child of anger ; 2. A child under anger.

God's children are never 'children of wrath,' Eph. ii. 3, and anger, after

* That is, 'experiences' = trials of.—G.

their first conversion. But sometimes children under wrath, if they make bold with sin, so as they cannot use their right of sonship, to go boldly to the throne of grace. Because then, though they have the right of fear,* they conceive of God as angry with them, and cannot use it, so long as they live in any sin against conscience, and so continue, until they reform and humble themselves, as the church doth here ; after which they can and do rejoice again, claim their right, and are not either children of wrath, or under wrath. David, after he had sinned that foul sin, Ps. li. was a child under wrath, not a child of wrath. So, if we make bold to sin, we are children under wrath, for ofttimes God begins correction at his own house, if there be any disorder there, 1 Pet. iv. 17. You know God was so angry with Moses, that he was not suffered to enter into the land of Canaan, Num. xx. 12. And David, when he had numbered the people, God was angry with him, 2 Sam. xxiv. 1 ; and with the Corinthians also, for unreverent receiving of the Lord's Supper, 1 Cor. xi. 30. But here is a course prescribed to remove his fatherly anger, and to enjoy the beams of his countenance, and sunshine of his favour in Christ. If we humble ourselves, confess our sins, and fly unto him, as the church here doth, then we shall find this made good, 'For mine anger is turned away from him.' But it may be asked,

Quest. In times of affliction, how may we know God's anger to be removed, when yet we endure the affliction ?

Ans. The answer is, that God is infinitely wise, and in one affliction hath many ends ; as,

1. When he afflicts them, it is to correct them for their sins; after which, when they have pulled out the sting of sin by confession and humiliation, if afflictions continue, his anger doth not continue.

2. Affliction sometimes is for an exercise of patience and faith, and trial of their graces, and for the exemplary manifestation to others of God's goodness to them.

But even then they may know that things come not in anger unto them by this ; that after repentance God speaks peace unto their conscience ; so that, though the grievance continue, it is with much joy in the Holy Ghost, and peace of conscience, in which case, the soul knows that it is for other ends that God continues it. Therefore the first thing in any affliction is, to remove away the core and sting thereof by humbling ourselves, as the church here doth, after which our consciences will be at peace for other things. God hath many ends in correcting us. He will humble us, improve our afflictions to the good of others, and will gain himself honour by our afflictions, sufferings, and crosses. When God hath shed abroad his love in our hearts by his Spirit, then we can rejoice in tribulation, and rejoice under hope, Rom. v. 5. Though the afflictions continue, because the sting is gone, anger is removed.

'For mine anger is turned away from him.'

The last point we observe from hence, and gather from all these general truths, is this,

Where there is not humiliation for sin, and hearty prayer to God, with reformation of our ways, flying unto God for mercy, who is merciful to the fatherless, there God's wrath continues.

For as where they are performed his anger is turned away, so must it needs follow, that where they are not performed, his anger continueth. Therefore, let us examine ourselves. The Spirit of God here speaks of

* Qu. 'the right, of fear they conceive ?' &c.—ED.

'healing backslidings,' and of 'turning away iniquity.' Let us look well to ourselves, and to the present state of things, that our diseases be soundly cured, our personal diseases; and then let us be sensible of the diseases of the land, and pray for them. For there are universal diseases and sins of a kingdom, as well as personal. And we are guilty of the sins of the times, as far as we are not humbled for them. Paul tells those who did not punish the incestuous person, 'Why are you not humbled rather for this deed?' 1 Cor. v. 2. Where there is a public disease, there is a public anger hanging over upon that disease; the cure whereof is here prescribed, to be humbled, as for ourselves, so for others. Therefore let us beware of sin (if we would shun wrath), especially of idolatry, or else we shall be sure to smart for it, as Ephraim did, of whom the Spirit of God saith, 'When Ephraim spake trembling, he exalted himself in Israel; but when he offended in Baal, he died,' Hosea xiii. 1. Ephraim had got such authority, what with his former victories, and by the signs of God's favour among them, that when he spake 'there was trembling,' and he 'exalted himself in Israel;' but when he 'offended once in Baal,' that is, when he became an idolater, 'he died.' It is meant of the civil death especially, that he lost his former credit and reputation. We see then the dangerous effects of sin, especially of idolatry. Wherefore let us fortify ourselves against it, and bless God that we live under such a gracious, just, and mild king, and good government, where there are such laws against this great sin especially, and beseech God long to continue his life and prosperity for our good amongst us. For use then.

Remember, when we are to deal with God, *that he is the great Mover of all things;* who, if he be angry, can overturn all things, and cross us in all things; and can also heal us of all our diseases. But what must we do if we would be healed? We must take the course prescribed here, 'Take unto us words;' humble ourselves, and have no confidence in Asshur, munition, people, or in 'the works of our hands;' but trust in God, so shall we be happy and blessed. Whatsoever our enemies be, yet if we can make God our rock, fortress, and shield, then it is no matter who be our enemies. 'If he be on our side, who can be against us?' Rom. viii. 31. Let us all, ministers and all, reform ourselves, and stand in the gap, after the course here prescribed, and go to God in a right manner; so we may dissipate all the clouds of anger which may seem to hang over our heads, and find God experimentally making this promise good to us, which he made then to his people, 'I will heal their backsliding, I will love them freely: for mine anger is turned away from him.'

Therefore let us do as Jacob did with Esau, when he came incensed with mighty displeasure against his brother. Jacob comes before him humbly, prostrates himself before him, and so turns away his anger, Gen. xxxiii. 3. So when God is angry with us, and comes against us, let us humble ourselves before him to appease him. As Abigail quieted David, by humbling herself before him, when he had a purpose to destroy her family, 1 Sam. xxv. 23, *seq.,* so let us come before God in humility of soul, and God will turn away his anger. As when there was a great plague begun in the army, Aaron stood with his censer betwixt the living and the dead, offering incense and making atonement for them, whereby the plague was stayed, Num. xvi. 48; so in any wrath felt or feared, for ourselves or the State we live in, let every one hold his censer and offer the incense of prayer, 'Take with you words,' Rev. viii. 4. God is wondrously moved to pity by the incense of these sweet odours offered up by

Christ unto the Father. Believe it, it is the only safe course to begin in heaven. Such a beginning will have a blessed ending. Other courses, politic and subordinate helps must also be taken, but all is to no purpose, unless we begin in heaven; because all things under God are ruled and moved by him; who, when he is favourable, makes all the creatures pliable unto us, but especially makes this good, 'I will heal their backsliding, I will love them freely; for mine anger is turned away from him.'

THE SEVENTH SERMON.

I will be as the dew unto Israel: he shall grow as the lily, and cast forth his root as Lebanon. His branches shall spread, and his beauty shall be as the olive tree, and his smell as Lebanon.—Hosea XIV. 5, 6.

The church, as we heard, had been humbled, and therefore is comforted. It is usual in the Scriptures, especially in the prophetical parts thereof, after terrible threatenings to come with sweet promises; because God in all ages hath a church.* Therefore God in this chapter takes this course. He makes gracious promises to this people, grounded upon the former part of the chapter, wherein God had dictated unto them a form of prayer, repentance, and reformation. 'Take with you words, and turn to the Lord: say unto him, Take away all iniquity, and receive us graciously,' &c. Whereupon a reformation is promised, 'Asshur shall not save us, we will not ride upon horses,' &c. Which was a reformation of that national sin which they were guilty of, false confidence. Now, as we have heard, God answers them to every particular. He makes a gracious promise, 'that he will heal their backsliding,' according to their prayer, 'Take away all iniquity.' And to that, 'receive us graciously,' he answers, 'I will love them freely, for mine anger is turned away from him.'

Now, it cannot be but that God should regard the desires of his own Spirit, when both the words and Spirit proceed from him. Therefore he goes on more fully to answer their desire of 'doing good to them,' saying, 'I will be as the dew to Israel,' &c.

In which words the holy prophet doth first, by a metaphor and borrowed speech, set down the ground of all happiness. So that there is here given a more full satisfaction to the desires of the church.

1. The cause of all—'I will be as the dew,' &c.

2. The particular persons to whom—'to Israel.'

3. The fruit of this follows—'he shall grow as the lily, and cast forth his root as Lebanon.'

Now the words read are a fuller satisfaction to the desires of God's people, which were stirred up by his own Spirit. 'I will be as dew unto Israel.' Where,

1. You have set down the cause of all, which follows. God by his gracious Spirit will be ' as the dew unto Israel.'

2. And then upon that, the prosperous success this dew of God's Spirit hath in them, ' They shall grow as the lily.'

Obj. 1. Aye, but the lily grows, but hath no stability. Everything that grows is not well rooted. Therefore he adds, in the second place, ' They

* Joel ii. 27, 28; Hos. ii. 14, 15; Isa. i. 18, 19; Deut. iii. 1, *seq;* Jer. iii. 12; Jer. xxx. 1, *seq.*

shall cast out their roots as Lebanon;' that is, with growth they shall have stability; not only grow in height speedily, but also grow fast in the root with firmness.

Obj. 2. And likewise, as everything that grows in root and firmness, doth not spread itself, he says, he shall not only grow upward, and take root downwards, ' but his branches shall spread;' whereby he shall be more fruitful and comfortable to others.

Obj. 3. Oh! but everything that grows, is rooted and spread, is not for all that fruitful ; therefore, he saith, they shall be as the olive tree, ' His beauty shall be as the olive tree for fruitfulness.'

Obj. 4. Yet, though the olive be fruitful, it hath no pleasant smell nor good taste. Therefore he adds another blessing to that. They shall, in regard of their pleasantness to God and man, that shall delight in them, be ' as the smell of Lebanon;' which was a wondrous pleasant, delightful place, which yielded a pleasant savour round about. So we see what a complete kind of growth this is, wherein blessing upon blessing is promised. The Holy Ghost cannot enough satisfy himself in variety of comfortable expressions. Nothing is left unsatisfied that the heart can propound. He will make them grow, be stedfast, fruitful, delightful, and pleasant. So that we have here to consider:

1. The favour and blessing that he promiseth, to be ' as the dew to Israel.'

2. The excellency of it in divers particulars.

3. The order wherein it is promised.

Before we come to the words themselves, if we remember and read over the former part of the prophecy, we shall find it full of terrible curses, all opposite unto that here promised : to shew,

We can never be in so disconsolate a state, but God can alter all.

He hath a right hand as well as a left ; blessings as well as curses ; mercy as well as justice ; which is more proper to his nature than that. Therefore let Christian souls never be discouraged with their condition and state whatsoever it is.

Reason. For, as there are many maladies, so there are many remedies opposite to them. As Solomon saith, ' This is set over against that,' &c., Eccles. vii. 14. If there be a thousand kinds of ills, there are many thousand kinds of remedies. For God is larger in his helps than we can be in our diseases and distresses, whatsoever they are, Zech. i. 19, 20, 21. Therefore it is good to make this use of it, to be so conceited of God, as may draw us nearer unto him upon all occasions.

Again, we see here how large the Spirit of God is in expressions of the particulars. ' I will be as the dew unto Israel: and he shall grow as the lily, and cast forth his roots as Lebanon. His branches shall spread, and his beauty be large,' &c. Whereunto tends all this largeness of expression? God doth it in mercy unto us, who especially need it, being in a distressed, disconsolate estate. Therefore they are not words wastefully spent. We may marvel sometimes, in Isaiah, and so in some other prophets, to see the same things in substance so often repeated, though with variety of lively expressions, as it is, for the most part, the manner of every prophet. Surely, because it is useful and profitable, the people of God need it. There is, nor never was any man in a drooping, sinking condition, but he desires line upon line, word upon word, promise upon promise, expression upon expression.

Obj. One would think, is not a word of God sufficient ?

Ans. Yes, for him, but not for us. We have doubting and drooping hearts, and therefore God adds sacraments and seals ; not only one sacrament, but two ; and in the sacrament not only bread, but wine also ; to shew that Christ is all in all. What large expressions are here, thinks a profane heart, what needs this ? As if God knew us not better than we know ourselves. Whensoever thou art touched in conscience with the sense of thy sins, and knowest how great, how powerful, how holy a God thou hast to deal with, who can endure no impure thing, thou wilt never find fault with his large expressions in his word and sacraments ; and with the variety of his promises, when he translates out of the book of nature into his own book, all expressions of excellent things to spread forth his mercy and love. Is this needless ? No ; we need all. He that made us, redeemed us, preserves us, knows us better than we know ourselves. He who is infinite in wisdom and love takes this course.

And mark again, in the next place, how the Holy Ghost fetcheth here this comfort from things that are most excellent in their kind. ' They shall grow as the lily,' that grows fairly and speedily ; ' and they shall take root as Lebanon.' To shew that a Christian should be the excellent in his kind, he compares him in his right temper and state, to the most excellent things in nature ; to the sun, to lions, trees of Lebanon, cedars, and olive trees for fruitfulness ; and all to shew that a Christian should not be an ordinary man. All the excellencies of nature are little enough to set out the excellency of a Christian. He must be an extraordinary singular man. Saith Christ, ' What singular thing do ye ?' Mat. v. 47. He must not be a common man. Therefore, when God would raise his people, he tells them, they should not be common men, but grow as lilies, be rooted as trees, fruitful as olives, and pleasant, beautiful, as the goodly, sweet-smelling trees of Libanus. How graciously doth God condescend unto us, to teach us by outward things, how to help our souls by our senses, that when we see the growth, fruitfulness, and sweetness of other things, we should call to mind what we should be, and what God hath promised we shall be, if we take this course and order formerly prescribed. Indeed, a wise Christian, endowed with the Spirit of God, extracts a quintessence out of everything, especially from those that God singles out to teach him his duty by. When he looks upon any plant, fruit, or tree that is pleasant, delightful, and fruitful, it should put him in mind of his duty.

' I will be as the dew to Israel,' &c.

These sweet promises in their order follow immediately upon this, that God would freely love them, and cease to be angry with them. Then he adds the fruits of his love to their souls, and the effects of those fruits in many particulars ; whence first of all we observe,

God's love is a fruitful love.

Wheresoever he loves, he makes the things lovely. We see things lovely, and then we love them ; but God so loves us that in loving us he makes us lovely. So saith God by the prophet, ' I have seen his ways, and will heal him ; I will lead him also, and restore comforts unto him and to his mourners,' Isa. lvii. 18. And from this experience of the fruitfulness of God's love, the church is brought in rejoicing, ' I will greatly rejoice in the Lord ; my soul shall be joyful in my God : for he hath clothed me with the garments of salvation, he hath covered me with the robe of righteousness, as a bridegroom decketh himself with ornaments, and as a bride adorneth herself with her jewels,' Isa. lxi. 10. Thus he makes us such as may be amiable objects of his love that he may delight in.

Reason. For his love is the love, as of a gracious, so of a powerful, God, that can alter all things to us, and us to all things. He can bring us good out of everything, and do us good at all times, according to the church's prayer, ' Do good unto us.'

Use. Wherefore, seeing God can do us good, and since his love is not only a pardoning love, to take away his anger, but also so complete and fruitful a love, so full of spiritual favours, ' I will be as the dew unto Israel, and he shall grow up as the lily,' &c., let us stand more upon God's love than we have formerly done, and strive to have our hearts inflamed with love towards God again, as the prophet David doth, ' I love the Lord, because he hath heard my voice and my supplications,' Ps. cxvi. 1. It may be for outward condition that even where God loves they may go backwards so and so; but for their best part, their souls, God will be as the ' dew to them,' and ' they shall grow as Lebanon.' God will be good to them in the best things; and a Christian, when he begins to know what the best things are, concerning a better life, he then learneth to value spiritual blessings and favours above all other whatsoever. Therefore God suits his promises to the desires of his children, that he would water their dry souls, that he would be as the dew unto them. God's love is a fruitful love, and fruitful in the best things. As we know what David saith, ' There be many who say, Who will shew us any good? Lord, lift thou up the light of thy countenance upon us. Thou hast put gladness in my heart, more than in the time that their corn and their wine increased,' Ps. iv. 6, 7. So God fits his gracious promise, answerable to the desires of a gracious heart,

' I will be as the dew to Israel.'

2. To come to the words, in particular, for this is the ground of all that follows, ' I will be as the dew unto Israel.'

Quest. How will God be as the dew to Israel?

Ans. This is especially meant of, and performed to, the church under the New Testament, especially next unto Christ's time, when the dew of grace fell in greatest abundance upon the church. The comfortable, sanctifying, fruitful grace of God is compared to dew in many respects.

First, *the dew doth come from above.* God sends it, it drops from above, and cannot be commanded by the creature. So all other gifts, and especially this perfect gift, the grace of God, comes from above, from the Father of lights. There is no principle of grace naturally within a man. It is as childish to think that grace comes from any principle within us, as to think that the dew which falls upon a stone is the sweat of the stone, as children think that the stone sweats, when it is the dew that has fallen upon it. Certainly our hearts, in regard of themselves, are barren and dry. Wherefore, God's grace, in regard of the original, is compared to dew, which should teach us to go to God, as the church doth here, and pray him to deal graciously with us, to do good to us, for this cause laying open our souls unto him, to shed his grace into them.

Secondly, *the dew doth fall insensibly and invisibly.* So the grace of God. We feel the comfort, sweetness, and operation of it, but it falls insensibly without observation. Inferior things here feel the sweet and comfortable influence of the heavens, but who sees the active influence upon them? which, how it is derived from superior bodies to the inferior, is not observable. As our Saviour speaks of the beginnings of grace and workings of it, ' The wind bloweth where it listeth, and thou hearest the sound thereof, but canst not tell whence it cometh or whither it goeth: so is every one that is born of the Spirit,' John iii. 8. It works we know not how. We feel the work, but the manner of working is unknown to us. Grace, therefore, is wrought undiscernibly. No man can see the conversion of another; nay, no man almost can discern his own conversion at first. Therefore, this question should not much trouble you, Shew us the first hour, the first time of your conversion and entrance into the state of grace. Grace, to many, falls like the dew, by little and little, drop and drop, line upon line. It falls sweetly and undiscernibly upon them at the first. Therefore, it is hard to set down the first time, seeing, as our blessed Saviour speaks, grace at the first is wondrous little, likened to a grain of mustard-seed; but though it be small at first, yet nothing is more glorious and beautiful afterwards, for from a small seed it grows to overspread and be great, shooting out branches, Mark iv. 31, 32. And as the root of Jesse was a despised stock, and in show a dead root, yet thence Christ rose, a branch as high as heaven; so the beginning of a Christian is despised and little, like a dead stock, as it were; but they grow upward and upward still, till they come to heaven itself, Prov. iv. 18. Thus we see there is nothing in the world more undiscernible in the beginning than the work of grace, which must make us not over-curious to examine exactly the first beginnings thereof, because it is as the falling of the dew, or ' the blowing of the wind.'

Thirdly, Again, as it falls undiscernibly and invisibly, so *very sweetly and mildly*, not violating the nature or course of anything, but rather helping and cherishing the same; or if it make any change in anything, it doth it mildly and gently. So usually, unless it be in some extraordinary case, God works upon the soul by his grace mildly and sweetly. Grace works sweetly upon the soul, preserving its freedom; so as man, when he begins to be good, shall be freely good, from inward principles wrought in him. His judgment shall like the course he takes, and be clean opposite to others that are contrary, from an inward principle; as free now in altering his course, as formerly he was in following the other. There is no violence, but in regard of corruption. God works strongly and mildly: strongly, for he changeth a stone into a fleshly heart; and yet sweetly: he breaks not any power of nature, but advanceth it. For grace doth not take away or imprison nature, but lifts it up, and sets it at liberty. For it makes the will stronger and freer, the judgment sounder, the understanding clearer, the affections more orderly. It makes all things better, so that no violence is offered to nature.

Fourthly, Again, grace is compared to dew, *in regard of the operations of dew*. For, what effects hath dew upon the earth?

(1.) *It cools the air when it falls*, and then with coolness it hath a fructifying virtue; for falling especially on tender herbs and plants, it soaks into the root of them, and makes them fruitful. So it is with the grace of God's Spirit. It cools the soul, scorched with the sense of God's anger; as indeed all our souls will be, when we have to deal with God, who is ' a consuming fire,' Heb. xii. 29, till we take that course to look upon him in Christ for the pardon of sin; after which his grace and the sense of it cooleth, assuageth, and speaks peace to an uncomfortable, disconsolate heart. This voice, ' Son, be of good comfort, thy sins are forgiven thee.' Oh, this hath a cooling in it! and this also, ' This day shalt thou be with me in paradise.' Oh, how it cooled and cheered the good thief, and comforted him! And so when God says unto the soul, ' I am thy salvation;' Oh, when the soul feels this, how is it cooled and refreshed!

(2.) And the soul is not only cooled and refreshed, but *it is also sweetened and made fruitful with comfort to the soul.* If we were to see a man in the pangs of conscience, stung with fiery temptations, as with so many fiery serpents and poisoned darts, which drink up the spirits, and presents God a consuming fire ; and hell beneath, full of insupportable torments, set on by the insupportable wrath of God : then we should know what it were to have grace in this efficacious manner, cooling and refreshing the soul, that hath these fiery darts stuck into it of violent strong temptations, which to the present sense are the flashes and beginnings of hell. Oh, it is an excellent thing to have the grace of God in such a case to assuage and cool the maladies of a distressed soul, which for the present seems to burn in a flame of wrath ! As it cools, so also it makes the heart fruitful, our hearts of themselves being as the barren wilderness and wild desert. Now God by his grace turns 'the wilderness into water-springs,' as it appeareth in many places of the prophets. Saith God, 'For I will pour water upon him that is thirsty, and floods upon the dry ground ; I will pour my Spirit upon thy seed,' &c., Isa. xliv. 3 ; xlv. 8. So grace, it turns the barren wilderness, the heart, dry of itself, and makes it fruitful. We know what Paul said of Onesimus, a fruitless servant, nay, a fugitive thief. He is unfruitful no longer, saith he, now that he is become a convert, another, a new man, now he will do good service, Phil. xvi. A man is no sooner altered by the dew of grace, but howsoever formerly he were a naughty, hurtful person, of whom every man was afraid because of his wickedness, yet now he is a fruitful person, and strives to bring forth fruits worthy of amendment of life, Mat. iii. 8.

Fifthly, And we may add one more, in the next place, *in regard of the unresistibleness thereof ;* for as nothing can hinder the dew from falling from the sweet influence of heaven unto us, or hinder the working of those superior bodies upon the inferior, or hinder the wind from blowing ; so who can hinder God's grace ? Job xxxviii. 37. They may, out of malice, hinder the means of it, and hinder the gracious working of the Spirit, by discouragements in others ; which is a sign of a devilish spirit, when yet God hath a hand in that too after a sort. For it raineth in one city, and not in another, by God's appointment ; but nothing can hinder, where God will have the dew and water, and shine of the influence of grace, work. Nothing in the world can stop it. So it is said in that excellent prophecy of Christ and his kingdom, 'He shall come down like rain upon the mown grass, as showers that water the earth,' which as they cool and fructify, so come they unresistibly, Ps. lxxii. 6.

Use. Let none, therefore, be discouraged with the deadness, dryness, and barrenness of their own hearts ; but let them know that God doth graciously promise, if they will take the course formerly set down, to be ' as the dew unto them.' Therefore let them come unto the ordinances of God, with wondrous hope, confidence, and faith, that he will be as dew unto them ; that, seeing he hath appointed variety of ordinances, the word and sacraments, he will bless those means of his own ordaining and appointing, for his own ends. He that hath graciously appointed such means of grace, will he not bless them ? especially having promised, 'I will be as the dew unto Israel.' Therefore let us attend upon the ordinances, and not keep away, though our hearts be barren, dry, and unfruitful. God is above the heart, and able to turn the wilderness into a fruitful place. He can make the heart a fit habitation for himself to dwell in. Let us by faith attend upon the ordinances. If we find not comfort in one ordinance, let us go unto another, and another. Comfort and help shall come, especially if, with the church, we 'go a little further,' Cant. iii. 4 ; for the promise is, ' I will be as the dew unto Israel.'

But mark the order wherein he makes this promise.

First, He gives grace to pray to him. ' Take away all iniquity, and receive us graciously ;' ' Do good to us.'

Then, *second, he gives a spirit of reformation,* promising amendment ; whereupon this followeth, 'that he will forgive their sins, love them freely,' &c., and be ' as the dew unto Israel.' He will be as the dew unto Israel ; but he will give them grace first to be humbled, confess sin, and pray to God for grace and forgiveness. There is an order of working in the soul. God giveth justification before sanctification ; and before he freeth from the guilt of sin, he gives grace to confess sin. ' If we confess our sins, he is faithful and just to forgive us our sins, and to cleanse us from them,' saith St John, 1 John i. 9. Where these go before, grace will follow ; and where they do not, there will be no sanctification. Therefore let us consider the order ; for wheresoever God 'takes away iniquity,' and heals their souls, in regard of the guilt of their sins, unto those he will be as dew. Therefore, if we have still barren souls, without desires or strength to goodness, certainly our sins are still upon the file ;* for justification is never without holiness of life. ' Whosoever is in Christ, he is a new creature,' 2 Cor. v. 17. When this is done, God will be ' as the dew ;' because he doth pardon our sins for this cause, that he may thereby fit us to be entertained in the covenant ; and are we fit to be in covenant with him, until our natures be altered ? Therefore, whensoever he enters into covenant with any, he changeth their natures, that they may be friends, and have communion with him. Then the same soul which crieth, ' Take away all iniquity,' desireth also the dew of grace to make it better. This order is not only necessary on God's part, but in regard of the soul also. For was there ever any soul, from the beginning of the world, that truly desired forgiveness of sins, which did not also therewith desire grace ? Such a soul were but a hypocritical soul. For if it be rightly touched with sorrow, it desires as well ability to subdue sin, as forgiveness of sin ; holiness and righteousness, with forgiveness, Luke i. 75.

Use 1. Therefore, lest we deceive ourselves, let this be an use of trial from the order, *that if we find not grace wrought in our natures to restrain sin, and alter our former lewd courses, our sins are not yet forgiven.* For, wheresoever God takes away sin, and ' loves freely,' there also he gives the best fruits of his love, bestows the dew of his grace, to work upon and alter our natures. Christ came not by blood alone, to die for us ; but by water also, to sanctify us, 1 John v. 6. He will not only ' love freely,' but he will be ' as the dew,' where he loves freely. Therefore, if we have not sanctifying grace, we have not as yet pardoning grace. For we know the prophet joins them both together. ' Blessed is the man unto whom the Lord imputeth not iniquity, and in whose spirit there is no guile,' Ps. xxxii. 1, 2. If we retain a guileful, false spirit, our sins are not forgiven. We see both these are put together.

Use 2. And seeing all these good things come from God, it is necessary to take notice of what hath been said of God's goodness, *that we do not rob God of his due glory, nor ourselves of the due comfort that we may draw thence.* The Egyptians had the river Nylus, that overflowed the land every year, caused by anniversary winds, which so blew into the mouth of the river, that it could not discharge itself into the sea ; whereupon it over-

* See Note *b*, vol. I. p. 289.—G.

flowed the banks, and left a fruitful slime upon the ground, so that they needed not rain as other countries, because it was watered with Nylus. Hereupon they did not depend upon God's blessing, nor were so holy as they should; but were proud of their river, as is intimated by Moses unto the people. 'But the land whither thou goest in to possess it, is not as the land of Egypt, from whence ye came out, where thou sowest thy seed, and wateredst it with thy foot, as a garden of herbs : but the land whither ye go to possess it is a land of hills and valleys, and drinketh water of the rain of heaven : a land which the Lord thy God careth for,' &c., Deut. xi. 10, 11. They having more immediately rain from heaven, saw God's hand in watering it, whereas the Egyptians did not. And what makes a papist to be so unthankful ? He thinks he can with his own industry water his own ground with somewhat in himself. What makes another man thankful, on the other side ? Because he knoweth he hath all things by dependence from the first Cause : for as in nature, 'In God we live, move, and have our being,' Acts xvii. 28, much more in grace. We have all our nourishment, spiritual being, moving, and life from the dew of heaven. All our heat is from the Sun of righteousness,' Mal. iv. 2, which makes a Christian life to be nothing else but a gracious dependence. ' I can do all things,' saith St Paul,' Philip. iv. 13. Big and great words ! Oh, but it is ' through Christ that strengthens me.' These things must not be forgotten. For a child of the church is a child of grace. By grace he is what he is ; he hath all from heaven. Suitable to the former place is that in Ezekiel. ' And the land of Egypt shall be desolate and waste ; and they shall know that I am the Lord ; because he hath said, The river is mine, and I have made it,' Ezek. xxix. 9. He shall be desolate, because he boasts and brags of his river, and depends not upon God for the sweet showers of the former and the latter rain. They boasted because it was a fat, fruitful country, which the Romans called their granary. But we must look for all from heaven. God by his Spirit will be as the dew.

You know in paradise there were four rivers that watered the garden of God, that sweet place, and made it fruitful ; but the heads of all these rivers were out of paradise, Gen. ii. 10. So it is with the church of God, ' There is a river, the streams whereof makes glad the city of God,' as the Psalmist speaks, Ps. xlvi. 4 : many precious comfortable graces, the particulars whereof follow. But where is the head-spring of the river ? It is in heaven. We have all from God, through Christ the Mediator. So, though we have of the water and dew, yet notwithstanding the head and spring of all is from without the church ; in heaven, in Christ, in the Mediator. And, therefore, in all the excellent things we enjoy in the church, let us look to the original first cause, Christ by his Spirit. He is ' as the dew' to his church.

Use 3. This affords likewise an *use of direction,* how to come to have grace to sanctify and alter our natures.

Ans. Do as the church doth here ; desire it of God. Lord, teach me to see and know my sins : Lord, ' Take away all iniquity, and receive me graciously ;' Heal my soul, for I have sinned against thee. O love me freely. Turn away thy angry face from my sins, and be as the dew unto my barren soul ; my dead soul, O quicken it ; make good thy promise, come swiftly, come speedily, come unresistibly, ' like rain upon the mown grass,' Ps. lxxii. 6 ; as showers, to water with the dew of grace, and fructify my dry, parched soul. Thus we should be earnest with God for grace for ourselves, and for the churches abroad, for our church and state at home. Therefore, let such an use be made of it generally, as God, and not other foreign helps, may especially be trusted in: for it is the only way to destruction, to let God alone, and to trust to this body and that body. For in this case, many times, God makes those we trust in our destruction, as the Assyrians and Babylonians were the ruin of the ten tribes. But begin always first in heaven: set that great wheel a-working, and he will make all things comfortable, especially for our souls. Then we shall not only find him to make good this promise, 'I will be as the dew unto Israel;' but the residue which follow after.

'He shall grow as the lily,' &c.

Those unto whom God is dew, [he gives] a double blessing. He will make them grow, and so grow as they shall grow up as the lily. Thistles, and nettles, and ill weeds grow apace also, but not as lilies. But God's children are lilies, and then they grow as lilies.

Quest. How do Christians grow like lilies?

Ans. First, *for beauty and glory.* There is such a kind of glory and beauty in that plant, that it is said by our Saviour, that Solomon 'in all his royalty was not arrayed like one of these,' Mat. vi. 29. Because his was a borrowed glory from the creature, but the lily hath a native beauty of its own.

2. Again, the lily hath *a sweet and fragrant smell.* So have Christians a sweetness and shining expressed in their conversation; as we have it a little after, 'His smell shall be as Lebanon,' &c.

3. And then again, in regard *of purity and whiteness.* So, Christians are pure and unspotted in their conversation, and their aim is purity and unspottedness. Whiteness betokens an unstained conversation. So the people and children of God, they are lilies, beautiful and glorious in the eyes of God, and of all those who have spiritual eyes, to discern what spiritual excellency is ; howsoever in regard of the world, their life be hidden. Their excellency is veiled with infirmities, afflictions, and disgraces by the malignant church ; yet in God's esteem, and in the esteem of his children, they are lilies. All the dirt in the world cast upon a pearl cannot alter the nature of it. So, though the world go about to besmear these lilies with false imputations, yet they are lilies still, and have a glory upon them. For they have a better spirit and nature than the world hath. And they are sweeter in their conversation than the world ; for when they have begun to be Christians, they sweeten their speeches and discourses. There is no Christian who is not of a sweet conversation. So far as grace hath altered him, he is beautiful, lovely, and sweet, and hath the whiteness of sincerity.

4. Now as God's children are lilies, and then grow as lilies for sweetness, glory, and beauty ; so they are like lilies, especially in regard of *sudden growth.* When God gives a blessing, there is a strange growth on a sudden, as it is observed of this plant, that it grows very much in a night. So God's children, when his blessing is upon them, they thrive marvellously in a short space. To make this clear. When the dew of grace fell in our Saviour's time upon the Christian world, what a world of lilies grew suddenly ! Three thousand in one day, at one sermon, converted by Peter, Acts ii. 41. The kingdom of heaven suffered violence in John Baptist's time, that is, the people thronged after the means of grace, and offered a holy violence to the things of God, Mat. xi. 12. So when this dew of grace fell, it was prophesied of it, 'The youth of thy womb,' saith he, 'shall be as the morning dew,' Ps. cx. 3. The dew comes out of the womb

of the morning, for the morning begets it : ' Thy youth shall be as the dew of the morning,' that is, they shall come in great abundance, as we see it fell out in the first spring of the gospel. In the space of forty years, by the preaching of the apostles, what a deal of good was done through a great part of the world ! How did the gospel then break out like lightning, by means of that blessed apostle Paul, who himself carried it through a great part of the world !

And now, in the second spring of the gospel, when Luther began to preach, in the period of a few years, how many countries were converted and turned to the gospel ! England, Scotland, Swethland,* Denmark, the Palatinate, a great part of France, Bohemia, and of the Netherlands. How many lilies grew up here on a sudden ! Sudden growths are suspected, and well they may be. But when God will bless, in a short space a great deal of work shall be done. For God is not tied to length of time. He makes water to be wine every year in tract of time ; for he turns the water of heaven into the juice of the grape. So there is water turned into wine ; that done in tract of time, which he can do in a shorter time, as he did in the gospel, John ii. 1, &c. Where is the difference ? That he did that miraculously in a short time, which he usually effects in continuance of time. So now many times he doth great matters in a short time, that his power may be known and seen the more, as we see now in these wars of Germany (g) how quickly God hath turned his hand to help his church, and hiss for a despised, forgotten nation to trample down the insulting, afflicting, menacing power of the proud enemy. And he can do so still, if our sins hinder him not. Surely if we stand still and behold the salvation of the Lord, we shall see great matters effected in a little time. ' They shall grow as the lily.' The accomplishment of this promise is not wholly yet come, for there be blessed times approaching, wherein, when the Jews are converted, ' they shall grow as the lily ' in those glorious times there spoken of, at the conversion of the Jews and ' fulness of the Gentiles ' coming in, Rom. xi. 12, the accomplishment whereof we expect, to the rejoicing of our hearts, that they should at length prove indeed with us the true children of Abraham.

Use 1. Therefore, we should make this use of all. Labour that the dew of God may prove the dew of grace, that God would make us lilies. If we would be beautiful and glorious, have a lustre upon us, and be as much beyond others as pearls are beyond common stones, and as lilies are better than thorns and briers, let us labour to have the grace of God, so to be accounted lilies, whatsoever the world accounts of us.

Use 2. Again, if the work be wrought upon us, though the imputations of the world be otherwise, let us comfort ourselves, God accounts me a lily. Set this against the base esteem of the world, considering how God judgeth, and those who are led by his Spirit, who judge better of us. And in all association, combination, and linking in acquaintance, labour to join with those that are lilies, who cast a good and a sweet savour. For we shall gain by their acquaintance whom Solomon affirmeth to be better and more excellent than their brethren, Prov. xii. 26. What are other people then ? They are but thorns. Therefore, let not those which are lilies have too much or near acquaintance with thorns, lest they prick us, and, as our blessed Saviour saith, turning again all to be-rent † us, Mat. vii. 6. It is said of our blessed Saviour in the Canticles, ' He feedeth among the lilies,' ii. 16. And, indeed, where is there any true delight to be had under

* That is, ' Sweden.'—G.　　　　　† That is, ' rend.'—G.

heaven but in their company who are gracious ? What can a man receive from profane spirits in regard of comfort of soul ? Nothing. They are as the barren wilderness that can yield nothing. Their hearts are empty. Therefore, their tongues are worth nothing. But let our delight be with David, toward the most excellent of the land, Ps. ci. 6, and then we shall not only ' grow as the lily,' but, as it followeth, ' we shall cast forth our roots as Lebanon.'

' And cast forth his roots as Lebanon.'

Because we have spoken of growth, and shall have occasion to touch it hereafter, we will not be large in the point. God here promiseth a growth not only to the church, but to every particular Christian ; and it is very necessary it should be so. For without growth neither can we give God his due honour, nor he receive the smell of a sweet sacrifice from us, as is fit. Nor can we without it withstand our enemies, or bear our crosses that God may call us to. Again, without growth and strength we cannot perform those great duties that God requires at our hands, of thankfulness ; nor do things so cheerfully and sweetly as may be comfortable to us. In some* without growth we can do nothing acceptably either to God or his people. The more grace, the more acceptance, which is spoken that we may value the promises, this especially, that we shall grow up in grace and knowledge ' as the lily, and cast forth our roots as Lebanon.'

Quest. But how shall we come to grow ?

Ans. 1. Go to God, *that we may continually have from him the sanctifying dew of his grace.* Go first for pardon of sin, then for a heart to reform our ways, to enter in a new covenant for the time to come, that we will not ' trust in Asshur,' but will renounce our particular personal sins ; after which we shall find sanctifying grace, so as the dew of God's Spirit will make us grow. Therefore take this order to improve the promises. Go to God for his love in Christ, for the pardoning of sin, and accepting of us in him, that we may find a sense of his love in accepting of our persons, in the pardoning of our sin, which is the ground of love ; for then this sense of his love will kindle our love towards him again, feeling that we are in the state of grace. Then go to God for his promise in this order: Lord, thou hast promised that thou wilt be as the dew, and that we shall grow as lilies. Make good thy promise then, that I may find the effectual power of it transforming my soul into the blessed image of thy dear Son !

2. And know *that we must use all the means of growth, together with the promise ;* for, in the things of this life, if a man were assured that the next year would be a very plentiful year, would men therefore, because they were thus forewarned, hang up their ploughs, and not prepare their ground? No ; but they would the rather be encouraged to take pains, because they know that howsoever God be pleased to vouchsafe plenty, yet he will do it in the use of means, observing and depending on his providence. So when he hath made gracious promises of the dew of his grace, and of growth as lilies, &c., this implieth a subordinate serving of his gracious providence. Therefore it is a way to stir us up unto the use of all means rather, and not to take us off from them. Even as God, when he told the Israelites, ' I will give you the land of Canaan,' Gen. xvii. 8, did only promise it, leaving the remainder to their conquest in the use of means. Should this have made them cast away their swords? No ; but it was that they might fight, and fight the more courageously. So when God hath promised growth in grace, should this make us careless ? Oh no ; it should make us

* Qu. ' in sum ?'—ED.

more diligent and careful, and comfort us in the use of means, knowing that our labour shall not be in vain in the Lord, 1 Cor. xv. 58. Now, Lord, I know I shall not lose my labour in hearing, in receiving of the sacrament, in the communion of saints, and use of sanctified means, for thou hast made a gracious promise that ' I shall grow as the lily,' and that thou wilt be ' as the dew unto me.' Therefore make thy good work begun, effectual unto my poor soul, that it may flourish and be refreshed as a watered garden. But there are several sorts of growth formerly touched, either

1. A growing upward; or
2. A growing in the root ; or
3. A spreading and growing in the fruit, and sweetness.

Therefore Christians must not always look to have their growth in one and the same place, but must wisely consider of God's prudent dealing with his children in this kind, as will be further seen hereafter in the particulars.

' He shall cast forth his roots as Lebanon.'

That is, he shall cast and spread, and so put forth his roots as Lebanon. He shall grow upward and downward. In regard of firmness, he shall be more rooted. In what proportion ? Trees grow upwards, in that proportion they take root downwards, because otherwise they may be top-heavy and overturn, a blast of wind taking advantage of their tallness and weakness, to root them out the sooner. Therefore, proportionable to their spreading above, there must be a rooting in the ground. As the prophet speaks to Hezekiah of God's people, ' And the remnant that is escaped of the house of Judah shall yet again take root downward, and bear fruit upward,' 2 Kings xix. 30. There must be firmness in the root, as well as growth in the branches, for which cause God here promiseth to the church and every Christian stability and fixedness, that as he groweth upward like the lily, so he should grow downward, firm and strong.

Quest. Now, whence comes this rootedness and firm stability of God's children ?

Ans. Especially from this, that they are now in the covenant of grace, rooted in Christ, who is God-man, in whom they are firmly rooted. In Adam we had a root of our own, but now our root is in Christ. All grace is first poured into Christ's blessed nature, John i. 16, and then at a second hand, ' out of his fulness we all receive grace for grace.' Being rooted in Christ we become firm, for there is in him an everlasting marriage and union. ' The root beareth us, we bear not the root,' Rom. xi. 18. Christ beareth us, we bear not him. So now, in the covenant of grace, all the firmness is out of us. Even as salvation itself was wrought out of us by a mediator, so it is kept by a mediator out of us. All goodness, grace, and favour of God to us is not in us, but in Christ; but it is so out of us, as Christ and we are one. But now we only speak of the cause of our firmness and stability, that because we are in the state of grace we have an everlasting firmness, as we are in Christ Jesus. God now making a second covenant, he will not have it disannulled as the first was, for his second works are better than his first. His first covenant was, ' Do this and live,' Lev. xviii. 5 ; but his second is, ' Believe this and live,' Rom. x. 9. So as howsoever our state in grace be but little, yet it is of a blessed, growing, spreading, firm nature, so sure as what is begun in grace will end in glory. Where God gives the first fruits he will give tenths, yea, the full harvest and all, because by the covenant of grace we are one with Christ, who is an everlasting head that never dies. Subservient to this now we have promised in the covenant of grace that we shall never depart from him, and that he will never depart from us to do us good. He puts an awe-band into our hearts, that we shall never depart from him. But this point being often touched, leaving it, we will come to answer some objections.

Obj. 1. It may seem that these things are not so. God's children do not always grow and spread themselves, but they are often overturned and fall.

Ans 1. This is nothing. They are moved, but not removed. They are as Mount Zion, which cannot be removed, but abideth for ever, Ps. cxxv. 1, which, though it may be shaken with earthquakes, yet is not removed thereby. The gates of hell and sorrows of death may set sore upon them, but not prevail against them, Mat. xvi. 18. They may fall, but not fall away. They may be as a weather-beaten tree, but not as a tree pulled up by the roots. Therefore they are compared here to a tree whose root stands fast still. Thus much the church, after a sore trial and endurance of much affliction, confesseth, 'All this is come upon us, yet have we not forgotten thee, neither have we dealt falsely in thy covenant; our heart is not turned back, neither have our steps declined from thy way, though thou hast broken us in the place of dragons, and covered us with the shadow of death,' &c., Ps. xliv. 17, 18, 19.

And again, though they fall, yet they learn to stand fast by their falls, are gainers by their losses, and become stronger by their weaknesses. As tall cedars, the more they are shaken by the winds, the more deeply they take rooting; so Christians, the more storms and blasts they have, the more they are fastly rooted. That which we think to be the overthrow of God's children, doth but root them deeper. As Peter after his fall took deeper rooting, and David, &c., so after all outward storms and declinings, here is the fruit of all. They take deeper rooting, whilst their sins are purged away by their fiery afflictions, Isa. xxx. 15.

Qbject. 2. But why then are they not more comfortable in their lives, in feeling and seeing of God's wise ordering of things ?

Ans. 1. *First,* Because though God work strongly and surely in them, *yet he doth it for the most part slowly,* as the wise man speaks, ' all his works being beautiful in time,' Eccl. iii. 11. Therefore they apprehend not their comforts as they ought, and so go mourning the longer : the time of knitting divine experiences together not being yet come.

Secondly, Because the anguish of the cross, if it be quick and sharp, many times *takes away the apprehensions of God's excellent ends in the same ;* as the children of Israel could not hearken unto Moses, for anguish and vexation of spirit, Exod. vi. 9. ' No affliction,' saith the apostle, ' for the present is joyous,' though afterwards it brings forth the quiet fruit of righteousness, Heb. xii. 11.

Thirdly, Then again, *Satan's malice,* who casts in floods of temptations, *is great.* So that the soul cannot enjoy that sweet tranquillity and peace it otherwise might, casting in doubts and numbers of what-ifs into the soul. So that for a time, he causes a strong diversion in them, whence after that, there followeth peace again, when those temptations are seen and overcome.

Fourthly, It is long also of ourselves, who are not armed for crosses and afflictions, until we are suddenly surprised by them. And then leaving our watchfulness, and forgetting our consolation, we are struck down for the present by them, and cannot support ourselves against them.

Fifthly, and lastly, It comes also *from God's wise ordering and disposing providence,* who will not do all at once. Our comforts must come by degrees, now a little and then a little. Our experience, and so our comforts, come together, after we have honoured God in dependence upon his will and pleasure. And yet this hinders not, but a Christian grows still, though he be for the present insensible of it, as a man is alive and grows whilst he sleeps, though he be not sensible of it. Other objections have been formerly touched.

'He shall cast forth his roots as Lebanon.'

We see then that the state of God's children is a firm and a stable condition, whence we may observe the difference betwixt God's people and others. God's people are rooted, and spread their root; but the other have rottenness in their root, being cursed, without any foundation. For take a man who is not a good Christian, where is his foundation? Only in the things of this world. Now all here is vanity, and we ourselves by trusting vanity become vain, 'Every man in his best estate is altogether vanity,' Ps. lxii. 9, vanity in himself, and trusts in vanity. What stableness can there be in vanity? Can a man, *stare non stante*, stand in a thing that stands not in itself? Will a picture continue that is drawn upon the ice? Will it not fail and melt away, when the ice upon which it is drawn thaws? So all these who have not the dew of God's grace, they are as a picture upon the water, have no foundation, and stand upon that which cannot stand itself. Therefore the Scripture compareth them to the worst of grass, which hath no good root; grass upon the housetop, which hath no blessing of those that come by, but there stands perking up above others, Ps. cxxix. 6. So it is with men that have no grace, they can perk up above others; but as they have no stable root, nor the blessing of God's people, stability with the Spirit of God inwardly, and the prayers of God's people to water and bless them, so they perish and wither quickly. Nay, whole nations, if wicked, have no foundation. What is become of the great monarchies of the world, the Assyrian, Persian, Grecian and Roman monarchies? And for cities themselves, they have died like men, and had their periods. Only a Christian hath a kingdom, a stable condition which cannot be shaken, Heb. xii. 28. He takes his root strongly, and grows stronger and stronger till he grows to heaven, nay, indeed, while he lives, he is rooted in heaven before his time; for though we be in earth, we are rooted in heaven. Christ our root is in heaven, and his faith which is wrought from heaven, carrieth us to Christ in heaven; and love, that grace of union, following the union of faith, carrieth us to Christ also. Even before our time, we are there in faith, love, and joy. Therefore a poor Christian is firm and stable even in this life, having union with Christ. Though he creep upon the earth, and seem a despised person, yet his root is heaven, where he hath union with Christ. 'His life is hid with God in Christ,' who 'when he shall appear,' he shall appear with him likewise in glory, Col. iii. 3, 4. Therefore, if Christ be firm, the estate of a Christian must needs be firm, for he is a cedar. Another man is as grass or corn upon the house-top. 'All flesh is grass,' saith the prophet, Isa. xl. 6.

Obj. Aye, but they have wit, and memory, and parts, &c. Yet they are but as the flower of the grass, perhaps better than ordinary grass, 'but the grass withereth, and the flower fadeth.' What continueth then? Oh, the word of the Lord, and comfort and grace by that word, 'endures for ever,' 1 Pet. i. 25, and makes us endure for ever. This is excellently set down by the prophet David. We see there, the righteous man is compared to a tree planted by the water side, his leaf fails not, Ps. i. 3. So a Christian is planted in Christ, he is still on the growing hand, and his leaf shall not wither: 'Those who are planted in the house of the Lord, shall flourish in the courts of our God, they shall still bring fruit in their old age, they shall be fat and flourishing, they shall grow like a cedar in Lebanon,' Ps. xcii. 13.

Use 1. This clear difference should stir us up to *be comforted in our condition, which is firm and stable.* Why do we value crystal above glass? Because it is brighter, and of more continuance. Why do we value continuing things? inheritance above annuities? Because they continue. If by the strength of our discourse, we value things answerable to their lasting, why should we not value the best things? Our estate in grace, this is a lasting condition: for a Christian is like a cedar that is rooted, and takes deeper and deeper root, and never leaves growing till he grow to heaven. ' He shall cast forth his roots as Lebanon.'

Use 2. Again, let all them make use of it, *that find not the work of grace upon their hearts.* Oh! let them consider what a fading condition they are in. They think they can do great matters. Perhaps they have a destructive power. They labour to do mischief, to crush whom they will in this world. But what is all this? We see what the psalmist saith of a Doeg, a cursed man, who had a destroying power. ' Why boastest thou thyself in mischief, O mighty man? the goodness of God endureth continually,' Ps. lii. 1. Why boastest thou thyself, that thou canst do mischief and overturn God's people? &c. Know this, that the good will of God continues. Boast not thyself; thy tongue deviseth mischief, as a sharp razor; God shall destroy thee for ever. He shall cast thee away and pull thee out of thy dwelling, and root thee out of the land of the living. Those men that rejoice in a destructive power, in their ability to do mischief, and exercising of that ability all they can, they shall be plucked out of their place, and rooted out of the land of the living. And as it is in Job, they shall be hurled away as a man hurls a stone out of a sling, Job. xxvii. 21. Then what shall the righteous say? They shall see and fear, and say, ' Lo, this is the man that made not God his strength, but trusted in the abundance of his riches, and strengthened himself in wickedness,' Ps. lii. 7. He thought to root himself so fast, that he should never be removed; but at the last it shall come to pass, that all that see him shall say, ' Lo, see what is become of him! this is the man that trusted in his riches, and made not God his strength.' What is become of him? Saith David of himself, ' I am like a green olive tree in the house of God; I trust in the mercy of God for ever and ever,' Ps. lii. 8. Let them trust, if they will, in riches, power, strength, and favour with Saul and great men; yet notwithstanding, be Doeg what he will, ' I shall be a green olive planted in the house of God,' &c.

So here is a double use the Scripture makes of these things. 1. The godly man rejoiceth in his condition; and 2, Other men fear and grow wise, not to trust to their fading condition. They are, as the prophet speaks, ' as a bay tree,' Ps. xxxvii. 35, that flourishes for a time, and then after come to nothing, ' their place is nowhere found.' They keep a great deal of do in the world for a time, but afterwards, where is such an one? Their place is nowhere found, nowhere comfortably. They have a place in hell, but comfortably a place nowhere. This is the estate of all those who have not a good root. For, saith Christ; ' Every plant that my heavenly Father hath not planted, shall be rooted up,' Mat. xv. 13. It is true of every condition, and of every man, if God have not planted him in that excellent state, or do not in time, he shall be rooted up. For the time will come that the earth will hold him no longer. He roots himself now in the earth, which then shall cast him out. He cannot stay here long. Heaven will not receive him, then hell must. What a miserable thing is this, when we place and bottom ourselves upon things that will not last! when ourselves shall outlast our foundation! when a man shall live for ever, and that which he builds on is fading! What extremity of folly is this, to build on riches, favour, greatness, power, inheritance, which either must be taken from him, or he from them, he knoweth not how soon!

What makes a man miserable, but the disappointing of his hopes and crossing of his affections? Now when a man pitcheth his soul too much upon his worldly things, from which there must be a parting, this is, as it were, the rending of the skin from the flesh, and the flesh from the bones. When a man's soul is rent from that he pitcheth his happiness on, this maketh a man miserable ; for misery is in disappointing the hopes, and crossing the affections. Now only a Christian plants his heart and affections on that which is everlasting, of equal continuance with his soul. As he shall live for ever, so he is rooted for ever in that which must make him everlastingly happy. These things we hear, and they are undeniably true. But how few make use of them, to desist from going on in a plodding, swelling desire of an earthly condition, to overtop other men. Such labour to grow in tallness and height, but strive not to be rooted. Now that which grows perking up in height, overtopping other things, yet without root, what will become of it ? It will be turned up by the roots.

Now, how shall we grow to be rooted ? For to attain hereunto, it is not only necessary to apply the promises, and challenge God with them, but to consider also what ways he will make them good.

First, Labour to know God and his free grace in Jesus Christ. ' Grow in grace, and in the knowledge of our Lord Jesus Christ,' 2 Pet. iii. 18. They go both together. The more we grow in the knowledge of our Lord Jesus Christ, and of the grace of God in him, the more grace and rootedness we shall have. For that which the soul doth clearly apprehend, it fastens upon in that measure it apprehendeth it. Clearness in the understanding breeds earnestness in the affections, and fastness too. So the more we grow in knowledge, the more we root ourselves in that we know. And therefore the apostle prays for the Ephesians, that they might have the Spirit of revelation, &c., that they might know the height, breadth, depth, and length of God's love that passeth knowledge. ' For this cause I bow my knees unto the Father of our Lord Jesus Christ, of whom the whole family of heaven and earth is named, that he would grant you, according to the riches of his glory, to be strengthened by his Spirit in the inner man ; that Christ may dwell in your hearts by faith ; that ye, being rooted and grounded in love,' in the sense of God's love to us, and so of our love to him again (for we are not rooted in love to God, till we be rooted in the sense of God's love to us), ' that you may be able to comprehend with all saints the height and breadth,' &c., Ephes. iii. 14.

Second, And withal, labour to know the gracious promises of Christ. For we are knit to him by virtue of his word and promises; which like himself are ' yea and amen.' ' Jehovah, yesterday, to-day, and the same for ever,' 2 Cor. i. 20. So all his promises made in him, they are ' yea and amen,' in themselves firm, and firm to us in him. They are ' yea and amen;' that is, they are made and performed in Christ, in whom they are sure to be performed ; and thereupon they are firm too. God made them, who is Jehovah, and they are made in Christ that is Jehovah. So God the Father Jehovah, he promiseth, and he makes them good in Christ Jehovah, who is unchangeable.

Thirdly, But this is not enough. We must *labour to have our hearts stablished*, that they may rely firmly on that which is firm. For if a thing be never so firm, except we rely firmly on it, there is no stability or strength from it. Now, when there is strength in the thing, and strength in the soul, that strength is impregnable and unconquerable strength. In Christ they are ' yea and amen ;' in whom he stablisheth us, anoints us, seals us, and gives us the earnest of the Spirit in our hearts.

How doth God stablish us upon the promises ? The rest which followeth is an explication of this. When he gives us the ' earnest of the Spirit,' 2 Cor. i. 22, and seals us to be his, in token he means to make good the bargain, then we are established. But we are never firmly established till we get the assurance of salvation. Then, as the promises are yea and amen in themselves, so we are stablished upon them when we are sealed and have earnest of the Spirit. Let us labour therefore to grow in the knowledge of God's love in Christ, to know the height, breadth, depth, and length of it, and to grow in all the gracious promises which are made in Christ, who is Amen himself, as his promises are ; and then, when we are sealed and anointed by the Spirit, we shall be so stablished that nothing shall move us. Therefore let us use all means for the establishing of growth in us, the word and sacraments especially. For as baptism admits us into the house of God, so by the sacrament of the Lord's supper, the blessed food of the soul, we are strengthened. In the use of these means, let us make suit unto God to make good his gracious promise unto us, that we shall ' grow as lilies, and take root as the cedars in Lebanon.'

Let us know, that we ought every day to labour to be more and more rooted. Do we know what times may befall us ? We have need to grow every day, to grow upward, and in breadth and in depth. If we considered what times we may live to, it should force us to grow every way, especially in humility, that root and mother of graces, to grow downward in that ; to grow in knowledge and faith, until we be filled with the fulness of God.

Obj. A poor Christian ofttimes makes this objection, Oh! I do not grow! Therefore I fear my state ; I am oft shaken! Therefore this promise is not fulfilled to me!

Ans. To this I answer, Christians may be deceived ; for they do grow ofttimes in firmness, strength, and stability, though they do not spread out. They may grow in refinedness, that that which comes from them may be more pure, and less mixed with natural corruption, pride, self-love, and the like. This is a temptation that old men are subject to especially, in whom the heat of nature decays, who think withal that grace decays. But it is not so ; for ofttimes when grace is carried with the heat of nature, it makes a greater show, being helped by nature. The demonstration, but not the truth, of grace is thus helped. Therefore this clause of the promise is made good in old Christians. They are every day more and more rooted, firm, stable, and judicious, and more able in those graces which belong to their place and condition. Therefore they should not be discouraged though they be not carried with the stream and tide of nature, helped with that vigour that sometime was in them. They grow in judiciousness, mortifiedness, in heavenly-mindedness, and in ability to give good counsel to others. This is well, for we grow not in grace one way, but divers ways ; not only when we grow in outward demonstration, and in many fruits and actions, but when we grow in refinedness and judiciousness, as was said, then we are said to grow likewise.

Yet notwithstanding it should be the endeavour of all to grow what they can in grace. When, if they grow not so fast as others, let them know that there are several ages in Christ. A young Christian cannot be so planted and so deeply rooted as another that is of a greater standing. This should not discourage any, seeing there are 'babes in Christ,' 1 Cor. iii. 1, as well as 'strong men,' Rom. xv. 1. Therefore where there is truth of heart, with endeavour to grow better and better, and to use all means, let no man be discouraged. Remember alway this for a truth, that we may grow, and we ought to grow, and the children of God ordinarily have grown more and more, both in fruitfulness and stedfastness every way, but not with a like growth in measure or time. Therefore labour to make use of these promises, and not to favour ourselves in an ungrowing estate, for grace is of a growing nature. If it grow not in fruitfulness, yet it grows in the root; as a plant sometimes grows in fruitfulness, sometimes in the root. There is more virtue in winter time in the root than in the fruit which is gone. So a Christian groweth one way if not another; though not in outward demonstration, yet in humiliation. God sometimes sees it necessary that our branches should not spread for a while, but that we should grow in humility; by some faults and sins we fall and slip into, that we may see our own weakness and look up.

Let us labour therefore, who have so long enjoyed such store of blessed means, under the dew of God's grace and the influence of his Spirit, in the paradise of God, his house and church. Having so long lived in this Eden, let us labour now to spread and grow in fruitfulness, that so we may be filled with the fulness of God. It is the chief thing of all, to be rooted and grow in grace. You see, God when he would single out a blessing, he tells them not that they shall grow rich, that they shall spread out and grow rich in the world. No! But, you whom I love freely, take this as a fruit of it, 'you shall grow as the lily,' you shall grow fruitful 'as the olive,' &c. This is the comfort of a Christian. Though he grows downward oft in the world, and things of this natural life, yet he grows upward in another condition: as lilies and cedars, they grow downwards one way, but they grow upwards another. Perhaps they may decay in their state and favour, and in their practice and cunning in this life; but a Christian, if he be in the use of right means, and put in suit the gracious promises, he is sure still to grow in grace, in faith, in love, and in the inner man.

Is not this a comfort, that a Christian hath a comfortable meditation of the time to come in all his crosses? that it is for better and better still; that as in time he is nearer heaven, so he shall be fitter and fitter, and nearer and nearer still, with a disposition suitable to the place; that the time to come is the best time; and that he shall grow every way, in height, in breadth, in depth and length, and apprehension of God's love, and that the more he grows in knowledge of these things, the more he shall grow in all dimensions, being as sure of things to come as of things past, and that neither things present nor to come shall ever separate him from the love of God in Christ? Rom. viii. 35. What a comfortable state is a Christian in, who is always on the mending hand, that is such a child of hope, when the hope of the wicked shall perish! Let us labour, therefore, that we may be in such a case and state of soul as that thoughts of the time to come may be comfortable, that when we think we must be transplanted hence out of the paradise and Eden of God's church into a heavenly paradise, that all our changes shall be for the better. What a fearful thing is it to be in the state of nature! What foundation hath a man in that estate, who hath no root here, and that root he hath will fail him ere long? How fearful is it for such a man to think of a change, when it is not a change for the better ?

Here is wisdom. If we will be wise to purpose, let us be wise this way. Labour, in the first place, to prize God's favours, and to know how to come by them in the use of all means. Look to God for the performance of these gracious promises. For they are not of what we shall do in ourselves, but what God will do in the covenant of grace. And if a Christian should not be rooted and grow stronger and stronger, we should not fail, but God and Christ should fail, who is our root and bears us up. Therefore, God hath taken upon him the performance of all these things. What remaineth for us but a careful using of all means ? and in the use of all, a going out of ourselves to God, that he would be ' as the dew to us,' and cause us, by the dew of his Spirit, to grow more and more rooted in grace as long as we live in this world ? And then our rooting and stability lies upon God, not upon us. He fails if we fail, who hath undertaken that ' we shall grow as the lily, and cast forth our roots as Lebanon.'

THE EIGHTH SERMON.

His branches shall spread, his beauty shall be as the olive-tree, and his smell as Lebanon. They that dwell under his shadow shall return; they shall revive as the corn, and grow as the vine: the scent thereof shall be as the vine of Lebanon.—Hos. XIV. 6, 7.

WE have heard at large heretofore what petitions God put into the heart and mouth of his church, as also what gracious answer God gives his own petitions. He cannot deny the prayers made by his own Spirit; and as he is goodness in itself, so he shews it in this, that he goes beyond all that we can desire, think, or speak. His answer is more transcendent, as the apostle speaks. He does ' exceeding abundantly above all that we ask or think,' &c., Ephes. iii. 19, 20. For whereas they in particular and in brief say, ' Do good to us, and receive us graciously,' he tells them, ' He will be as the dew unto them.' And from thence, being dew to them, is their spreading and growing as a lily, and casting of their roots as Lebanon. ' And their branches shall spread,' &c. And all this to encourage us to come to so powerful and large-hearted a God, who, as he is able to do more than we desire of him, so he will also do it. ' He will be as the dew unto us.' This is the general of all, for all other fruitfulness comes from this: 1. God will be as the dew; and then, 2. They shall grow as the lily, and cast their roots as the cedars in Lebanon. They shall not only grow upward, but downward, for the lily quickly spreads itself forth; but they shall be like the trees of Lebanon for stedfastness, and then spread in breadth, grow in all dimensions, which is fulfilled of the church in general, and of every particular Christian, when once he is in Christ, using sanctified means. They grow, then, in the root, and upright, and in every dimension. ' His branches shall spread.' And then,

' His beauty shall be as the olive-tree.'

Which, though fruitful and excellent, yet because it hath no sweet smell, it is added,

' His smell shall be as Lebanon.'

These excellencies promised to the church of God are not all in one tree, but yet they are in some sort in every Christian. What agrees not all to one plant agrees to the ' plants of righteousness.' They grow upwards and downwards, spread, and are savoury and fruitful. All agrees to a tree of righteousness. We say of man, He is a little world, a compendium of this great world, as indeed there is a comprising of all the excellencies of the world in man, for he hath a being with those creatures who have only that, and therewith he hath growing sense and reason, whereby he hath communion with God, and those understanding spirits, the angels. So that he is, as it were, a sum of all the excellencies of the creatures, a little world indeed (h). The great world hath nothing, but the little world hath the same in some proportion. So it is in grace. A Christian hath all excellencies in him, that are in the world. There is not an excellency in any thing, but it is an higher kind in a Christian. He hath the beauty of the lily, and he grows up in spreading, smell, and fruitfulness. His wisdom exceeds that of all the creatures. There is not an excellency in nature, but we have some proportionable excellency in grace which is above it. God useth these outward things to help us, that we should do both body and soul good by the creatures. Whatsoever doth our bodies good, either by necessity or delight, they help our souls; as plants and trees not only refresh the outward man, and the senses, but also they teach our souls, as here the Holy Ghost teacheth them by outward things. First it is said,

' His branches shall spread.'

When God enriches the soul with saving grace, one shall grow every way and flourish abundantly, extending forth their goodness on every side largely to the knowledge and open view of others ; and then further,

' His beauty shall be as the olive-tree.'

What is the beauty of the olive-tree ? To be useful, fruitful, and to bring forth good fruit. Indeed, the glory of a tree is to be loaden with fruit, and useful fruit ; which is the best property of fruit, to be useful and delightful. So the glory of a Christian, who is a plant of righteousness, of God's own planting, is to abound in fruits of righteousness. Indeed, the olive is a very fruitful tree, and the oil which comes and distils from it hath many excellent properties agreeing to graces.

1. Amongst the rest, it is a royal kind of liquor, that will be above the rest. So grace it commands all other things ; it gives a sanctified use of the creature, and subdues all corruption.

2. And then it is unmixed. It will mingle with nothing. Light and darkness will not mingle, no more will grace and corruption ; for the one is hostile to the other, as Solomon speaks, ' The just is abomination to the wicked,' Prov. xxix. 27.

3. Further, it is sweet, strengthening, and feeding the life, as in Zechariah there is mention made of two olives before the Lord, which feed the two candlesticks, Zech. iv. 3. And olives of grace have always fatness distilling from Christ to feed his lamp with oil. God's church hath always oil ; and those that are olives, they keep the church by their particular calling.

1. He shall be fruitful as the olive ; and,

2. Abundant in fruit, as the olive.

3. Constant in fruit, like the olive.

For it bears fruit much, and never fails, no not in winter, and hath a perpetual greenness. Indeed, the child of God hath a perpetual verdure ; as it is, Ps. i. 3, ' His leaf never fails,' because that which is the cause of flourishing never fails him. Which causes are two,

1. Moisture.
2. Heat.

For we know, moisture and heat, these two are the causes of all kindly growth. If a tree have more moisture than heat, then it is waterish ; if it have more heat than moisture, then there is no bigness in the fruit. So true it is, that moisture and heat are the causes of fruitfulness in a good proportion. So God's children, having the Sun of righteousness always shining upon them, and being always under the dew of grace (the promise being, ' to be as the dew to Israel'), having all dew to fall upon them for moisture, and having the Sun of righteousness to shine upon them to make them fruitful, their leaf never fails, they never give over bringing forth fruit ; because they have in them causes perpetuating fruitfulness, though not alike ; because Christ by his Spirit is a voluntary, and not a natural, cause of their fruitfulness, that is, he is such a cause, as works sometimes more and sometimes less, to shew that grace springs not from ourselves, and to acquaint us with our own weakness and insufficiency. Heaven is the perfection of all, both graces and comforts. Wherefore Peter calls the state of heaven, ' an inheritance, immortal and undefiled, that fades not away,' 1 Peter i. 4. Why is that an estate of grace and comfort, more than this of this world ? Because it is a never-fading estate. There they are alway in one tenure ; and because Christ shews himself alway there. There is abundance of water to moisten them, and heat to cherish them. There is no intermingling or stopping in growth, as is here. Therefore it is an inheritance that fadeth not away, having the supply of a perpetual cause of flourishing.

This in some degree is true of the church on earth. It is the inheritance of God that fades not, and Christians therein are olives that bring forth fruit constantly, having a perpetual freshness and greenness. So the righteous man is compared to the cedars of Lebanon, Ps. xcii. 12, which bring forth much fruit in their age. He shall be fruitful as the olive. From all which this point, formerly touched, followeth :

That it is the excellency and glory of a Christian, to be fruitful in his place.

Both to be fruitful in his place as a Christian, and in his particular calling ; to be fruitful as a magistrate, as a minister, as a governor of a family, as a neighbour, as a friend ; to be fruitful in all. Because in religion, every near relation is as it were a joining together of the body in Christ, one to another, by which some good is derived from one to another. God uses these relations as conduits to convey graces. A good Christian, the meanest of them is a good neighbour, and doth a great deal of good, being fruitful as a neighbour, fruitful as a friend ; much more as a husband, as a magistrate, as a minister. These relations are a knitting to Christ, by which fatness and sap are derived from the head for the good of the whole body. Therefore a Christian in all relations is fruitful. When he comes to be a Christian, he considers, like good Mordecai, what good he may do ; as he told Esther, ' What if thou be called to the kingdom for this purpose,' Esther iv. 14 ? So a Christian will reason with himself, What if I be called to be a magistrate, or a minister, for this purpose ? What if I be called to be a friend, for such or such a purpose, to do this or this good ? Indeed such are gracious *quære's** made to a man's soul, to inquire for what purpose hath God raised me ? To do this or that ? To be idle, or barren, or noisome ? O no ; to be a plant of God's planting. My glory shall be my fruitfulness in my place.

* That is, ' queries.'—G.

Therefore let us every one consider with ourselves, wherefore God hath set us in the church in our particular standings. Wherein let us remember this, that howsoever God may endure barrenness out of the church, in want of means, yet he will never endure it under means. It is better for a bramble to be in the wilderness, than in an orchard ; for a weed to be abroad, than in a garden, where it is sure to be weeded out, as the other to be cut down. If a man will be unprofitable, let him be unprofitable out of the church. But to be so where he hath the dew of grace falling on him, in the means of salvation, where are all God's sweet favours, to be a bramble in the orchard, to be a weed in the garden, to be noisome in a place where we should be fruitful, will God the great husbandman endure this ? He will not long put it up. But that he exerciseth his children with such noisome trees to try them, as he hath some service for these thorns to do, to scratch them. So, were it not for such-like services for a time, he would weed them out and burn them. For whatsoever is not for fruit, is for the fire.

Yea, every tree that bringeth forth not good fruit, shall be hewn down and cast into the fire,' Mat. iii. 10.

And the more to stir us up hereunto, let us know that wheresoever the dew of grace falls, and where there is the means of salvation, that at that very time there is an axe, an instrument of vengeance, laid to the root of the tree, which is not struck down presently, but ' it is laid to the root,' Mat. iii. 10; that is, vengeance is threatened to the tree, to that plant which hath the means, and brings not forth good fruit in time and season. What is the end thereof ? To be hewn down and cast into the fire. As we see the church of the Jews, when Christ came, the Messiah, the great prophet of the church, never was there more means of salvation ; yet even then, what saith John Baptist ? ' Now,' even now, ' is the axe laid unto the root of the tree,' Mat. iii. 10 ; and indeed, in a few years after, the whole tree, the church of the Jews, was cut down. And, Rev. vi. 2, 4, we see, after the rider on the ' white horse,' which is the preaching of the gospel, there comes a ' red, bloody horse,' and ' a pale horse,' war and famine. After the ' white horse,' his triumphant chariot, the preaching of the gospel. If this take not place, that it win and gain not, what follows after ? ' The red and the pale horse,' war, famine, and destruction. It will not be always with us as it is ; for the gospel having been so long preached, we having been so long planted in God's paradise, the church, if we bear not fruit, ' the axe is laid to the root of the tree.' God will strike at the root, and root up all. Therefore let every one in their place be fruitful.

Every one that is fruitful, God hath a special care of. If any tree were fruitful, the Israelites in their conquest were to spare that, because it was useful, and they might have use of it, Deut. xx. 19, 20. So God will always spare fruitful trees, and have a special care of such in common calamities. Let us therefore be exhorted not only to bring forth fruit, but to bring forth fruit in abundance, to study to excel in good works. The word in the original is, ' a standard-bearer ' (i), to stand before others in good works. As it is in Titus, ' labour to be as standard-bearers,' Titus iii. 8, to go before others in good works. Strive to out-go others in fruitfulness ; for therein is the excellency. For those both in the sight of God and men are in most esteem who are most fruitful in their callings and places. The more we excel in fruitfulness, the more we excel in comfort ; and the more we excel this way, the more we may excel. For God will tend and prune good trees, that they may bring forth more and better fruit, John xv. 2. And the more majesty we walk with, the more we damp the enemies, seeing them all under our feet. A growing Christian never wants abundance of encouragements, for he sees such grounds of comfort, as that he walks impregnable and invincible in all the discouragements of this world, breaking through all. As Solomon saith, it is a comely thing to see a lion walk, Prov. xxx. 29, 30. So much more it is to see a valiant, strong, well-grown Christian, who is bold as a lion, abound in good works.

It is said, ' His beauty shall be as the olive, and his smell as Lebanon.' The olive of itself hath no sweet smell. Therefore it is made up by another resemblance,

' His smell shall be as Lebanon.'

Lebanon stood on the north side of Judea, and was a place abounding with goodly trees, and all sweet plants whatsoever, which cast a wondrous sweet scent and smell afar off; as some countries abound so in sweet fruits and simples, as oranges, lemons and the like, that the fragrancy of the smell is smelt of passengers as they sail along the coast (j). So was this Lebanon a place full of rare fruits and fragrant flowers, which cast a scent afar off. Now, hence the Holy Ghost fetcheth the comparison. ' They shall smell as Lebanon,' that is, as those plants in Lebanon which cast a sweet and delightful smell afar off. Whence we will only observe this;

That a Christian by his fruitfulness doth delight others.

He is sweet to God and man, as the olive and the vine speak of their fruitfulness. ' They delight God and man,' Judges ix. 9, 13. So a Christian, both alive and dead, he is pleasing and delightful to the spirits of others, to God, and all that have the Spirit of God. As for God himself, we know that works of mercy are, as it were, a sweet odour. He is delighted with good works, as with sacrifice, Philip. iv. 18, smelling a sweet savour from them ; and their prayers ascend as sweet incense before him, Ps. cxli. 2. Every good work is pleasing and delightful to God, who dwells in an humble heart, and broken spirit. ' The upright are his delight,' Prov. xi. 20. We see likewise how Christ commends the graces of his church, which whole book is full of praises in this kind one of another. The church sets out the praises of Christ, and Christ the praises of the church. The church is sweet : ' Oh, let me hear thy voice, for it is sweet and lovely,' Cant. ii. 14. The church's voice is sweet, praying to God, or praising him. So whatsoever comes from the Spirit of God in the hearts of his children, is sweet. God lays to heart the voice of his children.

And as it is true of God, so is it of God's people. They are delighted with the favour of those things that come from other of God's people. For they have graces in them, and therewith the Spirit of God, which is as fire to set a-work all those graces in them. For it is the nature of fire, where it encounters with sweet things, to kindle them, and make them smell more fragrant and sweet. So a spirit of love makes all sweet and pleasing whatsoever, in the children of God. It puts a gracefulness upon their words, making their reproofs, admonitions, comforts, and whatsoever comes from them, to have a delightfulness in them ; because all is done in love, and comes from the Spirit of God, which carrieth a sweetness in it, to all those endowed with the same Spirit.

Use 1. Let this be an encouragement to be in love with the state of God's children, that so our works, and whatsoever comes from us, as far as it is spiritual, may be acceptable unto God and to the church, while we are living, nay, when we are dead. The very works of holy men, when they are dead, are as a box of ointment, as the ointment of the apothecary ; as the wise man says of Josiah, whose very name was like the ointment of the apothecary.* So the name of those who have stood out for good, and have been good in their times, it carries a sweetness with it when they are gone. The church of God riseth out of the ashes of the martyrs, which hitherto smells sweet, and puts life in those who come after, so precious are they both dead and alive (*k*).

Use 2. And then, let it be an encouragement to be led by God's Spirit, and planted in God's house, and to be fruitful in our places, that so we may delight God and man, and when we are gone, leave a good scent behind us. Good men, as it were, with their good scent they leave behind them, perfume the times, which are the better for them dead and alive. What a sweet savour hath Paul left behind him, by his writings to the church, even to the end of the world! What fragrancy of delightful smells have the holy ancient fathers and martyrs left behind them! A good man should be like the box of ointment spoken of in the gospel, which when it was opened, the whole house was filled with the sweetness thereof, Mat. xxvi. 7, *seq.* So a good man should labour to be full of sweetness, willingness and abilities to do good, all kindled by a spirit of love in him ; that when he is opened, all should be pleasing and delightful that cometh from him. Christ never opened his mouth, but good came from him ; and the heavens never opened in vain. Therefore, in opening of our mouths, we should labour to fill the places where we are with a good savour. Oh, how contrary is this to the condition of many! What comes from them ? Filthy speeches and oaths ; nay, that which should be their shame they glory in. We see it is the glory of a tree to be fruitful, and to cast forth a good savour, like the trees of Lebanon. What vile spirits, then, are such men led withal, who delight to offend God and man with their impious speeches ! who yet are so bold as to shew their faces, to outdare others that are better than themselves. Such are contrary to all God's senses. The Scripture condescends so far to our capacity, as to attribute senses unto God, of feeling, smelling, and touching, &c. So God is said to look upon his children with delight, and to hear their prayers. 'Let me hear thy voice,' &c., Cant. ii. 14. And he tastes the fruit that comes from them. So, on the contrary, all his senses are annoyed with wicked men and vile persons, who are abominable to God, as the Scripture speaks. As a man that goes by a stinking dunghill, stops his nose, and cannot endure the scent, so the blasphemous breath of graceless persons, it is abominable to God, as it were; God cannot endure such an odious smell ; and for his eyes, he cannot endure iniquity, to look upon the wicked ; and for his ears, their prayers are abominable. How abominable, then, are their persons whence those prayers proceed ! They have proud hearts, hating God and man. Wherefore, praying out of necessity, not love to him, they are abominable. And so for feeling. Your sacrifices are a burden unto me, I cannot bear them, Isa. i. 11 ; and the prophet complaineth that God was burdened and loaded under their sins, ' as a cart pressed till it be ready to break under the sheaves,' Amos ii. 13. All his senses are offended with wicked men. This, hardened wretches think not of, that, whilst God fills their bellies with good things, go on in sin-security. But the time will come when they shall know the truth of these things, what it is to lead an odious, abominable life, contrary to God and all good men. Hence we see what we should be, that we may give a sweet scent : ' His smell shall be as Lebanon.'

---

* The passage is in Ecclesiasticus xlix. 1. This is the first reference that we have found in Sibbes to the Apocrypha.—ED.

Wicked men know this very well, that the lives, speeches, and courses of good men, for the most part, are fruitful beyond theirs. Therefore, what they can, they labour to cast aspersions upon them, that they may not smell so sweet. So, crying down those who are better than themselves, that they may be the less ill thought of, and setting a price upon all things in themselves, and their companions. Take me a knot of cursed companions, and they are the only stout, the only wise and learned men : all learning it must live and die with them ; and all other men, though incomparable beyond them in abilities, in grace, in fruitfulness to do good, they are nobody. And this policy the devil teacheth them. But this will not serve the turn ; for God, both in life and after death, will raise up the esteem of such who have been fruitful, when ' the memory of the wicked shall rot,' Prov. x. 7, and not be mentioned without a kind of loathing. Therefore let no man trust to this foolish policy, to cry down all others that are better than themselves, thinking thereby themselves shall be better esteemed. This will not do ; for as all other things, so our good name is at God's disposing. It is not in the world to take away the good name or acceptance of good people ; for they shall have, in spite of the world, a place in the hearts of God's people, who are best able to judge. The next thing promised is,

' They that dwell under his shadow shall return.'

The Holy Ghost, it seems, cannot express in words and comparisons enough, the excellent condition of the church, and of the children of God, when they are once brought into the state of grace. The former words concern the excellency of the children of God in themselves, and these the fruitfulness and goodness of them that are under them, who shall be brought into the families and places where they live. ' They that dwell under his shadow,' under the shadow of Israel, ' shall return and revive as the corn, and grow as the vine,' &c. For so it is most fitly meant of Israel. For formerly it is said, ' I will be as the dew unto Israel.' Originally it is meant of Christ's shadow ; but because whosoever dwells under the church's shadow dwells under Christ's, therefore it is most fitly applied to Israel. They that dwell under Israel's shadow shall return.' What returning ? Return to God by repentance. This is supposed ; for those that dwell in the church of God, if they belong to God, by the help of good means they shall attain to reformation and repentance. But it is especially meant of that which follows upon it, 'They shall return ;' that is, they shall revive, as a man's spirits after a swoon are said to return, and things after a seeming decay and deadness are said to be quickened and return again. So all that dwell under the shadow of Israel, they shall return to God by repentance. ' They shall return,' having a greater vigour and liveliness, recovering that which they seemed to have lost before.

' They that dwell under his shadow shall return.'

When God will bless any people, he will bless all that belong to them and are under them, because they are blessed in blessing them, even as we are touched when our children are stricken. God strikes the father in the child, the husband in the wife, the master in the servant, because there is some relation and dependence betwixt them. As it is in ill so it is in good. God blesseth the father in the child, the king in the subject, and the subject in the king. God blesseth one in another. And in blessing, because God loves the church, all the friends of the church are the better for it. They prosper that love the church, Ps. cxxii. 6, though they be not members of it. All that bless Abraham shall be blessed. Though they be not actually good, yet if they wish him well, a blessing is promised. So when

God blesseth a man to purpose, he blesseth all that belong to him. All that be under his shadow fare the better. The point to be handled is this,

That the church itself yields a shadow, being shadowed itself by Christ, who spreads his wing over it. Now, what is the use of a shadow?

1. It is for a retiring place to rest in.
2. It is for defence against the extremity of heat.
3. It is for delight, if the shades be good and wholesome.

For, as philosophers express the nature of trees, there be some trees which yield noisome shadows, some trees have a heavy, noxious, dangerous shadow, because there comes a scent from the tree, as naturalists observe, which annoys the brains. But he speaks here of good trees. Israel is a tree that yields a shadow unto all; that is, all that are under Israel shall rest quietly, and not be annoyed with the heat of God's wrath, and the like. They shall be delighted, having a sweet refreshing under the church.

God, in Scripture, is often said to be a shadow, and his people to be under 'the shadow of his wings,' Ps. xxxvi. 7. But God and the church are all one in this, for they that are under the church's shadow are under God's shadow; for the church is Christ's, and Christ God's. Therefore to be under the church is to be under God, and to be in the church is to be under God's protection. They both agree, as we see, Mic. v. 7. The church is said to be dew, because God bedews the church, and the church bedews others; and here the promise is, 'I will be as the dew unto Israel,' where the same name is attributed unto God. Christ is a vine, and the church is a vine, John xv. 1. Christ is a dew and a shadow. So is the church, because Christ communicates his excellencies to her, and she hers unto others. Therefore there can be no offence in applying this to the church, which is the proper meaning of the place; for the church is a shadow for rest and freedom from annoyance unto all that come under her.

Quest. To clear this a little. What solace and rest do men find under the shadow of the church?

Ans. There is a rest and a peace in the church, for all things are at peace with the church, even the very stones in the field, Job v. 23; nothing can hurt the children of the church, 'God will be and is a sun and shield unto them,' Ps. xxxiv. 11: a shield to keep off all ill, and a sun to confer all good unto them. So his promise is to Abraham, 'I will be thy buckler, and thine exceeding great reward,' Gen. xv. 1. A buckler to keep ill from him, and 'an exceeding great reward' for good. Therefore it is a sweet shadow to be under the church, where God is all in all to them, who makes all things work for good unto them, even the greatest evil. Now, what a delightful thing is it to have a resting-place with them which either suffer no ill, or God turns all ill to their great good! where God is a 'sun and a shield,' a 'buckler,' and an 'exceeding great reward,' as he is to his church and children!

And then, again, God is about his church as a 'wall of fire,' Zech. ii. 5, to protect it, not only as a shadow to keep off storms, but as a wall of fire to keep off and consume enemies. God, in regard of protection of his church, is a compassing unto them, as it is in Job. Saith Satan, 'Hast thou not made a hedge about him, and all that he hath?' Job i. 10. There was a hedge about Job, his wife, children, and goods, which the devil durst not enter, nor make a gap in, until God gave him leave. Therefore those that are under the shadow of the church, they are safe, and may rest quietly.

But this is especially understood spiritually. The church is a shadow, and herself under a shadow spiritually, that is, in regard of spiritual evils, from the worst enemies. For out of the church, where is any fence for the greatest ill of all, the wrath of God? In the church of God there is set down a way of pacification, how the wrath of God is taken off and appeased in reconciliation by the death and sufferings of Jesus Christ, whereby the believing soul attaineth peace and joy unspeakable and glorious. Out of the church there is no means at all to pacify the greatest ill. Therefore there is no true rest out of the church, nothing but stings and torments of conscience. And as there is a shelter against the wrath of God, which burns to the bottom of hell, so here is a remedy against death and damnation. For now death is made a friend to the church, and the children of the church, for the sting of it is taken away, so that it doth them more good than anything in the world, ending all their misery and sinning, and opening a passage unto eternal happiness. All other petty ills that attend upon death are nothing. There is a rest from all these whatsoever, for all afflictions have a sanctified use to God's people for their good. There is therefore a rest and refreshing in the church for all that come under it.

And as this is true of the church in general, so it is true of particular families, that are little churches. There is rest and happiness in them. God blesseth all under the roof of a godly man. Whosoever comes under that shadow comes for a blessing, or for further hardening. We see in the current of Scripture ordinarily that when God converted any one man, he converted his whole family. 'Salvation is this day come to thy house,' saith Christ to Zaccheus, Luke xix. 9. When salvation came to his heart, it came to his house; all was the better for it. So the jailor, when he believed, he and his whole house were baptized, Acts xvi. 33. When God blesseth the governor once, then it is supposed all the house comes under the covenant of grace. Abraham and his house were blessed, Gen. xxii. 17. But this holds not always, for there was a Ham in good Noah's family. Still there will be the ravens and wild beasts among the tame beasts. There will be an Ishmael in Abraham's family, a Doeg in the church of Judah, a Judas in Christ's family, and a Demas among God's people. That is, let the family be never so good, you shall have some by God's judgment naught in the same. As it is said of Jeremiah's figs, the good figs were exceeding good, and the bad exceeding bad, Jer. xxiv. 3. There is none so good as those that are in a gracious family, and none so naught as such who are naught there. Because they are cursed and under a curse, being bad under such gracious means, being like the ground which receives the rain and showers from heaven, and yet is not the better for it, and so is accursed, Heb. vi. 7, 8. If a man who is untoward were in a gracious family, it is supposed he would be better, but those who are naught, where they should be good, under abundance of means, such are in danger to be sealed to eternal destruction. Such being bad, are very bad, who though they break not out to dangerous enormities, because of the place, yet to have a barren, untractable heart under abundance of means, is to be hardened to destruction, without a special mercy to make it work afterwards. For some who have lived in gracious families, though for the present the seed fructified not, yet have afterwards found that seed fructify after a long time, and have blessed God that ever they came under such a shadow. Therefore, though such barrenness be a dangerous sign, yet must we not suddenly either condemn ourselves or others in this case. Because in the things of God in the church it is as in nature. The seed springs not as soon as it is sown. So that grace at length which hath seemed to lie dead, after many years may sprout out. Monica, St Austin's mother, was a gracious woman whilst he was an untoward young man, as appeareth by his own Confessions, yet his mother having prayed much for him, he was converted after her death, and became a glorious father and instrument of the church's good (*l*). It is ordinary amongst us. Many, when they have gone astray, reflect home upon themselves, consider under what means they have been, calling to mind the gracious instructions they have had, and so, by God's assistance, are new men. Therefore let none despair in regard of time or place, because God may have further aims than we can reach to. But unless God give a special blessing after such watering, it is for the increase of condemnation not to profit under such abounding means, but still to be like Pharaoh's lean kine, full fed and lean still, Gen. xli. 17, *seq.* For the promise is, 'Those that are under his shadow shall return.'

There is here a fit occasion offered to spend much time in pressing care upon those that are governors, that even out of love unto those that are under them, they would labour to be gracious; because if they be gracious, God will give them those that are in their family. The whole family was baptized when the master was baptized; and when any man was called, the whole family came within the covenant. When Shechem and Hamor were circumcised, all the city was circumcised also, Gen. xxxiv. 24. It is true especially of governors. There is no man hath grace for himself alone. God gives special graces to special persons, to be a means to draw on many others. Wheresoever grace is, it is of a spreading nature. It is said here of such, 'their branches shall spread.' It is communicative, and of a piercing nature, a little whereof will work strangely. As we know, a little short speech of a poor maid to Naaman the Assyrian,* how it wrought, and was the occasion of his conversion, 2 Kings v. 3. So a little savoury speech will often minister occasion of many heavenly thoughts. God so assists it with his Spirit, that it often doth a great deal of good.

Quest. But why are all in the family the better for the governor that is good ?

Ans. Because God gives them grace and wisdom to walk holy before them, and to shine as lights, expressing and shewing forth the virtues of God which they have felt ; as we see David professeth, Ps. ci. 2, to walk singularly and exactly in all things in the perfect way, that so he might please God and men, shining out before them in an holy, glorious conversation in the midst of his family. And as by their example, so by their authority, they use to bring all under them to outward obedience at the least, which bringeth a blessing to the family. Because, when grace is once kindled in the master, he will see all at least come to outward conformity. They cannot work grace in them ; but as the prophet speaks, they may compel them to use the means, or else not to suffer a wicked and untoward person to dwell under their shadow. We know why God said that he would not conceal his secrets from Abraham, because he knew he would instruct and teach his family in the fear of God, Gen. xviii. 19. So this may be said of every one that is an Abraham, a governor of a family. They labour to tell them all things that have done good to themselves. Therefore they are the better for living under their shadow. Nay, further, not only the governor of the family, but if there be any graciously good in the family, they do much good. Laban's family was the better for Jacob,

* Syrian.—ED.

Gen. xxx. 27 ; and Potiphar, he and the jailor both, prospered the better for Joseph's sake, Gen. xxxix. 5, 23; so Naaman, that great captain, fared the better for his poor maid, 2 Kings v. 3, *seq*. It is a true position. God stablisheth grace in none who are gracious for themselves merely, but for the good of others also that converse with them. Whether it be governor or servants, no man liveth to himself, and for himself only, but for the good of all within their reach.

Use 1. For use therefore, first, this shall be for encouragement to all governors of families, *to be good, if not for themselves, yet in love to those that are theirs*. It may be, some have no care of their own souls or good. But hast thou no care of thy children, of thy wife that lieth in thy bosom, or of thy servants ? If thou hast not a heart of stone or marble, surely thou wouldst desire that for them, that thou dost not for thyself. Think of this, at least thou wouldst have thy children good and prosper. Labour then, if we would have all prosper who come under our roof, that our families may be little churches of God, that all who come under our shadow may revive and return. Therefore, out of love to those that belong to us, let us labour to be good. Is it not a pitiful thing, that some who are governors of others, they look to them as to beasts, and use their service as a man would use the service of his beast ? They feed their bodies, and think they have no charge of their souls. Now this is one reason why all that come under the shadow of a good governor are the better ; because they take care for their instruction and best good; that they live in obedience to God's ordinances, and not like wild creatures, ruffians, vagabonds, Cains, and the like. What a strange thing is this, to have a care of the body, the worser part, and neglect the more excellent part, their souls !

Use 2. Make we also this use, of trial. Art thou a good and a gracious governor indeed ? *Then grace in thy heart is communicative.* It will spread over thy family. Thou wilt labour to make thy children and thy servants good ; to make all good that come under thy roof. Other things are not always communicative. Gold is a dead thing, and other goods thou mayest keep by thee, which do not spread. But if thou hast the best good, faith and love, with a gracious heart, this is like oil, or like fire, which will not be held in, but out; and shew themselves they will, and shine in their kind. So grace is a spreading, communicative thing. All that comes therefore under the shadow of a gracious family, are said to return and be the better for it. Make this therefore an use of trial, whether thou be a gracious governor or not. If thou canst say with Joshua (when he called the people together, saith he, Do what you will, I know what I will do, ' I and my house will serve the Lord.' If you will be, idolaters, or so and so; ' but I and my house will serve the Lord,' Josh. xxiv. 15). So certainly there is no man who in truth of heart fears the Lord, but he is able to say, ' I and my house will serve the Lord.'

Use 3. Lastly, for terror, *let us behold the dangerous and cursed estate of those that dwell out of Christ's shadow*, the church, and good means ; who lie open to the indignation of God and storm of his wrath; who howsoever they may bless themselves in a thing of naught, yet it is a fearful thing to lie under a curse ; and that soul must needs be barren where the dew of grace falls not, for God usually derives* spiritual and heavenly things by outward means. ' They that dwell under his shadow shall return.' They shall return to God ; and by returning to him, return as it were and revive ; as when in a swoon, a man's spirits return again, he is said to revive. But the ground

* That is, ' communicates.—G.

of returning is, that they shall return to God, and come under his roof in the church. But more immediately this is true, ' they shall return,' and shall quicken and revive in returning ; which we spake of in the beginning of the chapter. Only this shall be added to that, that a wicked man, out of judgment of the danger of his estate, may make a stop ; but turning is more than so. In this case a man turns his face to God and heavenwards; to good things formerly neglected, on which he turned his back formerly. What is turning, but a change of posture, when the face is turned towards that the back was to before ? So it is in this spiritual turning to God. When heavenly things are in our face, when God and Jerusalem, the church, are in our eyes, still minding heavenly things and not earthly, then we are said to return. And therefore these converts mentioned in Jeremiah are thus described in their conversion, ' asking the way to Zion, with their faces thitherward,' Jer. l. 5. Whereas before in the days of our corruption, we turned our backs to God; now when we return, ' we set the Lord always before us,' Ps. xvi. 8, in everything. This is properly to return, to revive and flourish also in returning. Thus we have heard how all who live under the shadow of Christ do return, and what use we should make of it.

THE ·NINTH SERMON.

They that dwell under his shadow shall return ; they shall revive as the corn, and grow as the vine: the scent thereof shall be as the vine of Lebanon. —Hos. XIV. 7.

OUR desire of good things is not so large as God is bountiful in satisfying our desires, and going beyond them, as we see in this chapter. Their hearts were too narrow to receive all that good which God intended them. ' Receive us graciously.' This was their petition : whereunto God answers, ' That he would be as the dew unto them ; that they should grow as the lily, and cast forth their root as Lebanon, and their branches shall spread :' that they should grow in all dimensions, upwards and downwards, and spread in beauty and smell. ' Their beauty shall be like the olive, and their smell like Lebanon.' And because he would be God-like, like himself, that is, thoroughly and abundantly gracious and merciful, he doth not only, as we have heard, promise a blessing to Israel himself, but unto all near unto him, and belonging to him. ' Those that dwell under his shadow shall return; they shall revive as the corn.'

We are all too shallow to conceive either the infinite vastness of God's justice to impenitent sinners, or his boundless mercy and goodness to his poor church and children. Therefore God, to help our weak conceit in this kind, borroweth all the excellencies of nature, and makes use of them in grace. He takes out of the book of nature, into his book, what may instruct our souls ; and therefore sets down the growing estate of a Christian, by all excellent comparisons that nature will afford ; many whereof we have gone over. The last we spake of was, that mercy which God superabundantly shews unto the friends and servants of the church, ' Those that dwell under his shadow shall return.' Now, those that shall thus return, they revive in returning ; for they turn to the fountain of life, to the Sun of righteousness. They come under God's grace. Therefore they must needs return and revive in vigour, as they return to God: which vigour is especially meant here, when he saith, ' Those that dwell under his shadow shall return.'

' They shall revive as the corn.'

Now, how doth the corn revive ? Not to speak of that comparison that the godly are corn, and not chaff, as the wicked are, who are driven to and fro, Ps. i. 4, without any solidity, which, though true, is not here especially aimed at. For it is supposed that they who are good and gracious, have a substance, solidity, usefulness, and goodness in them, like corn, not being empty chaff which the wind blows away. This is useful to mention; but to.come to the scope indeed* by the prophet.

1. ' They shall revive as the corn.' In this, first, that as the corn when unsown, it lies dead in the granary, fructifieth not, but when it is sown springs up to an hundredfold, as we read of in Isaac's time, who received so much increase, Gen. xxvi. 12. So it is with converted Christians. Before they were under any gracious means, or in a good place, they lay as it were dead, and did not spring forth. But afterwards, being planted and sown under gracious means, in good company, in a good family, then they increase and grow up and multiply. ' They revive like the corn.'

2. And then again, as it is with the corn, though it seem to die, and doth indeed die in some sort, covered with winter storms, ere it spring out from the oppressions of frost and snow, and hard weather, as if it were altogether perished ; yet, notwithstanding, it is all the while a-preparing for springing up again more gloriously. So it is with the church, which seems to die often in regard of spiritual mortification by afflictions, whereby it is dead to the world ; yet all this while there is a blessed life in the spirit, preparing the soul, under the hard pressures of all weathers, to a glorious springing up again. Therefore the church hath no hurt by afflictions, no more than the corn hath by the winter, which is as necessary for it as the spring-time or summer. For else, how should the earth be ripened and prepared ? How should the worms and weeds be killed, if it were not for hard weather ? So it is with a Christian : those afflictions that he suffers, and under which he seems to be buried, they are as useful to him as all his comforts. Nay, a Christian is more beholden to afflictions for his graces and comforts than he is to outward blessings. One would think that the goldsmith were a-spoiling his plate when he is a-burning of it, when all that while the dross is but a-consuming out of it; and the vessel so hammered and beaten out, is but a-preparing to be a vessel of honour, to stand before some great man. So it is with a Christian : an ignorant person looking but one way, thinks God neglects such a one ; and that if God cared for such a one, or such a one, would or could such and such things befall them ? they conclude hence, as the Psalmist saith, ' God hath forsaken him,' Ps. lxxi. 11, and forgotten him. And as Christ the head of the church was thought to be forgotten and neglected, even when he was most dear and precious unto God, so even they all this while. The Spirit of God is working an excellent work in them, preparing and fitting them for grace and glory. Therefore, in that respect also, ' They shall revive as the corn.'

3. Thirdly, ' They shall revive as the corn' in regard of fructification. It is true both of the church and of particular graces. We see one grain of corn, when it is almost perished and turned to froth, nothing in a manner ; presently out of it springs a stalk, and thence an ear, and in that many ears, God giving it a body sixty or a hundredfold, as he pleaseth. So it is with a Christian : when he is planted, he will leaven others, and

* Qu. ' intended ?'—Ed.

those, others and others. A few apostles leavened the whole world, scatter-
ing the gospel like lightning all over the same. So it is true of grace in
God's children; it is like a grain of mustard-seed at the first, yet it grows
up and fructifies, Mat. xiii. 31, from knowledge to knowledge, faith to
faith, and grace to grace; from virtue to virtue, from strength to strength,
from one degree to another; nothing less at first, and nothing more great or
glorious in this world in progress of time; nothing so admired of God, and
pleasing unto man, as this which makes one all glorious and without spot.

Oh, what can be said more to encourage us to come under gracious
means, to love God and his ordinances, good company, and the communion
of saints—considering they are such happy people! 'Those that are under
their shadow shall return,' revive, and be vigorous. 'They shall revive as
the corn,' which doth, when it seemeth to be dead, notwithstanding all
weathers, grow up and multiply. And whereas it seemed dead before
and lay hid, being sown it grows. So being planted in the church, we
shall grow. For there is a hidden virtue in the least grace, in the least of
God's ordinances, more than we are aware of. Saith Christ, 'Where two
or three are gathered together in my name, there am I in the midst of
them,' Mat. xviii. 20. Much more is this made good in great congrega-
tions and families. But this is not all; he saith,

'They shall grow as the vine.'

Howsoever, the church which is the mother church grows before in the
former words: the new church that comes under her shadow, shall grow
in the same manner. 'They shall grow as the lily; their branches shall
spread;' and more, it is said here, 'They shall grow as the vine.' It is a
comparison delightful to the Holy Ghost, to compare Christ to a vine; the
church to a vineyard, and Christians unto vines, but such as draw all
their moisture and fatness in them from Christ the true vine, their sweetness being a derivative sweetness,

'They shall grow as the vine.'

1. The vine we know is a fruitful plant, as we read in the Judges,
ix. 9, 13. The olive and the vine would not forsake their sweetness to
be a king; for it is said by them, that they revive God and man, being
pleasing to them. So every true Christian is like a vine for fruitfulness.
He is a tree of righteousness; a plant of God's own planting; a vine that
spends himself in bearing fruit.

2. Again, as it is fruitful, so it is exceedingly fruitful, abounding in fruit,
So Christians are vines, not only for a little fruit that they bear, but because they are abundantly fruitful, which is premised, that if they do as
they should do, they shall be vines abundant in the work of the Lord.

3. And further, the vine as we know is never a whit the worse for pruning; but is pruned and cut, as our Saviour speaks, 'that it may bring
forth the more fruit,' John xv. 2. So the church and people of God are
never a whit the worse for afflictions; for as the best vines need dressing
and pruning, the best ground ploughing, the best linen washing, the best
metal the fire, to consume away the dross, the best things we use having
something amiss, so the best Christians need dressing and purging from
the great Husbandman, whereby they are not the worse, but the better;
having thereby much corruption purged away from them. As the pruning
of the vine makes it not the worse, but draws wild things from it, which
would draw away the strength of the vine, a Christian is the better for his
afflictions, wherein the glory of the church especially consists. For the
church never thrived better than in Egypt, where they laboured to crush

and to cut the vine. God brought his vine out of Egypt for all this, maugre all the malice of the enemies. The church was never more glorious in its own seat than it was in Babylon under the captivity. How glorious then was the church in Daniel and others!

4. Again, to the outward appearance, the vine is a rugged, unseemly plant, being not sightly and beautiful to look on; yet it is abundantly fruitful under that unsightliness. So if we look to the outward state and face of the church, it is nothing else to look to but a deformed company, defaced by affliction, lifeless here, as it were, 'having their life hid up with God in Christ,' Col. iii. 3, as the apostle speaks. Their life here is covered over with many afflictions, crosses, infirmities, and disgraces, whereunto they are subject, like unto other men. Therefore as it was the state of the Head to have no outward form or beauty, though inwardly he was all glorious, so the beauty of the church is inward; for outward show, it being unsightly like the vine, crooked and uneven, there being nothing delightful in it, unless it be in regard of the fruit that comes from it. So it is with the church of God and particular Christians; who, though in outward government they have not that policy and outward glory other governments have, yet there is an inward secret work of God's government of the church by contraries which exceeds all other policies, wherein he brings glory from shame, life by death. He brings down and lifts up. When he is about his excellent work he humbleth first. This is an ordinary way. Therefore we must not take offence at any outward deformity that we see in the church, and in God's children, when they seem to be trampled upon. They are but as vines, unsightly to the eye; they have a life, though it be a hidden one.

It is excellently set down by Ezekiel, Ezek. xv. 3, what the vine is of itself. It is serviceable for nothing. We cannot make a pin of it. It is such a brittle wood, as is good for nothing but to bear fruit. So, take a Christian that professeth religion, if he be not fruitful in his place, of all men he is the worst; of all men he is either the best or the worst. As the vine, if it bear fruit, it is the best, though it be an unsightly tree; but otherwise it is fit for nothing but the fire. Therefore let no man glory in his profession, that he is baptized, hears sermons, and reads. But where is thy fruit? Wherefore serves the dressing and pruning of the vine but for fruit? If there be no fruit, a Christian is the worst man that lives; worst, in regard that he is bad under good means; and in condition, he is the worst of all men, his torment is the greater. Those that are barren and unfruitful under means, the time will come that they will wish they had never enjoyed such a testimony against themselves.

5. And further, a vine is so weak that it must be propped and supported along, or else it will lie on the ground. Such is the estate of the church, which must have something to fence it and underprop it. God is the strength of the church. It is a wondrous weak plant. The children of God are wondrous weak, and exposed to a wonderful deal of misery. In regard whereof, and of the injuries and weaknesses they are exposed to, they must have support. A Christian is compared to the shiftless things, sheep, lambs, and doves; and in the plants they are compared to the vine, which needs a strong support. And, as Solomon saith of the conies, though 'they are a weak people of themselves,' Prov. xxx. 26, yet notwithstanding they have a strong rock over their heads, where they are safe; though they be as weak as the vine. So God's people, though they be weak of themselves, yet they have a strong support to uphold them. God, by the

ordinances of magistracy and ministry, especially by his Spirit, keeps them up and supports them, that they spread in largenses and in fruitfulness.

Use 1. Is this so? Then let us examine ourselves, what our fruit is. If we be vines, what is our fruit? what comes from us? Certainly if we do not shew forth that fruit we should, in our lives and conversations, in our speech, carriage, and actions, when we are called to it, it is an argument that as yet the dew of God's grace hath never fallen upon us, so as it must before we come to heaven. As was said before, a man may endure a dead plant in his ground, but in his orchard he will not. He may endure weeds in pastures, in neglected grounds, but not in his garden. If we be lilies in God's garden, and vines in his orchard, we must be fruitful and grow, or else God will not endure us. Of all woes, the greatest woe lies upon them who enjoy plentiful and abundant means, and yet are not fruitful, Mat. xi. 21.

Use 2. That we are vines, and God's vines, it is in the next place an use of comfort, that God therefore will have a care of us if we be fruitful. He will have a special care of that place where his vines are planted. If we see many gracious persons and families, who are conscionable in their practice and conversation, we may rest assured that God the great husbandman will have a special care of those choice vines, and the places they live in. They carry the blessing of God with them wheresoever they go, with a shadow and protection, making every place the better for them. For God will care for those vines which bring forth much fruit; as it is in Isaiah, 'Spoil it not, for there is a blessing in it,' Isa. lxv. 8. If a Christian be fruitful, and labours to be more fruitful, God gives a prohibition—'He is my vine, do him no harm.' 'Touch not mine anointed, nor do my prophets no harm,' Ps. cv. 15. Satan himself, and all creatures in heaven and in earth, have a prohibition to touch his vines no further than shall be for their good. Will a man suffer men to come into his orchard to break down his vines? He will not. Surely though the sins of this nation be very great, yet one thing ministereth hope; God hath a great many vines under his shadow and protection, many conscionable magistrates, ministers, and people of other professions, governors of families and the like, which walk holily. God will spare the vineyard, even for the vines that bear fruit. A notable place amongst others we have, Cant. ii. 15, 'Take us the foxes and the little foxes that spoil the vine; for our vines have tender grapes.' There is in every church not only gross papists, and foreign enemies, that would root out all, if it were in their power, but subtle foxes also; men that pride themselves in devilish policy, to undermine the church and children of God; who wheresoever they see vine or grapes, they malice that. Both the means, and grace wrought by the means, is the object of their cruelty. Subtle foxes they are; who account it a great deal of glory to be accounted politic men; to do mischief secretly and closely in the church. Will God suffer these foxes? No; he will not. 'Take us the foxes, the little foxes that destroy the vines,' Cant. ii. 15. God hath young growing vines, so as he will not only care for the great vines, but for the tender vines also. Christ hath a care of his lambs; as he said to Peter, 'Lovest thou me,' &c., 'Then feed my lambs,' my little ones, John xxi. 15. So Christ speaks in the gospel of these little ones. 'I tell you (of a truth) that the angels of these little ones behold the face of my Father,' &c., Mat. xviii. 10. And so he speaks in another place. 'A bruised reed will he not break, and smoking flax will he not quench, until he bring forth judgment unto victory,' Isa. xlii. 1, 2. So likewise he promiseth, ' that he will carry the lambs in his bosom, and gently lead them that are with young,' Isa. xl. 11.

Use 3. The next use shall be for encouragement unto weak ones. Should tender and weak Christians then be discouraged, for whom God is so careful? Surely no. Put case they bring forth but little fruit ; yet, O destroy it not, for a bleasing is in it. Therefore let us not be discouraged, if we be God's vines ; which is known and discovered, not by the abundance of fruit only, but by the kind of our fruit also. If it come from the Spirit of God, and relish of the Spirit, though it be not in such plenty, yet a vine is not a thorn. A Christian is not to be discouraged, though he bring not forth abundance of fruit at the first. There are different degrees and tempers of soil, and of ages in Christianity; which is spoken to encourage those that are good ; and yet are discouraged, because it is not with them, as with some other Christians of their acquaintance. Know, that there is no set measure of grace necessary to salvation, but truth. God doth assign us a measure of grace according to his good pleasure, and according as he hath purposed to make us profitable to others in the use of means. Those whom he means to use for suffering or doing of great matters in the church, those he fits suitably for that he means to call them to ; others have not that abundance of grace, out of God's wisdom, who knows best how to dispense his own graces to his own glory. If we allow not ourselves in our weaknesses, but groan under them, hate them, and strive against them, reaching towards perfection; in this case our weaknesses shall not hurt our salvation, but God will perfect his power in our weakness, 2 Cor. xii. 9.

So we see it is not the multitude of fruit, but the sincerity of it. If it be true, that makes a Christian. If there be truth of grace, it will out and spread the branches ; it shall not always be so with us. Sincerity and endeavour to grow, with a desire and thirst after growth, makes a man a Christian. Therefore, as was said, we must not be discouraged, though our growth and spreading be not like others. Every Christian hath his measure. Though every one be bound to go further and further, from faith to faith, and grace to grace ; yet there is a blessing in a little, and a promise also to him that useth it well. ' To him that hath, it shall be given,' Mat. xiii. 12. Christ hath a care that the foxes do not hurt the little tender grapes. Let none therefore be discouraged for their non-proficiency in the ways of God, so as to go back and leave off. He knows best, when and how to take away the baits, snares, and temptations that are set to catch them and discourage them. Let God alone with his own work, who is the great vine-dresser. Do thou thine own work ; attend upon good means ; wait upon God ; and then let the malice of the world and the devil be what they will, he will have a care of his vines ; and the more care, the more young and tender they are, &c.

These considerations may affect us, not only to take good by the vine for our bodies, but for our souls also, and so the same thing may cherish both body and soul. A Christian by grace hath an extracting virtue to draw holy uses out of everything ; as the Holy Ghost here compares us to a vine, to teach us these and the like things now unfolded. The last thing promised is,

' The scent thereof shall be as the vine of Lebanon.'

This Lebanon was a mountainous place, on the north side of Judea, wondrous fruitful in all kind of trees, in cedars, and goodly vines ; so it did abound in spice, and all goodly things. Therefore, to shew that a Christian should be the best of his rank, he fetches comparisons from the best things in nature.

'The scent thereof shall be as the vine of Lebanon.'

Now the vine of Lebanon had a sweet scent in it, both to draw to the liking, and then to delight in the taste and taking thereof. So it is with the graces of God in his children, they carry, as it were, a sweet scent with them, both to draw others to delight in, and taste of the same things.

Quest. But how comes it to pass that Christians send forth so sweet a scent?

Ans. Because they are in Christ, in whom the ointment and all sweetness is in fulness. From him the Head, first, and from thence it is derived unto the members; all who* must partake of this ointment. As it is said of the head of Aaron, that that ointment which was poured on his head ran down to his skirts, and all his rich attire about, Ps. cxxxiii. 2. So that sweetness in Christ is poured on the skirts, all along upon his members; even the meanest Christian receiveth 'grace for grace,' John i. 16, sweetness from Christ. The virgins, that is, such as defile not themselves with idolatry, and such other lewd courses, they follow after Christ in the smell of his sweet ointments, Cant. i. 3. It is spoken of Christ, who carrieth such a sweet smell with him, as 'all his garments smell of myrrh, aloes, and cassia,' &c., Ps. xlv. 8. So sweet is the smell of Christ, when he is unfolded in his benefits and offices, that the pure and holy virgin souls of the saints follow after it. 'His name is as an ointment poured out,' Cant. i. 3; that is, himself is his name, and his name is himself, as the Hebrew proverb is: Christ made known in the unfolding of the word, that is, his name. When the box is opened, all in Christ is like ointment. In the preaching of the word, all is sweet, and nothing but sweet in Jesus. Now a Christian, being a member of Christ, and a virgin soul following Christ, must needs draw sweetness from him, casting out that scent unto others, drawn from him, because they partake of Christ's anointing. What is the name of a Christian, but a man anointed with Christ's ointment, one anointed to be a king and a priest in some sort? Rev. i. 6. Therefore they carry the favour of him wheresoever they go. Aaron the high priest had sweet garments, Exod. xxxix. 26, which made a savour where he went, having bells and sweet pomegranates at the bottom of his garment. He had not only bells to discover him, but sweet pomegranates also. So it is with every Christian. Not only the minister, but every Christian, is a priest under the New Testament, and carrieth a savour with him; graces that spread and cast a sweet scent in all places wheresoever, which they exercise upon all good occasions. As St Paul expresseth it, 'They savour the things of the Spirit,' Rom. viii. 5. Those who are in Christ, they have the Spirit of Christ, or they are none of his. And having the Spirit of Christ, they savour of the things of the Spirit; that is, their thoughts, speeches, actions, and conversation are savoury. Those 'that are in the flesh,' saith the apostle, 'cannot please God,' Rom. viii. 8, they are unsavoury. A carnal man hath no savour in his speeches. They are either worldly or civil, without spiritual savour; because he hath nothing of the Spirit of Christ to savour of. 'His heart,' saith Solomon, 'is little worth,' Prov. x. 20. The like we may say of his thoughts, actions, and affections; they are unsavoury and little worth. He hath a dead heart to goodness; and thence whatsoever goodness cometh from him is forced, and against the hair, as we say. But a Christian having the Spirit of Christ, and therewith communion with Christ, all his discourses and actions are for the most part savoury; those he acteth

* That is, 'all of whom.'—ED.

as a Christian.   Therefore from his communion with Christ, it is said here, ' His smell shall be as Lebanon.'

' The scent thereof shall be as the vine of Lebanon.'

Delightful both to God and holy, blessed spirits, likewise to the church and to the angels which are about us, and pleasing to our own spirits ; for there issueth a wondrous contentment even to the conscience of a person, which is fruitful and abundant in goodness.   That soul receiveth an answerable proportion of comfort.   As it is with heat, that accompanieth fire alway, so there is a kind of heat of comfort which naturally accompanieth the heat of any good action.   There remaineth a sweet relish to the conscience of the performer, reflecting, with humility upon himself, with thankfulness to God, from whose dew, as we have heard before, cometh whatsoever is good.   Reflecting on this with an eye to the principal cause, it breeds a great deal of comfort to the soul.   As it was said of Josiah, the memory of Josiah was like the ointment of the apothecary ; whereas, on the contrary, it is said, ' The remembrance of the wicked shall rot,' Prov. x. 7. God threateneth the Jews that they should be a hissing to all nations, and that they should be abominable to all kind of people, Deut. xxviii. 37 (for what is so odious now as the name of a Jew ?), yet certainly this whole promise shall be verified even of them, this whole chapter having an eye unto the calling of the Jews.   The time will come that the scent of these odious people, who are now the object of hatred unto all people, ' shall be as the vine of Lebanon.'

Use 1. If this be so, it cuts off a carnal exception of senseless persons, that think they can stop men's mouths with this, I cannot make so much show as you, but I hope I have as good a heart to God as you or as the best.   But a Christian is a vine that brings forth grapes and much fruit, and casts a scent from him, as ' the scent of Lebanon,' upon all fit occasions ; for his words should be ' as the apples of gold set with pictures of silver,' Prov. xxv. 11.   He is seasonable in his actions of consolation, and bringeth forth his fruit in due season, as the promise is, Ps. i. 3 ; for Solomon sheweth that everything is made beautiful in his season, Eccles. iii. 11.   Those, therefore, that have not a good word to speak, but rather express the contrary, rotten, unsavoury discourse, vain in their conversation, savouring nothing that is good, how have they as good a heart to God as the best ?   No ; this is not to be a Christian, who should savour like Aaron's garments, or like these graces coming from his Head to him ; who should spread abroad his sweetness unto others, ' shining out as a light,' Philip. ii. 15, amongst others.   Therefore, away with this base plea.   A rotten speech argueth a rotten heart.   What can come out of a vessel but such as is within it ?   If the issues be naught, what is the vessel but naught ? If all be unsavoury outward, what is there but a rotten heart within ?

Use 2. Again, if Christians should cast a scent and savour, this should move and stir them up, if they will answer their title to be Christians, sweet, anointed persons, priests to God, to labour more and more to be spiritual, and savour the things of the Spirit, and to labour for more and more communion with Christ in the use of all sanctified means, that they may have the Spirit of Christ in their conversation, shewing forth the humility, patience, love, and obedience of Christ.   As Peter speaks and exhorteth us, ' to shew forth the virtues of him who hath called us from darkness into his marvellous light,' 1 Pet. ii. 9.   Then we answer our title, and ' cast forth a scent like Lebanon,' when inwardly and outwardly all things join to make us fruitful and savoury before God and man.

Quest. What will come of it if we be fruitful and savoury ?

Ans. 1. God will be more pleased in all our actions, and will ' smell a sweet savour of rest,' as it is said of Noah, Gen. viii. 21, after his coming out of the ark ; for God delights in his own graces, which he admireth in us.   As he said to the woman of Canaan, ' O woman, great is thy faith, be it unto thee as thou wilt,' Mat. xv. 28.   God, as it were, stands admiring his own graces, he is so delighted with the faith, love, prayers, and patience of his children, which is further excellently expressed in the Canticles, ' Who is this that cometh up out of the wilderness like pillars of smoke, perfumed with myrrh and frankincense, and all the spices of the merchant ?' Cant. iii. 6.   Christ there is brought in admiring* at his church and children, conflicting through all the miseries and incumbrances of this world, which hinder and oppose their journey to heavenwards, wherein they thrust forth all the practice of their holy graces, which smell like spices.   Then let us not envy God, the saints, and holy people the sweetness of our graces, but let our scent smell abroad to the content and comfort of all, that they may delight in these graces that come from us, in our humility, patience, faith, love, sincerity, and all these graces wherein we resemble Christ and shew forth his holy virtues.   Therefore, for our own comfort and delight of all, and to assure ourselves of heaven and of the love of God whilst we live here, let us labour to be fruitful in our conversation, and to cast forth a scent in regard of others, which hath an attractive, drawing force.   For when they see a holy, fruitful, and gracious conversation, it casts forth a scent, and makes others like religion.   So God is glorified, and religion is adorned.   What greater ornament to religion than to see a fruitful, gracious Christian, who hath ability and a heart to do good upon all occasions, with an humble, meek, peaceable spirit, taught of God to be so for the good and love of others ?

There must be pomegranates with bells, a sweet conversation with words, a little whereof will do more good to others than a great many words.   A good conversation is sweet, and hath a kind of oratory joined with it. Therefore, if neither for God, or Christ, or others, yet for our own sakes, and the reflection of that good scent upon ourselves, let us be fruitful.   A man cannot grow in fruitfulness but he must needs grow in comfort, peace, and joy.   Nothing cheereth and solaceth the heart of a Christian more than this, the conscience† that God honoureth him to be fruitful, to do good, and cast a sweet savour, to draw others to good things.   This will comfort us upon our deathbeds more than all other things.   Therefore, in all these respects, for love of God, others, and ourselves, which are delighted with the expressions of our graces, let us labour to be fruitful trees in God's garden, and to bring forth much fruit, that we may send forth ' a scent like Lebanon.'

Now, who would not be in such an estate and condition as this, as to have title to all these gracious promises, for ' the dew ' of grace to fall upon him, ' to grow as lilies ' in height, and to spread as other plants do, to grow upwards and downwards, to be ' rooted as cedars ' and ' fruitful as vines ' ?   The Spirit of God sets himself here to shew spiritual things by earthly comparisons, to make us the more capable of them.   The misery of the contrary condition may well stir us up to seek after the forementioned. For what a misery is it to have the curse of God upon one's soul, to have it like the barren wilderness, void of all grace and comfort that may delight others, or is spiritual, savoury, or savingly good.   So all these promises tend

* That is, ' wondering.'—G.   † That is, ' consciousness.'—ED.

to encourage us to be in the condition of God's children, that when we are in that estate we may comfort ourselves, and be able to claim our part, portion, and interest in these excellent promises.

Thus, by God's blessing, we have passed over the particulars of God's gracious promises to his church and all that shall come under the church, all which should encourage us to go to God, and do as the church doth here, ' take words to ourselves,' and desire God ' to take away all iniquity, and heal all our backslidings,' and that we may renounce all vain confidence, as the church doth here, who is taught to trust horses no longer, ' Asshur shall not save us.' And then let us, as was said, cleave unto the blessed promises, that we may improve them and make them our own every day more and more. Therefore, let us have in the eye of our soul the excellency of growth, or else we shall not value these promises. Let us consider what an excellent condition it is to grow, flourish, and be fruitful, having a due esteem of all these promises beforehand. Do but consider how excellent a Christian is that groweth above others, what a majesty he hath in his carriage, how undauntedly he walks in all oppositions whatsoever, as a lion in his courses, Prov. xxviii. 1 ; how he overlooks hell, wrath, death, damnation, and all ; what a sweet communion he enjoyeth with God in all the disconsolations that the world puts upon him. He carrieth his heaven in his heart and a paradise within him, which is planted with all graces ; whereas another man carrieth his hell about him.

Wherefore, let us take such courses to help ourselves as the church doth here, trust in God, and not in man or in the arm of flesh, and be encouraged, from all that hath been said, to have a good conceit* of God, to be fruitful, and draw on others to goodness, that God, his saints, and angels may be delighted with the scent of our graces, and ourselves comforted ; that we may rejoice in our portion and lot that God hath dealt so graciously to us, and glory more that he hath made us members of Christ and heirs of heaven than in any condition of this world. O the incomparable, excellent state of a Christian, above all the glory of this world! who not only groweth, but shall grow to heavenwards still ; and as he hath begun to hate sin, shall hate it more and more. God hath undertaken it shall be so. Ephraim, after all these sweet promises and dew of grace, shall say, ' What have I any more to do with idols ?' &c., the prosecution whereof must be referred † until the next time.

THE TENTH SERMON.

Ephraim shall say, What have I any more to do with idols ? I have heard him and observed him: I am like a green fir-tree: from me is thy fruit found. —Hos. XIV. 8.

WE have heard at several times heretofore, how God, out of the largeness of his goodness, goeth beyond those desires which he putteth into his people's hearts. They briefly entreat him to ' do good ' to them, and to deal graciously with them ; and he answereth them largely, ' That he will be as the dew to them, that they shall grow as the lily, and cast forth their roots as Lebanon.' All set out by most excellent comparisons, helping grace by nature, our souls by our bodies, and our spirits by our senses. As we have

* ' That is, ' conception.'—G.   † That is, ' delayed.'—G.

souls and bodies, so God applieth himself to both : ' His branches shall spread ; his beauty shall be as the olive, and his smell as Lebanon.'

Then in the seventh verse, his gracious promise reacheth unto those who dwell under the church. ' Those that dwell under his shadow shall return, they shall revive as the corn, and grow as the vine,' &c. The new church that shall come under the shadow of the old, shall flourish as the ancient did. ' They that dwell under his shadow,' that is, under Ephraim's and Israel's shadow, ' shall return,' and be partakers of the same dew of grace.

Now this eighth verse containeth a further gracious promise to Ephraim, upon his repenting and former resolutions. Ephraim said, ' Asshur shall not save us, we will not ride upon horses : neither will we say any more to the work of our hands, Ye are our gods.' Now what saith God here, repeating the words of Ephraim? Ephraim ' shall say' is not in the original ; but only set down to express what the meaning is ; whereas Ephraim said, ' What have I any more to do with idols ? ' Ephraim shall have this answer, ' I have heard him, and observed him, I am like a green fir-tree : from me is thy fruit found.'

As though the Lord had said, let not Ephraim think that when he hath forsook idols, he hath forsaken his comfort, as though there were no comfort in walking according to the rule of my word and laws. Let him know, that instead of these poor and base comforts, either in gross idolatry, or other more cunning idolatries whatsoever, which formerly took him up, that now he shall exchange them for more solid and substantial comforts. For ' I have heard him and observed him.' So that let him see what he loseth in parting with base corruptions, worldly lusts, pleasures, and the like, he shall find it more abundantly supplied in a far more excellent manner in me, and in the fruits and effects of my love unto him ; so as he shall find that there is nothing lost by entering strictly into my service. And whereas formerly he walked in a vain shadow, in relying on ' Egypt, Asshur, and the works of his own hands ; ' now he shall have a far more excellent shadow, which no storm, nor rain, nor injury of weather can pierce through. ' I am like a green fir-tree unto him.' Not such a shadow as those his idols were, who could not keep off the storm of God's wrath from him ; nor such a shadow as Jonah's gourd was, which flourished for one day, and was nipt the next, Jonah iv. 7. No ; I will be constant and permanent as myself, ' I will be as the green fir-tree ; ' a constant shadow to keep back all annoyance whatsoever ; not like the cursed noisome shadow of idols, under which Ephraim rested before. But ' I will observe and regard him, and be like a green fir-tree unto him.' I will not only be a shadow and shelter of defence unto him from injury and molestation, that he may rest quietly ; but he shall be also fruitful. Though the fir-tree be not so fruitful, yet ' from me is thy fruit found.' Whatsoever he is in himself, yet this shall not be matter of discouragement unto him. I am all-sufficient, there is enough in me to supply him with ; ' from me is thy fruit found.' But to take them in order.

' Ephraim shall say, What have I any more to do with idols,' &c.

Some think the words come upon Ephraim's observing and hearing of him ; so as when God is seen in his most excellent majesty and glory, and observed as he is just, merciful, and wonderful, terrible in himself, that this manner of hearing and observation causeth flesh and blood so to stoop and reform, as they yield themselves, and resign up all unto God ; seeing htat miserable condition they are in, and what an infinite distance there is betwixt their impurity and God's most excellent holiness. As we read of Isaiah, when he had seen God in his throne of majesty, ' Woe is me !' saith he, ' for I am undone; because I am a man of unclean lips, and I dwell in the midst of a people of unclean lips : for mine eyes have seen the King, the Lord of hosts,' Isa. vi. 5. And so of Job, ' I have heard of thee by the hearing of the ear, but now mine eye seeth thee ; wherefore I abhor myself, and repent in dust and ashes,' Job. xlii. 5, 6. Which, indeed, is true in the general, that a man then truly repenteth and turneth unto God, when he knoweth God and himself to purpose, and never effectually until then; for Christ, who cannot lie, and is truth itself, calleth this kind of knowledge eternal life. ' This is life eternal, to know thee to be the only very God, and whom thou hast sent, Jesus Christ,' John xvii. 3. But, though this be a general truth, yet we take it here rather for an encouragement unto Ephraim, as before, that nothing is lost by cleaving unto God's ways, and forsaking of sin. Now whereas, ' Ephraim shall say, what have I any more to do with idols ? ' In the words we may consider.

1. *The manner of expression, with a great indignation of soul,* ' What have I any more to do,' &c.

2. *The matter so hated with indignation, is idolatry,* their former idols, ' Ephraim shall say, What have I any more to do with idols ? '

Ephraim, we see, renounceth idolatry. But in what manner is this done? with an high indignation of zeal and hatred : ' What have I any more to do with idols ? ' He doth not say, Now that Ephraim hath left idolatry, I will supply all these comforts that they had by idols. But Ephraim loathes idolatry. Therefore he saith, ' What have I any more to do with idols ? ' It is a figurative question, implying a strong denial with a strong indignation. ' What have I any more to do with idols ? ' I have had too much to do with them : I have now nothing to do with idols. It is a negation and denial, with as great aversation * and abomination as can be possibly expressed : for in such questions, the denial is set forth more strongly by a negation, and with a greater emphasis, than by any affirmation is possible to express. So elegant is the Spirit of God, in setting forth spiritual things in a heavenly and transcendent manner.

' Ephraim shall say, What have I any more to do with idols ?' &c.

Hence, in that Ephraim shall say thus, and say it with such vehemency of spirit and indignation, we may observe in general,

There is excellent use of the affections.

God hath planted the affections in us, to be as the wind, to carry the soul to and fro, forward or backward : for affections are planted in the soul, answerable to things aimed at by it. For, as in the nature of things, there be good and bad, delightful and hateful, hurting or pleasing ; so answerably God hath framed the soul to the nature of things. For good things, God hath planted affections in us to join, clasp, embrace them and welcome them ; as love, joy, delight, and such like. And for evil things, he hath planted affections to avoid them ; as indignation, hatred, and the like. Indeed, religion is mainly in the affections, whereof there is excellent use. Take away them, and take away all religion whatsoever. A man, were it not for his affections, is like *mare mortuum*, the dead sea that never stirreth. Therefore it is but a doting, idle conceit of these rigid men, that take away affections ; much like the folly of them, who, because they have been drunk with wine, do therefore cut up all the vines. But the way were, to moderate the excess, not to cut up the vines. So for the affections, we

* That is, ' aversion.'—G

must not root them up, or cut them down, but order them aright. For what doth the first commandment require, Thou shalt have no other gods but me; but a right ordering of all the affections of the soul, joy, delight, trust, and fear, and the whole frame of them to be carried to God? For the inward worship of God is nothing else but the excellent working of these affections suitably to the law, with the detestation of the contrary. It is not knowledge that makes a man a good man, but the affections. The devil and wicked spirits know much; but they have no love, joy, or delight in them. Therefore we must value ourselves and things, as we are in our will and affections; for so God valueth us, and we should value others thereby. This well done would bring us a wondrous deal of comfort, and stop our too much and rigid judging and censuring of others.

'Ephraim shall say, What have I any more to do with idols?'

Now in particular we see here, that Ephraim not only leaveth idols, but there is planted in him a sound indignation against them; whence we may learn,

That it is not enough to leave sin, but we must loathe sin also.

A notable place to this purpose, we have in the prophecy of Isaiah, what they should do after their conversion, in the case of hatred to idolatry. 'Ye shall defile also the covering of thy graven images of silver, and the ornament of thy molten images of gold: thou shalt cast them away as a menstruous cloth; thou shalt say unto it, Get thee hence,' Isa. xxx. 22. There is a hatred and a strong loathing indignation against sin, when it is discovered in the pollution and vileness thereof; which affection of hatred, God hath planted to draw the soul away from anything that is truly hurtful to it. It is not enough to leave sin for some by-ends, as fear of punishment, shame, and the like; but we must loathe it also. The prophet David, when he professeth his love to the law, how proveth he it? 'I hate and abhor lying,' Ps. cxix. 163. And so again, 'Do not I hate them, O Lord, that hate thee? and am not I grieved with those that rise up against thee? I hate them with perfect hatred, I account them mine enemies,' Ps. cxxxix. 21. Here is hatred, and perfect hatred with abomination.

Reason 1. The reason is, because God is a Spirit, John iv. 24; *and looks to the bent of our spirits,* seeing what we love and what we hate. Therefore the strength of this consideration draweth the soul to hate and love, with God, as he hates and loves; and as much as may be, to hate sin as he doth.

Reason 2. And then again, *he requireth our heart especially.* 'My son, give me thy heart.' Give me thy love in that which is good, and hate that which is ill. What ill we leave, we must hate first; and what good we do, we must first love, or else we shall never do either of them acceptably to purpose. What the heart doth not, is not done in religion. If it hath no hand in the avoiding of ill, it is not avoided. If it have no hand in the doing of good, it is not done before God. Therefore in true conversion, there must be a loathing of sin.

Reason 3. Thirdly, because in all true conversion there *is a new nature put in us.* Now the new creature, which partaketh of the divine nature, whereby we resemble God, it hath an antipathy to the greatest ill, which is sin, the cause of all other evils whatsoever; which maketh us opposite to God, defileth the soul, and hindereth our sweet communion with him. A new creature, we know, hath a new disposition, and is opposite to the works of the flesh; they are contrary to one another. So that we see it clear, that we must not only leave but loathe sin.

Quest. But how may we know, discern, and try this true hatred of sin ?

Ans. First, true hatred is *universal.* He who hates ill truly, hates it universally in the whole kind. As we see in wicked men and devils, who hate God and all goodness. So on the contrary, those that are good hate all ill whatsoever, whether it pleasure or displeasure them ; they stand not upon it, they hate the very nature of all ill. Those whose obedience and affections are partial, they hate some evils, but not others, which is not true hatred wrought by the Spirit of God, for that is universal to the whole kind.

2. Then also, wheresoever true hatred is, *it is unplacable and unappeasable.* There's no true end of sound hatred, but by the abolishing altogether of that thing it hates ; as we see the hatred of Satan to the church and people of God is unappeasable and unquenchable. Nothing in the world can stay Satan's hatred, nor the hatred of his instruments, who hate the remembrance of God's people. Therefore the very name of Calvin and Luther must be put out of their books, to satisfy their hatred, not only when they are dead, burn their bones, but abolish their memory, if they can, (*m*). So there is the like disposition in God's people to that which is ill. A godly disposition, it hateth sin even to the death, and is not quiet until all sin be abolished. Whereupon it is never quiet in this life, but desires heaven, not enduring patiently the least relics and rags of sin ; desiring that that which it so hateth, might have no being at all. Those who mince and cull things, who are so gentle and tender towards their sins and corruptions, in themselves and others ; is this that hatred which is unappeasable, and never rests, till it see either a thorough reformation, or abolishing of what it so hateth ? Wherein it is a more rooted affection than anger. For hatred is a rooted offensive displeasure, against persons and things ; and so rooted, as that nothing in the world can root it out. Anger may be appeased. It is appeased in God, and it may and must be in men. But hatred is implacable, aiming at the annihilation of the thing so hated.

3. Again, where true hatred and indignation is, there *the nearer the ill is to us, the more we hate it, &c.* As we hate it in itself, so we hate it the more, the nearer it is to us. As a toad or any venomous thing, the nearer it is to us, we loathe and abhor it the more, so certainly, whosoever hates and abhorreth sin as sin (as it is a hateful thing to a renewed soul), so he hateth sin more in himself than in others, because it is nearest in his own bosom. Every man hates a snake more in his bosom than afar off, because it is more likely to do him harm there. Therefore those that flatter their own corruptions, and are violent against others, as Judah against Tamar, ' She shall be burned, bring her forth and burn her,' when himself had gotten her with child, Gen. xxxviii. 24. So many are severe in punishing of others, as if they were wondrous zealous ; but what are they in their own breast ? Do they reform sin in their own hearts and lives ? He that truly hates sin, he hateth his own sin more than others, because it is near him.

4. And so, in proportion, he that hates sin truly *will hate it in his own family, children and servants, more than in others abroad.* It was a great fault in David, that he cockered* up Adonijah, and others in his own house, whilst he was more strict abroad. Can men think to redress and hate sin in the commonwealth, and yet suffer it in their families ? True hatred is most conversant in its strength near hand. Those who suffer deboistness†‡ and profaneness in their families, and never check it in their children and servants, they hate not sin. Whatsoever countenance they may take upon

* That is, ' indulged.'— G.   † That is, ' debauchery.'—G.

them, of reformation abroad, it cometh out of by-respects, and not out of true hatred.

5. Again, he that hateth sin truly as sin, *will hate the greatest sin in the greatest measure*, because he hates it as it is hateful. Now in the nature of things, the greatest sin deserveth the greatest abomination, and aversation* from it. Therefore he who truly hateth sin, he hates the greatest sin most of all. Those therefore that are very nice in less matters, and loose in greater things, it is but hypocrisy. For he who truly hates sin as sin, where the greatest sin is, thither he directs the edge of his hatred, which is the strongliest carried against the strongest ill. And such a one will not respect persons in evil, but wheresoever he findeth it, if he have a calling, there will be an answerable hatred of it. Therefore if one be a minister of the word of God, he will do as good Micaiah did, and will not balk† Ahab for his greatness, 1 Kings xxii. 9, *seq.*; and like good John Baptist, he will tell Herod of his faults. Because he hates sin as sin, therefore, where he hath a calling to it, he will hate it proportionably in the greatest measure. Good Eli in this case was too indulgent over his sons, 1 Sam. ii. 27, *seq.*; but we must love no man so nearly, as to love the ill in them.

6. Again, a man may know that he truly hates sin, *if he can endure admonition and reproof for sin.* He that hates a venomous plant which troubleth the ground, will not be displeased if a man come and tell him that he hath such a plant in his ground, and will help him to dig it up: surely he cannot be displeased with the party. So here, if a man do truly hate sin, will he be angry with him that shall tell him that he is obnoxious to such an evil, which will hurt him dangerously, and damn his soul if it be not helped? Surely no. Therefore let men pretend what they will, those who swell against private reproof, they do not hate sin as sin. Only add we this caution: a reproof may be administered with such indiscretion, out of self-love, and with a high hand, as that a man may dislike the carnal manner of reproving; but if it be done in a good manner, he that hates reproof, because he loveth himself and his sin, pretend what he will, he hates not sin.

7. So, *if a man love to be flattered in his sin, it is a sign he hates not sin truly.* For there is naturally a great deal of self-love in man, which makes him that he loves to be flattered in his sins; whereupon he comes to be abused to his own destruction, especially great men. Now, it is a sign of an ill state of soul to be subject to be abused by flattery, and to hate instruction. Saith Paul, 'Am I your enemy, because I have told you the truth?' Gal. iv. 16.

8. Again, we may know what our hatred to sin is, *by our willingness or unwillingness to talk of it or mention it, or to venture upon the occasions thereof.* Where hatred is, there is outward aversation. We fly from what we hate, and shun to frequent places where we may receive offence. Whatsoever hath an antipathy to nature, that we hate and run away from. Therefore those that present themselves to the occasions of sin, upon no calling, say what they will, they feed sin, and live according to the flesh. Those that hate a thing will never come near it if they can choose. Therefore, those that present themselves willingly to places infected, where there is nothing religious, but scorning of religion, your common representations of abomination, pretend what they will, their intent is to strengthen their own corruption, against the good of their souls. This is the issue. Those that hate sin will hate all that which may lead to it, the representations of

* That is, 'aversion' = turning from.—G.   † That is, 'avoid.'—G.

sin also. Can a man hate sin and see it acted? Wickedness is learned when one seeth it acted, as one of the ancients saith well. Therefore let us by these and the like trials take notice what our hatred to sin is.

Only this our zeal and indignation to sin must have a mitigation and be regulated, lest, like an exorbitant river, it exceed the bounds. Therefore, not to follow the school niceties in the exactness of differences, we will touch the mark a little, how this zeal and hatred to sin, in reproof especially, must be qualified; wherein we must consider divers things.

1. First, *our calling must be respected.* For howsoever we must carry an universal hatred to sin thus far, that we must not do it, yet in the discovery of hatred and dislike to others, we must consider what calling we have, and how far we go.

2. And it must be done *with a sweet temper*, keeping our distance, and reserving the due respect unto those in whom we shew our dislike. As we see Nathan, when he came to tell David of his fault, how he doth it, what art he useth! It must so be done as that it may appear to be done out of pure zeal, that it is no wild-fire nor no heat of nature; but that it cometh merely from the Spirit, and in much love, with mildness and pity, in which case it carrieth a wondrous authority. The discovery of hatred to the faults either in a minister or in a magistrate, though they must be truly dealt with, and have their faults told them, yet there must be respect had to their place, by reason of the weakness of men. As it is with the body, great men have their physicians as well as meaner, only their physic must be more costly, because perhaps of the tenderness of their constitutions; but as for their bodies, they must not be suffered to perish, nor will not. So for their souls, they must have that which other men have to help them, but it must be done with reservation and respect; as Paul, speaking to Festus the governor, calleth him 'most noble Festus,' &c., Acts xxvi. 25. Pressing also goodness in some sort upon king Agrippa, 'O king Agrippa, believest thou the prophets? I know thou dost,' Acts xxvi. 26. So we see how we may examine whether our hatred to sin be true or not.

Let every one therefore make use of it in their calling. Those that are entrusted with God's message, let them know that God's ambassadors are to be faithful in their message, for they serve a greater Lord than is upon the earth; and let them shew their true hatred of ill, and the danger of sin, wheresoever they find it. And for those that are governors of others, let them not think that they hate sin in themselves except they hate sin also in all that belongs to them, and reform it. For we see here an evidence of conversion. When Ephraim was converted, 'What have I any more to do with idols?' and, 2 Cor. vii. 11, there is an excellent description of the nature of repentance, by many parcels. The Corinthians had repented: how is this evidenced? 'Oh, behold,' saith he, 'this selfsame thing, that ye sorrowed after a godly sort, what carefulness it wrought in you; yea, what clearing of yourselves; yea, what indignation; yea, what fear; yea, what vehement desire; yea, what zeal; yea, what revenge!' What revenge and indignation against sin! A kind of extremity of hatred, a hatred quickened and kindled, the height of hatred. What indignation! Insinuating that wheresoever there is the truth of conversion, there will be indignation against sin in ourselves. As David confesseth of himself, having sinned, 'So foolish was I, and ignorant: I was as a beast before thee,' Ps. lxxiii. 22. When he suffered such a thought to lodge in his breast, that it was better with the children of the world than with the church of God, he was troubled for it. But when he went into the church of God, and saw the end of wicked men, then he saw his own foolishness in being so deceived, and speaks against himself with indignation. So wheresoever there is true conversion, there is hatred with indignation against ourselves. As in that place before alleged, they shall say unto their idols, 'Get thee hence,' Isa. xxx. 22, what have I any more to do with you? Which is a phrase of speech shewing a disposition of hatred to the utmost extension, 'Get you hence.' So Christ to the devil, 'Get thee behind me, Satan.' This is the right temper of a truly converted Christian, expressed by divers phrases in Scripture: by a denial of our lusts, by killing and crucifying, by pulling out the eye, and cutting off the right hand. Which phrases, do they not imply a great strength of hatred and indignation, when we must, as it were, pull out our own eyes; that is, our beloved sins, which are as dear to us as our eyes, and as useful as our right hands unto us? Yet these must be cut off, mortified, crucified, and denied, Col. iii. 5. Therefore let us not deceive ourselves; but let us judge of the truth of our conversion by our true hatred to sin in ourselves and others, and in all who are committed to our charge.

If this be so, what shall we judge of a cold, lukewarm temper? It is the nature of cold, to gather heterogeneal bodies together. As we see in the ice, there are straws, and stones, and heterogeneal things incorporated, because the cold congeals them together; but where there is fire, there is a separating of the dross from the good metal. So where the Spirit of God is, it is not so cold as to jumble sin and sin, this and that together; but it purgeth away that which is ill, and that which is good it makes better. For in what proportion the fire of God's Spirit stirs up that which is good, in that proportion there is a hatred of that which is ill. They are unparalleled affections. Those that love God, they hate evil. Those that are alike to all things, do shew that they have not this active true hatred against sin. No! 'Ephraim shall say, What have I any more to do with idols?'

Quest. But now, How shall we come to get this hatred against sin, and holy revenge and indignation against ourselves for that which is amiss in us?

Ans. First, we must every day labour to get a *clearer sight of the excellency of that which is good, and a nearer communion with God by prayer and meditation.* And then, when we have been with God, it will work an abomination of whatsoever is contrary unto him. Thus Moses, when he had talked with God in the mountain, at his return, seeing them dancing and sacrificing to the calf of gold, Exod. xxxii. 19, what did Moses? He brake the tables asunder. So it is with those that have communion with God, who is 'light itself, and in whom is no darkness,' 1 John i. 5, who is holiness and purity itself. Those who have effectually conversed with God in his ordinances, meditation, prayer, and the like, when they look upon sin, which is contrary to God, they look upon it with a more perfect hatred. So Isaiah vi. 5. When God appeared to the prophet, and touched his tongue* with a coal from the altar, saith he, 'Woe is me, for I am undone, because I am a man of unclean lips,' &c., 'for mine eyes have seen the King, the Lord of Hosts.' Thus, when once he had communion with God, he began to loathe himself. So, if we would hate evil, let us labour more and more to be holy, and to increase in that divine affection of love. For in what measure we love that which is good, in that measure we hate the evil: as it is, Ps. xcvii. 10, 'Ye that love the Lord, hate evil;' insinua-

* Lips.—G.

ting, that all that love the Lord hate evil. All those that are near unto God, they hate all sin. The more they grow into communion with God, the more they grow in the hatred of all that is contrary. Let us therefore never talk of love to God, and of piety, and such like ; for if there be any grace or communion with God, we hate all sin in that measure as God hateth. He who hath no zeal to reform that which God hateth, he hath no love at all.

2. Again, the way to stir us up to hate sin in ourselves and others, and out of that hatred to reform it, is to set before us, *what it is in itself; that it is* the loathsomest thing in the world, worse than the devil himself : for it is sin which makes him a devil. That corruption, pride, worldliness, and profaneness, which we cherish, is worse than the devil himself, because this made him a devil. Let us make sin therefore as loathsome as we can, and then we shall hate it : and let us present it to our souls, as the most dangerous thing of all, the ill of ills, which bringeth all other evils upon us. This may appear more ugly in our sight, in that the foulness thereof could not be expiated but by the death of the Son of God. And consider what great torments he hath prepared for that which we so cherish. This proud, sinful, and carnal disposition of ours, so opposite to all goodness, God hath appointed to punish it with eternal separation from his presence. It maketh God hate his own creatures. ' Go, ye cursed, into everlasting fire, prepared for the devil and his angels,' Matt. xxv. 41.

3. And to stir us up to reform sin in all that belong unto us, we must consider *the dangerous condition that they live and die in, in whom this is not reformed.* Eternal torments, and separation from God. These things may help to work in our hearts a hatred of sin : and from this hatred, a reformation of it, with a zeal and indignation. Therefore let us labour more and more for this temper of soul, that we may be like God, and carry the characters of the children of God in us. There is no affection will distinguish us from hypocrites more than hatred, which cometh of love, which is the first-born and breeding affection of all others. For why do we hate any thing, but because it is opposite to that we love ? Why do we hate ill, but because it is opposite to God and to Christ, whom we love ? Amongst others, take we along this consideration with us, that it is the spear which wounded our blessed Saviour ; and that it is that he hates most which we love most. Consider the holiness of God, that he would punish it in his own Son, ere it should not be punished.

4. And consider that *it is the bane of all our comfort, this which we so cherish, and that it embitters all things to us.* We cannot rejoice, no, not in the good blessings of God, whilst we are guilty of sin ; neither can we pray comfortably whilst our hearts regard it, Ps. lxvi. 18. In this case, that which should rejoice the heart, communion with God, is terrible to us. What have I to do to take his name in my mouth, when I embrace such sins ? Ps. l. 16. The day of judgment is terrible also ; for how can a man think comfortably thereof, if therewith he expect a heavy doom for his sins he liveth in ? So we may say of the day of death. None of these can be thought upon without terror, when therewithal it cometh to one's mind, the cutting off from their sins, and the ' terror of the Lord' against all sin whatsoever, 2 Cor. v. 11. It should be the joy of our hearts to think of these happy times : therefore, there must needs be a great deal of sin and atheism in our hearts when we cannot think comfortably of them. For either we believe not these things, and so are plain atheists ; or else, if we believe them, we are exceeding foolish to lose future joys for the poor ' pleasures of sin for a season.'

5. Let us labour to *grow in grace more and more;* for the more we grow in the love of God and good things, the more we shall hate sin. For, whatsoever may be said for the growth in love, and cherishing of it to good things, the same may be said for the hatred of ill, in a contrary sense.

6. The last place shall be, *to place and drive our affections a contrary way, to translate and place them on a contrary object, when they are stirred up to evil attempts.* As, when hatred is stirred up, direct it to its proper object, sin; when love is irregular, think with ourselves, that God hath not planted this affection for this object, but to carry me another way; I must love God above all, and all that he loveth, for his sake. Hath God put love and hatred into my heart, to hate my brother whom I should love, and to love the devil, and hate God? Oh no! I should love God above all, and my brother as myself; and hate the devil and all his works, whom I have renounced in my baptism. Therefore, in distempers of the affections, make a diverson, and turn them the right way. As physicians use to do, when the distempered blood runs dangerously one way; if they cannot stop that, they open a vein to drive the course of the blood another way. So it is Christian policy, when the affections run dangerously one way, then to reflect thus upon ourselves: Aye, But is this the end why God hath placed this affection in me? Certainly no! He hath planted this affection in me for another purpose. Therefore, I will hate that which I should hate; sin in general, and my own sin most of all, which makes me hate my brother. This should be our daily task and study, to take off the affections where they should not be placed, and to fix them where they should be placed; and there to let them go amain, the faster the better; restraining them where they should not run out.

Thus we ought to temper ourselves, and to work in ourselves as much as may be, a sound hatred to all sin, not only of the second table, but of the first also. The church here saith, ' What have I any more to do with idols?' Now I hate all vain inventions. And think not, with Gallio, that this belongeth not to us; if we be magistrates, and called to do it, to stand for the cause of the church and true religion.

' What have I any more to do with idols?'

The last thing to be observed from Ephraim's manner of expressing his indignation is—

Obs. That where love is not well contracted and begun, it will not hold to the end, but will end in eternal hatred.

The serpent and Eve* had some poor acquaintance together, as the issue proved. What did it end in? ' The seed of the woman shall break the serpent's head,' Gen. iii. 15. This association and acquaintance ended in everlasting war and breach. So all covenants, leagues, and associations with those we should not join with, can never soder† handsomely together, but will end in everlasting hatred. What a strict league was in former times betwixt Ephraim and idols! But when Ephraim's eyes are opened to see his idols devils, he detests and loathes all abominations, and is of another mind. ' What have I any more to do with idols?' He abominates them, as the word importeth.

Let us therefore beware with whom we join in intimate league. For what makes miserable so much, as the renting ‡ of the affections from that they were strongly placed on? when love is rent from the thing beloved? If we place our affections, for some by-respects, upon wicked persons, this

* Printed ' Hevah.'—G.   † That is, ' solder.'—G.   ‡ That is, ' rending.'—G.

will cause so much the more torment and indignation against ourselves, that were so foolish to suffer our affections to enter so deeply where they should not. Those that glory in their league with antichrist, and wonder at the beast, Rev. xvii. 8, *seq.*, thinking him a demi-god : will this be alway so ? Oh, no ; when God opens the eyes of any of his people, they shall hate them for ever. So wicked persons, that now are led on to this and that wicked course : shall this be always so ? Woe to thee, if it be ! But the time may come that thou shalt say, ' What have I any more to do with idols,' or with such an one's acquaintance ? I cannot endure to look on him : he tainted me, and misled me, and tempted me. Now we must be two, part we must, and I would we had never met together. Therefore, before we place our affections on any, consider who they be, whether we be likely to live with them for ever or not ; whether there be any evidence of grace in them. If not, let them be two to us. For whatsoever vanity is in the things or persons we love, if we belong to God, we must be separate from them, unless we will be damned. Therefore we must be wise to prevent the danger betimes. Ephraim might have known before the danger of idolatry, had he been wise and prudent ; but it is well he knows it now at length, which causeth him so to abominate idols. ' What have I any more to do with idols ?' Thus much is spoken, because of the lukewarmness and cold temper, neutrality and halting of a great many in the world, having so many sinful combinations and associations one with another, as if these things were not material.

Now, let men consider what a disposition this is, and how it stands with that disposition which must be in those that are members of Christ, and look for heaven. Let a Christian always remember what he is, and what he hopes for, and this will put him in a right temper. 1. What he is : a king, and an heir of heaven, &c. 'After which he should reason with good Nehemiah, ' Shall such a man as I fly ?' shall such a man as I do this ? I am redeemed from my sins, and advanced to be a king to rule over my lusts, to be an heir of heaven and eternal happiness in the world to come, to reign with Christ ; and shall I do thus and thus ? Doth this stand with my new temper, this sin, this filthiness, this base action and thoughts that I am tempted to and encumbered with ? Shall such a man as I follow these base actions, ways, and companions ? Consider we this well, and then it will breed Ephraim's resolution, ' What have I any more to do with this base lust ?' What hath it to do with me, or I with it ? Is this and this action befitting a king, and an heir of heaven, and a new creature ? And if a man be in authority, then let him consider what Mordecai said to Esther, ' What if thou be called to the kingdom for such a purpose ?' Esther iv. 14. What if thou be called to this place or dignity for this purpose, to reform such and such abuses ? Think with thyself, not only in particular what thou art, but in thy place, what if thou be called to reform such abuses : such unsound doctrines ; to stand for God and for the truth. This will breed this resolute indignation of Ephraim in us, ' What have I any more to do with idols ?' All which is for the manner of Ephraim's indignation : a strong negation of an abominated thing. ' What have I any more to do,' &c. The next, which is the substance and matter abominated—idolatry—must be reserved for some other time.

THE ELEVENTH SERMON.

Ephraim shall say, What have I any more to do with idols?   I have heard him, and observed him: I am like a green fir-tree: from me is thy fruit found.—Hos. XIV. 8.

WE have heard at several times heretofore how graciously God deals with his people, alluring them by many free and gracious promises to his service; the particulars whereof we heard heretofore at large.

This 8th verse hath reference unto that which went before, ver. 3. There Ephraim renounceth his former idols. 'Asshur shall not save us,' &c.; and here, 'Ephraim shall say, What have I any more to do with idols?' Unto which the answer is, 'I have heard him, and observed him: I am like a green fir-tree unto him: from me is thy fruit found.' Now, in that 'Ephraim shall say, What have I any more to do with idols?' this in sum is only the first part of the third verse, repeated in another manner: That Ephraim shall and will go on in abominating idols, be constant in his former resolution.   Therefore, in that Ephraim shall, by the Spirit of grace, go on in renouncing all false confidence, God sheweth here that Ephraim shall lose nothing by it, for he intends here the continuance of time.   'I have heard him,' and I do hear him, and I will hear him, and respect him, and be like a shady green fir-tree to shade him, causing him also to be abundant in fruit.   'From me is thy fruit found.'

'Ephraim shall say, What have I any more to do with idols?'   Here we considered the manner of expression, and then the matter itself.

'Ephraim shall say, What have I any more to do with idols?'

To come, therefore, to the matter itself specified, idolatry, against which Ephraim's indignation is directed:

'What have I to do with idols?'

In handling whereof we must take in all these four together, that is—

1. *False doctrine*, which is the foundation of *idolatry*.

2. *Idols themselves;* or,

3. *Idolatry*, which they tend to (for he which hates idols, hates them because he hates idolatry); or,

4. *Idolaters;* as if he had said,

What have I any more to do with idolatrous doctrines, opinions, or conceits, or with idols framed according to these conceits, or with idolatry or idolaters?   For these go together.   No man worships idols, but because he is poisoned in his conceits; and idols are forbidden, because idolatry is dangerous; and communion with idolaters is forbidden, because of idolatry. So that the doctrine, idols, idolatry, and communion with them, all these are objects of Ephraim's abomination and indignation.

'Ephraim shall say, What have I any more to do with idols?'

It were to misspend precious time, appointed for better uses, to tell you of the abominable distinctions of the papists, of *Latria* and *Dulia*, (*n*) or to insist upon a discourse of heathenish idolatry; truths, but not so profitable for us to spend time in.   Therefore, we will rather come to shew the reasons why Ephraim so abhorreth idolatry, idols, and conceits of all.

1. To begin, in the first place, with idols.   When Ephraim is truly converted, he hates them, because idols *are abominable to God*, unto whom

Ephraim is now converted. Ephraim hates idols, for idolatry is spiritual adultery. Religion is, as it were, a conjugal act of marriage ; so that a breach in religious worship is a breach of spiritual marriage. Now, the worshipping of idols being a breach of the conjugal act of marriage betwixt God and the soul, spiritual adultery, it must needs be abominable. For adultery is an abominable, filthy thing ; much more spiritual adultery. Therefore, saith Ephraim, ' What have I now any more to do with idols ? '

2. And then again, idolatry *frameth base conceits of God.* Whereas, on the contrary, we should elevate and raise up our hearts unto him ; idolatry pulls him down, and conforms him to our base conceits. Were it not a wrong to man to make him like a swine, or an ape, or some such ridiculous creature ? Who, in this case, would think himself well used ? There is not such disproportion betwixt any creature and man as there is betwixt the great God of heaven and earth, and the best creature that can be made to resemble him. Therefore, it is an abominable abuse and dishonour to the great majesty of God to be represented any kind of way.

3. Again, *consider the opposition between any representation of God, and God.* They are corruptible things ; God is incorruptible. They are visible ; God is invisible. They are vain and nothing ; God a being of himself, who giveth being unto all things. God is the living God, and the cause of all life. To be brief : the Scripture, to shew God's hatred of them, calleth them dunghill-gods, and Abel, as it is in this book, vanity, nothing, a name to alienate the affections from them. (*o*)

4. Yea, further, because *God is a jealous God,* Exod. xxxiv. 14, and will not give his glory to another. Ephraim, therefore, as soon as he cometh to know God, he hateth idols ; because he knows God, being a jealous God, could not endure them, Isa. xlii. 8.

Now, idolatry is committed when either we set up false gods in place of the true God, or when we worship the true God in a false manner.

Quest. But now another question may be moved, Whether the papists be idolaters or not ? For we live amongst many of them ; therefore we cannot be too wary of them.

Ans. The answer is affirmative. They are idolaters, and worse in some sort than the heathen idolaters were. Only change the names of the popish saints which they in popery worship, and the names that the heathen worship, and they will be all one. Now, names be no realities.

How may this be cleared ?

First, *they give the honour due to God to others,* which is idolatry. The religious worship only due unto God, they give unto other things. Christ, when he said, ' Him only shalt thou serve,' Mat. iv. 10, excepted the least divine worship from the creature. The devil, we know, would have had him fall down before him ; but Christ's answer is, ' Him only shalt thou serve ;' that is, him only shalt thou religiously prostrate thyself unto. So that religious worship is proper to God only. Now, this they give to saints ; for they pray to them, which is religious worship.

Obj. But they object, that they pray not directly to them, but to them as mediators, that they may pray to Christ for them.

Ans. 1. First, *they raise them above their degree, to make them mediators,* and so dethrone Christ of his office of Mediator, at least join copartners with him.

2. But this is not all. *They pray directly to saints* to help them against several ills, as they have several saints for several evils. Whatsoever they

say, who are not ashamed of lying to further their designs, yet their books and writings do testify the contrary.

3. Then again, *they vow to saints*, as in the form of their vows is seen. I vow to the Virgin Mary, &c. Now, a vow is a religious act. They vow to saints, and burn incense unto them, erect temples, and set apart days for their worship, and so break all the four commandments of the first table. In a good fashion, it is not unfit to remember them, that their memorial may be kept; but we are not to worship them.

4. And, besides saints, *they have other false gods;* for their head of the church is an abominable idol, unto whom they ascribe that which is proper unto Christ, to be the head of the church, which hath no influence from him, but all from Christ, the spiritual head thereof. Therefore the apostle complaineth of such ' who hold not the head,' &c., Col. ii. 19. Those of the Romish Church ' hold not the head,' hold not Christ, because they attribute that to saints and men which is proper to Christ only. They make the pope judge of all controversies, who must give authority to the word, and determine Scripture to be Scripture. What a shameful thing is this, to make him judge of the Scriptures, which must judge him at the last day. A pitiful thing it is to see ' a man of sin' go about to judge the righteous law of God, and to determine of that which must ere long determine him unto eternal torments, without particular repentance. Yet, being spiritually drunk, this folly they are given to, that they will be judge of that which must be judge of them. Many ways they make him an idol, ascribing that to him which is proper to Christ.

5. So likewise, *they make their sacraments to be idols.*

For, 1, they ascribe to the *water in baptism* power of conferring grace.

Now, grace is God's creature only; for all the creatures in heaven and earth cannot confer the least dram of grace. It is a thing of God's making. Now, to raise an element to confer grace, and then to trust in it, *ex opere operato*, for the conferring of it, is to make an idol of it.

2. And for *the bread*. None of all the heathens ever had such an abominable idol as the mass, a breaden god, for they worshipped living creatures, and there is not the worst living creature but it is better than a piece of bread; and yet they worship that, for, by their own confession, if the intention of the priest be not to the action, there is nothing but bread. How may the minds, then, of men be tormented when they may or shall think perhaps the priest hath no such intention, and so are in danger of idolatry. For, saith the psalmist, ' their sorrows shall be multiplied that hasten after another god,' &c., Ps. xvi. 4. So certainly the sorrows and scruples of those that are idolaters shall be multiplied. They cannot but be much tormented in soul sometimes. Coster *(p)*, himself a forward Jesuit, acknowledgeth ' that if, upon the words of consecration, the bread be not turned and transubstantiated into the body of Christ, we are the most abominable idolaters of the world.' But we make the minor and assumption, long since proved by the late worthies of our church * *(q)*, but there is no such transubstantiating of the bread into the body of Christ. Therefore, by their own consent, they are the most abominable idolaters of the world, worse than the heathen.

3. And in their *equalising traditions*, which are but the inventions of man's brain, *with the Scriptures*, they commit idolatry, in that they make their very church an idol. But what should we speak of their church,

* B. Jewel, D. Rainolds, D. Fulk, D. Whitaker, D. Willet, Perkins, &c. See Note *q*.—G.

when they have the pope, who is their church virtually? for what is said of the one may be said of the other. When they come to the issue, the church is nothing but the pope. Whatsoever their church or councils say, he is the whole church. Many ways they are gross idolaters, especially the common people. For though they say they give not *Latria*, worship to the image, but *Dulia*, service, but can the common people distinguish, who give worship to all alike? To say we worship not the image, but God before the image, was the heathen's excuse, as we may see in Arnobius (*r*). Can the common people distinguish? No; for they are ignorant images themselves. In this they are worse than the heathens, because they have more light, and still the more light the more sin. For they have been foretold that the whore of Rome should be the mother of all fornications, the spiritual Babylon, Sodom, and Egypt in regard of idolatry, the mother of all these abominations, Rev. xvii. 5. Now, for them who have been forewarned hereof, and in so much light still, to continue idolaters, and persist in false worship, is to be worse than the heathens, who had not the like light and warning.

Ques. But what is the reason that they are so impudent and audacious?

Ans. 1. First, to answer with the Scriptures, *they are drunk with the whore's cup*, Rev. xvii. 2; and we know a drunken man dares do anything.

2. And then, again, as the psalmist speaks, because those who worship idols *become blockish and stupid like unto them*, for an idol is a blockish, dead thing, so idolaters are stupid, dead things in a sort, who are seldom converted, partly because they are drunk, and partly because they are stupid, like the idols they worship, Ps. cxv. 8.

Use 1. If this be so, as it is too true to the eye of the whole world, then *how ought we to bless God, who hath brought us out of this palpable Egyptian darkness, out of spiritual Sodom,* as Lot was out of that Sodom! Gen. xix. 17. Oh, we cannot be thankful enough, nor ought we to desire to return to Sodom again, or unto Egypt. Where, then, is place left for neutrality? Those neuters, that will be of neither religion! Is such a disposition from the Spirit of God, which maketh Ephraim say here, 'What have I any more to do with idols?' Ephraim would not be a neuter. Therefore, what shall we say unto them that present themselves to Masses, in their travels especially? Is this to say with Ephraim, 'What have I any more to do with idols?' We must 'believe with the heart, and confess with the mouth, to salvation,' Rom. x. 9. If a man might escape with having his heart to God-wards, and his body prostrate, where were confession? In Elias's time, God told him, that there were left seven thousand in Israel, who had not bowed the knee to Baal, that is, who made no bodily prostration, 1 Kings xix. 18. Therefore, as the papists do not join with us, so neither ought we with them, if we hold the contrary religion false. In this case we should not present ourselves with them in any service.

Use 2. Again, if this be true, *what do we think of reconcilers of religion?* A thing impossible, as the apostle sheweth. 'For what communion hath God with Belial? Christ with antichrist?' 2 Cor. vi. 14, 15. What communion? The question is a strong negation, as that of Ephraim here. 'What have I now any more to do with idols?'

Obj. But some may say, We differ from them only in circumstance.

Ans. We may ask any man who hath his brains in his head, *whether idolatry be a circumstance or not?* it being clear that they are as great idolaters as the heathens, in many instances. If any affirm that idolatry is a circumstance, there is no disputing with such a one. That which is the sin, which makes God abhor and desert his own people, is that a circumstance ?   Is that a circumstance, which is the chief sin against the first table ?   Granting that they are idolaters, that the pope is 'antichrist,' and Rome to be ' Babylon' (s), and Babylon to be the ' mother of all fornication,' this must needs follow, that there can be no reconciling of these two religions.   We may come near them, and become papists, but they will never come near us, to be good Christians.

Use 3. Again, if this be so, that popery be idolatry, and that we must beware of all idolatry, let us take heed, therefore, *that we have nothing to do with them more than we must needs.*   Converse with them in our callings, we may ; because, as an ancient father saith, we be compossessors of the world, and not of religion.   We must go out of the world, if we will not have to do with them sometimes in the places where we live ; but amity is very dangerous with such.   The Scripture runs much upon it.   Should we love them whom God hates ?   It was Eve's fault, that without a calling she ventured to talk with the serpent.   We should therefore shun conversing and parley with them as much as may be.   As there were rails set about Mount Sinai, to keep off the people from touching the mountain ; so God hath set hedges about the second commandment, to keep us off from offending in it, as it was usual with God in this kind.   As, when he would keep them far from murder, he forbade them to kill the dam with the young, Deut. xxii. 6, and not to seethe a kid in his mother's milk, Exod. xxiii. 19 ; only to restrain them from murder, that abominable sin.   Such precepts the Jews call ' the hedges of the commandments' (t).   So for idolatry, the Scripture would have us ' hate the garment spotted with the flesh,' Jude, verse 23 ; ' to defile the coverings of the images, to account them as a menstruous cloth,' &c., Isa. xxx. 22 ; and ' to have nothing to do with the unfruitful works of darkness,' Eph. v. 11 ; [and] to hate all monuments of idolatry.   As Augustine saith of monuments, ' Any monument moves and stirs up the mind ;' so anything that may move or stir us to idolatry, we should abhor, and keep afar off from it.

And therefore the commandments are set down in the highest pitch of the sin, to shew that we should avoid all the degrees under that which leads to so great a breach, and that we should hate all those steps and leadings to the sin itself.   We should therefore beware of popish writers, and do with them as was done with the magic books in the Acts, burn them all, lest they corrupt ourselves and others, Acts xix. 19.   Learn we this of the papists, who hate our books, burn them, or lock them up safe ; yea, hate the very names of Luther and Calvin, much more their books.

In this case it is with the soul of man as with water, that relisheth of that soil through which it runs, if it run through a hot soil, as baths through a sulphury soil, it tastes of that.   So the spirit of a man tastes of those authors he runs through.   Therefore such who converse much in popish writings, unless ministers who have a calling that way to confute them, are in danger to be ensnared by them.

Use 4. And then, again, if we must hate all idolatry, *we must take heed of occasions.*   Not like some looser Christians, which make no matter of crucifixes.   How doth the spirit of Ephraim here agree with such ?   A crucifix is but a teacher of lies, representing only the outside, and that falsely ; for there is no expression in Scripture, what kind of man Christ was.   And if there were, yet the apostle sheweth, ' that we must now no more know him any more after the flesh,' 2 Cor. v. 16.   Not as such a man, as tall and fair, &c. ; but know him as the Mediator, as king of heaven and earth, avoiding all lewd, base conceits of him. People in this kind are too bold, and run too near popery. A father saith well, ' No man is safe that is near danger.' We are commanded to ' fly from idolatry,' 1 Cor. x. 14. We must not come near the pit's brink, lest we fall in. Run and fly from it as from a serpent, dally not with the occasions.

But to leave this gross idolatry, to speak of something which more nearly concerneth us, and which we are prone to. Though we hate the gross idolatries, yet there be some we are more nearly addicted to ; as,

First of all, there is a proneness in us, in our worship, *to conceive false conceptions and ideas of God ;* and so in place of worshipping God, we worship an idol of our own brain.

Quest. It may be said, How shall we conceive of God when we worship him ?

Ans 1. First of all, negatively, do not dishonour God *in imagining any character of an infinite incomprehensible God,* but conceive of him as an infinite essence.

2. And then, *conceive not absolutely of God,* but of God distinguished in three persons, the Father, Son, and Holy Ghost ; or else we conceive an idol. For there are three persons in one common nature ; and in our prayers we must not conceive the nature without the persons.

3. In the third place, we must not in our prayers conceive of God, *without Christ the Mediator.* For even as God was only to be known and spoken to towards the tabernacle ; so Christ is the tabernacle now, where God manifests his gracious presence, and will be worshipped in him the Mediator. For God, considered out of Christ, is a ' consuming fire ; ' without Christ, no converse with God. Let us therefore take Christ along with us, when we go to God. Go to him by God in our nature, our Immanuel ; and so we shall conceive of God aright, and not worship an idol of our own brain.

4. Again, there is another thing which is a common abuse among Christians, wherein they come near to idolatry, *when they transform God to be like themselves in their affections,* as it is the property of all unregenerate men to do so. Idolatry is so natural, it cannot but transform God to be like itself. As for instance, a man that is not a gracious man, in the pride of his sinful course, thinks that God is like unto him. ' Thou thoughtest that I was like unto thyself ; therefore I will come against thee,' &c., Ps. l. 21. As oppressors, and such who grow great by ill courses, they justify thus much. Would God let me alone if he did not approve of my courses? So they make God like themselves. And so the good fellows of the world, they make God to allow all their dissoluteness, because he lets them alone. So those that are fierce and cruel by nature, who delight in cruelty, vexation, and blood, they transform God, as though he delighted in such things, and make him a God of blood. So others transform God to be all mercy. This is to make God an idol, and as ill as if they transformed him into this and that creature ; worse than the heathens, in regard of their light under the gospel ; yet this is the disposition of many Christians now-a-days.

Quest. What was the reason why the heathens worshipped Bacchus and Venus, such abominable gods ?

Ans. They, to countenance their lusts and drunkenness, deify them : an abominable sin of the heathen, for which God gave them up to other sins. Doth not our sin come near theirs, when we make God to countenance our sin, and cite Scripture for it, as if God can countenance sin in his word ?

This is to transform God into our own abominable conceits. Those, therefore, who bless themselves in any sinful course, they are guilty of idolatry
in the worst kind that may be ; for it is as ill to transform God to allow of
such courses, as to transform Christ to die for such who go on in their sins
without remorse, or to transform him into the likeness of such and such
vile creatures.

5. Further, there is another sort of idolatry Christians are subject unto—
to set up somewhat in their hearts higher than God. There is no man without grace, but he doth so until his conversion. Nay, when a man is
converted, he is prone to this, to idolize and set up something above that
which should be in the heart. Hereupon Paul, Col. iii. 5, calleth covetousness, idolatry ; because a covetous man placeth those affections upon his
own wealth, which should dwell in God : for, ' he saith to the wedge of
gold, Thou art my confidence,' Job xxxi. 24, thinking his wealth shall bear
him out in any ill cause whatsoever. And then, again, that time which he
should spend in thinking of God and of a better life, he buried those
thoughts in his muck and wealth, toiling and moiling in the world, when
he should serve God. Thus the covetous man is an idolater.

6. And there are some guilty of idolatry, likewise, in another kind, *such
as have men's persons too much in admiration,* that deify them, especially if
they be in great place : such who will offend God before they will offend
them ; and whereas for God's glory they should deny themselves, they
deny themselves, and make themselves fools, for men ; and to please them
by whom they hope to rise, deny both wit and honesty. This is abominable
idolatry, and such are as far from heaven and salvation, as those that fall
before an idol, if they repent not. Oh, if these men that study to please
men, and deny themselves for them, would be as careful to please God, as
they have been to please men, how happy, and what excellent Christians
would they be ! As a great man-pleaser in his time said, ' If he had served
God as well as he had served his master the king in that time, God had
not left him so in his old years' (*u*).* To set up any man so high in our
affections, as for him to deny ourselves, crack our consciences, and do
things unlawful, will be misery in the end. ' If I please men,' saith Paul,
' I am not the servant of Christ,' Gal. i. 10. He meaneth sinful pleasing,
for there ought to be service and respect. Due honour must be given
unto those who carry God's image, our governors, yea, great respect and
honour, and nothing in this kind can be too much ; but to go beyond our
bounds herein, is to commit idolatry. As the heathen did, when the
government of Rome was turned into an empire, some of their emperors
were made gods by them after Augustus's time, wherein they could not
have devised to have done them greater wrong, for they came most of them
to fearful ends (*v*). It is ill for any man to have God his co-rival ; for no
greater misery can befall a man, than to be set up in God's room, so to rule
a man's honesty, will, and conscience at his pleasure ; for God is a jealous
God, and will not endure such idolatry.

7. And so, in the next place, they frame Christ an idol, *in taking him
without his cross.* They will be of the true religion ; but when they come
to suffer anything, if it be but a frown, a reproach or disgrace, they give
out and fall back. Such, they frame to themselves an idol, a false Christ ;
for the knowledge of Christ is never without the cross, some cross or other,
some persecution or other in some kind. ' All who will live godly in
Christ, shall suffer persecution,' 2 Tim. iii. 12. A man may live godly,

* A Scottish Regent before his execution. See Note *u.*—G.

and not suffer persecution ; but he that will live godly in Christ, so as he sheweth his nature to be altered, carrying an antipathy against all false courses, and so as the world may conceive that he is such an one, it is impossible that he should live in the world without persecution, because he shall meet with those that are of an opposite disposition. Therefore, to frame a smooth Christ, all comfort, is to frame a false Christ, and a false religion,—to frame an idol that hath no truth in it, that never was, nor never will be to the end of the world.

8. Again, unconverted persons especially are prone to another idolatry, *to set up their own wits and wills instead of God's.* So as there is not a greater enemy to religion than our own conceits and wills, which will have a model of religion of our own brain, which must stand, let what will come of it. This is the fault especially of great learned persons, who take upon them conceits and apprehensions of things, and then doat upon these brats of their own brain. And so for will, to have our own will in all things ; as the speech is, ' My mind to me a kingdom is.' I will have my will, whatsoever come of it. This is idolatry ; for whosoever will come to heaven must deny his will. The first lesson in Christ's school is self-denial, Mat. xix. 21, 24 : denial of wit and will, to have no more wit and wisdom, especially in divine things, than God will teach us ; and no more will, which is distinct and opposite to Christ's will, but to bring our wills to his in all things. When men will go about great affairs, and set upon things in their own wit and strength, never praying nor depending upon God for a blessing, this is a kind of idolising of parts to work out things by policy, strength, wits, and parts. As that heathen atheist could say, ' Let cowards pray, if they will ;' but his success was answerable. So is it not the common atheism of the world ? They go about things in confidence of their wit and parts, and so hope to attain a glorious issue ; whereas God, who overthrows Babels, takes delight to confound all their devices. It is his daily practice ' to send the rich empty away, and exalt the humble and meek,' Luke i. 52. Those who set upon things rashly without prayer, as though they were lords of all, and without dependence upon God, promising themselves good success, they make idols of themselves. As a proud man is an idol, ' he worships himself,' whilst he leans to his own wit, plots, and parts. Carnal men thus idolise themselves.

9. Again, you have some who are none of the worst who commit this great sin of idolatry, *by trusting to the outward performances and tasks of religion*, thinking that God must needs be bound unto them, when they have done so many tasks, read, and prayed, or heard so many sermons, or done a good deed. But here lieth the spiritual subtlety, in that they set up these things too high, when, if they find not that success they look for, then they inwardly murmur against God ; when rather all these things should be done with a spirit of humility and subjection, using them only as means whereupon we expect God's blessing, craving his assistance and strength to do them in a holy and a self-denying manner. When we do otherwise, and trust to the outward tasks and performances we do, we make them idols. And you have many that go along with outward performances who never come to a dram of grace, because they trust to the outward performances, and look not to the life and soul of them, which is the Spirit of God assisting, quickening, strengthening, blessing them. The life of a Christian is a perpetual dependence upon God in the use of means, and not an idolising of them, to be careless when he hath done his task.

10. But a more subtle idolatry than this is of another kind, *when we trust too much to the work of grace, and rely not upon God in Christ*, in the matter of justification and acceptation to life everlasting, which is a fault, both,

1. Before conversion.

2. After conversion.

First, *before conversion*. When we think we have not done so much good, and been sufficiently humbled, and therefore that God will not be merciful to us, as if Christ must take us with dowry of good deeds, or else he cannot ; whereas all grace is promised upon our entry and coming into the covenant of grace, upon our believing, when we come with empty hearts and hands. 'The poor,' saith Christ, 'receive the gospel ; and those that are lost, Christ is sent to save them, and to call in the weary and heavy laden,' Mat. xi. 5, ix. 13, xi. 28.

2. And *after conversion*. Those that are in the state of grace oftentimes want that comfort in the main point of justification and acceptation to life everlasting, which they should have, because they look into their imperfections, seeing this and that want, and so are swallowed up of discomfort ; whereas, if we had all the graces in the world, yet we must live by faith, relying upon the merits of Christ. For our good works bring us not to heaven, as a cause, but only are helps and comforts to us in our walking to heaven. For if we had all the sins of all men, yet Christ's all-sufficient righteousness is sufficient for to do them all away, if we can go out of ourselves, and cleave to that. Therefore, in trouble of conscience we must not look either to our good or our ill, but to God's infinite mercy, and to the infinite satisfaction of our blessed Saviour the Lord Jesus Christ ; there, as it were, losing ourselves, seeing our sins as mountains drowned in the infinite sea of his mercy. The blood of Christ ! That will pacify and stay the conscience. Nothing else can give rest to our souls. If we look to our works and to the measure of our sanctification, what saith holy Paul in the like case ? 'Yea, doubtless, and I count all things but loss, for the excellency of the knowledge of Christ Jesus my Lord, for whom I have suffered the loss of all things, and do count them but dung, that I may win Christ,' Phil. iii. 8, even his righteousness and best works. Therefore there is no regard to be had of them in that case. Wherefore when we would speak comfort to a distressed conscience, we must not look to his ill or good, but to the command, 'This is his command, that we believe,' 1 John iii. 23. And look to the all-sufficiency of God in Christ, and the promises, whereby we honour God in giving him the glory of his truth, and depart with comfort. Therefore, though we hate gross idolatry, yet we see there are many ways wherein the soul may be seduced, whereby we may come very near that sin which our soul hateth, by trusting too much to something out of God.

Use 5. If then the case be thus, *how shall we come to reform it*, for a use of direction, so as to fly from all idolatry, and to say with Ephraim, 'What have I now any more to do with idols ?'

First of all, *do but consider God's hatred unto all sorts of idolaters ;* for he accounts such to hate him, and so accordingly punisheth them. In the second commandment, those that are given to idolatry in any kind, are such as hate God, which is a horrible thing ; and yet, notwithstanding, this is the disposition of all such as are idolaters. So far forth as they are idolaters, they hate God, for the more we know God, the more we shall hate all idols, 'What have I now any more to do with idols ?'

2. Labour *to grow in the sound knowledge of God and of Christ, and of their all-sufficiency.* Mark St Paul's method, Col. ii., and in other places, when he would draw us from all outward things, he speaks gloriously of the fulness of Christ, ' In him dwelleth all the fulness of the Godhead bodily,' Col. ii. 9 ; and, ' In him you are complete.' When he would draw them from ' touch not, taste not, handle not, worshipping of angels, and from counterfeit humility,' Col. ii. 21, &c., he labours to dispossess them of these idolatrous conceits, and to possess them of the fulness of Christ. If in him we have fulness, why should we look for any thing out of him ? If we be complete in him, if all fulness be in him, why do we seek any thing out of that fulness ? Thus the holy apostle shutteth up his first epistle, ' Babes, keep you from idols,' 1 John v. 21. What is promised there ? Christ is eternal life, all is in him ; whereupon presently comes this, ' Babes, keep you from idols ?' If life and happiness, and all be in Christ, if we be complete in him, and the fulness of all be in him, why should we go out of him for anything ? When God would persuade Abraham to leave all idolatry, Gen. xvii. 1, and all things else, to depend wholly upon him, what doth he first possess him with ? ' I am God all-sufficient,' &c. Know God in covenant all-sufficient, and Christ in the fulness of his high perfections as Mediator, in whom is all fulness and life eternal, in whom we are complete ; we shall then be so far from going out of him for any thing, as we shall be of the same mind with Ephraim, ' What have I now any more to do with other intercessors and mediators ?' what have I to do with will-worship ? what need I go to other cursed means, when God is all-sufficient ? It is the scope of the new covenant of grace, that we should glory in God only, who hath made Christ unto us ' wisdom, righteousness, sanctification, and redemption,' 1 Cor. i. 30. And all this, because that whosoever glorieth in him, should not go out of him for any thing. The more we know therefore the fulness of Christ, and 'God's mercy in him, the more we shall abhor all idolatry, with the kinds and degrees of it.

3. Another help and means to cure this disposition in us is, *to know that we are naturally wondrous prone to it in one degree or another.* It is reckoned up, Gal. v. 20, as a work of the flesh ; and, naturally, man hath a working fancy, to set up somewhat in his heart and understanding above, and besides God, imaginations to adulterate things. Men live by sense, and imagination is next to sense, so that naturally all men are idolaters before conversion, in one kind or other, and doat so upon their own, that they will not be driven out of themselves unto God in Christ, without a great deal of grace. As men naturally love the child of their own body, so men love the children of their own brain.

Quest. What is the reason that it is so hard to convert a papist ?

Ans. Because it is will-worship, a device of their own brain, suiting their natural will and appetite. And what makes them so furious, as all idolaters are cruel : though they be mild of their own nature, yet as idolaters, they are cruel. It is because it is a device of their own brain, a brat, a child of their own begetting, wherefore they strive to maintain it, because it is their own. Let us therefore conceive thus much, that it is no easy matter to free the soul from idolatry, and all the degrees of this cursed disposition. This will make us beg earnestly the Spirit of God, by which only we shall subdue this idolatrous proud conceit, Rom. viii. 5, and lay ourselves open to Christ, to be disposed of as he pleaseth. Beg the Spirit only, whereby we shall mortify the cursed deeds of the flesh, for nature will never subdue nature. The Spirit of God therefore is that which can, and must free us from all dregs and tainture of this cursed disposition, which the Jews were so scourged for, and hardly* driven from.

4. Again, consider *God's punishments in this kind.* As we see, Rev. ix. 20, where the Turk is said to be raised up against all these idolaters, that would not be kept from worshipping the devil and the image of the beast; yet for all this, it is said, 'they did not repent.' And so the Jewish church was still punished with enemies raised up against them for their idolatry. And it is to be expected that the idolatry of these western churches will at length pull down antichrist himself, which must be before the conversion of the Jews. For what hinders their conversion now? The world is full of idolaters, even Christians; and therefore there must be a confusion of antichrist's idolatrous worship before the conversion of the Jews, who will not return whilst that scandal is in their eye. Therefore, that we may help forward that glorious work, let us labour as much as we can to purge the church of this, in drawing others from idolatry, that we may help to make way for those glorious times a-coming; for this Scripture specially hath relation unto the calling of the Jews, not to be fulfilled till then, when 'Ephraim shall say, What have I now any more to do with idols?' with that for which we have been so plagued for in former times.

5. And withal let us consider this, that the end of all false worship, when it is left, *is grief and shame, befooling and shaming of ourselves for it.* 'Ephraim at length shall say, What have I any more to do with idols?' to cherish pride and self-conceit? which, if ever I come to heaven, I must renounce, hating myself for my own pride and folly.

6. And so for idolaters themselves, why *should we consort ourselves with these, of whom we shall say one day, What have we any more to do with them?* We must be separated from them here, or in hell live with them for ever. What will then be the hell of hell? Mutual cursing of one another. Thy familiarity and acquaintance, thy provocations and allurements, brought me into these torments! If we belong to God, late or soon, there must be these speeches, 'What have I now any more to do with such and such lying vanities?'

Therefore let us not think will-worship a slight matter; for, we see, popery is nothing else but a bundle of man's devices. We see in Scripture, when the dearest friends of Christ came unto him with devices of their own, and good intentions, Christ notwithstanding saw the devil in them. Peter made a great confession, 'Thou art the Son of the living God,' Mat. xvi. 16, and then he came 'Master, spare thyself,' ver. 22; whereunto Christ replied, 'Get thee behind me, Satan,' ver. 23. God is never more provoked than when men think to honour him with their own devices; stablishing a false, and neglecting his own true, worship. And there is usually little amendment of these kind of persons, because they carry with them a show of wisdom, as Paul saith, Col. ii. 23, and great humility; which things being so carried with a show of some grace and wisdom (though they be desperate folly in the conclusion), men hardly will part withal. As we see of corporal adultery, few of them are reclaimed, because it hath a bewitching, alluring power; which is most true of the spiritual adulterers. There are few of them reclaimed, until God, by some severe judgment, alter and bring down the proud imagination to serve him as he will be served; so as to say with Ephraim here, 'What have I now any more to do with idols?'

Well, that we may abhor idolatry the more, consider two or three direct
* That is, 'with difficulty.'—G.

places. ' Who required these things at your hands ? ' saith God, Isa. i. 12. When we think to please him with voluntary devised things, this will strike them dumb then. The things that God requires being so easy and so few, yet we to omit them all, and to devise new things of our own, our reward shall be, ' Who required these things at your hands ? ' And then again saith God, ' In vain they worship me, teaching for my precepts the devices of men,' Mat. xv. 9. See then the vanity of idolaters, who, though they would do nothing in vain, yet do all their will-worship in vain. It is not only idolatry, but obstinate idolatry, the Romish doctrine. ' We would have cured Babel, but she would not be cured,' Jer. li. 9. Is this a light cause of our coming out of Babylon? Do we leave them for trifles, when they stand guilty of abominable idolatry? You may see here, if so be Ephraim out of holy affection say, ' What have I now any more to do with idols ? ' what to think and judge of those that would bring God and idols together. If Ephraim had been of the temper that many men now are, he might have said, ' Tush ! what need we care for idols, crucifixes, and the like ? There is not such a distance betwixt them and us, why may not both religions stand together? This new-fangled niceness is but the distempered devices of some few giddy-headed men, who know not what they would have.' This is the wisdom of many men in our times, who reckon that there is not an eternal, irreconcilable distance between light and darkness, the service of God and that of idols. ' We cannot serve two masters,' saith Christ, Mat. vi. 24. Yes, they say, we may serve two masters, Antichrist and Christ, God and Belial. Oh! but what saith Ephraim? ' What have I now any more to do with idols ? ' There can be no mixture, you know, where there is abomination. That church, Rev. iii. 15, which was neither hot nor cold, may parallel many now in our times, who are neither hot nor cold, papists nor protestants, but politic atheists, who will be both or neither, whatsoever may best serve and advance their worldly ends. How doth God look upon such? Saith he, ' I will spue them out of my mouth.' God hates such most of all : ' now I would thou wert either hot or cold.' If this be the affection of God's people toward idols and idolaters, an utter aversation ; and shall we think to jumble and mingle contrary things together, to serve God and the devil, Christ and antichrist ?

Thus we see what to think of the temper of these men. In lighter matters indeed we may enjoy our own private opinions in some things. As St Paul saith in lesser things, ' If any man be otherwise minded, God shall reveal it unto him,' Phil. iii. 15. But when he comes to the point of justification by Christ in God's worship, what saith he ? ' If any man be otherwise minded, God shall reveal it ? ' No. But ' if I, or an angel from heaven, teach otherwise, let him be accursed,' Gal. i. 8. Now, when men teach another doctrine and worship, joining with gross idolaters in that worship, there we must be of Paul's spirit, ' If I, or an angel from heaven, teach otherwise, let him be accursed.' The Holy Ghost at first appeared in the form and shape of a dove, Mat. iii. 16, which is a meek and mild creature, that hath no talons to hurt with. Yet notwithstanding, at another time, he appeared in ' fiery tongues,' Acts ii. 3, to shew that the same Spirit that in lesser things maintaineth peace and love, when it is set against any sin, especially against that sin of sins, idolatry, which brings God's vengeance upon kingdoms and states, and roots them out ; there the Holy Ghost must appear in fire. That element must be in the hearts of people against sin. That, though to persons that have their slips, and in lesser matters, there must be the spirit of a dove, yet there must be in men the spirit of courage, indignation, abomination, and hatred unto the idolatry of the times, that we may say from our hearts with Ephraim, ' What have I now any more to do with idols ? '

Therefore, *let us join with those that we shall live for ever with in heaven*, and go in the best courses, and we shall never need to fear separation, nor want encouragements to well-doing. Thus shall we neither grieve nor be ashamed to say with Ephraim, ' What have I now any more to do with idols ?' At the length the kings of the earth, who adore the whore, they shall come and eat her very flesh, Rev. xvii. 16. So it will be the end of those that reign in other men's consciences, and in a manner will be accounted gods, that all which is gotten with wrong to God, shall be renounced with grief, shame, and detestation of the persons of those that make idols of others, and will be made idols in the hearts of others ; thinking themselves not enough respected, unless they command the conscience. The end of such cannot be good. All this must end in loathing, shame, and detestation. ' What have I now any more to do with idols ?' said Ephraim ; and what have I now any more to do with such and such profaneness, hypocrisy, double-dealing, and the like ? shall such persons, thus sinful, say one day, with shame and horror of conscience. Wherefore, let us meet God betimes, and renounce our idols of all sorts, that God may come ' to hear us, observe us, and be as a green fir-tree unto us,' &c. Whereof, if God please, we shall hear more the next time.

THE TWELFTH SERMON.

Ephraim shall say, What have I any more to do with idols ? I have heard him and observed him : I am like a green fir-tree: from me is thy fruit found.—Hos. XIV. 8.

THE words, as we heard heretofore, are a gracious answer unto the prayer which God himself, by his Spirit, had dictated to Ephraim : as likewise a reward of Ephraim's reformation. Aided by grace, Ephraim shall say, ' What have I now any more to do with idols ?' ' God will hear him and observe him, and be like a green fir-tree unto him.' For, saith God, ' from me shall Ephraim's fruit be found.' Whereby we see, that whensoever God doth alter the soul by his grace, there he also breeds divorce and division between it and all idolatry ; a disposition in some sort like himself, having those sympathies and antipathies he hath towards sin and goodness. Now, because God is a jealous God, and cannot abide idols ; therefore Ephraim, being sanctified by the Spirit of God, is minded as God is, ' What have I any more to do with idols ?'

1. God hath framed the soul, *that it may enjoy the chief good*, and avoid the chief ill especially ; for petty goods and petty ills are not so behoveful. Yet notwithstanding, God will have us avoid all ill, and embrace all good, and he hath made the soul into an answerable condition. Therefore hath he planted affections therein tending to good ; as love, and joy, and delight, especially made for the embracing of the main good, thereby to go out of itself, and close with that main chief good, in closing wherewith it may be happy.

2. And then, *to avoid the chief ill, sin and damnation*, he hath planted affections of aversation, abhorring, hatred, grief, and the like. Thus hath he framed the soul for these main ends, without which affections the soul were as *mare mortuum*, that dead sea. The affections are the wings and the wind of the soul, that carry it unto all which it is carried unto. Especially, when the wind of God's Spirit blows upon it, then it is carried out of itself; for of itself it cannot love or hate as it should; but God must raise the affections, and lay them down again. We have not the management of our hearts. Grace teacheth us to do all.

The particular then here is, *indignation and hatred*. ' What have I now any more to do with idols?' So that the proper affection in God's children, which should be conversant about that which is ill, and sinfully ill, is hatred and indignation. Here is hatred with indignation, the extent of the affection.

Reas. 1. The reason whereof is, when God's children are once converted, *they have a new nature put into them*, like unto Christ, whose Spirit they have. What he hates, they hate. He hates all sin, and nothing but sin. He hates the devil himself for sin, and no further.

2. Then, again, when once they are God's children, *they have a new life put into them*, which hath antipathy to all that is contrary to it. Every life in any creature hath antipathy to every enemy thereof. There is antipathy in doves to birds of prey; and in the lamb to the wolf, because they are enemies to the life and being of them. So in the soul of a Christian, so far as grace is renewed, there is an antipathy, aversation, and abhorring of that which is contrary. What have I to do with sin in any kind? When grace hath altered the disposition of a man's heart, then sin and he are two; two indeed, in the most opposite terms that may be. What have I any more to do with my former delightful sins? We are two now, for we were before nothing but sin. And, indeed, where this hatred is not, there men may leave sin, because sin leaves them; but this is not enough, God would have us to hate it with indignation. ' What have I now any more to do with it?'

Quest. But how should we come to have this true hatred of sin, as Ephraim should have?

Ans. 1. Amongst those helps formerly named, this is a main one, to represent to the soul (as the soul is quick and nimble in such apprehensions) *the odiousness of sin*, that it is a truly hateful thing; and therefore, that our affection of hatred cannot be better set nor employed upon any object than that of sin. For let us consider that it is not only ill in itself, defiling the soul and hindering communion with God; but it is also the cause of all ills, being the ill of ills, as God is the good of goods. For our troubles and terrors of conscience, we may thank sin, and for all that we suffer every day in our conditions of life. What is all, but the fruit of our own ways? ' Wherefore suffereth living man?' saith the prophet; ' man suffereth for his sin,' Lam. iii. 39. ' Thine own inventions have brought these things upon thee; therefore they are bitter unto thee, they shall pierce thy bowels,' Jer. iv. 18. Shall we not, therefore, hate that which is the cause of all mischief to us? If we had an enemy, especially if he were a soothing false enemy, that under pretence of love should seek our bane and ruin, and join with our worst enemies, would we not hate such an enemy? Sin is the greatest enemy which we have in the world, and doth us more harm than the devil himself; for it betrays us to the devil, and, under pretence of favouring and pleasing our nature, betrays us. It is a false, deceitful enemy, which cometh not in an ugly shape, but closes with the soul in a kind of conjugal love, Delilah-like enticing and alluring us, whereby it hath the more advantage and strength, in that it appears in a lovely, pleasing, and not in an imperious, commanding manner. Therefore, it should be the more hateful to us. Shall we not hate such an enemy as always dogs us, and hinders us? hinders us from doing anything well, and puts us on to all that is ill. It is such an enemy, that we cannot go about to pray, or do any good thing, but it hangs upon us, and clogs us in all our performances. If a man knew that such an one as made love to him and all his were his great grand enemy, aiming at his destruction, would a man ever love such a man? Thy base, false, revengeful, covetous, worldly heart, it joins with Satan, without which he could not hurt thee. Shall a man cherish that which betrays him to his worst enemy, the devil? and then, should he cherish that which makes a breach betwixt him and his best friend? If a man saw one so maliciously evil towards him, as to sow dissension by all means he could betwixt him and his best honourable friend, by whom he was maintained in all things, would not a man hate such a one? What doth sin else but breed division and enmity betwixt God and us? And further, when it hath moved us to do ill, it crieth for vengeance against us at God's hands. Conscience, soundly awakened, is always clamorous to pull somewhat from God against us. Are not sinners justly called fools? Either men must be atheists to deny all, or else, if they cherish sin, they must needs be fools, and stark mad, if they confess this, that they join with that which is their chief enemy. Therefore, learn to be wise to salvation; make not with Solomon's fool a sport of sin, Prov. x. 23, of swearing, of defiling ourselves and others, seeing God threateneth damnation unto such.

Ans. 2. And then again, *avoid all parley and intercourse with sin in the first suggestions*, or with wicked persons that may draw us away. Use sin ruggedly and harshly, as they do here. ' What have I to do with idols?' Do but entertain parley with it, and it is of such an insinuating nature, that it will encroach daily, and spread over the soul suddenly, betraying it to the devil. Therefore, use it hardly in the first beginnings, and avoid Satan in the first suggestions, if we love the peace of our souls; as Ephraim here, ' What have I any more to do with idols?' For as we say in case of honesty, they come too near that come to have the refusal. They should not have so much hope from a chaste person. There should be such a modest carriage as should not give any one the boldness to adventure in that kind. So if a man carry himself remotely from sinful courses, he shall have a great deal of peace from wicked men, who dare not so much as adventure to draw away such a one. They know he is resolved. Therefore, constant resolution against all sin and wicked men will breed a great deal of peace, so as to say with Ephraim, ' What have I any more to do with idols?'

Ans. 3. And *we must know that this hatred comes from the life of God in us.* Therefore we must by all means maintain spiritual life; and then, as we grow spiritual, we shall grow in the detestation of sin, a sense of joy in good things, with a hatred of all that is contrary. A man can never hate sin till he hath the Spirit of Christ in him. For there be three queries, whereof this is the last.

1. The first is set down, ' No man said, What have I done?' Jer. viii. 6. When conscience in a man is awakened once, he saith, Oh! what have I done? what case am I in?

2. The second query of a wakened conscience is, ' What shall I do?'

As that, 'Men and brethren, what shall we do to be saved?' Acts ii. 37. He that truly saith, 'What have I done?' if conscience be awakened, will also say, 'What shall I do?' You shall not need to drive him when the question is answered, 'What shall I do to be saved?' that is, by casting myself upon God in Christ.

3. We need not put the question, he will say of himself, 'What have I any more to do with that which is contrary to that which saves me?' 'What have I to do with idols?' This comes in in the last place. 1. A man is awakened out of his natural condition. 2. Then he goes to God in Christ. And then, 3. There is a spiritual life wrought in him, which stirs him up to hate all that is contrary unto it. 'What have I now any more to do with idols?'

'For I have heard him and observed him.'

'I have seen and observed him,' some read the words, but very few (w); which is thus a very good and pious construction of them. 'What have I now any more to do with idols?' As if Ephraim should say these words, 'I have seen him and observed him;' that is, because I have seen him and observed; therefore, 'What have I now any more to do with idols?' As soon as a man comes to hear God speak, and to observe God, down goes all idols; for, indeed, the respect to idolatry, and anything that is naught, it falls down in the soul, as the knowledge of the true God is lifted up, and as affection to good things are raised up in the soul. 'What have I to do with idols any more?' 'I have seen and observed him.' As Job said of himself when he had seen God, 'I abhor myself, and repent in dust and ashes,' Job xlii. 6; much more all false courses. I abhor them all, now that 'I have seen and observed him.'

This is a safe, pious, and good sense; but the words, under correction, are fitliest applied unto God himself, as if God rather than Ephraim said thus, 'I will hear him and observe him;' I will do thus and thus; 'I will be as a green fir-tree,' to shade him from danger, and to make him fruitful.

Obj. But you will say, Ephraim cannot cast away idols till God respect him first. Therefore, this is promised in the second place. 'Ephraim shall say, What have I to do with idols?' And God shall say, 'I have seen him, heard him, and observed him,' when he hath cast away idols.

Ans. To this the answer is: Indeed, in the order of nature, God doth first stir us up to pray to him, and promiseth us respect and hearing of our prayers, after which we cast away idols; but the experience of it is after we have done the deed. After that we have found God experimentally gracious, protecting and hearing of us, then we cast away idols. So this experience a Christian finds when he abominates and rejects ill ways. Then he finds God all-sufficient, as indeed God is never fully felt and known till we renounce all other helps. So the general point is,

Obs. That nothing is lost by renouncing idolatry and carnal confidence in any worldly thing.

For God makes a supply in himself. 'I will hear him and observe him.' Nothing is lost, for God will be true of his promise. 'Seek ye first the kingdom of God and his righteousness, and all other things shall be ministered unto you,' Mat. vi. 33. The truth of God, and then his mercy, makes this good. Is not God merciful to his children when they renounce all false confidence? In regard of the truth of his promise and mercy, he will make good this, that nothing is lost by cleaving to him. We read in the story of our own times, in King Edward the Sixth's reign, the same day that there was reformation of idolatry in London, purging of churches from roods* and idols, the same day was that noble victory and conquest in the north parts over the enemies (*x*). So God answered their care in reforming things amiss with good success.

On the contrary, when we go on with favouring abuses and corruptions, yet expecting good success, it is in vain. Let Ephraim come to say, 'What have I to do with idols?' and see then whether God will respect him or not. Do nations or persons think that God will respect them or bless them, whilst they do that which is abominable to him? No; when Ephraim saith, 'What have I to do with idols?' then presently comes, God 'will hear and observe him, and look to him;' as you have it in that gracious promise, 'The eyes of the Lord are open unto all them that fear him, and his ears are open to their prayers,' Ps. xxxiv. 15. His eyes and his ears. Indeed, God is all eye and all ear. The best friend in the world cannot have his eye always upon us. The mother's eye cannot be always upon her child. She must have a time to sleep, when neither her eyes nor ears are open to her child's prayers. It may cry, and die in crying sometimes, before she can help it. But if we renounce sin, we have a gracious Father 'who will hear us, observe us, and see us,' and not only hear and see, but, as the Scripture phraise s, do that that follows all this. Where he sees, he will pity and relieve; and where he hears, he will pity and protect.

'I have heard him, I have observed him.' God will hear, when once we renounce sin. 'If I regard iniquity in my heart, God will not hear my prayers,' Ps. lxvi. 18, saith David. But when I do not regard iniquity, God will hear my prayers. Then a man may know that God will hear him, when once he hath renounced sin, and comes with clean hands and heart to God. As it is in Isaiah, they were corrupted in their course, and yet came to God, Isa. i. 11, *seq*, but he rejects all; so in the last of that prophecy, he accounts of their sacrifices as of the cutting off of a dog's neck, because their hands were full of blood, and they were full of sin, Isa. lxvi. 3. Reform abuses, let there be personal and national reformation; and then come and reason the matter with God, and see whether he will regard us or not. The Spirit, it is said, makes requests for the saints, and 'God knoweth the meaning of the Spirit, because it makes request according to the will of God,' Rom. viii. 27. The same Spirit that stirs us up to amend our lives, and fly idolatrous courses, the same Spirit stirs us up to pray to God, according to the will of God; and then God hears the desires of his own Spirit. Of all judgments in the world, this is the greatest, to pray and not to be heard; for when we are in misery, our remedy is prayer. Now when that which should be our remedy is not regarded, what a pitiful thing is that? Now, here is an excellent blessing set down, to pray, and for God to hear, 'I will hear him, and observe him.' Because then, God and Ephraim were of one mind, and join in one, therefore God cannot but hear and regard Ephraim, being of his mind, to love and to hate what he loves and hates. As soon as ever the prodigal began to hate his former courses, the father came out to meet him, Luke xv. 20, *seq.*; and so of David, 'I said I will confess my sins to God,' Ps. xxxii. 5. I said, that is, in my heart, I resolved to confess to God, and thou forgavest mine iniquity. God heard his resolution. We cannot else entertain a full purpose to go to God, unless there be a cessation from sin. The prodigal, for all his contrition, was afraid to be shaken off his father, for his dissolute life. Oh, but the father provides a banquet. So it is when we turn to God, and re-

* That is, 'crosses,' as in Scotland, Holyrood = holy cross.—G.

solve a new life, to cast away our idolatries, and former abominations ; presently, ' God hears us, and observes us,' and is ready to meet us.

There is an excellent place, even touching Ephraim himself. ' I have surely heard Ephraim bemoaning himself: Thou hast chastised me, and I was chastised, as a bullock unaccustomed to the yoke : turn me to thee, and I shall be turned ; thou art the Lord my God, &c. Is Ephraim a dear son ? is he a pleasant child ? for since I spake against him, I do earnestly remember him still ; therefore my bowels are troubled for him : I will have mercy upon him,' Jer. xxxi. 18. If Ephraim begin to bemoan himself for his folly, presently follows, that God's bowels are turned to him ; so it is said of Ephraim here. After he had renounced idols, God's bowels are turned towards him, ' I have heard him, and observed him.' Which yields us a sweet and comfortable consideration, *to turn to God from all our sinful courses*, because God is so ready to forgive, and to forgive great sins. What if our sin be idolatry, the grand sin of the first table ? Yet if Ephraim say, ' What have I do with idols ?' (though it be spiritual adultery), yet if Ephraim begin to renounce idolatry, God will say, ' I have heard him, and observed him.' If your sins were ' as red as crimson,' saith God, ' I will make them as white as wool,' &c., Isa. i. 18. Crimson sins, double-dyed sins, it is no matter what they are, if we come to God. There is more mercy in him than sin in us. If Ephraim say, What have I to do with my former evil courses, ' God will hear him, and observe him.'

It is never better with a Christian, than when he hath renounced all wicked courses, (though he thinks himself undone if he leaves his former Delilah delights). But there is no such matter, for we shall find an hundredfold more in God, as Christ speaks, ' Whosoever leaves father or mother, brother or sister, house or kindred for me, shall have a hundredfold in this world,' Mat. xix. 29 ; that is, they shall have it in contentment and grace, in peace of conscience, and perhaps in the things of this life in another kind. What lost Abraham when he obeyed God, and forsook his father's house ? God was all-sufficient for him. He grew a rich man. And what lost he by giving Isaac to God ? He received his son again, of whom there came an innumerable seed. And what lost holy David, in waiting for the time that he should come unto the kingdom, without making haste ? He came quietly to the possession of the crown ; whereas Jeroboam, who made more haste, after God had told him he should reign, he was cursed in his government, and none of his posterity came to good. There is nothing lost by depending and waiting upon God, and renouncing of carnal confidence. We think naturally we are undone. Oh, there is no such matter, as David speaks, ' When my father and mother forsaketh me, yet the Lord taketh me up,' Ps. xxvii. 10. As we know in the gospel, when the blind poor man was excommunicated and cast out, after he had spoke somewhat stoutly to the Pharisees, ' Will ye also be his disciples ?' John ix. 27, yet then Christ takes him presently into his company, being expelled by them. What lost he by this ? So when Israel had lost all their fleshpots in Egypt, they had no loss, for God provided them manna from heaven, and what lost they by that ? They had angels' food instead of their garlic and onions.

' I have observed him.'

That is, I will have a special eye to him ; I will look to him in all conditions and states whatsoever. God never slumbers nor sleeps. Like the master of the house in the parable, who, when the poor man came for bread, Luke xi. 5, all the rest being asleep, is awaked, and raised up by the importunity of the poor man.   So the great master of the family of heaven and earth, that governs all, he wakes day and night, and never sleeps ; herein going beyond the care of the dearest friends we have in the world, for they must have a time to sleep.   The mother, though she love the child as her own bowels, yet notwithstanding she must have a resting time, and perhaps in that time the child may miscarry ; but God always observes ; his eye is always upon his children, they are before him, written ' in the palms of his hands, he hath them in his eye,' Isa. xlix. 16 : as in Exodus, you have there God brought in observing the children of Israel.   ' I have seen, I have seen the affliction of my people Israel,' Exod. iii. 7.   They thought themselves neglected of God, but he tells Moses, ' I have seen, I have seen,' I know it very well ; he adds knowledge to sight.   So there is no affliction in this world to God's children, but God in seeing sees.   As before, he hears the groans and sighs ; so he sees the most intimate inward affliction whatsoever that afflicts the soul ; as they were grieved in very soul at the tyranny of Pharaoh.   Oh, but God in seeing he sees, whose eyes are ten thousand times brighter than the sun !   This is a consolation, when one thinks that no man sees and regards ; alas, what shall become of me !   Why should any man say so, that hath God to go to, who is all eye, and all ear !   God hears and sees ; his ears are always open, as it is often shewed, especially, Ps. xxxiv. 15.

It is said, ' His ears are open to their prayers, and his eyes to see their afflictions.'

Quest. But with what kind of eye doth God see the afflictions of his children ?

Solution. He sees them with a tender, compassionate eye ; for he aboundeth in those affections which he hath put into a father and mother. There is no mother would suffer her child to miscarry, if she could help it. God sees surely* some afflictions are for our good, or he would relieve us ; for as he hath a compassionate eye, so he hath a tender heart, and a powerful hand.   He sees wicked men also ; but his eyes in regard of them are ' like a flame of fire,' not only because he is quick-sighted, but because he sees with a revengeful† eye ; and as his eyes are like a flame of fire, so likewise he hath feet of brass to tread them to powder, Rev. i. 14, 15.

Use 1. And this likewise is no little part of our comfort ; for when we suffer anything in this world, it is from ill men for the most part, except it be in those afflictions wherein we more immediately deal with God, as in sickness, &c.   But in persecution in the world, our trouble lies with men. Therefore it is our comfort, God sees our trouble, and their malice ; and as he is ready to help the one, so he is to revenge the other.

Use 2. And as it is a point of comfort, so of great encouragement to be bold in God's cause.   What ! shall we be baser than the base creatures ? Take but a dog in his master's sight, you see how he will fight.   Take the meanest and basest creature, when it hath a superior nature to itself, that it ‡ is wiser and greater, that encourageth and sets it on, that it knows will see it take no harm, these base creatures will be courageous ; which otherwise if it had none to set it on, had no courage at all, at least not so much.   And shall we in the sight of God, and when we are set in his quarrel, and have his encouragement and his command, with promise of his presence and assistance, flinch and fly off then ?   It argues a great deal of atheism and infidelity of heart.   God sees me and looks on me while I fight, and while I stand for his cause.   God's cause is true and just, God

* That is, ' assuredly.'—G.   † That is, ' avenging.'—G.   ‡ Qu. ' it knows?'—ED.

sees me, and he sees who opposeth me. In regard of the eye of God therefore, let us be courageous in these things that are agreeable to the mind of God, whatsoever they be, whether matters of justice or piety.

Use 3. Again, if God have such an ear to hear us, let us have an ear to hear him, and an eye to look to him. Let us have Moses' eye to look on him who is invisible, Heb. xi. 26. His eye is upon us, and let our eye be to him ; both may be together. When these two eyes meet ; when my heart tells me that God seeth me, and that I see God looking upon me, this makes courageous. Therefore as God hears and sees us, so we must have an eye to see him that is invisible. And so we pass from these words, ' I have heard him and observed him ; ' and what the prophet's meaning is. ' I have heard him, and will hear him ; I have observed him, and will observe him.' For they contain a perpetual action in God; not that he hath, and will not do it now, but what he hath done and will do. That he sets down here in borrowed speeches, for he saith also,

' I will be like a green fir-tree to him: from me is thy fruit found.'

God will be ' like a green fir-tree ' in regard of shadow. A fir-tree is a high tree, a goodly, smooth tree, barren in regard of fruit, but it hath thick leaves, which hinders rain from falling upon those who rest under the shadow thereof, and likewise keeps the sun from annoying them. So it is a fit tree for shadow, and the fitter, because it hath no fruit. For usually those trees which spend not themselves this way, they spend themselves in leaves, and have a perpetual greenness, which is supplied with that which should be fruit in fruitful trees. Therefore he sets it down by this comparison of a fir-tree, that so God will keep back all showers, tempests, and storms, and all annoying heat, and he will do it perpetually, as the fir-tree hath a perpetual greenness ; and he will do it with pleasure and delight, as it is a delightful shadow. But because the fir-tree hath no fruit on it, God will not only be a shadow to his children to keep ill from them, but he will be a fruitful tree to them. 'From me,' saith God, ' shall thy fruit be found;' that is, whatsoever good thou doest, thou shalt have it from me. All fruitful comfort comes from me, and all grace. Whatsoever is good for thee, for prosperity of soul or body, all is from me. So we see how God conveyeth himself and his mercy here by sweet comparisons, dealing very familiarly with us, and speaking to us in our own language. We will take both in order as they lie.

God will be as a fir-tree in regard of shadow to the passenger, and keeping off of storms. The great God, and the good God, who is goodness itself, hath provided in this world not only good for us, but hath also promised defences against all annoyances. In the comparison itself, we will observe somewhat concerning the goodness of God ; for as in this life we are subject to many inconveniences, wants, and necessities ; so God hath supply for all, even outward necessities. We are subject to cold, for that we have the element of fire ; we are subject to storms, he hath provided garments, and skill to make them ; so in our travels, he hath provided some trees especially to shelter us. We cannot name any inconvenience of this life, but the rich God in his goodness hath provided a suitable supply. Doth God take care for this fading, perishing life, which is but as a vapour? and hath he good things for it, and fences from the ill and annoyances of it, till we have fulfilled our pilgrimage upon earth ? And will not that God have a care of our best life of grace that shall end in glory, that we shall have all things necessary for life and godliness, which hath the promise, not of this life only, but of a better, 1 Tim. iv. 8. He that is so good to this natural life, will be much more in things concerning a better life, which he would have us mind more. ' I will be as a green fir-tree unto him.'

God will be as a fir-tree, especially in regard of shadow, to keep from all annoyance both of storm and of the sun ; for the sun in those hot countries annoys them very much, as the spouse complains of her blackness, 'because the sun had shined upon her, Cant. i. 5, ' to be black as the tents of Kedar,' &c. Whence we may observe by the way,

There is not the most comfortable refreshing creature in the world, but take it in excess, it harms and annoys.

What more comfortable than water ? yet if it prevail and abound, it is a destroying creature, as we see in the deluge and divers inundations. What more comfortable than fire ? and what more terrible if it exceed ? What more cherishing, refreshing, and quickening than the sun ? Yet in the excessive heat thereof, it scorcheth and parcheth things. So in the sun of prosperity and all other good things in the world, it is best to have and enjoy all things with moderation ; for if we have grace to qualify them, all things are good ; otherwise the excess hurts us. Therefore beg of God wisdom to temper and moderate the best good in this world, which otherwise hurts us. For even the excessive heat of the sun in those countries makes them glad of the shadow of the fir-tree.

Thus God doth not only give a shadow, but a comfortable shadow and defence to his people, which is therefore called ' the shadow of his wings.' ' How oft,' saith Christ to Jerusalem, ' would I have gathered thee, as the hen gathereth her chickens under her wings ? ' Mat. xxiii. 37. It is not only a shielding from hurts, and dangers, and storms, but a sweet defence, with rest, and quiet. As those that are weary compose themselves to rest under a shadow, so in God is our rest ; ' Come unto me,' saith Christ, ' all ye that are weary and heavy laden, and ye shall find rest to your souls,' Mat. xi. 28. All rest is in Christ, and in God's mercy in Christ. We see, then, after we have forsook idolatry, God is to us instead of all the good we had by idols. We lose nothing by it. ' God will be as a green fir-tree.'

Whence the point is, *there is a protection, rest, and defence provided for God's people, when once they have renounced their idolatry and sinful courses.*

Those who refuse the shelter of idols, God will be a shelter unto them, ' a green fir-tree unto them,' another manner of shelter than that which idols or any other creature can give them. Every man will have some shelter, shield, or other to cover him, this or that great man to shield or shelter himself under. A rich man, he hath riches ; another, this or that defence. Every man that hath any wit about him will have some shelter, and not lie open to all storms when they come. But the only true shelter is God himself to a Christian. All other refuges are but shadows, that is, they are nothing, but like Jonah's gourd, which may shelter for a time, but there is a worm of vanity that will eat them out. Riches and the favour of men may shelter for a time, but there is a worm at the bottom which will root them out. Death will consume them and those they depend upon. But God is a true shelter to his people, an everlasting habitation, as it is written, ' Thou art our habitation from generation to generation, Ps. xc. 1. We dwell in him as in our rock and castle. He is an everlasting habitation, not only a shadow, but a tower and a castle to dwell in. Therefore the only wise man is the Christian. For, as Noah, when the flood came upon the old world, and swept them away, had an ark to save himself in, so have all God's children a house to get over their heads in the worst times, which is God's blessed protection, in whom they are safe. Let us think often of these things. What a blessed thing it is to be in the state of a Christian, that hath alway a certain and sure protection, quiet, and rest in God! And what a fearful thing is it to be as the Ahithophels of this world! to be as Cain, Judas, or Saul! who are shrewd in counsel and policy, and yet, when conscience is awakened by the storm of God's wrath, want a shelter, whilst he who is above conscience, and should be a shelter to them, frowns upon them. What a pitiful state is this! The wickedest man in the world, though he have never so great dependence, parts, and strength from human helps, yet when the storm of God's wrath comes, he is as a naked man in the midst of a storm, and knows not whither to go. Therefore let us be wise to have God for our shelter, if we would not be like these miserable politicians and worldlings.

Now, from this, that the shadow is comfortable in those hot countries, where the sun is directly over their heads, comes these sweet phrases in the Psalms and other Scriptures: 'Thou shalt keep me under the shadow of thy wings. As the apple-tree amongst the trees of the forest, so is my beloved amongst the sons. I sat down under his shadow with great delight,' &c., Cant. ii. 3. The church speaks of Christ, 'I sat under his shadow with great delight, and his fruit was sweet to my taste.' The like you have in many places in the Psalms. I will name one or two, more pregnant than the rest, to help our memories, and to breed a deeper impression of so comfortable a point. Ps. lxiii. 7. There the psalmist speaks of resting under the shadow of God's wings. And so in that other sweet and excellent psalm, in the greatest extremities of God's people, 'He that dwelleth in the secret place of the Most High,' that is, God, 'shall abide under the shadow of the Almighty,' Ps. xci. 1. He says after, 'I will say of the Lord, He is my refuge and fortress;' for where God tells a man that he is a hiding-place and a shadow, there faith adds the application presently; and then he goes on, speaking of himself, 'He shall cover me with his feathers; under his wings will I rest; his truth shall be my buckler. Thou shalt not be afraid of the terror by night; nor of the arrow by day; nor of the pestilence that walketh in the dark. A thousand shall fall,' &c., vers. 4-7. So that we see how God doth that to our souls and conditions that the fir-tree, which is God's good creature, doth to the body in the time of storm and heat, that is, he doth refresh us under the shadow of his wings. He is a sweet, comfortable, and gracious God unto us. This, you see, is a clear truth; yet, because it is so comfortable, we will enlarge it further. Look what God speaks, 'The Lord will create upon every dwelling-place of mount Zion, and upon her assembly, a cloud and smoke by day, and the shining of a flame of fire by night; for upon all the glory shall be a defence,' Isa. iv. 45. See what a comfortable shadow God is! He saith, 'He will create.' If they want the comfort of the fir-tree, and such like shadows, he says, 'God will create,' that is, make them of nothing. He will 'create upon every dwelling-place of mount Zion,' where his children dwell, and upon their assemblies, 'a cloud and a smoke by day;' that is, when they are annoyed by the sun, God will create a cloud to keep the rage and the scorching heat of the sun from them, and then a 'shining flame of fire by night,' because in the night we need light, for 'upon all the glory shall be a defence,' that is, upon all the glorious saints of God. They are glory, for there is a Spirit of glory put into them, 1 Pet. iv. 14. The people of God, in whom God will glorify himself, are glorious, and shall be further glorified, and they shall in the mean time have a defence by day and by night from all dangers whatsoever.

Thus it is clear that God will be a shadow to his people, as the fir-tree, which is an allusion to that grand passage of his providence in conducting the children of Israel out of Egypt, where God, to guide them, provided a ' cloud by day, and a pillar of fire by night,' Exod. xiv. 20. The same pillar which was lightsome to the Israelites, was dark to the Egyptians, which cloud and pillar of fire continued, God conducting them, till they came into the land of Canaan. He shadowed them by day with a cloud, and lighted and heated them by a pillar of fire at night, thus conducting them till they came to Canaan. So we, passing through the wilderness of this world till we come unto our celestial Canaan, heaven, God will be a ' cloud' by his gracious special providence, to keep all ill whatsoever from us, and a ' pillar of fire' to lighten and direct us till we come to our heavenly Canaan, where he will be all in all, when we shall need neither sun nor moon, nor have anything to annoy us, Rev. vii. 16. There the noonday shall not burn us with heat of the sun, nor the fire by night. When we are in heaven there shall be no annoyance of the creature. There shall be no more want of light, because we shall have all light and refreshing there for ever and ever. For, as it is written, then ' all tears,' all sorrow, and cause of sorrow, shall be for ever wiped away, an allusion whereunto we have comfortably set down, Ps. cxxi. 7. The more we shall enrich and refresh our memories with thinking of these things, the more comfort will sink into our hearts. The 121st psalm is all spent on comfort in this kind. ' I will lift up mine eyes to the hills, whence cometh my salvation. My help cometh from the Lord, who made heaven and earth,' all my help is from him. ' He will not suffer my foot to be moved ; he that keeps Israel will neither slumber nor sleep.' ' He will not slumber ;' that is, his eyes are always open to see, as his ears to hear. ' Behold, he that keepeth Israel doth neither slumber nor sleep. The Lord is thy keeper, thy shadow, so that the sun shall not smite thee by day, nor the moon by night. The Lord shall preserve thy going out and thy coming in, from this time for ever.' Thus we see this Scripture is a large gloss and commentary upon this truth, that God, with a special providence and protection, cares for his children, to keep them from all ill. He will be as the fir-tree to them in regard of shadow. Whence we observe in special,

That this life of ours, whilst we come to heaven, is subject to scorchings and many annoyances, and those both outwardly and inwardly, from ourselves and from others.*

First, for *outward annoyances*, how many of them is our poor life subject unto ! and for inward terror and boiling heat of conscience, when God in anger discovers himself unto us, and sets our sins in order before us. Oh then, if we have not a shadow ; if God in mercy through Jesus Christ be not a shadow to keep that boiling heat from us, what will become of the poor conscience ? especially if Satan adds his poisoned fiery darts, poisoning, inflaming the conscience with temptations to despair, Ps. l. 21, as if God had forsaken and were angry ; or when God seems angry, then he seems like a consuming fire. Oh, who can abide it, when all these fiery temptations are joined with God's anger ! Yet the dearest of God's saints are subject to these inward boiling heats of God's anger. ' My God, my God, why hast thou forsaken me,' said the head of the church himself, Matt. xxvii. 46 ; and see how Job complains, ' Thou hast set me as a butt to shoot at,' Job xvi. 12. And, in regard of this spiritual desertion, David complains much throughout the Psalms. So this our life is subject to out-

* That is, ' until.'—Ed.

ward and spiritual annoyances from God, from Satan, and from ourselves and the world ; every way annoyed with scorchings and heat, what need [of] a shadow, a protection, a defence else ?   That supposeth this.

If this be so, then consider how fearful the condition of those people is, that are not under the shadow of the Almighty ; who have not God as a fir-tree to shadow and cover them ; that he is not a cloud by day to, and a pillar of fire by night ; that have not him for a hiding-place to spread the wings of his mercy over them.   What is the state of such people ? surely howsoever God feed them, and fills their belly with good things in this world for a time ; yet their case will be fearful, when God lets loose con-science, and Satan's fiery darts against them.   Judge then hereby what our state is by nature without God.   The same sun which cherisheth and com-forteth, also tortures and scorcheth us : so God is a sun, a quickening sun to his children, Mal. iv. 2, yea, a vigorous sun, who hath healing under his wings ; but to the wicked he is a scorching and consuming fire, Heb. xii. 29. 'It is a fearful thing to fall into the hands of the living God,' Heb. x. 31, who is so dreadful.   He will not be a shadow to the wicked in an excellent man-ner.   He indeed permits them to have many shadows in this world, many sweet comforts, and keeps them also from many dangers ; but they have not that worthy portion which Hannah had from her husband, 1 Sam. i. 5, love at the hour of death.   And in time of temptation, when these comforts leave them, what shadow have they then ? none at all, but are as naked men in a storm, subject to the fury of God's eternal wrath.   The things which are most comfortable to God's people are most terrible to them, as it is said in one of those plagues poured out upon antichrist (for all the vials there spoken of tend to the punishing of antichrist), there is a vial poured forth upon the sun, Rev. vi. ; which reflecting and lighting upon them, causeth them to blaspheme, they were so scorched with it.   The sun, by probable interpreters, is said to be the word of God, which, when it is opened, is sweet and comfortable to God's people, but shining upon men that are naught, especially at the hour of death, in affliction and in dis-tress, it speaks no comfort to them, but causeth them to despair, rage and storm.   Nay, profane men, when they are at the best, they rage and storm at the direction of the sun, because it discovers to them that which they would not have known.

Use 1. Now, what use should we make of this ?   Will God be a shadow to his people to keep them from all evil, as his promise was to Abraham in the covenant of grace : ' I will be thy buckler,' to keep ill from thee, and ' thy exceeding great reward,' Gen. xv. 1.   And in the Psalms, God pro-miseth to be a sun for good, and a shield to keep off all ill, Ps. lxxxiv. 11. Will God bestow good, and keep off ill from us ?   Then labour to come willingly under the shadow of the Almighty, to serve him, and to make God in covenant our God, that he may be a ' shield and a hiding-place ' unto us, and a shadow in all extremities whatsoever.   Those that attend upon great persons, they do it upon this hope : Oh, if I belong to such a great person, he will shelter me, that every base person shall not wrong me ; I shall now have some prerogatives.   Doth carnal policy teach poor creatures who are subject to abuse it, to get some shelter of great, noble men to be privileged? and shall not spiritual wisdom teach us to get under the great God, under the shadow of his wings ?   None can come near to annoy us without his special will and leave, as in the story of Job.   The devil durst not annoy him, Job i. 12, nor enter into the swine, Mat. viii 31, much less hurt God's children.   Shall we not, therefore, get under the service of our God ? can any man shelter us better ? There is no service to that of a king ; but is there any service to the King of kings, and Lord of lords ? Will he suffer his children to be abused in his own sight, or his followers disgraced ? Surely no. Therefore make this use of it, to get into the service of the great God, which is a rich, secure, and safe service.

Use 2. Again, it yields us an use of resolution, for to obey God, and to go boldly on in a good course. What should we fear, when God is our master ? He will shield us, and keep us safe, and give his angels charge over us, to shew that he hath a care over us. Indeed, he hath many keepers under him, but he is the grand keeper, who sets all a-work. For angels, magistrates, ministers, and our friends keep us ; but God's Spirit within us, and his gracious good providence without us, are our chief keepers. Therefore let all our care be to serve God, and to be in his ways. He will keep us in his ways. What an encouragement is this to be in good courses, where we may look for the shadow of the Almighty God, without tempting of him ! If a man be in an ill way and course, he cannot look that the Almighty should shadow him. His heart will tell him, now God may withdraw his shelter and wing from me ; he may leave me naked to the devil and to the malice of men ; he may strip me of all comfort in my soul and conscience, and give me up to terrors of heart out of his way. If I trust him now, I tempt him, because he will be a defence only in his own ways. Therefore let us labour always to be in those ways, and then God will be as a green fir-tree unto us.

Use 3. And, last of all, let it be an use of comfort unto us, for all the time of our life to come. Whatsoever may come, we yet pass under a buckler. Let a whole shower and shot of arrows * fall upon us, we have a buckler. ' Thou, Lord, art my buckler ; thou, Lord, art my defence, my hiding-place, my castle,' Ps. xviii. 1, 2. We are subject to a world of dangers whilst we live here, but we have God instead of all, to keep off all. He is a buckler, a shield, a shadow, and a hiding-place. Let what ill soever be presented to our thoughts, there is in God some fence against it. For this purpose we have many excellent passages in Ps. xviii., which was made after a great deliverance. ' I love the Lord, my buckler, my shield, my defence,' as if he should say, I have in my lifetime been annoyed with many troubles, but I have found experience of God in all. ' He is my buckler, my shield, my fence,' everything to me. So let us comfort ourselves in this. Let come what will come, all shall come well to God's children. He will keep them, if not outwardly, yet in that they most desire to be kept in. He will preserve their spirits ' from every evil work,' 2 Tim. iv. 18, from doing ill, and from desperate falling from God ; and he will guard them inwardly, ' by the peace of God which passeth understanding,' Philip. iv. 7. It shall guard their hearts ; they shall have inward peace in the midst of all the troubles of this world: a great comfort ! What a rejoicing is it to a poor passenger, when he passeth by the highway side in a hot, burning day, or in a storm, to see a goodly high tree, with spreading boughs, that he may hide and repose himself under it from the storm or heat. This pleaseth him marvellously, as Jonah's gourd did him. Do these outward poor contentments so refresh us in this world ? and shall we not think that God, which provides such poor contentments for this sorry life in this world, will he not provide a shadow in regard of the main dangers ? Surely he will, if we trust him, and shew our trust by casting ourselves upon him in obedience suitable to our calling. Saith the apostle,

* Qu. ' a whole shower of shot and arrows ?'—G.

' I am persuaded that neither things present, nor to come, nor life, nor death, nor anything, shall be able to separate us from the love of Christ Jesus our Lord,' Rom. viii. 38, 39.   Therefore let us be afraid of nothing that can befall us.   God will be a shield and a buckler, and all in all to us in a good way.   We have abundance of comfort everywhere in Scripture, and want nothing but faith to apply it home in practice.   Therefore we ought to beg of God so to enlarge our faith, that as his promises and comforts are very large, so may our vessels be to retain all these excellent comforts and sweet promises.

All other comforts in the world are but like Jonah's gourd ; for all other shadows yield only a shadow for a while, and then the sunshine or east wind is like a worm to nip them asunder.   Never trust, then, or lean to such shadows as these be, of friends, riches, &c., which are shadows men ordinarily rely upon.   I have such and such a friend, a place, and the like, my mountain is thus and thus strong.   All these are Jonah's gourds.   There is a worm of vanity will be at the root of all, and consume all.   All other shadows are but mere shadows.   What is more transient than a shadow ?   But God's shadow is like a green fir-tree.   It never fails nor forsakes us, as all other shadows and contentments do whatsoever.   But God saith, ' He will be like a green fir-tree unto thee.'   Yet this is not all, nor enough, for after this he adds,

' From me is thy fruit found.'

God is not only to his children a fir-tree in regard of shadow, that tree abounding in leaves very thick, whereby we are kept from annoyance of scorching heats of troubles and terrors of conscience and persecution, &c. This is not all, but he saith also,

' From me is thy fruit found.'

A fir-tree, though it be for thickness of the leaves a very good shade, yet it is a barren, fruitless tree ; but God is such a tree as hath both shadow and fruit.   In God there is a supply of all wants whatsoever.   All the scattered excellencies of all creatures being united in God, and eminent in him, it is in him, and in him in a divine, gracious, eminent, and comfortable manner.   All the creatures, as they come from God, are his creatures, neither is there any creature but hath somewhat of God in it.   Therefore, God vouchsafes to take names from the creatures.   To be a rock of salvation, he is as a rock to build on ; to be a shadowing tree, because he is a defence from ill ; and to be a fruitful tree, because he yields good, and comfort, and grace, as he doth fruit.   When we see anything that is useful, we may say, this we have from God in an eminent manner, this preservation and comfort.   Do I in my passage to heaven find such comfort in the creature ?   When I am passing through a wild place, have I such comfort in the shadow of a tree ?   or when I am hungry, am I so refreshed by a fruitful tree ?   What comfort, then, is there in God, in heaven, in glory, when there are such comforts in the way of my pilgrimage in this world ? Therefore, God is said here, both to be a fir-tree and a fruitful tree.   For then the passenger travelling through a wild, barren place, thinks himself made when he can retire from the scorching of the heat, and also therewithal find fruitfulness.   Shade and fruit concurring, he thinks himself marvellously happy.   This is the state of a Christian that hath God for his God, being in covenant with him.   He is not only a strong protection and defence from all annoyance (as God shadows us, and is a buckler from all evils, both inward and outward, from Satan, and all kind of evils and wrath), but he is also a fruitful tree too.   ' From me is thy fruit found.'

THE THIRTEENTH SERMON.

I am like a green fir-tree; from me is thy fruit found.—Hos. XIV. 8.

THIS holy prophet, as we heard heretofore, did prophesy more than sixty years among the ten tribes, even until the time immediately preceding their captivity and misery, in like manner as Jeremiah and Ezekiel did to the other Jews. Now, because in the worst times God always had a remnant, and yet hath, therefore it is the prophet's care, in this chapter which we have gone over, to instruct them in divers particulars of reformation, as we have heard at large, ' to return to the Lord,' ' to take words to themselves,' which words, as we have heard, are also taught them, backed with many sweet promises and encouragements in God's answer to their petitions: the last whereof insisted and stood upon was this, that God promiseth to be like a green fir-tree unto Ephraim, who personated all the ten tribes. Ephraim thought before to shadow and fence himself by idols, and league with other idolatrous nations, which were like Jonah's rotten gourd unto them, poor shadows and defences; but saith God, ' I will be a fir-tree' for shadow to Ephraim, to defend him from all dangers whatsoever; and then in the next place he adds,

' From me is thy fruit found.'

A fir-tree is a green tree, but it hath no fruit. The excellencies of the creatures are applied to God, but not the defects. Therefore, when comparisons are taken from the creatures and given to God, we must always except the defects, supplying the same by some other clearing comparison. So God is not only a fir-tree for shelter and defence, but he is a fruitful tree. So a fir-tree is not; and therefore without comparison, God hath more in him than any creature hath. For all that excellency which is in all the creatures is in him, and that in a far more eminent manner; therefore, he is both a shelter and fruit. If a passenger in distress have not only a fir-tree to shelter him and shadow him, but a fruit-tree also to feed him, he thinks he is made when God thus comforts him. So a Christian, he hath not only shelter from the wrath of God, but he hath also a place of rest and quiet, the mercy of God to keep him, and the word and sacraments to feed him. God is a fruit-tree as well as a fir-tree.

' From me is thy fruit found.'

That is, whatsoever is graciously or comfortably good to us, in us, or issues from us, is all from God. Hence first of all we observe for our instruction,

From a man's self comes nothing that is graciously good.

Whatsoever is savingly good is altogether from God. ' Without me,' saith Christ, ' you can do nothing,' John xv. 5. Saint Paul was wondrous chary * of this point. 1 Cor. xv. 10 he saith ' he laboured more abundantly than they all: yet not I ' (he recalls himself), ' but the grace of God in him that did all;' and of myself, as of myself, I cannot so much ' as think a good thought.' It is from God that we have means to make us fruitful, and from the gracious working of his Spirit comes it that they are effectual. That we think a good thought, or open our mouths to speak a good word, it is from God's Spirit enabling us thereto. ' Open thou my mouth,' saith the psalmist, ' and my lips shall shew forth thy praise.' We are tongue-

* That is, ' wary ' = circumspect.—G.

tied and our lips sealed unless God open them. We cannot speak one savoury, seasonable word to further our accompt. We may speak empty words, but never a word comes from the heart that is gracious and good, but it must be by the Spirit of God. It is he who works all our works in us and for us. ' He begins the good work in us, and perfects it to the day of the Lord,' Isa. xxvi. 12, Phil. i. 6. The truth of this is wondrous clear.

If this be so, then undoubtedly the differences in the graces of men, it is from another, merely from God and God's Spirit. There is indeed difference in men, but this is originally fetched from the grace of God's Spirit. The good use of freedom, that we talk so much of, it is from God, as well as the endowments of it. We have free will, but the use of it is not in our power, to use this or that at our pleasure; for ' it is God which gives the will and the deed,' Phil. ii. 13, of his good pleasure. Not only the deed, but the will too; we should make the will an idol else. For so many wills, so many idols, if we think one man in himself can difference himself by his will.

Again, in that God saith, ' From me is thy fruit found,' we may learn hence,

That fruit that is gracious comes from us and from God too.

It is our fruit and God's, so that there is a subordination of gracious works under God. The fruit we have is from God, yet it is our fruit too.

Quest. How can this be ?

Sol. Yes, easily. We speak the words, but it is God that opens our lips. We believe, but it is God that gives us grace to believe. We do the action, but God gives us grace to do it. God opened the heart of Lydia to believe, Acts xvi. 14, so that God and we meet together in the same action. We have parts, understanding, will, affections, bodies and souls. Therefore the actions are said to be ours, because God works in us as understanding creatures ; but God sets the wheel a-going, so that the actions are originally his, and ours subordinately under him, ' From me is thy fruit found.'

If so be that God and man join in one action ('From me is thy fruit found ;' as though he should say, Whatsoever thou hast or sayest that is good, it is from me ; here we see how, and why good works cannot merit, though they come from God, as all goodness doth), yet in regard they come from us too, we add some tainture thereunto from our corrupt nature. What God and Christ himself doth, is absolute and perfect, as justification ; but what fruit he works in us, there is somewhat of the old Adam in us, which taints the beauty of the work. It is God's fruit, coming from him, and yet our fruit also, coming from us ; which being so much tainted should humble us, in that we add nothing to the truth of God's work in us, but abasement and defilement by our corruptions. ' From me (saith God) is thy fruit found,' so much as is supernaturally good ; but because our nature is not altered on the sudden, but still tastes of the ' old leaven,' 1 Cor. v. 7, therefore there can be no meriting of salvation by any works we do, because they are not perfectly good.

Use 1. The clearing of these points, in our judgment, *they serve to work in us a deep humiliation,* seeing that we have nothing in ourselves but stains and defilements, all that is good in us coming from God, ' From me is thy fruit found.' What is from ourselves then, if all good in us comes from God ? We are a barren and a cursed soil, nothing that is good can come from us. Even as the earth was cursed after Adam's fall, and brought forth nothing but briers and thorns, so our soul naturally is a cursed soil in itself, and brings forth nothing but weeds and thorns. Our hearts are like the barren wilderness, full of evil, noisome lusts and affections. Therefore this serves to abase us, that we be not lifted up with any good in us ; for as that is altogether from God's Spirit, so likewise we of ourselves add nothing to it, but somewhat which may diminish the value thereof.

Use 2. Here, again, for matter of judgment, *you have a difference between the state of nature and the state of grace,* I mean of innocent nature, for in Adam we had a standing in ourselves, being trusted with our own good ; but now under the second covenant, under the second Adam, Christ Jesus, we have many graces to fit us for heaven, and many good works we do, but all the fruit we have and yield is from God. So that now this is a grand difference. Adam, as it were, had the keeping of his own happiness locked up in himself; but we have our happiness, graces, and whatsoever is good for us, shut up in Christ as the spring and fountain, which is the reason of the perpetual stability and permanent condition of God's children, once his and ever his. And put the case, we want this or that help, yet this prejudiceth not the perpetuity of the condition of God's children, because those graces which come immediately from God's Spirit, may be conveyed sometimes without means, as well as with them. Therefore, whatsoever decay is in the branches that are grafted into this noble Vine, Christ Jesus, in whom we bear all the fruit we bear, yet notwithstanding there is life everlasting for us in the root, which is by little and little distilled into us. The leaves may fall, outward things may decay, but there is life alway in the root of a Christian, because he is in Christ, and hath his fruit from him ; he cannot want fruit, no more than Christ can want influence and vigour, John xv. 5. Which shews us the excellent state of a Christian under the new covenant of grace, that now we fetch all out of ourselves, and it is happy for us that we do so. For without Christ we can do nothing. As without the soul the body can do nothing, so without the Spirit of Christ we can do nothing ; from him is all. This is the reason why we must not trust to any grace in ourselves, that comes from us, because grace comes from God in Christ. Trust God, the spring whence it comes, whose the fruit is : God the Father in Christ, from whom all fulness comes, and is derived unto us, or else we make but an idol of grace, if we trust too much to grace. Look to the spring whence all comes to us. ' From me is thy fruit found.'

Quest. Again, for further instruction, What is the reason that some have more grace than others, and more comfort, some having grace and comfort in one degree, and some in another ?

Sol. Hence it is : ' From me is thy fruit found.' It comes from the freedom of God in Christ, who according to his good pleasure gives the will and the deed, whence we have grace sometimes in the vigour, sometimes in a weaker and lesser degree, the fault being in ourselves too. Yet, notwithstanding, there is a liberty in the Spirit of Christ, to give a more or less measure of grace, to shew that our good we do springs not from ourselves. Which also is the reason of the difference betwixt Christians, because God will shew that he is the disposer and the dispenser of his own graces and comforts. And that is the reason also why we must perform this duty of waiting upon God in the use of means, though we find no sense of grace and comfort from him for the present, ' From him our fruit is found.' Wait his leisure. He suspends grace and comfort until a fit time, in regard of the degree ; but yet there is alway some grace left, though he suspends the increase thereof until a fit time, because he would have us know that it is of his giving. Christians who are acquainted herewith, they will not tie God to their time, but humbly go on in the use of means, who though they find not their spirits and their comforts enlarged so as at other times, nor so great, nor as other folks are ; yet can say, Lord, thou givest the will and the deed according to thy good pleasure, all comes from thee; therefore I will use the means and depend upon thee because I have all from thee freely. God gives a spirit of prayer, and then the thing we pray for, all is from him, ' From me is thy fruit found.' Do we find the ordinances fruitful, the preaching of the word to open our understandidgs, to kindle our affections, to enlighten our judgments? It is the Spirit of God that joins with the means, that are dead of themselves, to make them fruitful. What are the ordinances without God, but empty conduit-pipes of themselves ? Therefore, ' From me is thy fruit found.'

Use 3. This should teach and direct us also *in all things to look up to God in all use of means.* Lord, I may read, hear, and use helps and means long enough, to little or no purpose, unless thou give a blessing. Paul may plant and Apollos may water, but if thou give not fruit from heaven, all is to no purpose, 1 Cor. iii. 6. We forget this, and therefore prosper accordingly. We think we can work fruit out of the means, by our own wit. Oh ! it is not so ! Whatsoever. is comfortable or gracious in the use of means, it is merely God's blessing. And therefore seeing all our fruit whatsoever, that is good, comes from God, let us stir us up to practise the spiritual worship of God, to adore God, to beg of his fulness in Christ Jesus, and likewise to resign ourselves in all conditions unto him. Lord, I put myself upon thee ; all my fruit is from thee ; thou canst sanctify any condition unto me. This adoration and resignation are parts of the spiritual worship of God. And likewise the service of the Lord in fear and reverence, that inward service of the Spirit ; all depends upon this, that all our fruit is from God. Therefore I must serve him, and serve him as he must be served, in spirit and truth, John iv. 24. What makes a man reverence another ? I depend upon him ; without him I sink. Will this make a man serve man ? And will it not make us serve God, and serve him with fear ? What breeds an awful fear ? This, that if he withdraw his influence, I fall into sin, despair, and discomfort. So that the ground of all fear of God, and service springing from this fear, it is from hence, that from him all my fruit, all my grace and comfort, is found; therefore I must have grace to serve him, as a God in fear. For if the soul be not possessed and seasoned with this heavenly doctrine, that all comes from him, then surely where is God's service ? What becomes of it ? Where is that adoration and magnifying of God in our hearts ? Where's that putting off ourselves upon him in all conditions ?

Use 4. Again, this enforceth another part of God's spiritual and heavenly worship, *cleaving to God in our affections,* especially these two, in our faith and love ; that as all comes from and by Jesus Christ, so thereby we may draw from him the fruit of grace and comfort. So that this spiritual cleaving and uniting of our souls to Christ, it comes from this, that I have all from him, therefore I must cleave to him ; seeing whatsoever is spiritual, holy, and comfortable I must have from him. Therefore if we would worship God in spirit and truth, as we should do, and set him up in his due place in the soul, let us labour to have our judgments sanctified in this, that all comes from God. If we were surely grounded in the goodness, mercy, and riches of God's grace, and knew that all our fruit comes and is from him, this would make us to conclude that therefore it is reason that we should worship him and depend upon him strictly. As the prophet speaks of idols, that they can neither do us good nor harm, Jer. x. 5, enforcing that they should not fear them, so we may say of all other things distinct from God, they can neither do good nor harm, except God enable them. Will you be slaves to men? They cannot do good nor harm, but as God uses them, whose creatures they are. Therefore the worship of God is also founded hence, that God does all good or harm. If men do it they do it from him, he gives them leave; as it is said of Shimei, God bid him rail on David, 2 Sam. xvi. 10. If they do us good, they are his conduits, whereby he deriveth good to us; therefore all is from him. We see then how all the true and hearty worship of God comes from this, 'From me is thy fruit found.'

Use 5. This should make us likewise, as to worship God in spirit and in truth, so *to be resolute in good causes*, whatsoever come of it. Look for a ground, and then be resolute; because all comes from God, who will stand by us in his own cause and quarrel.

But if I forsake this and that support, I shall lay open myself to injuries and wrongs.

Mark what the Spirit of God saith, 'Ye that love the Lord, hate that which is evil,' Ps. xcvii. 10. But if I hate that which is evil, idols, &c., as Ephraim here doth, I shall be despised and trampled upon. No! saith he, 'God preserves the souls of his; he will be a shield and a buckler; a sun and a shield; and no good thing shall be wanting to them that lead a godly life,' Ps. lxxxiv. 11. God will be a sun for all good, and a shield to keep off all ill; therefore let us be resolute in good causes. Whence comes all shifting, halting, imperfect walking, and inconstances in the ways of God, but from this, that men know not where to have men? They are not grounded on this, that whatsoever is fruitful and good comes from God, who will give whatsoever is fruitful and good in depending upon him. This made the three children in Daniel courageous. They knew they should have fruit from God; that is, grace, comfort, and peace, the best fruit of all. And therefore 'know, O king, that we will not worship thine idol, nor fall down before it,' Dan. iii. 18. So holy Esther, being well grounded, could say, 'If I perish, I perish,' Esth. iv. 16. I know the cause is good; and if all help in the creature be removed and taken away, yet I shall have fruit in God.

Let us therefore carry this about us, as a principle of holy life, to know that our good is hid up in God, and not in the creature; so that if all help were taken away, yet we have it immediately, purer and better in the fountain. What if there were not a creature in the world to help me? What if all were against me? Yet God may make all their powers and endeavours fruitful. There is such fruit from God, that he can make the worst things which befalleth us fruitful when he pleaseth. There is a blessing in curses and crosses, a good fruit in them! Who can do him harm that God turneth the bitterest things he suffers to his good? Let none be daunted in a good cause, but go on resolutely, seeing God hath all in himself. Was not Moses forty days without any earthly comfort on the mount? Exod. xxxiv. 28. And Christ also without natural sustentation so long? Mat. iv. 2. Did not God give light without a sun in the first creation? We are tied to means, but he is not. We think if such friends and helps be taken away, that then all is gone; but what were they? Were not they means which God used at his good pleasure, and cannot he give comfort without them? Yes, certainly! The greatest comfort and grace is ofttimes given immediately from God, when he salutes the soul by his own Spirit, as he did Paul and Silas in the dungeon; who, in the midst of discomfort, had their spirits enlarged to sing hymns at midnight, Acts xvi. 25, God reserving that comfort for that time. Therefore seeing all comfort is from God, and he is not tied to this or that means, nay, can bless all contrary means, is not this a ground of resolution?

Use 6. Therefore now make a use of comfort of it, seeing all fruit is from God, who is in covenant with his children in Jesus Christ, and who will improve all his attributes for their good, his wisdom, goodness, power, and mercy. Let them therefore *take comfort to themselves, that howsoever the world may take their friends from them, riches, liberty, and what you will, can they take God and fruit from them?* No! 'From me is thy fruit found.' If they could take away the Spirit of God, grace, and comfort from us, it were something; but can they do that? No! The worst they can do is to send us to heaven, to the fountain of all grace and comfort; so that in this world they cannot cast us into any condition wherein we cannot have communion with God, in whom all the scattered excellencies of the creature are gathered together, meeting as it were in a centre. It is he that comforts us in our friends, that shews bowels to us in our mothers, wisdom and care towards us in our parents. The bowels of a mother, the care of a friend, the strength of wise assistance, hath he not all in himself, if all be taken away? He hath all. Therefore let Christians comfort themselves, that they can never be in a condition wherein fruit shall be taken from them. The poor worldling labours all his life for fruit, riches, and friends; and when he dies, then his fruit faileth him and falls, his leaf withereth. What becometh of his fruit then? He laboured for that which yields him nothing but vexation and death. But a Christian doth otherwise; he labours for grace and comfort to keep his communion and peace with God; and when all is taken away, either by the injury and wrongs of men, or by the extremity of the times, or as all will, in the hour of death, his fruit is most after, in death, and after death, more than can be by our narrow hearts conceived in the excellency thereof. Oh! the excellent estate of a Christian! Imagine such a one to have a tree that grows in heaven, and sends forth fruit and branches to him in whatsoever state he is in. And so indeed God reacheth fruit from heaven to the soul, being in prison and misery. He reacheth from thence the fruit of grace, of spiritual strength and comfort: a blessed estate! Therefore let Christians comfort themselves in their condition, 'that all their fruit is from him;' and that God especially will then shew himself abundant when they stand most in need of him. Other trees bear no fruit in winter and in storms, but God giveth fruit most in the worst times. He is a God that comforteth the abject. As it is 2 Cor. vii. 6; and here is said, that 'in him the fatherless findeth mercy.' We have most fruit from him in the worst times. Then especially he delighteth to shew himself a God, when no comfort can be had from the creature.

Therefore do not despair, but lay up this against evil times; never fear for the time to come. Let the mountains be cast into the midst of the sea, and let the earth and all rage, as the psalmist says, and let things run upon a head; come what can come, God is where he was, and God's children are where they were, in regard of the main comfort, Ps. xlvi. 2. They cannot be in such a condition, as that they can be deprived of their God, and of his assistance : 'From me is thy fruit found.' Therefore care not for any condition that thou art in, this or that, thou shalt have that condition which shall be comfortable to thee, though many like beasts go on, and look for no fruit from God.

Use 7. And let this also be an encouragement, *to walk with God sincerely and uprightly in all times*, not fearing any creature, or danger from the creature, because our fruit is from God. What if we lose this or that? We know what was said to Amaziah by the prophet. But what shall become of the hundred talents? saith he. God is able to give thee much more, 2 Chron. xxv. 9. So in the loss of friends, having this and that took* from us, let us comfort ourselves. Aye, but God is not taken from us. He who derives † comfort by this or that friend, can supply it better by his own Spirit. And whatsoever we part with in a good cause, let us remember what Christ saith. 'He that parts with father or mother, with house or land for my ,sake, shall have a hundredfold in this world, and afterwards life everlasting, Mat. xix. 29. He shall have all made up in grace, which is a hundred times better than anything that is here. He shall have contentment, which is better than the things themselves. Sometimes he shall, missing one worldly comfort, have more friends stirred up; but howsoever, in want of one, he shall be supplied in another comfort that he never dreamt of in this world. So that God is abundant to them that stick close to him in sincerity; he shall find him abundant in the things of this life, in one comfort or other.

Therefore, by these mercies ,of God here mentioned, let us be entreated to be in love with the condition of a Christian life, and say, as Ephraim here, 'What have I any more to do with my former corrupt courses, or idols?' Give a peremptory answer to all sinful courses and suggestions, either from others or from our own corrupt nature. 'What have I any more to do with you?' No; God shall be my God: for if I can resign myself wholly to God, and renounce the creature and all things else, God will be as a 'green fir-tree,' and hear me. I shall lose nothing by it. Be then in love with a Christian course; for it is the sweetest and the safest course, and never wants comforts from heaven: and it is the most honourable course that can be, for it will hold our communion and peace with the great God of heaven and earth; for though we break with others, we shall be sure of him. In which case take heed of that base suggestion which the devil himself was ashamed to own, 'that we serve God for nought,' Job i. 9. What! shall we renounce idolatry and wicked courses, and think that God will not have fruit for us? Shall I think, if I leave my sinful gain, that I or my posterity shall beg or starve for it? Do we serve a God that hath no fruit, that is a dead tree, or a barren wilderness? No; we serve a God that had all in himself before he made the world, and hath all the excellency in himself contained in the creatures. It is not in vain to serve him. 'Doth Job serve God for nothing?' said the devil. Therefore it is a suggestion worse than Satanical, to think we serve God for nothing, or to think, like those hypocrites mentioned by the prophet, that God regards not our fasting or our devotion, Isa. lviii. 3. No; we shall not lose a good word for God. Not a tear, but he hath a bottle for it, Ps. lvi. 8; not a sigh, or a groan, or a farthing, not a minute's time well spent shall be lost. He will pay us for every ill word we endure for his sake, for every disgrace, loss, or cross. Do we serve that God there is no fruit in? 'From me is thy fruit found.'

Whatsoever our condition be in the world, let us comfort ourselves with these things; and think that it is not in vain to serve the Lord; for we

* That is, 'taken.'—G.   † That is, 'conveys.'—G.

cannot serve a richer, nor a more kind master and Lord. First of all, he gives us opportunity and means whereby fruit may be wrought in us, and then he works the fruit of grace and comfort in us, and afterwards rewards and crowns his own fruit. But we add imperfections and inventions of our own, and so mar or stain all. But we deal with a gracious God in covenant, who pities us as a father doth his children, accepts and rewards what is his, and pardons what is our own. Therefore let thus much be effectual for the guiding of our lives, and comforting of us in a good course. If we take ill courses, we must look for no fruit from God, but fruits of his displeasure ; if we eat of the forbidden tree, we shall eat and reap ' the fruits of our own ways,' bitter fruits. For in this case, Jesus Christ, who is a sweet Saviour, will be a judge to us ; and he who is ' the Lamb of God,' will be angry, so as we shall reap the fruit of his indignation. In the Revelation, divers are brought in desiring ' the hills and mountains to fall upon them, to cover them from the presence of the Lamb,' Rev. vi. 16. Let us not, therefore, turn a sweet Saviour to a rigorous Judge, by adventuring upon courses wherein we cannot look for fruit ; but let us commend ' our souls in well-doing unto him, as unto a faithful Creator and Redeemer,' 1 Pet. iv. 19. And as it is, ' Let us acknowledge him in all our ways,' Prov. iii. 6 ; for it is good to acknowledge and look to him, that is, look to him for strength, quickening, success, grace, and light to direct us : acknowledge him in all our ways, and treasure up this comfort, that ' all fruit is found from God.' If we take good courses, we shall ever be fruitful, and have fruit from him, ' out of his fulness ; for, saith he, ' From me is thy fruit found.'

THE FOURTEENTH SERMON.

Who is wise, and he shall understand these things ? prudent, and he shall know them ? for the ways of the Lord are equal, the just shall walk in them : but the transgressors shall fall therein.—Hos. XIV. 9.

THESE words seal up the whole prophecy ; for the prophet, immediately before prophesying of the captivity, discovers to them at length their sins, as we heard, their idolatry, adding new idols to their former idols, Baal to the calves. The princes removed the bounds, old orders and laws ; the prophets they were fools, and did not see the judgments of God hanging over their heads ; and none of them all could see their ' grey hairs,' Hosea vii. 9, that is, the signs of their own ruin. After which, out of a Christian love, care, and conscience of his duty, by direction of the Spirit of God, he prescribes an excellent way how they should carry themselves, by returning to the Lord. ' Take words unto yourselves,' renounce all false confidence in Asshur, and all domestic helps at home, horses and the like, and fly to God as your best sanctuary. Then he shews what God will do to them, answer all the desires he had put into their hearts. ' I will heal their backslidings, and love them freely,' &c.

Now, because these were great matters of great consequence, to make them either happy in the observing them, or miserable in neglecting them, you see how he shuts up all in a most weighty close. ' Who is wise, and he shall understand these things ? prudent, and he shall know them ? for the ways of the Lord are equal,' &c.

Wherein the scope of the prophet is to stir up a holy regard of what hath been spoken. He would not have all lost for want of attention or application; and therefore he here stirs them up to a holy use of all, which stirring up is excellently and figuratively clothed with an *epiphonemy*, or acclamation, 'Who is wise, and he shall understand these things ?' &c. He doth not say, Let men understand these things, but ' Who is wise, and who is prudent ?' let them consider of these things; and then the exhortation is backed with many reasons.

1. *It is wisdom and prudence* to regard these things I have spoken. 'Who is *wise?* and who is *prudent?*'

2. And then again, *they are the ways of God* that are spoken of, and they are straight and equal in themselves. 'For the *ways,*' &c.

3. And they lead *to happiness directly, without winding and turning.* A man is sure to attain his journey's end in them; and if they will take example of those who only are exemplary to them, he tells them, ' the just shall walk in them.' They shall not walk alone; they shall have the company of ' a cloud of witnesses,' who prosper and walk on cheerfully in this way, and attain happiness in the end.

4. Then the last argument is taken from the *contrary end of all them who cavil and snarl at God's ways and truth,* that think themselves witty to pick quarrels with somewhat in God's book, as it is a common fashion now-a-days to have a divinity of men's own. ' Transgressors,' such as are opposite to God's ways, ' they shall fall in these ways ;' that is, they take offence at these ways, and so fall into sin, and by falling into sin, fall into misery, till at last they fall into hell, which is the end of all quarrellers with divine truths. They fall and dash themselves upon them, and so eternally perish.

Now, these are strong and forcible reasons to enforce care and attention of what hath been spoken. It is ' wisdom and prudence ;' and ' the ways of the Lord' here ' are straight,' and then ' all godly people walk in them,' ' and those that stumble at them are sure to perish,' and do perish in them; not that they are a cause of their perishing, but by reason of the malice of men, finding fault and picking quarrels with them, they fall first into sin, and then into misery. Thus we have the scope of the words.

' Who is wise, and he shall understand these things.'

First of all, we must know that the prophet here in this figurative speech makes a kind of exclamation, ' Who is wise !' He doth, as it were, secretly mourn at the apostasy and fewness of those that be truly wise ; as if he had said, I have given you many directions, and shewed you what sins lead to destruction ; I have shewed what course ye are to take, and the bounty of God to those that return ; but ' who is wise and prudent to regard these things ?'

In the words, therefore, in regard of the speaker, the prophet, we may observe this ere we come particularly to them, *the character of a holy, merciful, gracious, and wise man ;* that when he hath spoken things to excellent purpose, he would not have those things lost, but out of mercy and compassion, mingled with a great deal of heavenly wisdom, would have the best fruit of all he hath spoken. Which was the custom of the men of God in the Scriptures, the Spirit of God leading them to strike the nail home ; when they taught truths, to lay the word close upon the conscience, as much as they could. What is the whole book of Deuteronomy, as the word signifieth,* but a repeating of the former laws ? Moses thought all to

---

* Deuteronomy, *i.e.,* Δευτερονόμιον = the Law again or repeated.—G.

no purpose, unless he repeated laws, and fastened them upon the soul. So our Saviour Christ still when he had spoken excellent things, saith, 'Let him that hath ears to hear, hear,' Mat. xi. 15. So saith Jeremiah, 'Who is wise to consider these things?' Jer. ix. 12; and the conclusion of that excellent psalm is just thus, 'Who is wise to consider these things?' Ps. cvii. 43. And saith Moses, 'O that they were wise, that they would think of these things,' &c., Deut. xxxii. 29. So everywhere in Scripture you have such fastening of things, where truths have been spoken, in application of them; which doth justify the course of God's messengers in bringing the word home unto men's consciences, because that which is spoken loosely in general, no man applieth in particular to himself. We who are messengers of God must therefore bring things home to the conscience. 'Who is wise, and he shall understand these things,' &c.

But that which more nearly concerneth us is, whereas first of all he propounds this exhortation, to regard these things under this holy acclamation, 'Who is wise, and who is prudent?' we see, first of all,

Obs. *That there are but few who are truly wise and prudent.*

Few that enter the right way; for our Saviour sheweth that 'narrow is this way, and few there be that find it,' Mat. vii. 14. The point needs not much proof, it is so plain and well known; wherefore it is now touched only, making way to other things. The reason hereof is clear.

Reason. Most men, we see, live by sense, will, and passion, and not by faith, whereby they enthral the wisdom they have, and make it prisoner to sinful passions and affections, rejecting thoughts of their own future happiness; and though it behove them in this world to be broken of their will, yet they will have it here, though they perish and be damned for it hereafter. This is the state of the unbroken heart of man, till he have grace in him. Yea, it is the state of all men, especially those that are puffed up, either by their own place, humour, or the flattery of others. They will have their will. *Mens mihi pro regno*, as one said. Now, this being the proud, poisonful nature of man, we must not think it a strange thing that there are so few wise and prudent; for a man cannot be wise and passionate; for his passion transforms him to be a beast, a devil. Now, because most men live by sense and by humour, which is a life they are nuzzled* in (especially those that are subject to flatterers), therefore few come to be truly wise and prudent, to have so much steadiness and sobriety of spirit as to deliberate what is to be done. They will not in cold blood give leisure to their humours (but feed them), to consider what is best. This being the humour of the world, no wonder that there be so few prudent and wise.

Use 1. Since things are thus, learn this of it. If there be so few prudent and wise, as the prophets complain in all times, 'To whom is the arm of the Lord revealed? and who hath believed our report?' &c., Isa. liii. 1, then *take heed of living by example*, that we be not led away with the sway and error of the times; for seeing there are few 'wise and prudent,' it is better and safer to follow one man reformed by judgment than a thousand others. One man is worth a thousand, who is led with judgment and by the Spirit of God.

Use 2. And likewise *take no scandal†* *if you see men run upon heaps in the broad and worst way*, for that men have always done. It is the complaint of all the prophets in all times, calling the better sort few. 'As the grapes after the vintage, like a few scattered ears of corn after harvest,' Isa. xvii.

* That is, 'nursed.'—G.   † That is, 'let it not be a stumbling-block.'—G.

5, 6. ' One of a city, and two of a tribe, a few of all,' Jer. iii. 14. Therefore now let us seal this truth with this exhortation.

Use 3. That we labour *to be of that few that are truly wise and prudent.* Examine, are we of those few or not, and what have we in us that may secure us to be of this small number? for if we be not, we shall never be saved. For Christ's flock ' is a little flock,' Luke xii. 32 ; and few there be that shall enter in at that strait gate. What hast thou, then, which may discover unto thine own soul that thou art of that number, and not of the common multitude that shall be damned? It is a thing worth the inquiring of our souls. What have we in us that may characterise us to be God's true servants, Christ's true children, and members of the church? and never rest in a common persuasion of common grace, which castaways may have as well as we. We must strive for some distinct grace, that reprobates cannot attain unto.

' Who is wise, and he shall understand these things? prudent,' &c.

But to come more particularly to the words, ' Who is wise, and he shall understand these things ? ' The holy man of God here in his exhortation, naming wisdom, singling out ' wise and prudent ' men, ' Who is wise, and who is prudent ?' he toucheth men upon the quick, right vein ; for who is there that would not be thought wise and prudent ? A corrupt man naturally rather desires to be thought sinful than weak; judge him as you will, so you judge him not to be an unwise, an unprudent man. A proud man, till he be subdued and humbled, had rather be thought dishonest than simple, because if he be dishonest, he thinks it is out of choice ; but to be simple, this argueth imperfection, and not freedom and bravery of spirit. Therefore, it being the natural desire and instinct of all men to be thought wise and to be so, he endeavours to work upon that affection in them, ' Who is wise ? ' &c. Well, saith he, I know you all desire to be thought ' wise and prudent men.' Would you make it good that you are so indeed? Believe my sayings ! This is the way ; whosoever is wise, let him understand these things ; and he that is prudent let him hearken to these things that I have spoken.

Man at first, when he had communion with wisdom itself, was a wise creature till he hearkened to Satan, and so lost all, ' becoming as the beasts which perish,' Ps. xlix. 12. Yet in that glorious building, since the corruption of nature, this amongst that rubbish is reserved, that above all things there is a desire to be happy and wise, which two desires are naturally the leading desires in men, to desire to do well, and to be wise. Therefore, the prophet here, upon that which is left in man's nature, takes advantage to build true wisdom and knowledge indeed.

To come, then, in brief, to shew what this wisdom and prudence is ; for there is some distinction between wisdom and prudence. *Wisdom* is a heavenly light set up in the soul by the Spirit of God, whereby it discerneth the general truths concerning God, ourselves, the state of the church, the privileges of Christianity, and such like. In sum, it is a right, divine apprehension of spiritual truths.

And *prudence:* this is a kind of sharpness of spirit, whereby the Spirit of God directs the soul, knowing the right general principles, to particular cases. Prudence is an application of the general knowledge of general things to particulars, and is an ordering of the life in particular exigencies and cases in a right order, according to the direction of the Spirit, as we have it, Prov. viii. 12, ' I wisdom dwell with prudence.' Divine wisdom, wheresoever it is, dwells with prudence ; that is, where God doth enlighten the understanding to conceive aright of the mysteries of salvation, there it dwells with prudence; that is, it directs the soul to an orderly carriage of life towards God and man, and in regard of itself, every way as it should do, in all estates, times, and conditions. That is meant here by prudence, a particular gift whereby a man is fit to consult and deliberate of things in particular to be done, in particular cases of conscience, and the like. Now, wisdom and prudence, they are both together in God's people, howsoever perhaps one is more excellent than another. Some are wiser, who have a deeper search of truths in general; and some are more prudent in their ways, that are weaker Christians for the main general truths. Yet there is not a good Christian but he hath so much prudence as will bring him to heaven. But God giveth extraordinary wisdom to some, because they are leaders of others. Yet though in God's dispensation there be a difference, yet in every Christian they are joined together. There is no Christian but he is wise for himself, which is prudence. This is, as it were, the salt which seasoneth all other graces and knowledge whatsoever; for what is knowledge without discretion but a foolish humour? what is patience but blockishness if a man do not discern how, why, and upon what ground to be patient? what is religiousness without this but superstition? and what is zeal but an indiscreet heat, if it be not seasoned with this prudence? yea, and what is constancy itself but an indiscreet rigour and stiffness without wit? So that it is the seasoning of all other graces whatsoever, that which puts bounds and measure unto all. Therefore, he joins it with wisdom, ' Who is wise? and who is prudent?' Good, as we say, consists of a whole, entire cause, unto which must be occurrence* of all circumstances together. One defect may make it to be sinful. So this is prudence, to observe a due order, clothed with circumstances of the manner and season of every good action and duty. Therefore, he joins here prudence, ' Who is wise, and he shall understand these things? prudent, and he shall know them ?'

Now, these be the two graces that lead and guide a man's life. There must be first a general understanding and light of the soul, and then there must be a particular light to apply this general to particulars. Prudence is, as it were, the steward of the soul, which dispenseth the light thereof, according to particular occasions.

Now, for wisdom and prudence, we will not insist long on them, only we will draw towards a right discerning of them, squared and proportioned to our understandings by resemblances of other things. For a man may know what they are in divine things by some proportion to human things, what they are there as to give a little light to it.

1. He is a wise, prudent man in the world that will be sure to make *the greatest his friend.* So God, being the greatest of all and most able to do us good, he is a wise and prudent man that makes him his friend, and cares not who he break with, so he break not with God.

2. And we account him also a wise and prudent man in the world, that, like the wise steward in the gospel, *provides for the worst times.* What course did he take for himself herein? He provides for, as he foresees, danger, Mat. xvi. 3. So spiritual wisdom and prudence will direct a man what is best for his latter end, his eternal rest and happiness in another world. Heavenly wisdom prefixeth to† a man a full view of his latter end, and that which followeth thereupon in another world, and so makes him provide beforehand and direct all things to that end. A wise man will not have things to seek when he comes to make use of them, like the foolish virgins, who had their oil to seek when they should have had it ready,

* That is, ' concurrence.'—G.　　　　　　† That is, ' sets before.'—Ed.

Mat. xxv. 8.　He is truly spiritually wise towards his latter end, that, as he knows there is a state to come, so is truly prudent to have all things ready against that time, that, considering the uncertainty of this life, he may not be surprised unawares, like those glorious* virgins who had a lamp without oil.

3. And amongst men he is also counted a wise and prudent man *that makes a right choice;* for this is wisdom when a man discerneth a difference, and answerably makes his choice. *Simile mater erroris,* saith one, Likeness is the mother of error (*y*).　There is a likeness between good and bad in the world, and between truth and error.　Now, he is a wise man who is not catched with these resemblances, but discerneth a difference between temporal and eternal things, shadows and substances, realities and appearances of things, and suitably chooseth eternals before temporals, the favour of God before the favour of men, and, in a word, those things which concern everlasting happiness before those that are perishing.　Wisdom is seen in choice.　By these few instances named, we may see what heavenly wisdom and prudence is, by proportion of wisdom and prudence in earthly things.　Now, considering that there is a better state in another world than in this, he must needs be a wise man that orders things so as that he may not lose eternity.　Most men in the world are penny-wise and pound-foolish, as we say, wise to a particular end, to get particular favours and riches, so to satisfy their intentions; but for the main, which is wisdom indeed, to look to their last estate and happiness, and to fit their actions and courses that way, how few are wise to purpose!　How few provide for eternity!　Therefore, no marvel the prophet saith, ' Who is wise? and who is prudent?' because men live by sense, and not by faith.

' Who is wise, and he shall understand these things? prudent, and he shall know them?'

Obs. Now, the next thing to be observed hence is this, *that the wise and prudent only know these things.*　There must be wisdom and prudence before we can know divine truths, and make use of them.

Obs. And then observe further, *that true wisdom and prudence carries men to God's word.*　' Who is wise to understand these things?'　By divine truth we grow wise and prudent, the Spirit joining with the same, and then we come to make a right use of them.　There must be first a spiritual wisdom and prudence, enlightened by the Spirit, ere we can make use of the word aright, to taste and relish it.　Because, though the word be light, yet light alone is not sufficient to cause sight, but there must concur unto the outward light an inward sight.　Grace must illuminate the understanding, and put a heavenly light into the soul.　As by the light within meeting with the light without, the eye being the instrument of sight, applying itself to the thing, thence comes sight.　So there be divine truths out of us, wherewith, when the Holy Ghost puts an inward light into the soul, sanctified wisdom and prudence, then the inward light meeting with the light without, we see and apprehend.　The Spirit, therefore, must join to work wisdom and prudence.　Naturally we are all dead, and have lost our spiritual senses.　Therefore the Spirit of God must work in us spiritual senses, sight, and taste, that we may see, discern, and relish heavenly things, which, ere we can do, there must be an harmony betwixt the soul and the things; that is, the soul must be made spiritual, answerable to the heavenly things pitched upon, or else, if the soul be not set in a suitable frame, it can never make a right use of them.

* That is, 'over-confident.'—Ed.

Now, when the understanding of a man is made wise by the Spirit of God, it will relish wisdom and prudence. For the Spirit of God, together with the Scripture, takes the scales off the eyes of the soul, subdues rebellious passions in the affections, especially that rebellion of the will, putting a new relish in all, so as they come to love, affect,* and joy in heavenly things. Now, when these scales of spiritual blindness are fallen off the eyes of the soul, and when rebellion is removed from the will and affections, then it is fit to join and approve of heavenly things, else there is a contrariety and antipathy betwixt the soul and these things. As the body, when the tongue is affected with some aguish humour, cannot relish things, though they be never so good, but affecteth and relisheth all things suiting that distemper; so it is with the soul. When it is not enlightened it judgeth all things carnally, there being an antipathy between the soul and divine truths brought home unto it. Perhaps a soul not enlightened or sanctified will apprehend the generalities of truth very well, but when they are pressed home to practice, then, unless the soul be changed, it will rise up and swell against divine truths, and reject the practice of them. Without subduing grace, to alter and change the soul, the affections thereof are like the March suns,'which stir up a great many humours, but not spending them, they breed aguish humours and distempers. So the light of the word in a carnal heart, it meets with the humours of the soul, and stirs them; but if there be not grace in the soul to subdue these affections, it stirs them up to be the more malicious, especially if they be pressed to particular duties in leaving of sinful courses. So that the Spirit of God must alter the understanding, and subdue the will and affections, ere there can be a conceiving of divine truths savingly. Therefore, before these acts, he joins these graces. ' Who is wise? and who is prudent?' &c.

Use. The use hereof is thus much: Not to come to the divine truth of God with human affections and spirits, but to lift up our hearts to God. Why, Lord, as things themselves are spiritual, so make me spiritual, that there may be a harmony between my soul and the things; that as there is a sweet relish in divine truths, so there may be a sweet taste in me, to answer that relish which is in divine truths; that the wisdom of thy word and my wisdom may be one! Then a man is wise. There is not the commonest truth, or practical point in divinity, but it is a mystery, and must be divinely understood, and must have prudence to go about it as we should do. Repentance and the knowledge of sin, it is a mystery till a man be sanctified in his understanding. He can never know what spiritual misery is till the inward man be enlightened and sanctified, to know what a contrariety there is between sin and the Spirit of God. As no man can know thoroughly what sickness is but he that hath been sick; for the physician doth not know sickness so well as the patient who feels it; so it is with a holy man, sanctified with the Holy Ghost. Tell him of sin, he feels it, and the noisomeness of it, the opposition of it to his comfort and communion with God. Only the spiritual enlightened man can tell what repentance, sin, sorrow for sin, and the spiritual health of the soul is. Therefore it is said here, ' Who is wise? and who is prudent? and he shall understand these things.'

* That is, ' choose ' = cherish.—G.

THE FIFTEENTH SERMON.

*Who is wise, and he shall understand these things? prudent, and he shall know
them? for the ways of the Lord are right, the just shall walk in them: but
the transgressors shall fall therein.*—Hos. XIV. 9.

At length, by divine assistance, we are come unto the conclusion of this
short chapter, wherein the Holy Ghost, from God, hath shewed such bowels
of mercy and tender compassion unto miserable sinners, encouraging them
to return unto the Lord by many and several arguments, being formerly
insisted upon.   Our last work was to shew you what wisdom and prudence
was, the difference of them, and how that none, without these endowments,
are able to know and make use of divine truths and mysteries of religion.
' Who is wise, and he shall understand these things? prudent, and he shall
know them?' &c.

We came then to shew, that there must be prudence and wisdom, before
we can understand divine truths; there must be an illumination within.
It is not sufficient to have the light of the Scripture outwardly, but there
must be a light of the eye to see; there must be wisdom and prudence
gathered from the Scriptures.   Now, wisdom and prudence, if they be
divine, as here is meant, it is not a discreet managing of outward affairs of
our personal condition, but an ordering of our course to heavenward.
Wherefore a man may know whether he be wise and prudent by his relish-
ing of divine truths, for otherwise he is not wise and prudent in these things
which are the main.

Now, having shewed that only the wise and prudent can conceive and
make a right use of these great things delivered, he comes to shew and
defend the equity of God's ways, how crooked soever they seem to flesh
and blood.   These things ought to be hearkened unto, because they are the
ways of God.

' The ways of the Lord are right.'

By *ways* here, he understandeth the whole law and gospel, the whole
word of God; which he calleth *right*, not only because,

1. They are righteous in themselves; but,

2. Because they reform whatsoever is amiss in us, and rectify us; and

3. Work whatsoever is needful for our good and salvation.

Now more particularly, God's ways are,

1. Those ways wherein he walks to us; or,

2. The ways that he prescribes us to walk in; and,

3. Our ways, as they are conformable to his.

Any of these are the ways of God; of all which more hereafter.

1. *The ways wherein he walks to us,* because many of them are untrace-
able, as unsearchable to us, are not here meant; as those of election, predestination and reprobation; the reasons whereof, if we take them comparatively, cannot be searched out.   Why God should take one and not another,
it is an unsearchable way.   But take a man single, out of comparison, the
ways of God will appear to be right, even in that harsh decree which many
men stumble so much at.   For none are ever brought in the execution of
that decree to be damned, but you shall see ' the ways of the Lord right,'
who a long time together offers them a great deal of mercy, which they refusing, and resisting the Holy Ghost, taking wilfully contrary courses, work
out their own damnation.   So that at length the issue of those unsearch-

able ways will appear to be right in every particular ; howsoever the com‑parative reason at the first, why God singles out one man and not another, will not appear.

2. As for the *ways of his providence*, in governing the world, and ruling of his church, this is the way of God which is right ; all which ways, though we cannot in all particulars see in this world, yet in heaven, in the light of glory, we shall see what cannot now be seen in the light of grace and nature. For there be mysteries in providence. Who can tell the reason why, of men equally good, one should be sorely afflicted, and the other should go to heaven without any affliction in a smooth way ? None can give a reason of it ; but we must subscribe to the hidden wisdom of God, whose ways are unsearchable in his providence. Yet are they most right, though they be above our conceit. If we could conceive all God's ways, then they were not God's ways ; for in his ways to us, he will so carry them, as he will shew himself to be above and beyond our shallow conceits.

But the ways especially here meant, are the ways which he prescribes us to walk in ; and they are,

1. What we must believe ; and then,

2. What we must do. There is,

First, obedience of faith, and then obedience of life.

These are God's ways prescribed in the word, and only in the word.

3. Now *our ways*, when they join with *God's ways*, that is, when our life, purposes and desires of the inner-man, in our speeches, carriage, and con‑versation, agree with God's ways, then in some sort they are God's ways, ' the just shall walk in them.' They shall walk in these ways, that is, in those ways which God prescribeth. As for those ways wherein God walks to us, we have not so much to do here to consider them. But by walking in the ways which he prescribes, we shall feel that his ways to us will be nothing but mercy and truth. ' The ways of the Lord are right,' Ps. cxlv. 17. Those ways that he prescribes to men to be believed and done, they are right and straight, that is, they are agreeable to the first rule of all. Right is the judgment and will of God. He is the first truth and the first good ; the prime truth and good, which must rule all others, *mensura men-surans*, as they use to speak in schools ; the measure that measures all other things. For all other things are only so far right, as they agree to the highest measure of all, which is God's appointment and will. So the ways of God are said to be right ; because they agree to his word and will. They are holy and pure, as himself is just, pure, and holy.

' The ways of the Lord are right.'

Right, as they agree to that which is right and straight ; and right like‑wise, because they lead directly to a right end. We know a right line is that which is the shortest between two terms. That which leads from point to point, is the shortest of all other lines. *So God's ways are right and straight.* There are no other ways which tend directly to happiness, with‑out error, but God's ways ; all other ways are crooked ways. So God's ways are right, as they look to God, and as they look unto all other inferior courses. They are right to examine all our ways by, being the rule of them. And they are right, as they look to God's will, and are ruled by him.

' The ways of the Lord are right.'

Hence observe we in the first place, that the first thing we should look to in our conversation, must be to know this for a ground.

Obs. That man is not a prescriber of his own way, and that no creature's will is a rul-.

We must embrace, therefore, no opinion of any man, or any course enjoined or prescribed by any man, further than it agrees with the first truth and the first right. God's ways are right; right as a standard, that is, a measure to measure all other measures by. So God's will and truth revealed is a right rule, and the measure of all other rules whatsoever. Directions therefore, which we have of things to be believed and done from men, must be no further regarded than as they agree with the first standard. Therefore they are mistaken, and desperately mistaken, that make any man's will a rule, unless it be subordinate to that which is higher, at which time it becometh all one with the higher rule. When a man subordinates his directions to God's, then God's and his are all one. Otherwise without this subordination, we make men gods, when we make their will a rule of our obedience. 'The ways of the Lord are right.' But of this only a touch by the way; the main point hence is.

Obs. The word of the Lord is every way perfect, and brings us to perfection.

As we may see at large proved, Ps. xix. 7, &c., where whatsoever is good, comfortable, profitable or delightful, either for this life or the life to come, is all to be had from thence. And the wise man saith, 'Every word of God is pure,' &c., Prov. xxx. 5: a similitude taken from gold, which is fined till it be pure, as it is expressed in another place, 'The words of the Lord are pure words, as silver tried in a furnace of earth, and purified seven times,' Ps. xii. 6. And so the apostle to Timothy. 'All Scripture is given by inspiration of God, and is profitable for doctrine, for correction, for reproof, for instruction in righteousness, that the man of God may be perfect, throughly furnished unto all good works,' 2 Tim. iii. 16.

Use 1. Since then the ways of God are so right, just, pure, and perfect, *this is first for reproof of them that add hereunto;* as our Romish adversaries, who do herein, by their traditions and additions, condemn God either of want of wisdom, love, and goodness, or of all. So as all defects charged upon the word, are charged upon God himself, who did not better provide and foresee for his church what was good for it. But the wise man condemneth this their audacious boldness, where he saith, ' Add thou not unto his words, lest he reprove thee, and thou be found a liar,' Prov. xxx. 6. They bar reading of the Scriptures, or to read them in English especially, lest the people become heretics. They think it safe to read their own books and idle dreams, but reject the word of God, and then, as Jeremiah speaks, ' What wisdom is in them ?' Jer. viii. 9. Surely none at all; for the only wisdom is, to be governed by God's most holy word.

Use 2. Again, *it is for instruction unto us, to rest and rely upon this so holy, right, pure, and perfect word.* Since it is so sure and firm, we are to rest upon the promises, and tremble at the threatenings, though we see not present performance of them, because not one of them shall fail. For, saith Christ, ' Heaven and earth shall pass away, but one jot and tittle of the law shall not fail,' Matt. v. 28. What maketh so many judgments to overtake men, but their unbelief? what made their carcases to fall in the wilderness, so as they could not enter into the land of Canaan, but their unbelief? for, saith the text of them, ' They could not enter, because of unbelief,' Heb. iii. 19. Infidelity, and not believing God, is the root and cause of all our woe. It began with our first parents, and it cleaveth too close unto us, even unto this day. This cometh from our atheism and selflove; that if a mortal man promise or swear unto us, we believe him, and rest upon his word; but all that the great God can do unto us by promises, commandments, threatenings, allurements, and gracious examples, will not make us give credit to his word, but rather believe Satan, and our own false and deceitful hearts. As, for instance, God hath promised, that ' if our sins were as red as scarlet, yet he will make them whiter than the snow,' Isa. i. 18; though they be never so strong for us, yet he hath promised ' to subdue them,' Micah vii. 19. If our wants be never so great, yet if we will trust in God, he hath promised to relieve us, and hath said, ' that he will not fail us nor forsake us,' Isa. l. 10 ; Heb. xiii. 5, if we cast our care upon him. So, for the threatenings, we must believe that there is never a one of them but they shall come to pass, as sure as the promises shall be made good. If these thoughts were firmly settled in us, that ' the ways of the Lord are right,' and therefore must be all accomplished in their time, it would make us restless to fly from sin, and the punishments threatened, which all ' lie at the door,' Gen. iv. 7, and will quickly be upon us, if they be not avoided by sound and hearty repentance.

Use 3. Lastly, if every commandment be right, sure, and just, then when God commandeth do it, though the apparent danger be never so great, and though it be never so contrary to flesh and blood, pleasure, profit, or preferment, yet *know it is firm and sure, and that our happiness stands in doing it, our misery in disobeying it,*—as we know it was with Adam. What a sudden change did his disobedience work in himself, all the world since being leavened with that miserable contagious fall of his ! And for the whole world this is a general, we never want any good, but for want of love and obedience unto it. ' Great prosperity shall they have,' saith David, ' who love thy law, and no evil shall come unto them,' Ps. cxix. 165. And we never had nor shall have any hurt, but from our unbelief and disobedience to the holy, pure, and perfect word of God, which is attended with comfort and prosperity here, and endless glory hereafter.

' The ways of the Lord are right.'

In the next place, if the ways of the Lord be right and straight, so straight that they lead directly to the right end, then it is clear,

Obs. That *the best way to come to a good and right end, is to take God's ways.* For it is a right way, and the right way is always the shortest way. Therefore, when men take not God's ways, prescriptions, and courses, they go wide about, and seldom or never come to their intended end. God's way is the right way, and therefore brings a man to his right end. Sometimes men will have their turnings, their *diverticula,* and vagaries, but they find by experience that God's ways they are the right ways, so as they never attain to comfort and peace until they come again into those ways. God until then suffereth them to be snared and hampered, and to eat the fruit of their own ways, and then they see the difference of God's ways and theirs, and that God's ways are the best, and the straightest ways unto true happiness.

Indeed, God suffers sometimes men that will have their own ways to come quickly to them, as some men hasten to be rich, and God suffers them to be rich hastily : yet they are none of God's ways which they take, but climb up by fraud and deceit. Aye, but that is only a particular end which God suffereth them to attain by byeways ; but what will be the upshot ? Where will all these ways end at length ? Surely in hell. For when a man goes out of the right, and straight, and direct way, to be great in the world, he is like a man who goes out of his way, which is further about ; who yet, when he is in that way, goes on through thick and thin, because he will gain some way. He goes on through thickets and hedges, fair and foul, where he gets many scratches, brushes and knocks. Doth any think in the world to attain his particular ends without* the direct ways of God ? God may suffer him to attain his particular end, but with many flaws, knocks, and brushes upon his conscience, which many times he carrieth with him unto his grave ; and finds it a great deal better, both to attain unto his particular ends by God's ways, and to have no more of anything in the world than he can have with a good conscience. For, though they be good men, ofttimes God suffers such men to have bruises in their conscience all their days, that they and others may know that the best way is the straight and right way, which at last will bring us best to our end.

Having thus made it good, ' that the ways of the Lord are right,' now, for conclusion of all, the prophet begins to shew the divers effects these right ways of God have in two sorts of people, the godly and wicked.

I. The just shall walk in them :

II. That the transgressors shall fall therein.

I. *The just shall walk in them.* Who be the just men here spoken of ? Such are just men who give to every one their due ; that give God his due in the first place, and man in the second place, whereby it is framed. ' The just shall walk in them ;' that is, they shall proceed and go on in them till they be come to the end of their race, the salvation of their souls. And, more particularly,

(1.) Just men first, are such, *who have respect unto all God's commandments*, Ps. cxix. 6. Though in their disposition they find some more hard to them than others, yet they do not allow themselves to break any, but strive so much the more earnestly and constantly to observe them, as they find their natures opposite to them. Now hypocrites, howsoever they do many things in show, yet, like Herod and Judas, their hearts run in a wrong channel ; they allow themselves to live in, and like of some sin. The young man in the gospel had not a respect unto all God's commandments, though Christ loved his amiable parts, Mat. x. 21. To this purpose James saith, ' Whosoever shall keep the whole law, and yet offend in one point, he is guilty of all,' James ii. 10. That is, he who alloweth himself in any one sin, he is guilty of all. Ask Judas, Is murder good ? He would have said, no : but he was covetous, and allowed himself in it, and so drew upon him the guilt of all the rest. God is he who forbids sinning against them all. He who forbids one, forbids all ; and being rightly turned to God, the same authority makes us leave all. It is not sin, but the allowance of it, that makes an hypocrite.

(2.) Again, *they do things to a good end,* the glory of God, and the good of man. For want hereof, the alms, prayers, and fasting of the scribes and Pharisees (because they did nothing out of love to God or man, but for vainglory and carnal respects), are condemned of Christ. So some are brought in at the last day, saying, ' Lord, Lord, have we not in thy name prophesied, and in thy name cast out devils, and in thy name done many wonderful works,' Mat. vii. 22 ; and yet Christ professeth not to know them, but calleth them ' workers of iniquity.' They had gifts and calling, and delivered true doctrine, &c. But here was their failing, ' They prophesied *in* his name, but not *for* his name.' Their actions were good in themselves, and for others, but the end of them was naught, and therefore both they and their works are condemned. Yet this is not so to be understood, but that God's children have some thoughts of vainglory, which accompanieth and creepeth into their best actions ; but they do acknowledge this

* That is, ' outside of.'—Ed.

for a sin, confess it, and desire the Lord to pardon and subdue it, and then it shall never be laid to their charge. Because having of infirmities is not contrary to sincerity, but allowing of them, and living in them; in which case the Lord is more pleased with our humiliation for our sin, than the motions to vainglory did offend him.

(3.) Thirdly, *a desire to grow in grace, and to become better and better*, is a sign of uprightness. Christian righteousness, as it sees still need, so it still desires more grace and less sin; because he who hath a true heart, seeth both the want and worth of grace, and feeleth his want. A man feels not the want of faith, humility, and love, till he have it in some sort, as it is said, Philip. iii. 15, ' As many as are perfect are thus minded,' to wit, so many as are upright: all is one.

(4.) Lastly, this just uprightness is known *by love of the brethren*. ' By this we know we are translated from death to life, because we love the brethren,' 1 John iii. 14. Contrary to which is that disposition which envieth at all things which suits not with their humours: as James speaketh of those who prefer men, and have their persons in admiration, in regard of outward things, despising inferiors, James ii. 2.

Use 1. If therefore we will ever be counted righteous persons, let us keep these rules set down here, have a respect to all God's commandments, do all things to the glory of God, desire to grow in grace, and love the brethren.

2. And so it is also for consolation unto such who are thus qualified; for unto them belongeth all the promises of this life, and of that to come. They are in a blessed estate, for ' all things are theirs,' 1 Cor. iii. 21, because they are Christ's. Therefore it is their bounden duty, having an upright heart, to rejoice in God, as the prophet speaks : ' Rejoice in the Lord, ye righteous, for praise is comely for the upright,' Ps. xxxiii. 1 ; lii. 9. None have cause to rejoice but upright men.

1. Because they of all others have title and right to joy. 2. Because they have command to do it, seeing heaven is theirs. All the promises are theirs, and they are heirs of all things. It is a comely service, and the work of heaven.

Obj. Against this some object. Oh, but I find many sins, passions, and infirmities in myself; how then can I joy in God ?

Ans. To this we answer briefly, that the passions and infirmities of God's servants are not contrary to Christian uprightness and righteousness; for St James saith, that ' Elias was a man subject to like passions and infirmities as we are,' James v. 17, yet he was a righteous man, though a man subject to the like passions as we are. Therefore the passions of Christians are not contrary to Christian, but to legal, righteousness. But ' we are not under the law, but under grace,' Rom. vi. 15. The first covenant of works bids us have no sin ; the other covenant bids us allow no sin. Thus much is for that question, What is meant by *just men ?* It remains now that we should further inquire into that mystery, how it is that just men walk in the ways of God, and prosper therein, when yet wicked men, called ' transgressors,' fall therein. But this being a mystery, by your patience we will take time to unfold what we have to speak hereof the next time, if God be so pleased.

THE SIXTEENTH SERMON.

The ways of the Lord are right: the just shall walk in them; but the trans-gressors shall fall therein.—Hos. XIV. 9.

God's children have their times of deadness and desertion, and again their times of quickening and rejoicing. Weeping doth not always remain unto them for their portion, 'but joy cometh in the morning,' Ps. xxx. 5. In the worst times the saints have always some comforts afforded them, which supporteth them against all the storms and tempests they endure. They have always a Goshen, Exod. ix. 22, to fly to. Others shall perish in that way, wherein they shall walk and escape.

'The just shall walk in them, but the transgressors shall fall therein.'

Thus far we are now come in the unfolding of this chapter, having shewed God's rich and incomparable mercies to miserable and penitent sinners; how ready God is to embrace such, as this rebellious people named were, with all the arguments used to make them return unto the Lord. We are now come at last unto the upshot of all, a discovery of the several effects and works God's word hath upon both sorts of people here named and aimed at.

'The just shall walk in them, but the transgressors shall fall therein.'

These were very bad times; yet there were just men, who walked in the ways of God: so that we see—

In the worst times, God will have always a people that shall justify wisdom.

God will have it thus, even in the worst times, that 'the just shall walk in them.' Though before he saith, 'Who is wise? and who is prudent?' yet here he shews that there shall be a number who shall 'walk in God's ways,' who though they go to heaven alone, yet to heaven they will. Though they have but a few that walk in God's ways with them, they will rather go with a few that way, than with the wicked on the broad way to hell. Alway God hath some who shall walk in his way; for if there were not some alway who were good, the earth would not stand; for good men they are the pillars of the world, who uphold it. It is not for wicked men's sake that God upholds the frame of the creatures, and that orderly govern-ment. We see all is to gather together the number of his elect, of whom in some ages there are more, and in some less, of them born, thereafter as God breathes and blows with his Spirit. For according to the abundant working of the Spirit, is the number of the elect. Yet in all ages there are some, because it is an article of our faith, to believe 'a holy catholic church.'* Now it cannot be an article of faith, unless there were alway some that made this catholic church; for else there should be an act of faith, without an object. Therefore we may always say, I believe that there are a number of elect people that walk in the ways of God to heaven-wards.

And what is the disposition of these some? To have a counter motion to those of the times and places they live in. Some are foolish, not caring for the ways of God, cavilling at them. But the 'just shall walk in them,' that is, they take a contrary course to the world, that slights wisdom. Thus in all times it is the disposition of God's children to go contrary to the world in the greatest matters of all. They indeed hold correspondency, in outward things, but for the main they have a contrary motion. As we say of the planets, that they have a motion contrary to the wrapt motion.

* Creed, Article IX. Cf. Pearson and Smith, *in loc.*—G.

Being carried and hurried about every twenty-four hours with the motion of the heavens, they have another motion and circuit of their own, which they pass also. So it is with God's people: though in their common carriage they be carried with the common customs and fashions of the times, yet they have a contrary motion of their own, whereby being carried by the help of God's Spirit, they go on in a way to heaven, though the world discern it not. They have a secret contrary motion, opposite to the sins and corruptions of the age and times they live in. Therefore, in all ages it is observed for a commendation to go on in a contrary course to the present times. Noah in his time, Lot in his time, and Paul in his time, who complains, 'All men seek their own,' Philip. ii. 21. It is a strange thing that Paul should complain of all men seeking their own, even then when the blood of Christ was so warm, being so lately shed, and the gospel so spread; yet 'all men seek their own.' And he speaks it with tears; but what became of Paul, and Timothy, and the rest? 'But our conversation is in heaven, from whence we look for the Saviour, the Lord Jesus Christ,' &c., Philip. iii. 20. Let all men seek their own here below, as they will, we have our conversation contrary to the world. 'Our conversation is in heaven,' &c. So that they hold out God's truth in the midst of a crooked and perverse generation, that is, when every man takes crooked ways and courses in carnal policy; yet there are a company that notwithstanding walk in the right ways of God, clean contrary to others. The just will walk in the right ways of God. As holy Joshua said, 'Choose you what you will do, but howsoever, I and my father's house will serve the Lord,' Josh. xxiv. 15. So when many fell from Christ for a fit, because his doctrine seemed harsh, Peter justified that way. When Christ asked him, Will ye also leave me with the rest who are offended? 'Lord,' saith he, 'whither shall we go?' We have tasted the sweetness of the word, and felt the power thereof: 'Whither shall we go, Lord? thou hast the words of eternal life,' John vi. 68. So God's people have an affection, carriage, and course, contrary to the world.

Reason. The reason is taken from their own disposition; they are partakers of the divine nature, 2 Pet. i. 4, which carrieth them up to Godwards against the stream and current of the time.

Use. The use hereof, shall be only a trial of ourselves in evil times, whether or not then, *we justify God's ways and the best things.* If we do, it is a sign we are of the number of God's elect, to defend and maintain good causes and right opinions, especially in divine truths, which is the best character of a Christian. Others in their own sphere have their degree of goodness, but we speak of supernatural divine goodness. A man may know he belongs to God, if he justify wisdom in the worst times, if he stand for the truth to the utmost, thinking it of more price than his life. It is the first degree to religion, 'to hate father and mother, wife and children, and all for the gospel,' Luke xiv. 26. Now when a man will justify the truth, with the loss of anything in the world, it is a sign that man is a good man in ill times.

Therefore, in ill times let us labour to justify truth, both the truth of things to be believed, and all just religious courses, not only in case of opposition being opposed, but in example, though we say nothing. Noah condemned the world, though he spake not a word, by making an ark, Heb. xi. 7; so Lot, Sodom, though he told not all Sodom of their faults. So a man may justify good things, though he speak not a word to any man, for such a one's life is a confutation and sufficient witness for God against the world. Therefore it is good, though a man do not confront the world in his speeches, yet notwithstanding, at least to hold a course contrary to the world in his conversation. We have need of a great deal of courage to do this ; but there is no heavenly wise man, but he is a courageous man. Though in his own spirit he may be a weak man, yet in case of opposition, grace will be above nature, he will shew then his heavenly wisdom and prudence, and of what metal he is made, by justifying wisdom in all times, ' The just shall walk therein.' But to come more directly to the words,

' The just shall walk in them.'

A just and righteous man that is made just by them, shall walk in them. Hence we may observe,

Obs. That first men must have spiritual life, and be just, before they can walk. Walking is an action of life. There must be life before there can be walking. A man must first have a spiritual life, whereby he may be just, and then he will walk as a just man. For, as we say of a bowl,* it is Austin's comparison, it is first made round, and then it runs round ; so a man is first just, and then he doth justly. It is a conceit of the papists, that good works do justify a man. Luther says well, that ' a good man doth good works.' Good works make not the man. Fruit makes not the tree, but the tree the fruit. So we are just first, and then we walk as just men. We must labour to be changed and to have a principle of spiritual life ; then we shall walk and have new feet, eyes, taste, ears, and senses ; all shall then be new.

Again, in the second place, the necessity of it appears hence, that there must be first spiritual life in the inward man, ere a man can walk, because there will not else be a harmony and correspondency betwixt a man and his ways. A man will not hold in those ways that he hath an antipathy to ; therefore, his nature must be altered by a higher principle, before he can like and delight in the ways of God. This is that which God's children desire first of God, that he would alter their natures, enlighten, change and quicken them, work strongly and powerfully in them, that they may have a sympathy and liking unto all that is good ; first they are just, and then they walk in God's ways.

' The just shall walk in them.'

Obs. In the next place, we may observe hence, *that a just man, he being the prudent and wise man, he walks in God's ways.* That is, spiritual wisdom and prudence, together with grace, righteousness, and justice, they lead to walking in obedience. Let no man therefore talk of grace and wisdom or prudence altering him, further than he makes it good by his walking. He that is just, walks as a just man ; he that is wise, walks wisely ; he that is prudent, walks prudently. Which is spoken to discover hypocrisy in men, that would be thought to be good Christians and wise men, because they have a great deal of speculative knowledge. Aye, but look we to our ways, let them shew whether we be wise or foolish, just or unjust. ' If a man be wise, he is wise for himself,' Prov. ix. 12, as Solomon saith, to direct his own ways ; ' The wisdom of the wise, is to understand his own way that he is to walk in,' Prov. xiv. 8. If a man have not wisdom to direct his way in particular, to walk to heavenward, he is but a fool. For a man to know so much as shall condemn him, and be a witness against him, and yet not know so much as to save him, what a miserable thing is this ? Now all other men that know much, and walk not answerable, they know so much as to condemn them, and not to save them. Our Saviour

* That is, a ' ball' for bowling.—G

Christ he calleth such ' foolish builders,' Matt. vii. 27, that know and will not do ; so unless there be a walking answerable to the wisdom and prudence prescribed, a man is but a foolish man.

Therefore let it be a rule of trial, would we be thought to be wise and prudent, just and good ? Let us look to our ways. Are they God's ways ? Do we delight in these ways, and make them our ways ? Then we are wise, prudent, and just.

' The just shall walk in them.'

As the just shall walk in them, so whosoever walks in them are just, wise, and prudent ; for is not he prudent, who walks in those ways that lead directly to eternal happiness ? Is not he a wise man, that walks by rule in those ways where he hath God over him, to be his protector, ruler, and defender ? Is not he a wise man, who walks in those ways that fits him for all conditions whatsoever, prosperity or adversity, life or death, for all estates ? He that walks therefore in God's ways, must be the only wise man.

Now, what things doth this walking in the ways of God imply ?

1. First, *perspicuity*. Those who walk in the ways of God, they discern those ways to be God's ways, and discern them aright.

2. Then when they discern them to be God's good ways, answerably *they proceed in them from step to step ;* for every action is a step to heaven or to hell. So a just man, when he hath discovered a good way, he goes on still.

3. And then *he keeps an uniform course*, for so he doth who walks on in a way. He makes not indentures* as he walks, but goes on steadily in an uniform course to a right end. So a just man, when he hath singled out the right way, he goes on in that steadily and uniformly.

4. And likewise where it is said, the just walks in them, it implies *resolution to go on in those ways* till he come to the end, though there be never so much opposition.

But how shall we know whether we go on in this way or not ?

First, he that goes on in a way, the further he hath proceeded therein, looking back, *that which he leaves behind seems lesser and lesser in his eye ;* and that which he goes to greater and greater. So a man may know his progress in the ways of God, when earthly profits and pleasures seem little, his former courses and pleasures seeming now base unto him. When heaven and heavenly things seem near unto him, it is a sign he is near heaven, near in time, and nearer in disposition and in wisdom to discern, because the best things are greatest in his eye and esteem. In this case, it is a sign that such a one is removed from the world, and is near unto heaven, having made a good progress in the ways of God.

It implies likewise in the *second* place, *an uniform course of life.* Such a one doth not duties by starts now and then, but constantly. Therefore we must judge of men by a tenure of life, what their constant ways are. Sometimes though they be good men, they may step away into an ill way, and yet come in again. Sometimes an ill man may cross a good way, as a thief when he crosseth the highway, or a good man steps out of the way ; but this is not their way, they are both out, and to seek, of their way. A wicked man when he speaks of good things, he is out of his way ; he acts a part and assumes a person he is unskilful to act ; therefore he doth it untowardly. But. a man's way is his course. A good man's way is good, though his startings be ill ; and an ill man's way is naught, though for passion, or for by-ends, he may now and then do good things. Therefore, considering

* That is, ' zig-zags.'—ED.

that the walking in the ways of God is uniform and orderly ; let us judge of ourselves by the tenure of our life, and course thereof. And let those poor souls who think they are out of the way, because they run into some infirmities now and then, comfort themselves in this, that God judgeth not by single actions, but according to the tenure of a man's life, what he is. For oftentimes God's children gain by their slips, which makes them look the more warily to their ways for ever after that. He that walks in the way to heaven, if he be a good man, he looks to make surer footing in the ways of God after his slips and falls. He labours also to make so much the more haste home, being a gainer by all his slips and falls. Let none therefore be discouraged, but let them labour that their ways and courses may be good, and not only so, but to be uniform, orderly, and constant, and then they may speak peace to their own souls, being such as are here described, ' The just shall walk in them.'

Third, again, he that will walk aright in God's ways, he must be *resolute against all opposition whatsoever*, for we meet with many lets, hindrances, and scandals,* to drive us out of the way. Sometimes the ill lives of those who walk in these ways, sometimes their slips and falls, sometimes persecution, and our own natures, are full of scandals, subject to take this and that offence, and then we are ready to be snared on the right hand, or feared and scared on the left. And our nature, so far as it is unsanctified, is prone to catch, and ready to join with the world ; therefore we have need of resolution of spirit and determination. As David, ' I have determined, O Lord, and I will keep thy laws ; I have sworn that I will keep thy righteous judgments,' Ps. cxix. 106. This is a resolute determination.

Fourth, and then again, pray to God with David that he *would direct our ways*. ' Oh, that my ways were so directed to keep thy laws !' Ps. cxix. 3. I see that my nature is ready to draw me away to evil, and perverse crooked courses. I see, though I determine to take a good course, that there is much opposition ; therefore, good Lord, direct me in my course, direct thou my thoughts, words, and carriage. Therefore, that we may walk stedfastly, let us resolve with settled determination, praying to God for strength ; otherwise resolution, with dependence on our own power, may be a work of the flesh. But resolve thus, these are right ways and straight, they lead to heaven, happiness, and glory ; therefore I will walk in them, whatsoever come of it. We have all the discouragement which may hinder us in the ways of God. For as we are travellers, so we are soldiers, warfaring men that meet with many rubs, thorns. Therefore to walk amidst such dangerous ways we must be well shod with the preparation of the gospel of peace, that is, patience, and reasons taken from thence. God hath provided spiritual armour in the word against all oppositions that meet with us, so that by resolution and prayer to him, using his means, we may go through all.

Now for a further help for us to walk constantly and resolutely in the ways of God.

1. Take first *the help of good company*. If we see any man to walk in a good way, let him not walk alone, but let us join ourselves with those that walk in God's ways ; for why doth God leave us not only his word to direct us which way to go, but likewise examples in all times, but that we should follow those examples ? which are like the pillar of fire which went before Israel unto Canaan. We have a cloud and a pillar of examples before us, (unto which he alludes, Heb. xii. 1), to lead us unto heaven, not only the word, but examples in all times. ' Walk, as you have us, for an example, Philip.

* That is, 'stumbling-blocks.'—G.

iii. 17, saith Paul. Therefore it is a character of a gracious disposition to join with the just, and those who walk in the ways of God. We see there is in all the creatures an instinct to keep company with their own kind ; as we see in doves, sheep, geese, and the like. So it comes from a supernatural gracious instinct of grace, for the good to walk and company with the good, helping them on in the way to heaven. It is therefore a point of special wisdom to single out those for our company, who are able to help us thither, as it is for travellers to choose their company to travel with.

2. Again, if we would walk aright in the ways of God, *let us have our end in our eye, like unto the traveller.* Look on heaven, the day of judgment, those times either of eternal happiness or misery, which we must all come to. The having of these in our eye, will stern* the whole course of our life ; for the end infuseth vigour in our carriages, and puts a great deal of life in the use of the means, breeding a love of them, though they be harsh. Therefore we must pray and labour for patience, to conflict with our own corruptions, and those of the times we live in. This is unpleasant to do ; but when a man hath his aim and end in his eye, this inspires such vigour and strength in a man, that it makes him use means and courses contrary to his own natural disposition, offering a holy violence unto himself. As thus, it is not absolutely necessary that I should have this or that, or have them all, or in such and such a measure ; but it is absolutely necessary that I should be saved, and not damned ; therefore this course I will take, in these ways I will and must walk which lead to salvation. Let us therefore with Moses have in our eye, ' the recompence of the reward,' Heb. xi. 26 ; and with our blessed Saviour, the head of the faithful, have before our eyes ' the joy that was set before him,' which will make us pass by all those heavy things that he passed through. Let us with the holy men of ancient time, have ' the prize of that high calling' in our eye, to make us, notwithstanding all opposition, press forward towards the mark.

3. And then again, because it is said indefinitely here, ' They shall walk in these ways,' remember always *to take wisdom and prudence along with you in all your walkings.* It is put indefinitely, because we should leave out none. For, as we say in things that are to be believed, Faith chooseth not this object, and not another ; so obedience chooseth not this object ; I will obey God in this, and not in this, but it goes on in all God's ways. Therefore, if we would walk on aright in God's ways, there must be consideration of all the relations as we stand to God. *First, what duties we owe to God in heavenly things,* .to please him above all, whomsoever we displease, and to seek the kingdom of heaven and his righteousness before all, that all things may follow which are needful for us, Mat. vi. 33. So, in the *next* place, when we look to ourselves, to know *those ways which are required of us in regard of ourselves ;* for every Christian is a temple wherein God dwells ; therefore we are to carry ourselves holily, to be much in prayer and communion with God in secret. A man is best distinguished to be a good walker by those secret ways betwixt God and his soul, those walks of meditation and prayer wherein there is much sweet intercourse betwixt God and the soul. Therefore, in this case a man makes conscience of his communion with God in his thoughts, desires, affections, using all good means appointed of God to maintain this communion.

4. Then we should look to our own carriage in the use of the creatures, *to carry ourselves in all things indifferently,* because wisdom and prudence is seen in those things especially, to use things indifferent, indifferently ;

* That is, ' steer, guide, regulate.'—G.

not to be much in the use of the world, in joy or sorrow, but in moderation to use these things, being sure to set our affections upon the main.

5. And so in things indifferent, not to do them *with offence and excess;* but to see and observe the rule in all things of indifferency.

6. And for our carriage to others in those ways, let us consider what we owe *to those above us,* what respect is due to governors, and what to others; what to those who are without; what to those who are weak. We owe an example of holy life unto them, that we give no occasion of scandal; and also to walk wisely towards them that are without, that we give no occasion for the ways of God to be ill spoken of.

7. And for all conditions which God shall cast us into, remember *that those be ways which we should walk seemly in.* If prosperity, let us take heed of the sins of prosperity, pride, insolency, security, hardness of heart, and the like. If adversity, then let us practise the graces thereof, take heed of murmuring and repining, dejection of spirit, despair, and the like. This is to walk like a wise man in all conditions, in those relations he stands in.

8. *For our words likewise and expressions to others,* in that kind of our walking, that they may be savoury and to purpose, that we labour to speak by rule, seeing we must give an account of every ' idle word' at the day of judgment, Mat. xii. 36. So that in all our labours, carriage, and speech, we must labour to do all wisely and justly. These are the ways of God, and ' the just shall walk in them.'

Negatively, what we must avoid in all our walking.

Remember in general, we must never do anything against religion, against conscience, against a man's particular place and calling, or against justice. Let us not touch upon the breach of any good thing, especially of religion and conscience. Thus a man shall walk in the ways of God, if with wisdom and prudence he consider what ways are before him to God, to himself, to others; in all conditions and states of life, to see what he must, and what he must not do, and then to walk in them answerably.

For our encouragement to walk in God's ways in our general and particular callings.

1. Know first, *they are the most safe ways of all.* Whatsoever trouble or affliction we meet withal, it is no matter, it will prove the safest way in the end. For as it was with the cloud which went before God's people, it was both for direction and protection; so the Spirit of God, and the ways of God, as they serve for direction, so they serve for protection. God will direct and protect us if we walk in his ways. Let him be our director, and he will be our preserver and protector in all times.

2. Again, they are *the most pleasant ways of all.* All wisdom's ways are paved with prosperity and pleasure; for when God doth enlarge and sanctify the soul to walk in them, he giveth withal a royal gift, inward peace of conscience, and joy unspeakable and glorious, with an enlarged spirit. God meets his children in his own ways; they are therefore to walk there. Let a man start out of God's ways, he meets with the devil, with the devil's instruments, and many snares. But in God's ways he shall be sure to meet with God, if he walk in them with humility and respect to God, looking up for direction and strength, and denying his own wisdom. In this case a man shall be sure to have God go along with him in all his ways. In God's ways expect God's company. Therefore they are the safest and the most pleasant ways.

3. And they are the *cleanest and holiest ways of all;* having this excellent property in them, that as they lead to comfort, so they end in comfort;

they all end in heaven, Ps. xix. 9. Therefore let us not be weary of God's ways, of Christianity and our particular callings ; wherein what we do, let us do as God's ways, having sanctified them by prayer, and do it in obedience to God. They are God's ways when they are sanctified. God hath set me in this standing, I expect his blessing therein, and what blessing I find, I will give him the praise. God hath appointed that in serving man I serve him ; therefore we must go on in our particular ways, as the ways of God, doing everything as the work of God, and we shall find them the comfortablest and pleasantest ways which end in joy, happiness, and glory.

Use 1. The use hereof may be first reprehension unto those *who can talk but not walk*, that have tongues but not feet, to wit, affections; that come by starts into the narrow way ; but yet be never well till they turn back again into the world, that broad way which leads unto destruction.

Use 2. Secondly, it is for instruction, *to stir us up to walk in God's ways ;* as Ps. i. 1, 2, ' Blessed is the man that walketh not in the counsel of the ungodly, &c. But his delight is in the law of the Lord, and in that law doth he meditate day and night.'

Use 3. Thirdly, this is for consolation ; if this be our walk, *then God will walk with us, and the angels of God shall have charge of us to keep us in all our ways*, Ps. xxxiv. 7; and though, like David, we slip out of the way, yet this not being our walk, we come to the way again. Though God's children miss of their way, yet their resolution, choice, and endeavour was to walk in the way ; therefore such are still in a blessed estate, and keep their communion with God. A man is not said to alter his way till he alter his choice and resolution. The best man may have an ill passion, and miss the way, but he will not turn from it willingly. And the worst man may have a good passion, and come into the way, but never continue in it to make this walk.* From all which it appeareth that they are only righteous persons who continue to walk in the ways of God. It is therefore consolation unto them who take that course. Though all the world go another way, yet they must imitate just men. And for us, we must imitate these just men, though they be never so few in the world and despised. If we would be counted the servants of God, we must imitate those that walk in those paths.

II. Now it is said that the other sort, wicked men, the ways of God shall have quite a contrary course in them.

' But the transgressors shall fall therein.'

As one and the selfsame cloud was both light to the Israelites and darkness unto the Egyptians, Exod. xiv. 20 ; so the same ways of God prove both light and darkness, life and death, to the godly and wicked. As the apostle speaks, unto ' the one they are the savour of life unto life, and unto the other the savour of death unto death,' 2 Cor. ii. 16. Therefore now here is the conclusion of all. If no warning will serve the turn of all what hath been given and said, yet the word of God shall not return empty, it shall effect that for which it was sent, Isa. lv. 11 ; one work or other it will do, even upon the most perverse.

' The transgressors shall fall therein.'

Obs. Whence we see and may observe, *that the same word which is a word of life and salvation to the godly, is an occasion of sin and perdition unto the wicked.* The same sun which makes flowers and herbs to smell sweet, makes carrions to smell worse. The same word which made the apostles believe and confess Christ, did also make many others of his disciples go

* Qu. ' to make it his walk?'—G.

back from him, saying, ' This is a hard saying, who can bear it ?' John xiii. 60. So, Acts xiii. 48, the same word which made the unbelieving Jews blaspheme, did make ' as many as did belong unto eternal life believe.' And when Christ preached, many blasphemed, and said he had a devil ; others trusted and defended him. So saith Paul, the same word to some is, ' the savour of death unto death, and to some the savour of life unto life,' 2 Cor. ii. 16 ; and so in another place he speaks of the same word, ' But we preach Christ crucified, unto the Jews a stumblingblock, and unto the Greeks foolishness ; but unto them which are called, both Jews and Greeks, Christ the power of God, and the wisdom of God,' 1 Cor. i. 23, 24. To this purpose, Peter speaks of Christ, ' Unto you therefore who believe, he is precious ; but unto them which are disobedient, &c., a stone of stumbling, and a rock of offence, even unto them who stumble at the word, being disobedient, whereunto also they were appointed,' 1 Pet. ii. 7, 8. The reasons are,

Reason 1. Because ' The natural man perceiveth not the things of the Spirit of God : for they are foolishness unto him ; neither can he know them, because they are spiritually discerned ; but he that is spiritual judgeth all things,' &c., 1 Cor. ii. 14.

Secondly, ' Because they who do evil hate the light,' John iii. 19, and therefore, cannot love what they hate. ' This,' Christ saith, ' is the condemnation, that light is come into the world, and men loved darkness better than light, because their deeds were evil.'

Thirdly, Because they are blinded, 2 Cor. iv. 4 ; therefore they are led away by the god of this world, Satan, so that they cannot perceive anything that is spiritual, for God hath not given them a heart to perceive, &c., Deut. xxix. 4.

Fourthly, Because they want faith, which is called ' the faith of God's elect,' Tit. i. 1 ; and we know, ' without faith it is impossible to please God,' Heb. xi. 6 ; for it is said that ' the word profited not those unbelieving Jews, because it was not mingled with faith in those who heard it,' Heb. iv. 2.

Fifthly, Because the word is like the sun, which causeth plants to smell sweet, and a dunghill to smell stinking. So it works grace in some, and extracts the sin and foul vapours out of others.

Use 1. The use is, first, reproof unto them who *stumble at the wholesome doctrines of the word;* of election, reprobation, predestination, and the like. Such indeed stumble at Christ himself. He is a stumblingblock unto them, as Peter speaketh, 1 Pet. ii. 8. They stumble at Christ who stumble at his word.

Use 2. Secondly, *not to love the word the worse, because evil men be made the worse by it ;* which shews rather the mighty power of the word which discovereth them, and will not let them be hid, unmasking hypocrites to themselves and others. As we must not like the sun the worse, because it makes carrion smell ; nor the fan, because it winnoweth away the chaff ; so must we not fall out with the word, because it hath these effects upon wicked men.

Use 3. Lastly, it is for consolation unto them that, when their sin is reproved, *fall not out with the word, but with their sin.* When they are excited to duty, they hate their corruption, and do endeavour to walk honestly without reproof. This shews the word is not the savour of death unto death to them, but the savour of life unto life ; which St Paul makes a sign of election, ' When they receive the word of God, as the word of God, with thanksgiving,' 1 Thes. ii. 13. This indeed is a matter of praise, to give God thanks for his good word, which saves our souls, and comforts us here in the way of all our pilgrimage, till we arrive at heavenly glory.

For conclusion of all, what then remaineth on our part to be done? Surely, to hearken no more to flesh and blood, to the world or the devil; but to hear what God saith in his most holy word, Ps. xxxii. 10, and to frame our hearts with a strong resolution to this ' *returning*,' here exhorted to. Oh, if we knew the many miseries and sorrows which attendeth wretched and miserable sinners, and sinful courses here and hereafter, it would be our first work to follow God's counsel to his people; to return from our sinful ways; to meet so gracious and merciful a God; that he may, as his promise is, ' heal our backslidings,' and be ' as the dew unto us,' to make us fruitful and abundant in every good and perfect work.

What can be said more for our encouragement than that which hath been delivered in this chapter? God, the party offended, who is Jehovah, God all-sufficient, exhorts us to return unto him, who is able and willing to help. And he also, out of his rich goodness, forewarneth us of the dangerous estate a sinner is in; who, being ' fallen by his iniquity,' ought therefore to pity himself. Return and not run on in a further course of disobedience and backsliding. And words are put in our mouths, dictated by God himself, which needs must be very prevailing with him. What an encouragement is this! Yea further, as we have heard, these petitions are all answered graciously and abundantly, above all they did ask; wherein God surmounteth our desires and thoughts, as we heard at large. Whereby we also may be confident to have our petitions and suits in like sort granted; if we go unto God with his own words and form prescribed. If we ' take with us words' of prayer, we shall be sure to vanquish all our spiritual enemies; for faithful prayer works wonders in heaven and earth, James v. 17. And that God doth not bid us be religious to our loss, he sheweth that we shall lose nothing by following his counsel, and walking in a religious course of life; having abominated our idols, ' He will observe us, and see us,' and be a shelter unto us, having a derivation of fruitfulness from his fulness. ' In me is thy fruit found.'

Lastly, we have heard who can make right use of these things delivered. Only ' the wise and prudent;' such only can understand heavenly things to purpose. ' His secret is with them that fear him,' Psa. xxv. 14; and ' wisdom is only justified of her children,' Mat. xi. 19. When others have no heart given them to perceive God's ways aright, as Moses speaketh, ' transgressors' fall in God's ' right ways,' whilst the just walk comfortably in them. O then let us hate sin every day more and more, and be in love with religion and the ways of God; for that is the true good, which is the everlasting good, that better Mary's part, which shall never be taken away, Luke x. 42. ' Whosoever drinks of this living water shall never thirst again,' John iv. 14. The best things of this world have but a shadow, not the substance of goodness. Let us then be wise for ourselves, and pity ourselves in time, ' whilst it is called to-day,' because, as our Saviour speaks, ' the night approacheth, wherein no man can work,' John ix. 4. O then let us often examine our hearts and covenant with them, let us see our sins as they are, and God's goodness as it is; that our ' scarlet sins' may be done away as a mist from before him, Isa. i. 18. O banish away our atheism, which, by our sinful conversation, proclaimeth us to be of the number of those fools, who have said in their heart that there is no God, Psa. xiv. 1. This serious consideration always makes first a stop, and then a returning; to believe indeed that there is a God who made the world, and a judgment to come.   This, God by Moses, calleth true wisdom indeed, ' To remember our latter end.'   ' Oh,' saith he, ' that they were wise, that they would think of these things,' Deut. xxxii. 29.   Of which things ? The miseries which attend sin here and hereafter; and the blessings and comforts which follow a godly life both here and hereafter, ' That they would remember their latter end,' the neglect whereof, Jeremiah sheweth, was the cause ' that they came down wonderfully, and had no comforter, because they remembered not their latter end.'*

Therefore, let us study this point well, that there is a God, and a judgment to come; and this will compel us, even out of self-love, to return from our sinful courses, and make a stop.   By this means, we shall not need a Philip's boy (z) to cry to us every day, we are mortal and must die; if our meditations once a day be both in heaven and hell.   These strong considerations (aided with strong rational reflectings on ourselves) will keep us within compass, overawe us, and make us quake and tremble to go on in sin; which is worse than the devil in this, that thereby he became a devil. This will drive us to fly unto God, that he may ' heal our backslidings,' who is described ' with healing under his wings,' Mal. iv. 2; who, in the days of his flesh, healed all miserable and ' returning backsliders,' who ever came unto him.   Therefore, let us lay to heart these things, that so we may be kept in soul and body, pure and unspotted, holy and without blame in his sight, until the day of redemption, ' When our mortality shall put on immortality, and our corruptible incorruption, to reign with God for ever and ever,' 1 Cor. xv. 54, *seq*.

* Qu. Isaiah? and the reference, xlvii. 7.—G.

NOTES.

(a) P. 256.—' Return,' &c.   It is very emphatical and significant in the original. Cf. Ackerman (*Prophetæ Minores*. . . . . Vienna, 1830); and Henderson (8vo, 1845), the latter especially, confirmatory of Sibbes.

(b) P. 286.—' It was well done by Luther, who, in a Catechism,' &c.   See his ' *Catechesis*' in Opera, *in loc*.

(c) P. 287.—' We have some bitter spirits (Lutherans they call them . . . . therefore to be in the sacrament).'   The reference is to the well-known dogma of *consubstantiation* as contrasted with, and even opposed to, the papists' *transubstantiation*. Both are explained in the following sentence from Barrow (Serm. 31, Vol. II.) : ' It may serve to guard us from divers errours, such as are that of the Lutheran *consubstantialists*, and of the Roman *transubstantiators*, who affirm that the body of our Lord is here upon earth at once present in many places (namely), in every place where the host is kept, or the eucharist is celebrated.'   Cf. Richardson, *sub voce*.

(d) P. 296.—' It was well spoken by Lactantius,' &c.   The thought is found several times in his *De Divino Præmio* and *De Opificio Dei* and *De Falsa Religione*.   Cf. Edition by Aldus, 1515, pp.240, 304, and 1, *seq*.

(e) P. 297.—' As the Jews call them, he hath hedges of the commandments.' Consult Kalisch (' Historical and Critical Commentary on the Old Testament . . . Exodus [8vo, 1855]) ; on Exodus xxiii. 19 ; and Maurer there ; and on Deuteronomy xxii. 6.'   For Rabbinical and other lore on the subject, Works of John Gregory, 4to, 1665, pp. 90—98.

(f) P. 303.—' And so we might go on in other resemblances.'   To all wishing to see the analogy carried out with wealth of quaint thought and illustration, we would commend the ' Soul's Sickness' of Thomas Adams (Works, Vol. I., pp. 471–506); also, as not at all inferior, and indeed abounding in even more recondite lore and unexpected flashes of wit, Bishop Gr. Williams, ' Of the Misery of Man,' in his ' Seven Golden Candlesticks.'   (Folio, 1635, pp. 565–661.)

(g) P. 337.—' As we see now in these wars of Germany.'   Cf. Memoir, Vol. I., pp. lvii.–viii.   The ' now' from 1620–21, onwards.

(*h*) P. 347.—'Man is, as it were, a sum of all the excellencies of the creatures ; **a** little world indeed.' This idea will be found worked out in quaint fashion by Bishop Earle, in his ' Micro-cosmography,' and by Capt. T. Butler, in his ' Little Bible of Man.' 1649.

(*i*) P. 349.—' The word in the original is a " standard-bearer," ' Titus iii. 8. . . . Cf. Ellicott, *in loc.*, together with extracts and illustrations given in Kypke, Observ. ii. 381 ; Loesner, Obs. p. 430. The word is προιστημι. The noun, προστάτης = a leader, champion. Wycliffe renders it ' Be bisie to be abouen other in good werkis ' (Hexapla . . . . Bagster) ; and, perhaps, ' standard-bearer' catches the idea, if it departs from the exact wording.

(*j*) P. 350.—' The fragrancy of the smell is smelt of passengers as they sail along the coast.' One of Richard Sibbes's hearers, John Milton (see our Memoir, Vol. I., p. liii.), has finely put this :—

> ' . . . . As when to them who sail
> Beyond the Cape of Hope, and now are past
> Mozambique, off at sea north-east winds blow
> *Sabean odours from the spicy shore*
> *Of Araby the blest.'*—*Paradise Lost*, B. IV., 159–163.

(*k*) P. 351.—' The church of God riseth out of the ashes of the martyrs, which hitherto smells sweet, and puts life in those who come after, so precious are they both dead and alive.' The sentiment is preserved by the poet, concerning the ' actions of the just,' in the familiar lines :—

> ' . . . . The actions of the just
> Smell sweet and blossom in the dust.'
>
> (*James Shirley*, ' Death's Final Conquest ').

Shirley was a ' student' of Catharine College, Cambridge.

(*l*) P. 355.—' Monica, St Austin's mother, ... he was converted *after* her death.' &c. This is a somewhat singular blunder on the part of Sibbes. Augustine was ' converted' *before* his mother's death, as the touching narrative in the ' Confessions ' has made immortal. Cf. B. VIII., 30 ; B. IX., 17, *et alibi*.

(*m*) P. 370.—' Calvin and Luther . . . . burn their bones,' &c. If this does not apply literally to Calvin and Luther, it yet holds good of many like-minded. Every one remembers what was done to Wycliffe's ' bones,' and also Fuller's characteristic conceits upon the scattered ashes, to which none will refuse Dr Vaughan's approving ' Well-spoken—Honest one ! ' Cf. Vaughan's John de Wycliffe, D.D., a monograph (4to. 1853), pp. 521, *seq*. To Wycliffe may be added Bucer, concerning the ' burning of whose bones I take the following verses from Faithful Teat's rare ' Ter Tria ' (18mo. 1669, 2d edition, pp. 142, 143).

> ' What though revengeful papists burne
> Dear Bucer's bones ? still hope's his urne,
> Till's ashes to a phœnix turne,
> And live afresh.' (From ' Hope.')

(*n*) P. 377.—' The abominable distinctions of the papists of *Latria* and *Dulia*.' That is, λατρεία and δουλεία, commonplaces in the popish controversy. Cf. Faber, ' Difficulties of Romanism,' and almost any of the standard treatises *pro* and *con*.

(*o*) P. 378.—' Calleth them dunghill-gods, and Abel, as it is in this book, vanity,' &c. The allusion of Sibbes in the former is perhaps to Beelzebub, worshipped by the Philistines of Ekron = the fly-god, *i. e.*, dunghill-bred fly. ' Abel ' means ' vanity,' and the reference is not to Abel—the proper name of Adam's second-born son—but to Hosea xii. 11.

(*p*) P. 379.—' Coster himself, a forward Jesuit.' That is, John Costerus or Costerius in his ' Comment . . . . pro Catholicæ Fidei Antiquitate et Veritate,' (Paris, 1569).

(*q*) P. 379.—' Late worthies of our church.' The following are the principal works on the popish controversy, by the eminent writers enumerated :—

1. Bishop Jewel.—(1.) ' Apologia Ecclesiæ Anglicanæ,' 1562. (2.) ' An Apology for Private Mass ; with a learned annswere to it by Bishop Jewell,' 1562. (3.) Various ' Answers ' to Hardinge and others.

2. John Rainolds, D.D.—' The summe of the Conference betweene John Rainoldes and John Hart, touching the Head and Faith of the Church,' &c., &c., 1584, and various editions.

3. William Fulke.—Very many works. For list, consult Watt's Bibl. Brit. *sub nomine*.

4. Dr William Whitaker.—Cf. our Memoir of Sibbes, pp. lxxxi–ii.

5. Andrew Willet.—His great work is his ' Synopsis Papismi,' 1600 ; but he is author of other masterly, if somewhat vehement, treatises on the controversy. Consult Watt *sub nomine*.

6. William Perkins.—His ' Works ' abound in confutations of popish errors, written with great intensity. He has one special treatise of rare merit, ' The Reformed Catholike ; or a Declaration shewing how neere we may come to the present Church of Rome in sundrie points of Religion ; and wherein we must for ever depart from them.' (Cambridge, 1597.)

(*r*) P. 380.—' To say we worship not the image but God . . . so we may see in Arnobius.' Arnobius here referred to was one of the apologists of Christianity in the African church during the third century. His ' Disputationum Adversus Gentes Libri ' (ex Editione Fausti Sabæi, Rome, 1542), remains a still vital book. It has passed through many editions. Again and again the question of image-worship comes up in it.

(*s*) P. 381.—' Rome to be Babylon.' Cf. Canon Wordsworth's conclusive little work, ' Babylon ; or the question considered, " Is the Church of Rome the Babylon of the Apocalypse ?" ' 12mo.

(*t*) P. 381.—' Hedges of the commandments,' Cf. note *e*.

(*u*) P. 383. ' As a great man-pleaser,' &c. Sibbes places in his margin, ' A Scottish Regent, before his execution.' This must refer to the Earl of Morton, Regent of Scotland, beheaded in 1581, on a very doubtful charge of treason. It is difficult to explain Sibbes's use of ' man-pleaser,' in relation to Knox's illustrious friend. But ' man-pleaser ' was a favourite term of reproach with the Puritans, which John Squier, in his extraordinary introduction to his sermon from Luke xviii. 13, thus sarcastically notices, ' If my text should lead me to avouch the dignity and authority of the superiours in our clergy, I should not escape that brand, behold a time-servant and a *man-pleaser* ' (4to, 1637, page 2). Better example far he might have taken from his contemporary, Shakespeare. I refer to the famous saying of Wolsey, (Henry VIII. iii. 2)—

> ' . . . . O Cromwell, Cromwell!
> Had I but serv'd my God with half the zeal
> I serv'd my king, he would not, in mine age,
> Have left me naked to mine enemies.'

(*v*) P. 388.—' Were made gods . . . came . . . to fearful ends.' This holds of nearly all the Cæsars. For ample proof, consult Smith's Dictionary of Greek and Roman Biography and Mythology, under the respective emperors, especially Caligula and Nero.

(*w*) P. 392.—' " I have seen and observed him," some read the words, but very few.' Cf. authorities cited in note *q*.

(*x*) P. 393.—' The same day was that noble victory and conquest in the north parts over the enemies.' The allusion is to the Battle of Pinkie, on September 10. 1547, between the English, under the Earl of Hertford, Protector, and the Scotch, when the latter were totally defeated. It was one of the most decisive victories, with least loss to the conquerors, of any in history. There fell scarcely two hundred of the English ; while, according to the lowest computation, above ten thousand Scots perished, besides fifteen hundred taken prisoners. 1547 (and according to Sibbes, 10th September) is usually reckoned as the ' completion ' of the English Reformation, although the reformed religion was not established until the accession of Elizabeth, in 1558.

(*y*) P. 415.—' Simile mater erroris.' This is a principle which is very often stated, in various forms, in the writings of Bacon.

(*z*) P. 433.—' We shall not need a Philip's boy.' The allusion is to the (I suppose), apocryphal story of Philippus II., father of Alexander the Great, having a boy appointed for the purpose of reminding him, by a daily repetition of it, of his ' mortality.' So sensual and volatile a nature was very unlikely to do so wise a thing.

G.

GOD'S PROVIDENCE UNFOLDED IN THE BOOK OF ESTHER

by

ALEXANDER CARSON

PREFACE

"Judge not the Lord by feeble sense,
   But trust Him for His grace;
   Behind a frowning Providence
   He hides a smiling face."

How true! O that we could always remember, and
believing see the glory of God. But alas! how soon does our
faith grow dim!
Friend, is it often so with thee? Dost thou oftentimes need a draught of the Water of Life to refresh
thee? Here, then, is the spring. Rest awhile, and draw
from the Book of Esther this sparkling truth: every event,
no matter how small or how sinful, works for thy good. In
this book, as in thy life, every passing instance lends its
weight. All works for the deliverance of the people of God.
Nothing is lacking. Had the most trifling incident refused
its aid, God's entire plan would have been deranged. But,
from first to last, every part is connected and influenced
by the hand of God.
He begins to deliver His people even before they come
into danger! In the beginning of the narrative the Babylon-
ian queen is deposed. Why? That God may place His instrument upon the throne.
Esther's marriage to the king was unlawful. God had
commanded that none of the daughters of Israel should be
given to a stranger. But this marriage, unlawful as it is,
is another of His many implements. Every instance, even the
blackest, is used by the God of heaven and earth. Lo, our
Lord controls all iniquity, even the sins of His people. He
turns iniquity by His hand, and uses sin to do His pleasure.
And was it a mere coincidence that "Esther obtained
favor in the sight of all them that looked upon her"? No.
Scripture tells us that 'the king's heart is in the hand of
the Lord, as the rivers of water; he turneth it whither-
soever He will.' And so doth He here, giving Esther favor
before the king. Thy rulers, thy friends; yea, the hearts
of all thy fellow men; thy God controls them.
What? Is even rebellion to be a tool in the hand of
the Almighty? Yes. Certainly the two chamberlains had no
thought for the glory of God when they laid their foul
plans. But still the Sovereign of Heaven takes their fiend-
ish impulse, brings upon it other circumstances of His
devising, and bends it perfectly to fulfil His purpose.

UNIVERSAL HISTORY OF PROVIDENCE

But we shall not here multiply examples. As our author has said, the entire book is a systematic unfolding of the decrees of God. Come, sit at the feet of this godly man. Take from his pages what he has received in turn from the pages of Scripture. "Learn (as he has learned) from this book to place unbounded confidence in the care of God in the utmost dangers; and to look to the Lord for deliverance, when there is no apparent means of escape."

In this book you shall "have an alphabet, by which you may read all the events of every day, of every age and nation. This is a Divine key which will open all the mysteries of Providence."

We will keep thee no longer. Here, take the key. And forget not to take another key, the work of this man of God. Let him lead thee through these pages into the darkest deeds, past the most trivial circumstances. See in them all the hand of thy God, shaping them for thy godliness and for His eternal glory.

Enter, and Godspeed!

BRADY SHAFER
ASSOCIATE EDITOR

PROVIDENCE UNFOLDED, &c.

THE great design of this portion of the Holy Scriptures is to display the wisdom, providence, and power of God, in the preservation of his people, and in the destruction of their enemies. We learn from it, that the most casual events which take place in the affairs of the world are connected with his plans respecting his people ; and that the most trifling things are appointed and directed by him to effect his purposes. It decides a question that philosophy has canvassed for ages, and never will fathom ; recording a number of events, the result of man's free will, yet evidently appointed of God, and directed by his providence. From this book the believer may learn to place unbounded confidence in the care of his God in the utmost danger ; and to look to the Lord of omnipotence for deliverance, when there is no apparent means of escape. It demonstrates a particular providence in the minutest things, and affords the most solid answer to all the objections of philosophy to this consoling truth. The wisdom of this world, with all its acuteness, is not able to perceive how God can interfere on any particular occasion, without deranging the order of his general plans. Philosophers account for the prosperity of the wicked, and the afflictions of the righteous, from the operation of general laws. A villain grows rich by industry, and oppresses the virtuous poor; a righteous man loses his all by a storm at sea, or is himself overwhelmed in the ruins of an earthquake. In all this the philosopher's god cannot interfere, for he is tied down by the order of a general providence. He is fettered by his own previously established laws, as effectually as the gods of the heathen were when they swore by the river Styx. He must quietly look on amidst all the occasional mischief resulting from his plans, which, though upon the whole the best possible, yet have many unavoidable defects. Storms and earthquakes result from the operation of general laws established at first by the Author of nature; and the Almighty, it is supposed, without unsuitably counteracting the order appointed by himself, can neither prevent them nor deliver from their dreadful consequences. Famine and war, with all the evils that destroy or afflict men, are accounted for on principles that exclude a particular providence. The arrogance of the oppressor cannot be restrained, nor the sufferings of the virtuous prevented, without an unbecoming deviation from the order of nature. Philosophy cannot see how her god could dispose every particular event without a miracle on every occasion of interference. On this supposition, she thinks that he must be continually suspending and counteracting the general laws which he at first established for the government of the world.

How different from this philosophic god is the Lord God of the Bible! Jehovah has indeed established general laws in the government of the world yet in such a manner that he is the immediate Author of every particular event. His power has been sometimes displayed in suspending these laws, but is usually employed in directing them to fulfil his particular purposes. The sun and the rain minister to the nourishment and comfort equally of the righteous and the wicked, not from the necessity of general laws, but from the immediate providence of Him who, in the government of the world, wills this result. Accordingly, the shining of the sun and the falling of the rain on the fields of the wicked, are represented in Scripture, not as the unavoidable effect of general laws, but as the design of supreme goodness. A fowling-piece well aimed will strike a particular object; but divine truth has assured us that a sparrow cannot fall to the ground without the permission of the Ruler of the world. This book teaches us that God exerts his particular providence in an inconceivably wise and skillful manner, even by the operation of his general laws, and by the exercise of the free determinations of men. The very laws that in the opinion of the philosopher, stand in the way of a particular providence, are here exhibited as the agents that he deputes to effect his purposes. The most astonishing interferences that ever were recorded are here effected solely through the operation of general laws, and the actions of voluntary agents. The people of God are delivered out of the most imminent danger, and their enemies most marvelously overturned, without a single miracle. The glory of the Divine wisdom, and power, and providence shines here the more illustriously, because God effects his work without suspending the laws of nature, or constraining the determination of the agents employed in the execution of his work. He saves them, and destroys their enemies without going out of the usual path of his providence. Had the earth opened and swallowed the enemies of the Jews, the power of Jehovah would have been displayed; but when he saved them by a train of events according to the general laws of nature, each of which separately viewed seems fortuitous, yet when seen in combination must necessarily have been designed to bring about the one great end; the existence of a particular providence is proved, and the nature of it is delightfully illustrated. It is not merely taught in doctrine, but it is exhibited in example. In the history of the deliverance of the Jews through the exaltation of Esther, we have the whole history of the world in miniature. The book of Esther is the History of Providence. In the inspired account which we have here of an interesting portion of Jewish story, we have an alphabet, through the judicious use of which we may read all the events of every day, of every age and nation. This is a divine key which will open all the mysteries of providence. It is God's commentary on all that he has done and on all that man has done, since the finishing of the works of creation. All is natural and seemingly fortuitous; yet if the whole had been a work of mere fiction for amusement, the events could not have been better adapted to the end. There is all the simplicity of nature, yet all the surprise and interest of romance. The grand object is evolved like the plot of a regular drama; every event recorded contributes its influence in producing the effect. There is nothing wanting; there is nothing superfluous. Had the most trifling incident refused its aid, the whole plan would have been deranged—the most fatal results would have succeeded. From the first to the last, all parts are connected and influenced like the machinery of a watch. By a thousand wheels the main-spring guides the index. We have first a train of events to raise up deliverance to the Jews, even before they were brought into danger; next, we have a train of events to bring them to the brink of ruin; then follow the surprising means of their preservation, and the destruction of their enemies. To one or other of these objects every circumstance recorded in the history contributes, and the whole forms one of the grandest displays of the wisdom, power, and providence of God, that is to be met with in the Scriptures, and is well calculated to represent that noble plan by which the kingdom of Satan is overturned, and God's people are delivered from the power of their great enemy, through the very means intended for their utter extirpation.

In reviewing the train of events that provided the means of deliverance for the Jewish nation, before they were brought into danger, the first thing that presents itself is the great feast of Ahasuerus. At first sight nothing could have been more unconnected with the intended object. It is quite a fortuitous and ordinary matter. A royal revel would appear calculated to defeat the designs of Jehovah, rather than fulfil them. But the wisdom and omnipotence of Jehovah can use ordinary events to effect his purpose, and can fulfil his will by a worldly assembly, or even by a synagogue of Satan, as well as by a church of Christ. He reigns as absolutely over his enemies

as among his friends. He works through Satan
and his emissaries, as well as through the ministry
of the angels of his presence ; and employs the
councils of sinners, as well as the loyal and loving
exertions of saints. The occasion of originating
this deliverance to the people of God was a feast
to exhibit the glory of a worldly kingdom, and not
a religious assembly. God employs his agents in
work suitable to their character. Had the wisdom
of men formed the plan of deliverance, the monarch
would have been made a proselyte to the religion
of the Jews, and the work would have been effected by him as a servant of the God of Israel.
But God does everything by him while he continues, as far as we are informed, altogether un-
influenced by the law of the Lord of heaven.
Had David sat on the throne of Persia, his zeal
for the preservation of Israel and destruction of
their enemies, could not have flamed with greater
ardor than that of Ahasuerus.

What was the particular occasion of this feast
we are not informed, and therefore it can be no way
useful for our edification. Commentators are
usually very obliging with their conjectures on such
an emergency, and edify us with many a shrewd
guess. But it is the duty of a Christian to learn
everything that the Scriptures record; and it is
equally his duty to remain in the most obstinate
ignorance of everything that they do not reveal.

Whether this was a birth-day, or a feast for commemorating the accession to the throne ; whether it was an annual festival, or an occasional revel, I know not—I care not.   What I know is, that God had evidently determined it as a link of the wonderful concatenation of ordinary events employed by him to effect his glorious purpose of delivering his people.   Though the free appointment of man, it was also the appointment of God.   It was necessary to give birth to the events that follow.

The whimsical, tyrannical, and indecent thought that struck the mind of the monarch in his wine, though originating with himself, was according to the appointment of a wise Providence.   Why did such a thought come into his mind ?   It was evidently contrary to the custom of Persia, for Vashti to make such an appearance, as the females on this occasion feasted apart.   It was extremely indecorous for the female majesty of the empire to be exposed to the formal survey of such an assembly, heated with wine.   The queen's disobedience of the orders of an absolute monarch, accustomed to universal obedience, shows how much the thing required was contrary to the general sentiments of decorum. Had such a thing been usual, it would not have been so offensive to the queen.   It may be said, it was a drunken frolic.   But was the king never drunk before ?   Is this the only time that he acted under the influence of wine ?   Why did the thought strike him now rather than at any other time of his drinking ?   Why is it that this is the only instance of the kind on record ?   God's intention undoubtedly was, that a thing might be enjoined on the queen with which she would not comply, that her disgrace might make way for the exaltation of the deliverer of his people.   Yet though in one point of view it was the appointment of God, in another it was the result of the actions of free and voluntary agents.   God's purpose is brought about by those whose only view is to fulfil their own purposes.   How inscrutable are the mysteries of Providence ! how unsearchable are his counsels in the government of the world ! Men are his enemies—they hate him, and disobey him ; yet in all their plans and actions they fulfil his will.   The regularity of the heavenly bodies in their courses is wonderful ; but they are not voluntary agents ; they are constantly urged on by the hand of their Creator.   But men think, and resolve, and act for themselves ; yet they fulfil the plans of Jehovah as much as the sun, moon, and stars.   His very enemies in opposing him are made the instruments of serving him.   How consoling to the believer is this view of Providence ! When he looks around him he sees everywhere men trampling on the laws of God, and openly putting dishonor on him. Is God disappointed in the end that he proposed by his works ?   is he really overcome and thwarted by the prince of darkness ? No ! Jehovah is executing his purposes even through the wickedness of men and devils : and all things that have taken place from the creation must minister to his glory. Though Satan has usurped the throne of God in the world for so many thousand years, yet in all this God has been executing his own plans ; and he now rules on earth as absolutely and as unreservedly as he does in heaven. This is a depth which we cannot fathom ; but it is a truth necessary for the honor of the character of God; and one of which the Scriptures leave no room for doubt. The sin and misery that are on the earth—the endless perdition of wicked men and devils—are subjects of melancholy consideration to the man of God ; but let him be consoled with the thought that Jehovah worketh all things according to the counsel of his own will, and that the darkest spots on the book of God may appear in the brightness of meridian light in the world of glory. "The Lord hath made all things for himself; yea, even the wicked for the day of evil," Prov. xvi. 4. The Apostle Paul declares that he was a "sweet savor unto God," as well "in those that perish," as "in those that are saved." A fool may ask, How can these things be so ? and the wisest man on earth cannot answer him. But is it not enough that God has said it ? Shall little children receive the word of their parents with the utmost confidence of conviction, when they testify the most incredible things, and shall we hesitate to receive the word of the God of truth ?

The queen's refusal is another providential circumstance which we are here called to observe and to admire. Notwithstanding the singularity, the indelicacy, and the unreasonableness of the command, it is remarkable that the queen should venture to disobey a despot heated with wine. She could scarcely expect to escape with impunity. Even Esther herself, with all her surpassing beauty, was exceedingly reluctant to venture uncalled into his presence. She was not willing to risk her life on his caprice, whether he would hold out the golden sceptre, or suffer her to perish in her rashness. What, then, must have been the danger of Vashti ? what must have been the intrepidity of the daring woman that refused to obey him ? Her conduct was singularly bold and imprudent. Her resolution was no doubt suggested by her pride, or by her sense of decorum ; but a regard to self-interest is usually stronger than these principles, especially in courts. Why, then, did her delicacy at this time prevail over her prudence ? Not one woman in a thousand would have acted in this manner, in the same circumstances. Why then did a woman of such spirit fill the situation of queen at this critical moment ? Why was not her beauty accompanied with an abject spirit of servility, as is usually the case among the slaves of eastern despots ? The reason evidently is, God had provided this high-spirited woman for the occasion which he meant to serve by her. He had determined her character and conduct as the means of executing his purposes; and by the ordinary course of events, his providence had given a consort to the monarch who was fitted for the part which he designed that she should act. As a voluntary agent she ignorantly fulfilled the will of Him whom she knew not, when she was influenced solely by a regard to her own feelings.

The advice of the king's counsellors on this occasion is also remarkable. The sycophants around despots are generally distinguished for caution. Even in their revels they are seldom off their guard. Now it was at the utmost hazard that they gave this advice. They must succeed, or fall. Though pure love could not influence the breast of a licentious eastern monarch, yet it is evident that Ahasuerus admired the beauty of his queen. The favorite mistress of despots is known to prevail against the most subtle and most powerful ministers. We see how readily this very monarch gave up to Esther the man whom he had most singularly honored and raised above all the princes of the empire. If the counsellors of the king should fail in displacing Vashti from the affections of their master, they were evidently planning their own ruin. Had the king refused to listen to their counsel, and the queen been restored again to power, their overthrow was certain. Why, then, did not the supple statesmen take the wisest course, and make their court to the queen by interceding for her pardon? After all the provocation of the king by the queen's disobedience, it was still possible that a man who admired her beauty, and had provoked her transgression, might not instantly put it out of his power to forgive her. She might have been disgraced in such a way as not to prevent her restoration, on repentance. Such a bold step in the ministers of a despot is certainly remarkable. But whatever might influence them, God had determined their counsel as the means of fulfilling his own.

That the king should subject her to a temporary degradation or disgrace, even though his own improper command was the occasion of her transgression, is very natural; but that, for the cold-hearted purpose of setting an example to the wives of the empire, he could consent to give up for ever one whom he so much admired, discovers more stoicism than is generally to be found in absolute monarchs. Their treatment of their wives is usually more influenced by passion than by a view to public good. In the heat of his fury it would have been less strange that he should have given orders for her death, than that he should divorce her for an example to the wives of his subjects. Yet, to the frigid morality of his wise men does this eastern sensualist sacrifice his beautiful queen. By a harsh decree she is divorced for ever. But this great feast—this capricious command—this imprudent disobedience—this rash advice—this unfeeling consent—this sacrifice of affection to policy—this harsh decree, are all necessary in the plans of Providence. Vashti must be removed, that Esther may be exalted to her place.

Let us next contemplate, for a moment, the elevation of a poor fatherless Jewess to the rank of queen of the Persian empire, and admire the wonderful providence of God in her destination. Is there any man so blind as not to perceive that it was entirely providential that one of the small number of captive Jews should be found more beautiful than all the virgins of a hundred and twenty-seven provinces? Can any one question that God gave her that exquisite loveliness for the very occasion? Known unto God are all his ways from the beginning; and in the formation of Hadassah he had an eye to the plan which he intended to execute through her. Had not God provided a Jewess of beauty surpassing all the virgins of the Persian dominions, the previous events would have been useless. Esther was found the most lovely of women, that through her beauty she might deliver the people of God.

In this circumstance we have a key to the Divine procedure in adjusting the various events in providence to the fulfilling of his plans and declaration with respect to the kingdom of his Son. All the persons who are called to take a part in the advancement or defence of the cause of God are gifted by him with the necessary qualifications. Many of these qualifications are given in their birth or education, though they may not for a length of time be called to use them. Sometimes they may even for years employ them in opposition to God. Such was the case with Paul, and doubtless some points of the character of this eminent apostle were bestowed on him in his very constitution, with a view to the service of Christ. He had many things by immediate gift; but he had some things by mental temperament and education. Any one who reads the History of the Reformation with an eye to this characteristic in Divine Providence, will see it surprisingly illustrated in innumerable instances. The character and circumstances of Luther alone will afford a multitude of such providential provisions. By a single gift was Esther fitted to be the deliverer of Israel : by a multitude of talents and acquirements, in the most wonderful complexity, was Luther fitted for the work to which he was called by God. Indeed, the history of the Reformation **bears a** very striking resemblance to this deliverance of the Jews. Without a single miracle, God wrought a deliverance as surprising as the preservation of Israel, and many of those employed to effect it were as ignorant of God as the king of Persia. He used the passions and the interests of worldly men in bringing about his purposes, as well as the love and zeal of his own people. The preservation of the cause and people of God at that period was as much the work of Divine Providence as the deliverance of the Jews from the destruction to which they were destined by the wicked Haman.

All the learning, ability, and acquirements—the riches, birth, rank, and influence, through which at any time the cause of God has been served, have been conferred by God, in his providential government, to fulfil the purposes of his grace. Not only does he gift his own people for this end, but many who belong not to any of the tribes of Israel have been made hewers of wood and drawers of water for the service of the temple. Many able defences of the Scriptures—many satisfactory vindications of their doctrines, and illustrations of their contents, have been afforded by Providence through the instrumentality of men as ignorant of the true grace of God as they who deny their authenticity. The very ravens are made to feed the people of God, rather than that they should want.

In God's conferring on Esther this exquisite beauty, that he might raise her to royal rank, and to influence over the throne itself, we may see that the same thing may, in one point of view, be the Divine appointment, and in another may be the sinful action of men. This is a doctrine clearly taught in the Scriptures. It is here exemplified in the government of Providence. It is a truth, however, that the wisdom of this world cannot fathom, and therefore cannot receive. That God should in any sense appoint, or intend to bring about, what he has in his word forbidden, is indeed one of the deep things of God. It is the abhorrence of the wise, while many even of those who have professed to have become fools that they may be wise, in effect deny it by their explanations. But this is a doctrine that the sagacity of men will never penetrate; it is a depth that human intellect will never be able to fathom? Who can by searching find out God? Can nothing be true of him and his ways but what is to be comprehended by such worms as men? Is it not enough to command our belief, that God has said it? Is he not virtually an atheist who requires more? A Christian who rests the reception of the Divine testimony on his ability to comprehend the thing testified, is more inconsistent than a deist. One who recommends any truth of Scripture on such grounds insults God. The voice of Providence

combines with that of Scripture in testifying to
the truth of the doctrine to which I have referred.
God evidently provided the beautiful Hadassah
for the bed of Ahasuerus. But does the Holy
One approve of this connexion? Are the se-
raglios of sensualists according to his word? Does
the divine law sanction the divorce of Vashti for
such an offence? What can be more abominable
in the eyes of God than this manner of choosing
a queen? What could be more hurtful to the
interests of men, or more repugnant to their
feelings? How unreasonable that a brutal sensualist should possess all the beauty of his vast
empire? How many of the fairest females were
thus lost to society, and consigned to perpetual
misery in the palace of the sensual despot? Can
anything be more palpably contrary to the end of
marriage, not only as it is declared in the word of
God, but even as it has been understood by
heathens? Yet God performed his purpose
through this great wickedness of men. He has no
share in human guilt, while the transgressors of
his law are made to fulfil his purposes. Such
wisdom is too wonderful for us; it is high; we
cannot reach it. But it is God's wisdom; let us
receive it with submission.

We may here see also the way in which God
regulates the events in his providence for fulfilling
his plans, by adapting them to the instruments

which he intends to employ in their execution. It was beauty that he gave to Esther, because beauty only could be the means of her elevation. All other accomplishments would have utterly failed. Had God given Esther greater riches than any subject of the hundred and twenty-seven provinces, she would not have been a single step nearer the throne. Had she been the daughter of the most powerful man in Persia, or a person of the highest birth, God, in his providence, could have made her a convert, or a friend to the religion of the Jews ; but this would not have forwarded her progress to the throne. Had she possessed all the wisdom of Solomon, or all the accomplishments of her sex, with the exception of beauty, she might as well have been an idiot or a rustic. Personal beauty only could raise her, and personal beauty the God of providence gave her, that she might be raised. This affords a key to God's plans in his providence, by which he governs a world that is at enmity with him. In this way he makes them obey his will who know him not, who hate him, and, what is still more strange, even while they fulfil his will, transgress his laws. How unsearchable are the counsels of Jehovah ! His way is in the sea, and his path in the great waters, and his footsteps are not known.

The providence of God appears conspicuous even in the ignorance of Mordecai and Hadassah. A marriage with a heathen was forbidden to the Jews. Now, had Mordecai and his kinswoman known their duty, her exaltation could never have taken place. But it seems very surprising that a man like Mordecai should be ignorant of this law of his God, or that he should know it, and join in the breach of it. Commentators are very willing to excuse him in this business. Mr. Scott says— " It does not seem to have been left to the choice either of Mordecai or of Esther ;" and Dr. Gill is willing to believe that the fair Jewess went by constraint. But, were this true, is it a justification of a breach of the law of God ? Why did Mordecai so uselessly hazard his own life and expose his whole nation to destruction, by obstinately refusing to honor Haman, and yield so readily to this vile prostitution of Esther ? If danger will warrant us to violate the law of God, we will never want a pretext. But there is no evidence that there was any reluctance in this business. There is no account of a search, nor of concealment on the part of Esther. So far from hiding Hadassah when the king's commandment was heard, it appears that Mordecai was uncommonly solicitous to promote her exaltation. Mr. Scott, indeed, attempts to plead his vindication in this, by alleging, that as he could not prevent her from becoming one of the concubines of Ahasuerus, he might thus endeavour to have her made queen.

But even this reasoning is not good. Had she been violated by the despot, she would not be justified in afterwards becoming his wife. Mordecai's zeal, then, to have her made queen is, in every point of view, unjustifiable. It was contrary to the law of God, yet it was in another point of view, God's own appointment. Instead of eagerly seeking a union with the king, Hadassah should have chosen the scaffold in preference. Her crime was much heightened by submitting to become his concubine before she became his wife. How many chances were against her that she might never have been called a second time into his presence?

Mr. Scott alleges, that " in her peculiar circumstances, the *ritual law of not giving their daughters to those of another nation* might not be thought obligatory." But can any circumstances justify the violation of a law of God? Very likely, indeed, Mordecai might have some way to excuse himself. The command, as contained in the law of Moses, could not be unknown to him. But, like many good men now, he might have some way of excusing himself from obedience. But whatever this might be, he must have deceived himself. Neither times nor circumstances can relieve from the obligation of obeying God's law. Could there be stronger circumstances to disannul the restriction as to marriage than those which existed in the return from the Babylonish, captivity? Wives had been married, and therefore ruined if the marriage is broken; children are born of these marriages, and, if the marriage will not stand, they must not only be bastardized, but even deprived of a father's roof, and education by him in the knowledge of the God of Israel. Yet all this was a matter of no consideration. Both wives and children must be disowned and driven away for ever. Let us read the Book of Ezra, and learn how sinful such marriages were accounted by all that feared God.

It is this wretched shift of times and circumstances that has subverted the whole order of Christ's house, and changed every ordinance of his kingdom. The laws of the kingdom are read in the Book of God; but, by some peculiarity in their situation, good men plead their excuse from observance, or, by forced explanations, conform the canons of Scripture to their own conduct. It requires but little ingenuity to devise a plausible pretext for not doing that to which we are averse, or for doing that we like.

Mordecai and Esther, then, were guilty in this affair. But this unaccountable ignorance of their duty prepared them to execute the part that God had allotted them in this wonderful display of his providence. Who can read this story without being convinced that this marriage was God's plan for delivering the Jews from the approaching danger? Can anything be clearer than that it was contrary to the law of God? In some point of view, then, God appoints what the sin of men effects. He ordains actions which are entirely free, and in which men have all the guilt. This is as clear as the authority of Scripture can make it. Ask me to explain it, and I confess myself a child. I would as soon attempt to fathom space, or calculate the moments of eternity. I believe it, I confess it before the world, I urge the reception of it on Christians, because God has testified it in his word. Let God be true, and all men liars.

From this we see that the very ignorance of duty in the people of God may sometimes be providential, and serve his purposes. I have no doubt that there are still in Babylon many Mordecais and Esthers, whose ignorance in their unlawful situation is turned to the glory of God and the good of his people. But the good effected by them in such a situation does not lessen their sin in violating the law of God. It is the hand of the Almighty that brings good out of evil, and makes the ignorance of his friends, as well as the wrath of his enemies, to praise him. He will pardon them, but they will suffer loss, both in this world and the next. Even in this world, the most gainful violation of God's laws is a loss to a Christian, and obedience, at the cost of the most expensive sacrifices, is a gain. What says the Lord Jesus to this question?—"Then Peter began to say unto him, Lo, we have left all, and have followed thee. And Jesus answered and said, Verily I say unto you, there is no man that hath left house, or brethren, or sisters, or father, or mother, or children, or lands, for my sake and the Gospel's, but he shall receive an hundred-fold more in this time, houses, and brethren, and sisters, and mothers, and children, and lands, with persecutions ; and in the world to come eternal life." The hundred-fold in this life cannot be of the things of this world, for then obedience would be a merely mercenary speculation. God does not bribe us to do our duty. It appears to me that it must be in the increase of light and enjoyment of God. The value of discovering God's mind in the Scriptures, and of beholding the glory of his character and ways, is incalculably great ; and no one who has experienced it would exchange it for kingdoms. He is a blessed man who is the least in the kingdom of God ; but there are many Christians who would not exchange with their brethren of the lowest attainments their views of divine things, as they have been taught by the Word and Spirit of their God, for all the glory of this world. The man who knows most of God is the first man on earth.

There is no reason, then, to envy the condition

of believers, who, from ignorance, can enjoy lucrative situations, even if there were no future loss. The peace of God, which will always be enjoyed in proportion to knowledge and obedience, is beyond all the treasures of the world. This view of things is highly·useful, for sometimes Christians may not only be tempted to envy the prosperity of the wicked, but even the condition of their brethren, whose ignorance allows them to possess more of the popularity, honors, and gains of the present world. Peter himself, when informed of the manner of his death, appears to have felt more from jealousy lest the beloved disciple might not be called to like suffering, than he did for the thing itself. "Lord," said he, "and what shall this man suffer?" It behoves us all to attend to the answer. "Jesus saith unto him, If I will that he tarry till I come, what is that to thee: follow thou me."

There is an obvious advantage in knowing and doing the will of God. Paul says, "If any man's work shall abide, which he hath built on the foundation laid by him, he shall receive a reward. If any man's work shall be burned, he shall suffer loss, but he himself shall be saved; yet so as by fire." He who got the greater number of talents, and made the best use of them, was made ruler over the greater number of cities. And what talent can be compared with the knowledge of the will of God?

Some people are willing to believe that whatever is lost by obedience to the will of God, will in some way be made up to them, even in this world, though it is their duty to obey without this consideration. But this view is false, fanatical, and hurtful. Though in every situation, we have a right to look to God, for this world as well as for the next, yet we know not to what sort of trials it may seem good to God to expose us. There is no safety in anything but in counting all things but loss for the excellency of the knowledge of Christ Jesus our Lord, and to be ready for him to suffer the loss of all things.

Sometimes the servants of Christ excuse themselves from complete conformity to his institutions, and vindicate the observance of the commandments of men in the things of God, by alleging the field of usefulness that accommodation in these things lays open to them. If they can point to any good done by them, they suppose that it is God's approbation of their situation. But in this they deceive themselves. Their conduct, as a transgression of the law of God, remains sinful, though his sovereignty turns their ignorance to his glory and the good of his people. Obedience is better than sacrifice, and to hearken than the fat of rams. It is a foul calumny on God to suppose that it is necessary to disobey him, in order to do good. This takes it for granted that his laws defeat their own end. When in the wisdom of God, he makes the ignorance of his people to serve his purpose, this no more excuses their ignorance and their conduct that results from it, than the good effects of the death of Christ will justify the crime of Judas Iscariot. God will, no doubt, forgive the ignorance of his people, but he will never hold it innocent. He will never approve it. Through the instrumentality of his people who understand not the nature of his kingdom, God provides that multitudes hear the gospel, who are to those in a scriptural situation altogether inaccessible. Yet this does not warrant the situation. Some of the people of God are in mystical Babylon, and, no doubt, will in some way serve God's purposes in that vile situation, yet the voice of God does not cease to sound in their ears, " Come out of her, my people, that ye be not partakers of her sins, and that ye receive not of her plagues." A Christian who knows his duty would not break the least of the commandments of Jesus, to enable him to turn the revenues of all the kings of the earth to the service of the cause of Christ. I might be asked, if all men would embrace my views of the nature of a church of Christ and his ordinances, and act on them with rigor, what would be the consequence? Millions who now constantly hear the gospel would be entirely shut up from it, and the hundreds of thousands of pounds that are raised annually for the spreading of the gospel, would fail. If none are to be embodied in the church except such as appear to be born again by the Spirit through the belief of the truth, how would the gospel be supported? How would it be spread over the world? And so asks the child, If the moon is not nailed to the sky, will it not fall? This is a preposterous fear. Leave God's province to himself; fill your own well. Follow Jesus, though it should leave the whole world to be involved in darkness. But there is no fear of such a result. Though God now makes use of the ignorance of his people to support and advance his cause; if they all knew their duty, he would give still more signal success. The silver and the gold are his. When it served him, Jesus said to a rich man, " Zaccheus, come down; for to-day I must abide at thy house." All the wealth of the world is at his absolute disposal, and the moment he needs it, he will call for it. Let not the servants of God do evil that good may come. Let them not disobey him, that they may put themselves in a condition to serve him. I would not set at nought the least of Christ's little ones. I will acknowledge all who know him, as far as I can know them, notwithstanding all the ignorance they may labor under. But I will not, out of complaisance, cease to declare what I learn from the word of God ; I cannot cease to call on Christians to follow Jesus. Their ignorance is sin. The good which they do through ignorance is no justification of it. Esther saved the Jews, but by being in a situation to do so, Esther transgressed the law of her God.

The providence of God is seen in every step of the progress of Esther to her destined elevation. As in the case of Joseph, when sold into Egypt, God provided friends for her in all who had the means of seeing her. He filled every heart with good-will towards her, at first sight. The king's chamberlain was pleased with her from the first moment of her arrival, and accelerated her progress by every means in his power. " So it came to pass, when the king's commandment and his decree was heard, and when many maidens were gathered together unto Shushan the palace, to the custody of Hegai, that Esther was brought also unto the king's house, to the custody of Hegai, keeper of the women. And the maiden pleased him, and she obtained kindness of him ; and he speedily gave her things for purification, with such things as belonged to her, and seven maidens, which were meet to be given her, out of the king's house ; and he preferred her and her maids unto the best place of the house of the women." When her turn came to approach the king, " she required nothing but what Hegai, the king's chamberlain, the keeper of the women, appointed ; and Esther obtained favor in the sight of all them that looked upon her." Surpassing as her beauty was, this universal favor cannot be ascribed to it. In courts, envy and intrigue often prevail over every claim. Had not God disposed the hearts of those who beheld her, some far inferior beauty might have been the general favorite.

Notwithstanding her incomparable beauty, it was possible that the king's affections might have been anticipated by some of those who had previous access, or, from caprice or peculiarity of taste, he might have preferred another. But the providence of God had ordered this also, and no one pleased the king before the approach of the lovely Hadassah ; and she obtained an instant preference. " So Esther was taken unto king Ahasuerus, into his house-royal, in the tenth month (which is the month Tebeth), in the seventh year of his reign. And the king loved Esther above all the women, and she obtained grace and favor in his sight more than all the virgins ; so that he set the royal crown upon her head, and made her queen instead of Vashti."

The conspiracy of two of the king's chamberlains is another event in which we may see the hand of God, for effecting the elevation of Mordecai, preserving him from the wrath of Haman, and investing him with authority for the defence of his people, as well as the destruction of their enemies. A plot for the assassination of the sovereign is indeed no unprecedented thing in the courts of absolute monarchs. It is granted, that the only impulse on the mind of the conspirators, exciting them to the murder of their master, was their resentment on account of whatever injury or provocation they had received. Their motives were not, in the remotest degree, to fulfil the counsel of God; nor are they sanctioned by him. They are therefore themselves solely responsible for their wicked intentions. But that this conspiracy was ordered of God, cannot surely be a matter of doubt with any who connect this fact with the others recorded in this history, and who believe the narrative to be the word of God. It is here as evidently brought in to contribute towards the general issue as any incident in a drama. Take it away, and the whole chain is broken. Let us then admire the wonderful ways of Providence, in bringing about events through the freedom and the sins of human action. Why did these officers receive provocation at this particular time? Why did they attend more to the gratification of their revenge than to their safety? Is a conspiracy to slay the sovereign the usual result of every great injury done by him to individuals? Why was not the conspiracy better conducted? why was it made known and frustrated? above all, why was Mordecai the man by whom it was discovered? why was he the man to whom it was known? Take away this link of the chain, and all the other links are useless. Whatever, then, was the means of bringing it to the knowledge of Mordecai, it was God that made it known to him, as much as if he had revealed it in a supernatural manner. Indeed, as Dr. Gill observes, " the latter Targum says, it was showed unto him by the Holy Ghost ;" for the wisdom of man cannot see how the providence of God can arrange human actions to fulfil his purpose without any miracle. How many chances were there, humanly speaking, that no conspiracy should have existed at this time, or that it should not have been found out ; or, if discovered, that Mordecai should not have been the discoverer? Was not the event evidently intended to lay a foundation for the future safety, elevation, and power of Mordecai? How encouraging is this document! The Lord's people are frequently in danger. Their enemies lay snares for them, which no human wisdom can enable them to escape. How consoling is it for them to reflect on this wonderful narrative !· Here is a fact that ought to encourage them in their most trying difficulties. *The Lord laid a plan, and prepared means for the deliverance of his people in the Persian empire, even before their enemies had prepared the plot for their destruction!* When therefore we are encompassed on every side, let us look to the hand of the Lord to execute the plan which he may have prepared for our deliverance. When Hagar cried unto the Lord, he showed her a well, which is as wonderful in Providence, if the fountain had been there from the creation, as if it had been opened by miracle.

Having considered God's wise and gracious provision for the safety of his people during the approaching storm, we shall now attend to the events by which it was raised. We may discover the hand of God in this, no less than the former. The providence of God brings his people into danger, not because he is unable to ward off even the appearance of it, but that he may glorify himself in their deliverance, and exercise their graces. Were they never in danger, they would be deprived of some of the greatest opportunities of praising the wisdom, kindness, and watchfulness of his providential care; his enemies would want an occasion of manifesting their enmity to them and him; and their faith would be without its necessary trials. But though, in one point of view, God wills the persecution of his people, the sin of the persecutor is all his own. He is ignorant of God's purpose, and his enmity to them arises from his enmity to him. Though he fulfils the appointment of God, yet he wickedly gratifies his own evil dispositions.

It is a curious fact, but not a singular one, that God raised up Haman to bring his people into danger, as well as Esther to deliver them. In this, as in other things, the Divine wisdom is distinguished from the human in a striking manner. No man would nurture the wretch whom he should know to be the future enemy of himself and his offspring. But God exalted Haman in the court of the great king, above all the princes of the empire, for the very purpose of giving him an opportunity of manifesting his enmity against his people, and of attempting the destruction of the whole nation. He puts his enemies in the most favorable situation to oppose him, that he may show with what ease he can discomfit the utmost efforts of their malevolence ; nay, he makes the very wrath of man to praise him, and the plans of his enemies to destroy his cause are made to effect its establishment.

The motives of Ahasuerus in the promotion of Haman were, no doubt, such as usually influence absolute sovereigns in conferring their favors, and in choosing the objects of their particular bounty. In the caprice of affection, they set no bounds to their liberality, and the most unworthy men in the empire are often their favorites. It is not strange, then, that it should have been so on the present occasion. But the direction of Providence is clear even amidst apparent casualties,

It was God raised Haman, as well as he had for a like occasion raised Pharaoh. The individual, the character, the crisis of his exaltation, the height of his elevation, are linked together by Providence for a good purpose. In such a light is this combination of circumstances exhibited in the inspired text. It is brought forward as one of the grand incidents which contribute their influence to bring about the result. "After these things did king Ahasuerus promote Haman, the son of Hammedatha the Agagite, and advanced him, and set his seat above all the princes that were with him." Why was Haman the favorite at this time ? Why was he raised to such a pitch of glory ?

The next event that presents itself to our con sideration, as contributing to bring the Jews into danger at this time, is the refusal of Mordecai to honor Haman, according to the king's commandment. Notwithstanding all that the commentators have said to justify Mordecai, I cannot but think that this part of his conduct arose from ignorance of his duty, and that he might lawfully have done the thing which he refused to do. Were it certain that Haman was an Amalekite, the fact would not vindicate a Jew in refusing him honor in the court of Persia. The command to extirpate the Amalekites was given to Israel only as a nation, and as living in their own land. "Therefore it shall be, when the Lord thy God hath given thee rest from all thine enemies round about, in the land which the Lord thy God giveth thee for an inheritance to possess it, that thou shalt blot out the remembrance of Amalek from under heaven ; thou shalt not forget it." Deut. xxv. 19.   What had Mordecai to do with this command in his present situation?   But if Haman was really an Amalekite, and if this was the ground on which Mordecai refused to honor him, whether it was valid or invalid, the providence of God is visible in the matter.   Why was the favorite an Amalekite? Why was one of that nation, at such a time, preferred to all the subjects of a hundred and twenty-seven provinces?   On this supposition, had he been a Persian, Mordecai would have honored him without scruple, and so no storm would have arisen against the Jews.

It is alleged in favor of Mordecai, that an idolatrous reverence might have been required. Dr. Gill makes wonderful stretches to justify or excuse his conduct.   As divine honors were given to the kings of Persia, he thinks that they might also have been exacted for their favorites ; but of this he gives no proof.   *It might be,* will prove nothing ; and nothing to justify such a supposition is in evidence from the passage.   On the contrary, the thing which he is said to have refused, is what he might lawfully have given.   The king's command enjoined all his servants to "bow down and reverence Haman." What should prevent any man to comply with this injunction of supreme civil power? But Dr. Gill's ingenuity finds even in this an argument on his side. The fact that "*the king had so commanded concerning him*, shows," he thinks, "that it was more than civil honor and respect, for that in course would have been given him as the king's favorite." But this would not have been in all cases a matter of course, and that it was enjoined, there is the evidence of this record. The king requires nothing but *to bow and reverence*. Even had Haman pretended to be a god, of which there is not the slightest evidence, this would not excuse any one from bowing to him according to the king's commandment. Caius made himself a god, but should this have hindered his Christian subjects to bow down to him and reverence him? Even if there was a danger that it might be mistaken by some for religious worship, let the principle on which it is performed be declared, but let not what is lawfully due be withheld.

Dr. Gill argues, that it must be more than civil respect that was required, because *that* the Jews did not refuse to give in the most humble and prostrate manner. This is just like saying that no Christian could refuse to uncover to the king, because Christians in general do this without scruple; yet William Penn would not uncover to King Charles. Besides, if Mordecai's conduct was influenced by a consideration of the nation of Haman, or anything in his individual character, this argument has no bearing. I cannot say why he refused: what I say is, that he might have lawfully yielded all that was required.

That nothing more than civil honor was required for Haman by the king's command, is clear from the 9th verse of the fifth chapter—"Then went Haman forth that day with a joyful and with a glad heart; but when Haman saw Mordecai in the king's gate, that he stood not up, nor moved for him, he was full of indignation against Mordecai." Here his offence was, that *he stood not up*, nor even *moved* himself to Haman. Can any sober mind interpret this of religious worship? was there any idolatry in rising out of respect to the second man in the Persian empire? Whatever ceremonial might have been in approaching great men in that country, on this occasion there is no ceremonial, for there was no approach. The great man is passing, and Mordecai will not stand up, nor even move to notice him. Dr. Gill himself admits that this was civil respect; but, then, Mordecai, it seems, refuses even this, lest it should be interpreted as religious worship. Was ever greater violence used in special pleading? So then not even the smallest respect ought to be given to heathen rulers who claim divine honors. But this, it seems, was only part of his reason. Mordecai was influenced, he says, partly by knowing that Haman had planned the destruction of the Jews. And would this justify him in refusing to obey the king's commandment? Another thing that weighed with Mordecai, he alleges, was, that he confided in Esther's influence to save the Jews, and therefore treated Haman with marked contempt. But may rulers be disobeyed when this can be done with impunity? Ought the man to be treated with contempt who is commanded by an absolute monarch to be honored above all his subjects? Is this the way in which Christians are to recommend the doctrine of Christ to the world?

But where is the necessity of arbitrarily supposing that this reverence must have had something idolatrous in it, when nothing but what is lawful is required in the words of the command? Was Mordecai perfect in knowledge, and infallible in conduct, that such a violent stretch must be made to justify him?

It is argued by Mr. Scott, that Mordecai was accepted of God in what he did, and therefore that his conduct must have been justifiable. But God's acknowledging him, and interfering to deliver him, are no proof that he approved of this part of his conduct. If God would not deliver his people from the consequences of their ignorance, they would soon be destroyed. Is there any passage in this history which, either by implication or expressly, commends Mordecai for not bowing to Haman? I admit that his motives may have been good. If he intended to honor God, his motives would be approved, though his conduct might be the effect of ignorance. We see from Rom. xiv. that God accepts his people even in their ignorance, when they are influenced by a regard to his authority. But this does not change error into truth, nor sin into duty. I think it is manifest that Mordecai acted on principle, for even when he saw the frightful consequences of his conduct, he persisted in it with the utmost steadiness. The text also seems to insinuate, that he considered his being a Jew as a reason for refusing honor to Haman. But whether this had an eye to the nation or character of Haman, or in what way he supposed his being a Jew could justify this conduct, is not said, and cannot be known.

It has also been very properly replied, that the homage required does not seem to differ from that paid to Joseph by his brethren and by the Egyptians, or from those forms of civil reverence which the greatest saints of whom the Old Testament gives an account, observed without scruple before their superiors. Ezra and Nehemiah, and even Mordecai· himself, must have rendered the

same homage to the king of Persia. It is answered, that in these cases, with respect to the
Persian monarch, the forms of approach may have
been dispensed with, in the approach of the Jews.
But this is gratuitous, and exceedingly unlikely.
It is not in evidence, and cannot be accepted as
proof. But what will utterly destroy this forced
supposition is, that Esther, in her first approach
to the king, must have complied with the ceremonial; and she could not have been excused by
her nation, for it was not known that she was
a Jewess. And in all this she followed the counsel
of Mordecai. What is still more, even after the
nation of Esther was known, she not only did
without scruple what Mordecai refused to Haman,
but she prostrated herself before the king. "And
Esther spake yet again before the king, and fell
down at his feet, and besought him with tears to
put away the mischief of Haman the Agagite, and
his decree that he had devised against the Jews,"
chap. viii. 3. Here she submits to the humblest
prostrations to the king. Mordecai refuses to
stand up, or even to move, in honor of Haman;
Esther prostrates herself at the feet of Ahasuerus.
It is utterly vain by special pleading to hope to
save Mordecai in this matter.

This point is of no great importance in itself,
but the forced interpretations and violent suppo-
sitions that are used in order to justify Mordecai,

is a specimen, in the disciples of Christ themselves, of the effects of human wisdom, to conform the word of God to itself, instead of implicitly bowing to its dictates. Had the learned and good men who have recourse to this criticism, in order to justify a man of God, met such an instance of outraging the inspired text, in the writings of the opposers of the doctrines of grace, they would have justly exclaimed with wonder, indignation, and horror. But they can consecrate the same licentious principle to make the text speak agreeably to their own wisdom. I have often observed, that in vindicating their own errors, the disciples of Christ avail themselves of the most licentious of the principles of criticism, which are the usual resource of the wildest heretics. On the contrary, the man of God ought to accustom himself in all things to conform himself to the word of God, to make his own wisdom bow to the Scriptures, and to receive implicitly whatever they teach.

Here, then, we see that even the ignorance of God's people is employed to fulfil his purposes. Mordecai's ignorance was sinful; but had he been better instructed in his duty, he could not have been employed on this occasion. Many a piece of service God has, in every age, allotted to some of his people, for which they are fitted by their ignorance. That he should bestow gifts on his people, to enable them to fill the station allotted to them, is not a matter of surprise to any ; but that the very ignorance of his people should fit them for certain situations for which he has designed them, could hardly be anticipated.

From this fact we may also perceive, that our ignorance of duty may frequently bring danger and persecution upon ourselves and the whole body of Christians with which we are connected. Haman's resolution to destroy the whole Jewish nation was occasioned by Mordecai's refusal to honor him. It is true, indeed, commentators are willing to believe that Haman's including the whole Jewish nation with Mordecai was influenced by the conviction that they were all of the same sentiment on this subject. This, however, is not only not in evidence, but it is direct contrary to the reason assigned by the Holy Spirit in the narrative. " And when Haman saw that Mordecai bowed not, nor did him reverence, then was Haman full of wrath. And he *thought scorn to lay hands on Mordecai alone ;* for they had showed him the people of Mordecai ; wherefore Haman sought to destroy all the Jews that were throughout the whole kingdom of Ahasuerus, even the people of Mordecai."

Mordecai is then fully chargeable with all the natural effects of his ignorance, even although a merciful Providence prevented the execution of the threatened vengeance. When an ill-informed Christian manifests a refractory, unsubmitting spirit towards his superiors, it brings odium and persecution on all connected with him. That God should give the government of the world to his enemies, and demand submission to the wicked, is not what the wisdom of this world could expect. If Christians will listen to the counsel of their own hearts, rather than to the dictates of the Divine word, they will think it very unreasonable that the children of the Great King, the heirs of God, should tamely yield to the evil men in power, and honor their persecutors. But such is the law of that kingdom which is not of this world. That spirit that refuses honor to worthless men in power is not the spirit of the gospel. That proud and insolent piety that refuses the customary tokens of respect even to majesty, was not practised by the patriarchs, nor was it inculcated by the apostles. If it finds shelter in the conduct of Mordecai, it ought to be known that it is sanctioned only by Mordecai's sin.

The next providential circumstance we shall review is Esther's concealing of her kindred. Had it been known to Haman that Esther was a Jewess, and the near kinswoman of Mordecai, he certainly would not have attempted any violent measures against either Mordecai or the Jews. Nothwithstanding his mortification on account of the insult, he would have found it prudent to smother his resentment, or to gratify it in a more indirect way.

He could not have expected to prevail, as long as Esther retained any share in the affections of the king. Mordecai's intention in enjoining Esther to conceal her descent, was, no doubt, lest her being a captive Jewess might prevent her advancement to the situation of queen. The odium of her religion, as well as the captivity of her nation, would appear to him to stand in the way of her elevation. God's intention by that concealment was to preclude a circumstance that would have prevented the danger of his people. He designed to bring them to the very brink of ruin, that he might manifest his power in their deliverance. It was ignorance and carnal policy in Mordecai ; yet in another view, it was ordained by God for a wise purpose.

From this fact we may see, that worldly policy in religion naturally leads to disappointment and trouble. When by their wisdom, Christians seek preferment, or endeavor to escape the cross, by concealing any part of the truth, they are generally preparing a scourge for their own back. Esther, by the advice of Mordecai, concealed her religion, for the purpose of obtaining a situation that would enable her to protect the cause and people of God ; but by that concealment the ruin of her whole nation would have been effected, had not a merciful God interposed to ward off the intended blow. Every means contrary to the word of God promise

affliction to the people of God. Believers who
conceal the truth to obtain any worldly advantage,
may congratulate their policy when they succeed ;
but let them look about, for danger and sorrow are
pursuing them. They have made a pit in which
they will sink, if a merciful God prevent not the
natural tendency of their conduct. From the
bold and independent spirit of Mordecai, we may
reasonably infer, that his desire of the advancement of his kinswoman was more influenced by
zeal for the good of his nation than by any views
of private advancement. The advantage of her
exaltation to the cause of the captive Jews, would
blind him to its sin. How often do Christians,
reasoning on the same principle, overlook the laws
of God ! Jesus Christ, by his apostles, separated
his disciples from the world for observance of the
ordinances of his kingdom ; but human wisdom
has violated this order, and sought protection and
power to the cause of God, through a marriage
with the world. In the writings of the apostles
we everywhere meet with the distinction between
Christ's people, who are called " Christians," " believers," " saints ;" and the rest of mankind, who
are called " the world," those who are without,
&c. But by the marriage of Esther with Ahasuerus, there is now no world : there are none without ; for every man in Christendom either belongs
to what is called the church, or may belong to it if

he chooses. That this marriage has produced some good effects, I am not the person to deny. It may often have been a shield to the people of God. But with all the advantages that it has ever had, the bans are forbidden, for the marriage is contrary to the word of God. None ought to have a place in the church of Christ but such as appear to be his disciples. When the Lord shall stand upon the wall that was made by a plumb-line, with a plumb-line in his hand, the high places of Israel shall be desolate, and the sanctuaries of Israel shall be laid waste, Amos vii. 7. The greatest possible good to the cause of God cannot justify the smallest deviation from his commands. Let the ark of God itself fall, rather than attempt to uphold it with a human hand.

Let us adore the mercy of our God, who steps forward in the time of our danger, to rescue us from the consequences of our own policy. He might justly have given up Mordecai and Esther, to reap the reward of their sin. But as their conduct was the effect of ignorance, he saves them from ruin, and promotes them to honor. Their devotedness to the cause of God is unquestionable. He forgets not the glory of his own name, and though his people are ignorant and sinful, he looks to the perfection of the righteousness of their Substitute, his own dearly beloved Son.

Not only was the great elevation of Haman providential; the commandment of the king for all to reverence him in a marked manner, was also directed by the Divine counsel. The favor of the king would indeed naturally have procured respect for the object of it; but the royal command made the neglect a breach of the laws of the king; and exposed it to the notice of the other servants, who made it known to Haman. " Why transgressest thou the king's commandment? is a question which shows that the offence was considered not a breach of courtesy merely, but the violation of the royal authority. Without this commandment, Mordecai might have escaped. That Haman was immediately informed of the people to whom Mordecai belonged, was also providential, for he had not previously known this. Had not this been discovered, the body of the Jewish nation would have escaped the danger to which Mordecai was exposed. But a wise Providence took care that this fact should not lie hid, that his name might be glorified in the salvation of his people, and in the destruction of their enemies. Why was Esther's descent unknown, though she was advanced to be consort to majesty, while Mordecai's was notified as soon as his offence? Yet the other servants themselves had not previously known this. It was on this very occasion that he himself discovered his kindred; " for he had told them that he was a Jew." Here we see, that as the caution of Mordecai in advising Esther to conceal her nation was the means of bringing it into the utmost danger of total extinction, his voluntary discovery of his descent was now to have the same effect. The utmost exertions of human wisdom may often be employed to bring about what they are intended to prevent.

But what above all calls for our wonder is, that a monarch, who ought to consider himself the father of all his people, shall, for no purpose but the gratification of a wicked favorite, give up a whole nation to perdition. If no sentiments of duty or of pity had any weight with him, why did not his interest as a sovereign forbid his compliance with the cruel request? Yet, in defiance of every principle of humanity, justice, and policy—without even the pretence of any misconduct—he gave the lives of the whole Jewish nation, "both young and old, little children and women," a present to his unprincipled favorite. The unsubstantial reasons alleged are not weighed, but received implicitly, without examination. After all, there is nothing in the history to show that Ahasuerus was a cruel or tyrannical man. His conduct in this instance is an easy, unsuspecting compliance, in a matter that required the utmost deliberation and caution. Let us attend a moment to the argument employed by the crafty favorite to overreach his master, and destroy the people of God. "And Haman said unto king Ahasuerus, There is a certain people scattered abroad, and dispersed among the people in all the provinces of thy kingdom; and their laws are diverse from all people; neither keep they the king's laws; therefore it is not for the king's profit to suffer them. If it please the king, let it be written that they may be destroyed, and I will pay ten thousand talents of silver to the hands of those who have the charge of the business, to bring it into the king's treasuries."

What was the head and front of the offence of this people? Their laws were different from those of all other nations. They would not observe the religious institutions that were ordained by man. The civil law of the countries of their captivity it was their duty to obey. Their God commanded them to "seek the peace of the city whither he had caused them to be carried away captive, and to pray unto the Lord for it," Jer. xxix. 7. But to neglect the ordinances of their God, or to observe the religious rites appointed by man, they had no license. Why were the Jews to be blamed for the singularity of their institutions, for their scrupulous separation from other nations, and for their firmness in refusing compliance with the rites of all other religions? If their laws were singular, were they not the laws of God? Why do kings and rulers pretend to interfere between God and his people? Why do wretched mortals assume an authority to set aside what God enjoins? Let

Christians in every country render to Cesar the things that are Cesar's, but to God the things that are God's. If rulers must usurp the throne of God, let them attempt to alter the rising of the sun, or regulate the changes of the moon; but let them not dare to meddle with the laws of the kingdom of Christ.

The allegations of Haman against the Jews are still substantially the ground of accusation against those who fully follow the churches planted by the apostles, and refuse compliance with all the institutions of man in the things of God. They are held up as a singular kind of people, who, by the peculiarity of their religious observances, and their uncompliant spirit with respect to every deviation from the ordinances of God, manifest disaffection to the government of the country. In their religious observances, they are accused as being "diverse from all people." Fear of this accusation, more, perhaps, than any other cause, keeps the people of God from discovering the ordinances of Christ, and induces them to accommodate, as far as possible, to some of the great sects in the countries where they live. Israel grew weary of the government of God, and desired a king, that they might be like other nations. How long will the children of God neglect the laws of his kingdom! when will they return to the order and ordinances of his house!

How grateful ought Christians to be who live in a land of liberty! What a blessing it is to have the exercise of their religion secured to them by the laws of the state! If any of them are so ill-informed as not to be impressed with the value of this privilege, let them think of the Jews in the time of Esther—let them think of the state of Christians in this country in ages past—and in some other countries at the present moment. What a wretched thing it is to live in a country whose rulers assume the authority of God, and dictate in the things of religion? What a revolting idea to live in a country where an incensed favorite may receive a present of the lives of a whole nation! How degraded is the state of man in a country where an insolent courtier offers the sovereign a price for the lives of a whole people!

Yet the Christian has nothing to fear in any country. If he is called to suffer, it will be for God's glory and his own unspeakable advantage. If God has no purpose to serve by the sufferings of his people, he can, even under the most despotic governments, procure them rest. Jesus rules in the midst of his enemies, and is master of the resolves of despots. He restrains their wrath, or makes it praise him. If he chooses, he can give his people power even with the most capricious tyrants. They are as safe in the provinces of the empire of Ahasuerus, as in the dominions of Great

Britain. The history of the book of Esther demonstrates that there is no danger from which the Lord cannot rescue his people, even through the medium of the ordinary course of events. Without a single miracle, he brings them from the very brink of ruin, and precipitates their enemies into the abyss. We see them, as a nation, formally given over to destruction by an irrevocable decree ; yet they escape without the suffering of an individual. " And the king took his ring from his hand, and gave it unto Haman, the son of Hammedatha the Agagite, the Jews' enemy. And the king said unto Haman, The silver is given unto thee, and the people also, to do with them as it seemeth good to thee." Even the power of the king himself could not revoke this grant. Letters were sent to all the provinces of the empire, to secure the entire extirpation of the hated race. The enmity of the nations to the Jews is stimulated by their avarice. They are permitted " to take the spoil of them for a prey." Can human wisdom descry any possible means of escape for the captives of Israel in the midst of their enemies ? Yet God is their deliverer !

Haman now thought his victory secure. The royal decree is obtained, and messengers are sent out with it to all the king's lieutenants in the provinces, in the languages of all the nations subject to Persia. " And the king and Haman sat down to drink, but the city Shushan was perplexed."

Little did that unthinking monarch reflect on the misery to which his rash indulgence of a favorite had consigned so many of his innocent subjects. Could absolute monarchs get a view of the mischief caused by the oppression of their wicked favorites, they would often shrink from it with horror. Many a bloody decree originates not so much in the cruelty of their nature, as in the seducing flatteries of their courtiers. They watch the pliant hour, and in the moment of good-humor, they obtain the fatal grant. From that moment they keep the matter at a distance from his ear, and divert his attention by the gratifications of intemperance and debauchery. How insensible is the mind of men in certain situations! "There is no flesh in man's obdurate heart, it does not feel for man." Despots and their sycophants sit down to their drunken banquets, after giving decrees that involve whole nations in misery!

As God can protect his people under the greatest despotism, so the utmost civil liberty is no safety to them without the immediate protection of his Almighty arm. I fear that Christians at present in this country have too great a confidence in political institutions, and in the enlightened views of the public on the rights of conscience. We hear more boasting of the march of mind than of the government of God. It is thought impossible, into whatever hands power may fall, that rulers in this country should ever attempt to effect uniformity in religion, or apply force in the affairs of religion. Such an opinion is as unfounded in the philosophy of human nature, as it is destitute of the authority of history and of the word of God. There are not wanting some symptoms of the rise of Haman, and if he does not at length obtain a present of the lives of his enemies, it will be owing, not to the light of our politicians, but to the overruling providence of God, in opposition to that light. At all events, let Christians confide in the power and watchfulness of their God, not in the schemes of fanatical politicians. Even at the present moment, I am confident that there are many places in the empire where there is not entire liberty of conscience. There may be the liberty of the statute book, when there is danger from the mob; and where there is not perfect safety for the Christian in exercising, and in publishing, and spreading his religion, there is not practical liberty of conscience. To have liberty of conscience, we must not only be freed from all force constraining us to profess a religion which we do not assume; we must also be safe in the most active and public efforts to spread our own.

Let us now attend to the providence of God effecting the deliverance of his people from this awful danger, and precipitating their enemies into the pit which they had prepared for others.

The disposal of the lots cast before Haman, to ascertain the most lucky day for striking the intended blow, attracts our attention as the first providential circumstance for the salvation of the Jews.   Even before Haman had obtained the royal consent for destroying them, he had used divination to discover the most fortunate time for executing his purpose.   Shall the oracle of Satan be compelled to speak for God?   Shall the god of this world lose all his sagacity when he comes to fix the destruction of the people of the Lord?   Why did he choose the last month in the whole year, when the execution of his plan would have been promoted by immediate despatch?   "The lot is cast into the lap, but the disposal of it is of the Lord."   He works his own will by the counsels of devils, as well as through the agency of the angels of his presence.   "In the first month, that is the month Nisan, in the twelfth year of king Ahasuerus, they cast Pur, that is, the lot, before Haman, from day to day, and from month to month, to the twelfth month, that is, the month Adar."   From the direction of this oracle, the day of execution was fixed on the thirteenth day of the twelfth month, that is, more than eleven months after the decree.   Whether the laws of nature, or the agency of infernal spirits, guided this answer, it was evidently ordained by God for the salvation of his people.   Had the day of execution been immediate, there was nothing to prevent Haman's wicked purpose from taking effect. But his very superstition is made to co-operate in God's plan for the preservation of Israel. When the devil himself is consulted, he gives the most foolish advice to his friends, when God has any purpose to fulfil by it. He that was a murderer of the saints from the beginning is here made an instrument to effect their preservation.

We have here a key to the providence of God with respect to the heathen oracles. Though they uttered the responses of demons, they were made the means of fulfilling the purposes of God. Satan by them ruled the world, but God in them overruled Satan himself. While the devil was the God of this world, and held men captive at his pleasure, Jehovah ruled the earth as absolutely as he did the angels of heaven. While men in general were serving the prince of darkness, the Lord effected his own sovereign purposes through their agency. Human wisdom may exclaim, How is this! Let it fathom the depths of the Divine wisdom before it repeats the question. If God is God, the rebellion of devils and of men must be in some way for his glory.

By a like expedient, Jehovah provided that Jonah should be cast into the sea. He raised a tremendous storm against the ship in which the refractory prophet was sailing. But what providence is in a storm? The philosopher sees in this nothing but what he calls nature, and the laws of nature. "But the Lord sent out a great wind into the sea." Although storms, and earthquakes, and pestilence, and thunder, and war, and famine, may all be brought about by natural causes, they are all the work of the Almighty. But when the storm is raised, how is it to manifest Jonah? It is through the impression of the heathen mariners that it was sent as a judgment. Why were they struck with this impression now? Did they look on all storms in this light? or did they judge from the peculiarly tremendous nature of this tempest? In whatever manner the impression came, it was to fulfil the purpose of God. But even with this impression, how is the guilty person to be detected? How are these heathens to find out the will of the God of Israel? It is through the means of their own superstition. It is by casting lots; and though God always disposes the lot, there is no reason to believe that he will always in this way manifest a guilty person. Were this the case, rulers would have no difficulty in detecting guilt, and discriminating between the guilty and the innocent. But the heathen mariners acted on their own superstitious opinion, which was nothing better than the origin of dueling; and in this instance God spake through their oracle: "So they cast lots, and the lot fell upon Jonah." Here, then, we

see the way of Providence. The Ruler of the
world effects his purposes by every agent, and
makes use of the opinions and motives, of the resolutions and actions, of all men. Nay, he over-
rules their very crimes to fulfil his plans. In these
sentiments of the heathen mariners, however erro-
neous they are in some respects, yet it is pleasing
to see the strong conviction of an overruling Providence. This is strikingly obvious, both in their
opinion of the cause of the storm and in their expedient of the lots. As Ælian has observed, " Atheism is the refinement of speculation, and not the dictate of human nature. No one of the barbarians,"
says he, " ever fell into atheism, or started a doubt
as to the existence of the gods. They have no
such discussions as, Are there gods ? and if there
are gods, do they take care of us ? Neither Indian,
nor Celt, nor Egyptian, ever conceived such a
notion as Epicurus and the atheistic Grecian sages."
Now, this observation of the heathen historian is
of great importance. In whatever way the impression has been received, it is general, that Divine
Providence rules in all the affairs of men. This
view of nature is only stifled by some of the greatest fools in human shape, who style themselves
philosophers.

But let us return to the history of Mordecai.
How wonderful is the providence of God in restraining Haman from taking immediate vengeance, on

receiving a fresh insult, as he returned in triumph from Esther's banquet! "Then went Haman forth that day joyful, and with a glad heart: but when Haman saw Mordecai in the king's gate, that he stood not up, nor bowed for him, he was full of indignation against Mordecai. Nevertheless, Haman refrained himself!" *Haman refrained himself!* There is something more wonderful in this than even in a miracle. In my view, Almighty power would not have been so illustriously displayed, had God interfered to save Mordecai, by causing the earth to open and swallow his adversary, as by ruling his impetuous passions without interfering with the freedom of his determinations. Haman has a royal irrevocable decree for the destruction of the whole Jewish nation; he is elated beyond measure by being the only person invited to the queen's banquet with the king; he is again insulted by the man whom he so much abhorred; his mind is full of wrath; yet he refrains from immediate violence! Where did he learn his self-command? Look at the mouths of the hungry lions with Daniel before them; look again at the enraged Haman, and Mordecai untouched in his presence. God, who stopped the mouths of lions, and preserved his children in the furnace, manifested here a more wonderful power in directing the free will of a bloody persecutor, armed with the authority of the Persian empire. It was Haman's own action—"he restrained himself!" yet it was the working of the providence of God. Not so wonderful would it be to see a ship standing motionless in the midst of the tumult of the waves, or the raging billows rolling to the shore without touching the rocks, as to see Haman restraining himself on this occasion. Let the children of God read, and believe, and rejoice. When their enemies are maddened with rage, their God can make them restrain themselves, even without changing their heart. By his inscrutable providence, they willingly resolve to refrain from injury, or to delay vengeance, even while they feel no pity.

We may recognize the hand of Providence in overcoming the fears of Esther when solicited to approach the king in behalf· of the Jews. By going uncalled into the inner court, she would subject herself to death by law. Judging from the manners of our own country, we may think that her risk was small. But in estimating her danger, we ought to take into account the caprice of despots in countries where polygamy prevails. This moment they devote to destruction the object on which they doated the moment before. Besides, Esther had reason to apprehend an alienation of affection, or at least a coldness, as she had not been called into his presence for thirty days previously. Here, indeed, is another providential circumstance that ought to excite our wonder. Whatever was

6*

the reason why the king had so long neglected her,
the thing was undoubtedly a part of the Divine
plan, that Esther's danger might be increased, her
faith put to the severer trial, and his own power
more fully manifested in obtaining for her a gracious reception. Let the children of God look at
this and take a lesson. When he calls them to
arduous duties, instead of smoothing the way and
removing the appearance of difficulty or danger, he
often, by his providence, throws obstacles in their
way. A wife, in following Christ, instead of de-
lighting her husband, may give him the greatest
offence. Children may make their very parents
their enemies by their obedience to their heavenly
Father. Instead of inducing his disciples to discover his laws and ordinances, by the prospects
of greater acceptance with the world, he promises
them nothing but ridicule and hatred. Instead of
flattering every instance of obedience with additional honors and rewards from men, the discovery of the laws and institutions of Christ's kingdom
may be followed by the loss of all things. God
will not bribe his people to serve him. He will
not secure their allegiance by hiding them from
danger. They must give their life, if he calls for
it, or give up the hope of the heavenly inheritance.
They must count the cost, and be willing to incur
it; they must take up the cross and follow him.
They are not to fear him who has power to kill

the body, but rather him who can punish both soul and body in hell for ever. Jesus must be obeyed in the prospect of every danger. He that loves his life, shall lose life eternal. Yet, in general, it may be observed, that when Christians are made willing to face every danger for Christ's sake, the greatest real dangers that they may have dreaded are turned away from them. When God has tried them sufficiently, he removes the trial. Esther's apparent danger was heightened by her long neglect. Yet, after all, her God procured her acceptance with the king.

It is absurd in any at this time to underrate the trial of Esther. She must herself, doubtless, have been a better judge of the extent of her danger than we can now possibly be ; and she estimated it so highly, that at first she altogether refused to comply with the request even of Mordecai, to whom she had in all other things paid the deference due to a father. "All the king's servants, and the people of the king's provinces, do know, that whoever, whether man or woman, shall come unto the king into the inner court, who is not called, there is one law of his to put him to death, except such to whom the king shall hold out the golden sceptre, that he may live ; but I have not been called to come in unto the king these thirty days." Her life, then, was actually forfeited by the act ; and to spare her was the pardon of a criminal condemned to die.

Besides, she must, in this approach to the king, appear in a new character, as a captive, as a Jewess, as one of these already given up to death in the grant to Haman. In such circumstances, she might well be apprehensive that by her death he might make way for a successor. What trust is to be put in the affections of a capricious despot? What confidence is to be placed in the unfeeling man who could give up the beautiful Vashti? Might not some reasons of state operate to the destruction of Esther?

Her apprehensions of the magnitude of her danger appear evidently in the preparations with which she thought it necessary to approach him. All the Jews in Shushan fasted three days, night and day, before she ventured on the dangerous service. It is also evident, in the words in which she expressed her determination, that having counted the cost, she was prepared to give her life as a sacrifice for her friends. "If I perish, I perish." She consented not to undertake this mission till she overcame the fear of death.

What a blessing is marriage according to the institution of God! Was she truly a wife who could not trust her life with her husband? Better to be the wife of a Christian peasant, than the queen of a Persian despot. In the midst of all her regal honors, what happiness could Esther enjoy in her situation? Yet with what preposterous artifice did she and her guardian court the dangerous height! The prospect of wretchedness will not deter the fallen human mind from seeking the glories of this world, even at the expense of the soul. Man is a strange compound of meanness and of pride.

Let us take a glance at the arguments by which Mordecai prevailed on the queen to undertake to intercede for the Jews. They are such as were calculated to produce the desired effect, and were, no doubt, suggested by a gracious Providence. The faith manifested by Mordecai in the Divine protection, approaches to that of Abraham himself. If, then, faith is the gift of God, there is no doubt that Providence directed the resolution of Esther. "Then Mordecai commanded to answer Esther, Think not with thyself that thou shalt escape in the king's house more than all the Jews. For if thou altogether holdest thy peace at this time, then shall there enlargement and deliverance arise to the Jews from another place ; but thou and thy father's house shall be destroyed : and who knoweth whether thou art come to the kingdom for such a time as this ?" Notwithstanding the greatness of the danger, Mordecai appears confident that his God would raise up deliverance from some quarter. He rightly interprets the intention of Providence in raising her to royalty for this very occasion. Here we have a beautiful example of the view of

Providence entertained at that time by the people of God. Mordecai knew well the events that led to the exaltation of Esther. He knew that she was raised in the ordinary course of human affairs. He knew that her exaltation was owing to the divorce of Vashti, and to her own surpassing beauty. An atheist would have no difficulty in accounting for it. Yet Mordecai believed also that God raised her, and justly concluded from the present danger, that his purpose in raising her was for the very purpose of interceding for the Jews. At all events, he concluded, that as she had it in her power to make an effort for their preservation with probable hopes of success, should she refuse to make trial of her influence, she might expect that God would signally punish her, and save his people in some other way.

Let all Christians learn from this, not to be backward in using their influence to protect the people of God, and serve the interests of his kingdom. If they hide their face, God will provide other instruments, and they shall not be without chastisement. If from apprehensions of danger they decline any service that the providence of God lays before them, the very thing that is dreaded may come upon them, and others may be honored to do the work in safety. " Thou therefore," says God to Jeremiah, " gird up thy loins, and arise, and speak unto them all that I command thee : be not dismayed at their faces, lest I confound thee before them. For behold I have made thee this day a defenced city, and an iron pillar, and brazen walls, against the whole land ; against the kings of Judah, against the princes thereof, against the priests thereof, and against the people of the land. And they shall fight against thee, but they shall not prevail against thee, for I am with thee, saith the Lord, to deliver thee." Jer. i. 7—19.

By the gospel the elect of God are to be saved from a greater destruction than that which threatened the Jews in the time of Esther. The gospel is to be spread over the world by the means of the disciples of Christ. Let them therefore brave danger, and shame, and loss, in publishing the glad tidings of salvation. Why have eighteen centuries passed since the giving of the command to preach the gospel to all nations, while many have not yet heard of the name of Jesus? The Lord's time indeed may not be come, but this does not excuse the indolence of his servants. The commandment is come, which is the only thing with which we are concerned. The Lord, will, no doubt, raise up instruments to effect his purpose in the proper time, but this will not make up the loss, or excuse the neglect of his slumbering servants.

By the institutions of Christ, his children are to be nourished and advanced in the knowledge of him. But the nature of his kingdom is yet little understood; and every one of his ordinances having been changed in Babylon, still remained incrusted with superstition and human inventions. The children of God, then, are deprived of much of that wholesome nourishment which the pure ordinances of God are calculated to yield. Let allegiance to Jesus and the love of his people influence his disciples, who know his will, to zeal in making it known to others. Let no mistaken complaisance, with respect to the corruptions of divine institutions, prevent them from denouncing everything contrary to the word of God. Let not the emolument of office, the reproach of the world, or deference to the prejudice of God's people, induce them to practise what is not taught in Scripture, or to decline adopting everything enjoined by the authority of Christ. Has he not himself said—" And why call ye me Lord, Lord, and do not the things that I say? Ye are my disciples if ye do whatever I command you."

Let not Christians, who know the law and ordinances of Jesus, fear to exert themselves in their defence. The corruptions of the ordinances of Christ are sanctioned by so many prejudices, and strengthened by so many interests, that Christians in general are irritated when they are called to inquire. The wise virgins have laid themselves down to slumber, and they are peevish with those who attempt to awake them. If they do arise for a

moment, it is usually to plead for a little more
sleep, and to remonstrate against the violence and
cruelty of the untimely intruders. He who will
revive all the ordinances of Christ, and denounce
everything human in religion, must be prepared
for a kind of martyrdom even from Christians.
This is much more painful than the enmity of the
world; but even this he is not to fear. If believers, from the apprehension of becoming unpopular
even with the churches of Christ, hide their knowledge, or decline to employ their talents according
to their opportunities, let them learn from the lesson of Mordecai to Esther, that God can do his
work without them; and that in some way they
may expect the Divine displeasure. There cannot
be a doubt that a Christian consults his good, upon
the whole, by boldly and unreservedly doing the
will of God. The more he shows himself dead to
censure and to praise, the more he disregards gain
and loss, when they stand in the way of duty—the
more he will have reason to rejoice in the end. Let
his ambition always be fired with the hope of ruling over ten cities. Esther, to save the people of
God, flung herself at the feet of the despot, at the
hazard of her life; but, instead of being put to
death, Esther met with a most gracious reception.
A day will come at last, when obedience to the
most disagreeable of Christ's commandments will
appear great gain.

We may also perceive here the good effect of wholesome admonition on a stumbling servant of God. The fear of man had prevailed over the love of her brethren, in the mind of Esther. But faithful admonition kept her from falling. How forcible are right words! From the suggestion of Mordecai, it appears, that though the royal decree consigned the whole Jewish race to death, yet that she counted on safety in the palace, as the wife of the king. But Mordecai undeceives her on this, and took away her flattering hopes. By declining to do duty, she put herself from under the Divine protection, and engaged the displeasure of Providence to seek her out for destruction. Notwithstanding all her confidence in her situation, he denounces death to her and her father's house, if she declined the dangerous service. It is always under some false confidence that the children of God decline to obey him. To expose them, is, by the Divine blessing, the means of recovering the stumbling individual. Let not the servants of Jesus perceive one another going astray, or halting on the Christian race, without endeavoring to recover them. By the words of Mordecai, through the Divine blessing, Esther was brought from a state of abject timidity, to the confidence and boldness of a martyr. "If I perish, I perish!" Such ought to be the resolution of all God's servants. They should count the cost, and be willing to part with property, fame, popularity, friends, relatives, life, for the sake of the Lord Jesus. "If any man come to me," says Christ, "and hate not his father and mother, and wife and children, and brothers and sisters, yea, and his own life also, he cannot be my disciple. And whosoever does not bear his cross, and come. after me, cannot be my disciple." Luke xiv. 26, 27. An apostle says, "As Christ laid down his life for us, we ought also to lay down our lives for the brethren."

An incidental remark or an allusive application of the words in which Esther expressed her devotedness, may not be useless. People in a certain state of mind are represented as saying—"If I perish, I will perish at the feet of Jesus !" Surely there can be no similarity between the situation of a person approaching a despot, contrary to law, at the hazard of life, and that of one approaching the merciful Redeemer, by the command of God, with the assurance of pardon. There is no possibility of perishing at the feet of Jesus. Men perish through unbelief, in refusing to come to him. " Ye will not come to me that ye may have life." Whosoever comes to Jesus shall not be cast out.

From the conduct of Mordecai on this occasion, we may see that confidence in God does not preclude the use of means. Mordecai had immediate recourse to the influence of Esther, though, it is evident, he ultimately relied on the power and providence of God.   It is obvious, from his observations, that he expected preservation from God through the use of means, even had Esther declined the intercession.   "If thou altogether holdest thy peace at this time, then shall there enlargement and deliverance arise from another place." Let us learn from this, that as God has promised to protect us and provide for us, it is through the means of his appointment, vigilance, prudence, and industry, that we are to look for these blessings.

We shall now view the providence of God in the reception of Esther.   Life and death are on the countenance of the despot, and according to the will of God he frowns or smiles.   Had God designed her death, she would have found the king in another temper.   But is not the king's heart in the hand of the Lord ?   Does he not turn it as he pleases ?   Esther is received most graciously, and accosted in the most affectionate manner.   The coldness that had overlooked her for thirty days, gives place to the utmost warmth of affection, and, instead of the denunciation of death that she at first feared, she now hears the expressions of the most extravagant bounty.   " Now it came to pass on the third day, that Esther put on her royal apparel, and stood in the inner court of the king's house, over against the king's house ; and the king sat upon his royal throne in the royal house, over against the gate of the house.   And it was so, when the king saw Esther the queen standing in the court, *that she obtained favor in his sight ;* and the king held out to Esther the golden sceptre that was in his hand. So Esther drew near, and touched the top of the sceptre. Then said the king unto her, What wilt thou, queen Esther? and what is thy request? it shall be even given thee to the half of the kingdom." *"And it was so, when the king saw Esther the queen standing in the court, that she obtained favor in his sight."* This favor was the spontaneous affection of the king's own heart; but in another point of view, it was God who gave her that favor. Who is so blind as not to see the hand of God in this? who is so stupid as not to ascribe the glory to the Almighty in this matter? who does not here recognise Joseph's God? "But the Lord was with Joseph, and showed him mercy, *and gave him favor* in the sight of the keeper of the prison." Who does not see the Lord that always interfered for Israel, and will always interfere for the deliverance of the true Israel of God? Who gave favor to the Israelites in the sight of the Egyptians on their leaving of Egypt? "And I will give the people favor," says God, "in the sight of the Egyptians ; and it shall come to pass, that when ye go ye shall not go empty."

Christian, see here the security of God's people in doing duty; see the encouragement to confidence in his protection. From this learn the importance of humbling thyself before thy God in the hour of trial. See the duty of fasting and prayer in the time of trouble and of danger; see the resource of God's people in the time of their calamity. If we need the protection of men, let us first ask it from God. If we prevail with him, the power of the most mighty and of the most wicked must minister to our relief. Esther and her friends first cried unto the Lord, and humbled themselves before him, and then she went to the king. "Then Esther bade them return Mordecai this answer, Go, gather together all the Jews that are present in Shushan, and fast ye for me, and neither eat nor drink, three days, night or day; I also and my maidens will fast likewise; and so will I go in unto the king, which is not according to the law; and if I perish, I perish." How often do Christians look first to the means of deliverance! how often do they try every resource, before they go to God with a simple and confident reliance on him! how is their unbelief rebuked here! What encouragement does this hold out to confidence in God in the utmost danger! Only let us believe, and all things are possible.

Esther's delay in preferring her request is another providential circumstance. It is strange that she did not hastily take the advantage of the good-humor of the monarch, before she gave him time for reflection and bad counsel. She might not find him again so complaisant. Her impatience also to be delivered from a state of suspense must have favored an immediate application. Yet without any assigned reason, she declined an explanation, not only at that time, but also at the first banquet. Whatever may have been Esther's design, the design of Providence is obvious. Had she at that time declared her request, Haman would not have had an opportunity of performing his part in the drama. This man of glory and of guilt must be allowed another scene on the stage of time, to exhibit his character in all its bearings, and to show the disappointment and misery of the enemies of God. His vanity is not yet at the highest pitch; he must be brought to the pinnacle of vain-glory. When he arrives on the summit of earthly magnificence next to majesty itself, he must grasp at the shadow of royal splendor. But in the grasp he must begin to totter to his fall. The crown he had devised to wear for a day, he must fix on the head of his greatest enemy. He must be made to minister to the man of God, whom he thought to destroy. Then shall he fall, never more to rise at all: he must prepare a gallows for Mordecai, but he must himself be hanged thereon.

Thus it shall be with the proud and prosperous wicked. Though they may not, like Haman, meet a retribution in this world, their honor will be succeeded with everlasting shame and misery. From the pinnacle of earthly glory they shall be hurled into the depths of hell. This prosperity is not to be envied by the poorest Christian. "Fret not thyself because of evil-doers, neither be thou envious against the workers of iniquity, for they shall soon be cut down like the grass, and wither as the green grass." Psal. xxxvii. 1, 2.

How vain is earthly glory! How irrational are the struggles of statesmen and courtiers for the giddy height of power! This moment their counsels may direct the destinies of nations; the next they may be hurled into the abyss of eternal misery. This day they may sit at the helm of empire; to-morrow they may appear before the dread tribunal of God. Now they are at the head of nobles and princes, and attract the notice of admiring millions; in an instant their souls may be required of them, and they may be covered with shame and everlasting contempt. Look at Haman. Was ever statesman or courtier more highly honored and advanced? He is drunk with worldly glory, but his soul is still thirsty. To what purpose is he mounting yon dangerous height? It is that he may tumble into the abyss below. While his happiness appears to the beholder to be complete, his own bad passions make him miserable. Infamy and ruin hover over him while he ascends, and he falls a monument of the vanity of earthly glory.

What a sudden and dreadful reverse ! what a lesson to all the children of pride ! what an example to statesmen and courtiers !

We may here see also, that even in this world the most successful ambition is always disappointed in the hope of happiness from the enjoyment of its object. The scholar, the man of science, the senator, the warrior, having gained the utmost eminence to which their throbbing hearts aspired, are not only unsatisfied with glory, but are perhaps more miserable than the lowest of the class to which they belong. There is still something that makes disappointment prey on their souls. In all his glory Haman confessed himself miserable, on account of the disrespect of an insolent Jew. " And Haman told them of the glory of his riches, and the multitude of his children, and all the things wherein the king had promoted him, and how he had advanced him above the princes and servants of the king. Haman said, moreover, Yea, Esther the queen did let no man come in with the king unto the banquet that she had prepared, but myself ; and to-morrow am I invited with her also with the king. Yet all this availeth me nothing, so long as I see Mordecai, the Jew, sitting in the king's gate."

All men are in the pursuit of happiness, and all, by nature, seek it in the things of this world ; but in them it never can be found. Even the acquisition of the things in which they suppose happiness to consist will disappoint them in the enjoyment. Man, at enmity with God, cannot be happy. The curse denounced against sin has entwined itself with all human enjoyments. It is seen not only in the thorns and briars, but also in the most voluptuous enjoyments of that royal luxury that crops the sweetest buds of a terrestrial paradise. It lodges not only in the cottages of the poor, but seats itself on the thrones of princes. Solomon has found that all earthly enjoyments are but vanity of vanities. Sinner, return to God through Jesus Christ. There is no real happiness either in this world or the next, but in the favor of Him from whom you fly. Ye children of pride, see in Haman the disappointment of your hopes! How unsatisfactory are your present enjoyments! how soon must you exchange your earthly splendor for the abodes of endless and unmixed misery! The basest of your menials, if he knows the Saviour of sinners, is a happier man than you. Seek happiness, then, where it is to be found—in the knowledge of God. "Behold the Lamb of God, that taketh away the sin of the world!" Until you are delivered from your sins, the curse of God rests on you, and Divine wrath must pursue you both in this world and the next. Lay them on the head of the Lamb of God, and be free from guilt, pollution, and misery. "The blood of Jesus Christ cleanses from all sin." Mordecai, with the threatening of death against himself and his whole nation before his eyes, was evidently a happier man, from confidence in the Divine protection, than Haman in the midst of the unbounded profusion of royal power. The children of God are, indeed, frequently sorrowful, but, paradoxical as the assertion may appear, if they enjoy their privileges *they are always rejoicing.* "Though now, for a season, if need be, they are in heaviness, through manifold trials, yet even now they rejoice with a joy unspeakable and full of glory." They endure as seeing him who is invisible. Moses chose rather to suffer affliction with the people of God, than to enjoy the pleasures of sin for a season, esteeming the reproach of Christ greater riches than the honor of Egypt : for he had respect to the recompense of reward. Even in the midst of all the afflictions to which he may be called for Christ's sake, the Christian has peace and joy. He is given strength for his day—faith in proportion to his trials. "Beloved," says the apostle Peter, "think it not strange concerning the fiery trial which is to try you, as though some strange thing happened unto you ; but rejoice, inasmuch as ye are partakers of Christ's sufferings, that, when his glory shall be revealed, ye may be glad also with exceeding joy. If ye be reproached for the name of Christ, happy are ye; for the Spirit of glory and of God resteth upon you."

In this history of providential interposition, there is nothing more wonderful than the process that led to the exaltation of Mordecai. We already noticed the circumstance that put him in the way of royal notice. He had discovered a conspiracy against the life of the king. But why was he not rewarded immediately on the discovery? why was he so long neglected or forgotten by the king? The smallest services to majesty usually meet an immediate and a magnificent retribution. Why was the greatest service that could be rendered to man overlooked till it was entirely forgotten? Is the saving of the life of a sovereign of so little estimation? Are absolute monarchs wont to disregard the saviours of their lives? Shall such profusion of royal bounty be showered on the head of Haman, while Mordecai remains unrewarded? What can account for this strange conduct? One thing can account for it, and nothing but this can be alleged as a sufficient cause. The thing was overruled by Providence, for the fulfilment of the Divine purposes. God not only works his will through the actions of all men, but their very abstaining from action is employed by him for the same purpose. Had Mordecai been suitably rewarded at the time of his service, there would have been no opportunity for the wickedness of Haman, and the danger of Mordecai, to be so wonderfully manifested. Had Mordecai been already advanced, Haman would not have sought his ruin. But by the delay, Haman is insulted; Mordecai is brought to the brink of ruin, from the wrath of the haughty favorite. Who is so blind as not to see the hand of God in this?

But if the reward of Mordecai at the time of his service would have been unsuitable to God's design in manifesting the wickedness of Haman, and his own power in the defence of his people, to have delayed it for a single day longer would have been ruin to the unbending Jew. His immediate death is planned by his enemies, and the next day would have seen him hanged on a gallows fifty cubits high. Haman was to ask the life of his enemy from the king, and to ask it was to obtain it. "Then said Zeresh his wife and all his friends unto him, Let a gallows be made of fifty cubits high, and to-morrow speak thou unto the king, that Mordecai may be hanged thereon; then go thou in merrily with the king unto the banquet. And the thing pleased Haman; and he caused the gallows to be made." Mordecai, what miracle shall deliver thee now? Shall God speak from heaven, or destroy thine enemies with his thunder? shall the earth open, and swallow them up that seek thy life? shall the angels of the Lord carry thee away, and hide thee from thy pursuers? No! thy God will save thee by his providence, in a way suitable to the rest of his conduct manifested in this book. Death hovers over thy head, but he shall not strike thee; the wings of Providence shall overshadow thee, and turn aside the dart; thou shalt have both life and glory without a miracle. But if thou wast neglected at the time of so eminent service, what probability is there that thou shalt now be thought of? What friend of thine shall thy God send to the king, to remind him that he owes thee his life? who shall put him in mind of his obligation at this critical moment? Another day, and thou art a dead man! But thy God is not asleep, nor unmindful of thee in the time of danger. What is it that he cannot make the minister of his mercy to his servants? A remarkable interposition of his Providence shall bring thee into notice this very night. Though thou hast no friend to speak for thee, thy God shall cause the thoughts of the king to roam in the paths where he shall find thy claims displayed. Even in the unseasonable hour of night, the memorial of thy good deed shall come before him. The king lies down, but he cannot sleep; nor shall he sleep till he hears of Mordecai. "On that night could not the king sleep; and he commanded to bring the book of records of the chronicles; and they were read before the king. And it was found written, that Mordecai had told of Bigthana and Teresh, two of the king's chamberlains, the keepers of the door, who sought to lay hands on the king Ahasuerus. And the king said, What honor and dignity hath been done to Mordecai for this? Then said the king's servants that ministered unto him, There is nothing done for him." Astonishing! *"On that night!"* O, gentle sleep, why didst thou forsake the king's couch on that critical night? There is indeed nothing strange to find thee leaving the bed of state, and fluttering with thy downy wings over the sooty cribs in the cottages of hardy industry. But why did thy caprice choose to leave the couch of Majesty in the critical moment? Didst thou not act as the minister of Heaven? Sleep, it was God drove thee on that night from the bed of Ahasuerus.

Let us here learn to trace the hand of God in the most trivial events. There is nothing fortuitous—nothing without God. Who would think of ascribing to God so seemingly unimportant a matter? Yet this link is essential in the chain of the wonderful providences by which the Ruler of the world executed his plan on this memorable occasion. Take this away, and the whole chain is useless. Another night would have seen Mordecai on the gallows, or in the grave. This fact teaches us, that there is nothing really casual as to God, even in a restless night of a human creature. How wonderful is the providence of Jehovah! how minute, how amazingly diversified, are its operations! The eye of the Lord beholdeth, and his wisdom directeth, all the events with respect to all the creatures in the universe. This would be too much trouble, and too mean an employment, for the God of the philosophers. But the God of the Scripture not only created all things at first, and established laws by which he governs them, but he continually worketh in his Providence. It is in him we live, and move, and have our being. It is by his immediate power that creation is sustained in existence, that every function of animal life is performed, and that every motion in the universe is effected. The blindness and enmity of the mind of man wish to put him at a distance, and to consider him no farther the governor of the world, than as the Author of the general laws of nature, according to which all events take place. But the Bible brings God before us in all things that occur. Of the innumerable insects that inhabit a blade of grass, there is not one whose vital functions are not carried on by the power of God. To him the lion roars for his prey, and he feedeth the ravens. He ever works without weariness. Epicurus removed his gods to a distance from the earth, that they might feast without disturbance from the tumults of men. He gave them a luxurious ease, far above the clouds, and did not interrupt their festivities with the government of the world. And infidel philosophy, in modern times, does nearly the same, under the name of Christianity, by ascribing to God only what it calls a general providence. This is not the God of the Bible. The Christian may recognize his God as shining in the sun, breathing in the air, and living in all life. His immediate power is as necessary to sustain all things in existence, and to effect every change in their state, as it was to create them at first. His Providence is as necessary for the care of a microscopic insect, as for regulating the motions of a solar system.

Why then, O monarch of the east, did thy sleep forsake thee on that memorable night? When it fled, why didst thou not pursue it, and with thy instruments of music force it back to thy royal chamber? Call thy minstrels, and woo it with softest sounds of sweetest melody; lure it to thy couch with the voice of song. Come forth, ye harmonious choirs; raise your most enchanting airs, and lull your monarch in repose. Tell me, ye wise men of the world, why nothing could amuse the king at this time but the chronicles of his kingdom? Is this the usual requiem of an eastern monarch? Is a dry register of facts a likely expedient to hush the restless thoughts, and induce the gentler influences of sleep? Tell me, Ahasuerus, why that thought passed across thy mind at this time ? Where shall I find its origin ? Out of a million of millions of thoughts, this appears the least likely to strike thee at such a time. Thou art silent, O monarch ! on this thou knowest no more than the bed on which thou dost lie. It came, but whence it came thou knowest as little as thou dost of the birth-place of the wind. And why didst thou yield to it when it came ? What made thy free will prefer to indulge this thought ? Was not the thought thine own ? Was not compliance with its suggestions thine own action ? Of this it is impossible for thee to doubt. How then can this thy thought be ascribed to God ? In what mysterious sense can this action be the appointment of God ? All is light, yet all is mystery. The facts are as certain and as obvious as the mind of man can wish ; yet to adjust their boundaries is as impossible as to draw a line between the colors of the rainbow. The most obvious truths may be incomprehensible to man. This thought, and the action which was its result, are the king's ; yet they are the instruments through which the Almighty Ruler of the world performs his purpose. Take these away, and you destroy the whole chain of Providence exhibited in the Book of Esther. But even when the book of the chronicles comes, are there not a thousand chances that the suitable part may not turn up ? What directed the reader to the proper place? In so extensive a subject as the annals of the Persian empire, what probability is there that the reader will happen on the few lines that record the service of Mordecai? He might have read till morning without touching this subject. What finger guided him to this story? Is it not more likely that the curiosity of the king would prompt him to hear some of the transactions of former reigns? This was the hour for the deliverance and exaltation of Mordecai, and it was the finger of God that pointed to the record of his service. Every step we advance in this wonderful history, we see a display of an overruling Providence. The Book of Esther is a book of wonders without a miracle.

The king hears the record of the conspiracy, and inquires about the reward of his services. He takes it for granted that he must have received a suitable recompense in honor and dignity; but finds that he is yet unrewarded. Strange! very strange! inexplicably strange! But God's design is clear. The Divine plan required that Mordecai's exaltation should be delayed till now. But it shall be delayed no longer. God's providence requires that this very moment Mordecai shall be raised; for Haman is at the door to demand his life. Keep Mordecai's services another hour unknown to the king and the servant of God is given into the hand of his enemy. How injudiciously are royal favors often conferred! The man who deserved of the king more than any subject in his empire is neglected, while that worthless minion, Haman, rose almost to royal honors!

In the preservation of the life of the king, we may learn the duty of the servants of God to their civil rulers. Mordecai was in the land of the captivity of his people, yet, instead of forwarding a scheme for the murder of the sovereign, he saved him by a discovery of his danger. Christians ought to stand at the utmost distance from every scheme that tends to overturn or embarrass civil government. Their duty and their safety in every country demand submission to the ruling powers.

There is something worthy of admiration in the conduct of Mordecai during the time of his being neglected after his important service. We find no unbecoming intrusion on the notice of majesty, no cringing at the knees of Haman and the minions of a court, to forward his claims to preferment. Yet, when honors came, they are received without any affectation of stoical indifference; he appears in the splendor of royalty, and becomes greater and greater in the Persian empire. Unlike an Aristides or a Diogenes, he spurns not the favor of the king, nor returns a rude reply to the kindness of majesty. A Christian ought never to show himself lower than an heir of heaven; but to

affect a disregard to all worldly comfort, is the affectation of philosophic pride.

While in Mordecai we find something to blame,
we may find in him much more to praise. God accepted him as his servant, though he was ignorant
of some points of duty. In him we find the strongest faith in the Divine protection, and the most
heroic devotedness to the cause of God and his
people. Should not this be a lesson to us all?
and while we faithfully bear our testimony against
errors of every kind, let us be willing to acknowledge the servants of God in all the various deno-
minations where they are to be found. We have
all our own errors ; and though this ought not to
induce us to look on error as innocent, it ought
to keep us from despising the weakest of the people of God. Is it not a most surprising thing,
that any Christian can find a difficulty in recog-
nising those whom God has recognised and sealed
with his Holy Spirit ?

At the critical moment of the king's inquiries
about Mordecai, Haman had come into the outward court, to solicit for his immediate execution.
Mark the Lord of providence in every step. Had
not the king been kept from sleep—had not the
book of records been called for his amusement—
had not the account of the conspiracy turned up
to the reader—Mordecai would now have been
given into the hand of his enemy.

Mark the providence of God, also, in having Haman at hand, that by his mouth the honors of Mordecai might be awarded, and that by his instrumentality they might be conferred. Why did the king think of referring the reward of Mordecai to another ? Why did he not himself determine the dignities to be conferred on his preserver ? Or, if he refers to another, why does he not immediately leave the matter to those now about him ? why does he ask, Who is in the court ? why was Haman there at this moment ? why was he the only one that waited so early on the king ? why did Ahasuerus put the question in such a manner as to conceal the object of the royal favor ? why does the king, instead of plainly naming Mordecai, use the periphrasis, "The man whom the king delights to honor ?" why did this form of the question allow Haman to suppose that he was himself the happy man for whom the honors were intended ? At this time the king knew nothing of the designs of Haman, and had no design to insnare him. Every circumstance here is wonderfully providential. From this we see that God can make the greatest enemies of his people the means of advancing their interests. Whom then ought the Christian to fear, but God ?

Behold the retributive justice of God in the death of Haman ! One of the chamberlains, who probably had seen it when he went to call him to the feast, mentioned the gallows that Haman had prepared in his house to hang Mordecai. "The king said, Hang him thereon."

But we are not yet done with the wonders of Providence in this affair. Even with all the good intentions of the king, how can the Jews be preserved? The first decree could not be revoked; how then could a handful of Jews, scattered over all the provinces of the empire, stand up against their enemies in all nations? Although they had the royal license to defend themselves and destroy their adversaries, how could one small nation, so widely dispersed, escape destruction, when impunity invited the assault, and instigated malice? Their escape is secured by the awe inspired into the nations by the elevation of Mordecai. The God who so often filled the hearts of the most numerous armies with the dread of his people, few in number, now filled the nations of the Persian empire with the fear of them. "The Jews gathered themselves together in their cities throughout all the provinces of the king Ahasuerus, to lay hand on such as sought their hurt; and no man could withstand them: *for the fear of them fell upon all people.* And all the rulers of the provinces, and the lieutenants, and the deputies, and officers of the king, helped the Jews; because the *fear of Mordecai fell upon* them. For Mordecai was great in the king's house, and his fame went out throughout all the provinces: for this man

Mordecai waxed greater and greater. Thus the Jews smote all their enemies with the stroke of the sword, and slaughter, and destruction, and did what they would unto those that hated them." Fear not the malice of your enemies, ye children of the most High. Your God can deliver you out of their hands. Lift up your heads, Christians, for your redemption draweth nigh. Ye shall yet " have light, and gladness, and joy, and honor."

But in the book of Esther we are not only to attend to the wonderful interpositions of Providence manifested in the facts of the history. From the manner of revelation, in innumerable other instances, we are warranted to consider this history as prophetical and typical. In the deliverance of the Jews on this occasion, we may see God's method of preserving his church in the time of the fourth beast ; and the final triumph of the saints of the Most High. When the Reformation opened the gates of Babylon, many Christians have remained there, or in some of its provinces. They are thus exposed to loss and danger ; but they shall not be destroyed. Their enemies plot their ruin, but the mischief will ultimately fall on their own heads. In Haman we see a striking type of the man of sin ; he seeks to destroy the whole Israel of God ; but his effort will only bring on his own ruin. All must honor this wicked Haman. He indeed seeks divine honors, and there is a

temptation here to stretch the type to the antitype, and find Haman guilty of claiming divine
worship. But this is not in evidence, and there is
no necessity that there should in all things be a
perfect correspondence between the type and the
antitype. This likeness is seen sufficiently in the
honors that his imagination suggested for the man
whom the king delights to honor, when he supposed that he was himself the person. It is astonishing that he presumed to award royal honors
to any subject of the empire. Was not this likely
to awaken the jealousy of a despot ? Yet such was
the arrogance of this man of sin, that Haman answered the king, " For the man whom the king
delighteth to honor, let the royal apparel be
brought which the king useth to wear, and the
horse that the king rideth upon, and the crown
royal which is set upon his head ; and let this
apparel and horse be delivered to the hand of
one of the king's most noble princes, that they
may array the man withal whom the king delighteth to honor, and bring him on horseback through
the streets of the city, and proclaim before him,
Thus shall it be done to the man whom the king
delighteth to honor." Can there be a more correct figure of the blasphemous pretensions of the
man of sin, who has usurped the honors of God ?
These honors, however, were without scruple
awarded to Mordecai by the king. " Then said
9

the king to Haman, Make haste, and take the apparel and the horse, as thou hast said, and do even so to Mordecai the Jew that sitteth at the king's gate ; let nothing fail of all that thou hast spoken." And if Mordecai is a type of the Son of God, how justly were these honors awarded ! The Father delights to have him honored even as himself.

In the unchangeable laws of the Medes and Persians, we may see one of the features of the kingdom of the man of sin, whose infallible decree cannot be altered. Yet notwithstanding the irreversible decree that determines the destruction of all heretics, the providence of God has made other provisions for their safety. The decree never dies, but it may slumber. Other laws may be made by the state to counteract it.

In the fall of Haman, let us anticipate the overthrow of all the opposers of the kingdom of Christ. All the schemes devised for overturning Christianity, will not only prove abortive, but will finally bring down vengeance on the heads of their authors.

We may here see how God can bring down the man of sin by the ordinary course of providence, without employing a single miracle. He can make his very enemies the instruments of effecting his designs. By them he usually cuts off those whom he devotes to temporal destruction ; and by them also he can deliver his own people. When Haman was cut off "many of the people of the land became Jews ; for the fear of the Jews fell upon them." How well does this correspond with the increase of the true kingdom of Christ by genuine converts, when destruction shall have fallen on mystical Babylon ! No king but the Messiah can reign in the midst of his enemies, and perform his will by those who design to oppose it.

This history, that has been thought by some unworthy of a place among the inspired writings, discovers, when attentively considered, the most surprising series of events brought about without a miracle, that ever was exhibited to the consideration of the human mind. Among the most admired works of genius, of all ages and countries, we will not find that the invention of man has been able to form a story, and connect a series of surprising events, like this true history. Homer, and Virgil, and Milton, and all the writers of epic poetry, have been obliged to use supernatural agency upon all critical occasions. To interest their readers, they must depart from the ordinary course of nature, and employ means that never really existed. Gods, and demons, and muses, are so necessary to the poet, that they still have their impression on the phraseology of poetry. If you prevent him from invoking the inspirations of his muse, from conversing familiarly with Apollo and the nine, from mounting to the top of Parnassus, and from drinking of the Pierian spring, you deprive him of the chief resources of his art. To have recourse to his machinery, is universally granted to be his privilege, as often as there is a " *dignus vindice nodus.*" But the book of Esther presents us with the most interesting and surprising narrative; it gives us a series of wonders in producing danger and deliverance, yet the means employed are so much in the ordinary course of nature, that a careless reader scarcely perceives the hand of the Lord. Every event appears the natural and obvious result of the situation in which it is produced, but to create and combine these situations is as truly a work of Divine wisdom and power, as to create the world, or to fix the laws of nature. It is thus God rules the world; he is continually working, yet blind men perceive him not. Nature or chance is worshipped instead of Him whose power is necessary to the life, motion, and existence of every being.

This book, then, whose inspiration has lately been called into question, by ignorance, speaking from the chair of learning, commends its claims to me, in the most convincing manner, by its own internal evidence. No human pen could have produced it. The characteristic feature which I have pointed out proves it to be a child of God. Had man been its author, it would have been crowded with miracles. I challenge the world to produce anything resembling it in this point, from the writings of uninspired men.

There is another feature in this history that proves it to be of heavenly birth. *There is no instance in which it gratifies mere curiosity.* While it informs us of facts, it informs us no farther than they contribute to the design of the Holy Spirit, and are important for instruction. In this feature it shows its resemblance to the teaching of our Lord, and to the writings of the apostles. So far from gratifying idle curiosity, our Lord declined compliance with respect to some points in which human wisdom would think it important to be informed. His communications manifest a striking reserve ; and even when pressed, he could not be induced to reply to any curious questions. In the writings of the evangelists and the apostles, how often do we wish that they had been a little more communicative ? And, assuredly, had they spoken from their own wisdom, they would have made a larger Bible.

Now, with this in his view, let any one read the Book of Esther. In how many points do we wish more information ! Facts are stated simply where we would wish to see them standing in connection with their origin. To see this argument illustrated in a striking light, let any one cast his eye over Gill's Commentary on this book, that he may see, from the Talmuds and Rabbinical writings, the

additional information that human wisdom seeks
in vain in the book of God. There is not one
point interesting to curiosity but what is supplied
by their traditions or their conjectures. Had the
book of Esther been written by the wisdom of men,
it would have manifested its origin by gratifying
curiosity in a similar way. Let us illustrate this
remark by a reference to a few particulars in this
history. The first I shall mention is the account
of Mordecai's conduct in reference to the marriage
of Esther. How human wisdom endeavors to justify or excuse him in this business, may be seen by
looking into almost any of the commentaries. But
this history relates the fact, without any observation either in justification or condemnation of him.
We are left to acquit or blame him, according to
the light of the Scriptures.

With respect to the conspiracy against the life
of the king, who is it that would not wish a little
more information ? What uninspired writer would
not have given us at least a sketch of the cause of
the discontent of the conspirators, and of the means
by which it was discovered to Mordecai ? What
a human author would have done on this subject,
we may see from what human wisdom has actually
supplied. Dr. Gill tells us that the Jewish writers
say that the two conspirators were Tarsians, and
spake in the Tarsian language, supposing that
Mordecai did not understand it, but that he being

skilled in languages, understood what they were saying. According to Josephus, it was discovered to Mordecai by Barnabazus, a servant of one of the chamberlains. The latter Targum says, that it was revealed unto him by the Holy Ghost, but the Spirit of God, speaking by the writer of the book of Esther, deigns not to inform us how Mordecai came to know the matter. He only declares that the thing was known to Mordecai.

The account of the rise of Haman affords us another specimen of this Divine wisdom. In giving an account of the rise of a favorite, every historian informs us of the ground of his acceptance with his sovereign; but not one word on this head here. We are merely told, "After these things did king Ahasuerus promote Haman, the son of Hammedatha the Agagite, and advanced him, and set his seat above all the princes that were with him."

Whether the conduct of Mordecai, in refusing to reverence Haman, was blameable or justifiable, and the grounds on which he acted, are things that no human author would have overlooked. But whether he was right or wrong, or what was the principle on which he refused obedience, in this instance, to the royal mandate, this book says nothing. It merely states the fact—"But Mordecai bowed not, nor did him reverence." In order to justify him, the Targum and Aben Ezra say, that

Haman had a statue erected for himself, and had images painted on his clothes. Dr. Gill, who does not rely on this, strains hard to make out a good case for his client from the passage itself, and from conjecture. He thinks Haman claimed divine honors, because they were given to the Persian kings, and *might have been given to their favorites*. But there "*might have been*," is a very bad foundation for an argument, though it is sufficient to remove a difficulty in a case that is attested by other credible testimony. This disposition to acquit the hero in an interesting narrative, in every part of his conduct, whatever may be its success in this instance, proves clearly that if the writer had not been guided by Divine wisdom, he would have given us a few remarks in justification of Mordecai.

The last instance to which I shall allude is the account of the affair that brought Mordecai into royal notice. We are not told what diverted the monarch from sleeping, nor what induced him to call for the book of the chronicles of his kingdom, nor what led to the reading of one passage more than another. Human wisdom would have gratified us on all these points, but the Spirit of God says no more than, "On that night could not the king sleep, and he commanded to bring the book of records of the chronicles ; and they were read before the king. And it was found written, that

Mordecai had told of Bigthana and Teresh, two of the king's chamberlains, the keepers of the door, who sought to lay hands on the king Ahasuerus."

But though I perceive internal evidence in this book, confirming its authenticity and inspiration, I do not submit to the dogma on which some modern critics seem to act, that the authority of the canon is not sufficient to entitle a book to be admitted to the rank of inspiration, and that it is necessary for each book to be separately tried on the independent evidence from its own contents. Modern critics, in acting on this principle, resemble the lawyers, who excite litigation in order to obtain clients. They have an opportunity of displaying the treasures of their learning, and the reach of their ingenuity, in defending the claims of the Scripture without the authority of the canon. In judging of this internal evidence, they lay down first principles that are not entitled to that rank, and overlook first principles that demand universal respect. A first principle of the latter description is, that testimony is a sound source of evidence, and that the books of Scripture are to be received on the authority of the canon. In ascertaining whether the book of Esther, among other books, is inspired, we have to inquire, Was it in the collection called Scripture in the days of our Lord? If it was, its inspiration is past dispute. Jesus

Christ recognised the Jewish Scripture as the word
of God.   The apostle Paul represents it as one of
the chief privileges of the Jews, that they are the
depositaries to whom were intrusted the oracles of
God, and neither the apostles nor their Master
charge them with unfaithfulness in their trust.
Now, the book of Esther, as Dr. Gill observes,
has been generally received as canonical both by
Jews and Christians.   "It stands," he says, "in
Origen's catalogue of the books of the Old Testament ; nor is it any material objection, that it appears not in the catalogue of Melito, since in that
list is comprehended under Ezra, not Nehemiah
only, but Esther also, which Jerome mentions
along with it."

As in rejecting the inspiration of this book,
some modern theologians disclaim a first principle
entitled to the most confident reception, so they
admit some first principles that are mere figments
of the imagination.   Why is the book of Esther
denied as a book of Scripture ?   Because it has
not the name of God in its whole compass.   Here
it is taken as a first principle, that no book can be
inspired, that does not contain the name of God.
But where have they got this axiom ?   It is not
self-evident, nor asserted by any portion of Scripture, and is therefore entitled to no respect.   Whether a book may be inspired, though the name of
God is not mentioned in it, depends not on any

self-evident first principles, but on matter of fact. And matter of fact determines in this instance, that a book may be inspired, although it does not express the name of God.

This objection, though it affects an appearance of wisdom, manifests a very inadequate conception of the nature of the word of God. It considers every book in the collection as an independent whole, standing unconnected with the other books. But the Bible is like the human body; all the books together form one whole, and there is no reason that one book should serve the place of another more than that the hand or the foot should perform the duty of the eye or of the ear. It is enough if the whole will of God is learned from the book as a whole. If it is contended, that every book of Scripture must contain the name of God, a like demand may be made with respect to every chapter, or any small division. The prophecy of Obadiah contains but one chapter; must it prove its divine origin by containing a whole body of divinity? Let the Christian form his views of the characteristics of Scripture from itself, and not from the arbitrary conceits of his own mind.

But if God is not expressly named in this book, he is most evidently referred to by periphrasis, and the strongest confidence in him is manifested by Mordecai. The faith of that illustrious ser- vant of God is among the most distinguished examples of faith that the Scriptures afford. "Then Mordecai commanded to answer Esther, Think not with thyself that thou shalt escape in the king's house more than all the Jews. For if thou altogether holdest thy peace at this time, then shall there enlargement and deliverance arise to the Jews from another place ; but thou and thy father's house shall be destroyed ; and who knoweth whether thou art come to the kingdom for such a time as this ?" Is not this a reference to God, and confidence in him as the God of Abraham, Isaac, and Jacob? *"From another place."* Can there be any doubt as to the place from which he expected deliverance? Is not this an obvious reference to God? Does not this reasoning to persuade Esther, express the fullest confidence that the Jews would be eventually delivered, though the danger was so great and so inevitable, that no human eye could discern the means of preservation, should not Esther undertake the intercession? As Abraham counted him faithful who had promised, and believed that though Isaac should die on the altar, he should by him be the father of the Messiah, so Mordecai believed that when every apparent means of safety failed, God would on this occasion be the deliverer of Israel. Is it not from the retributive justice of God that he threatens destruction to Esther and her father's house, should she decline the intercession through unbelief? The very Providence that is illustrated in this book is exhibited in the faith of Mordecai. He looked for deliverance through means, and if all apparent means should fail, still he believed that Providence would raise up means.

How clearly and strongly is this view of Providence expressed in the question to Esther—" And who knoweth whether thou are come to the kingdom for such a time as this ?" He justly concluded, from the occurrence of such a danger, that the reason why Providence had raised her to the rank of queen, was to be the deliverer of her people. Mordecai's view of Providence is that which is inculcated in all the wonderful events of this singular narrative. It is the view of Providence which I wish to press on all my brethren in Christ. If times of trouble are before us, what better preparation for it, than the study of the book of Esther? If the great Antichrist, under any form, is yet to meditate the destruction of the whole Israel of God —if there is any just apprehension from the prophecies of Scripture, that great calamities are still before the Church of Christ, ought not every Christian to be nourishing his faith with this wonderful display of Providence, as the deliverer of those who put their trust in him? Surely there can be no harm in watchfulness and apprehension, when the enemies of the cross are so rapidly increasing, and when indecision and lukewarmness so fearfully characterise the great body of the people of God. All the other symptoms of danger are not so dreadfully alarming as that spurious liberality that begins to look with complaisance on the enemies of Christ ; an affectation of that love of man that manifests disaffection to some parts of the character of God.

Esther also manifests confidence in God, and a resolution to die for his people, if that should be the result of her application in their favor. She approaches the king, not confiding in her charms, nor hoping to escape destruction from the love or pity of a husband, but in the way of Divine appointment, in the time of danger, by much fasting and prayer. This is an exhibition of a true servant of God. The power of Jehovah, and the love of his people, are strongly manifested in the conduct of these two illustrious Israelites. If God is not mentioned by name, he is seen in all their conduct.

In the exhibition of the conduct of Esther on this occasion, we have a strong internal evidence of inspiration. Had human wisdom formed a heroine, it would have been likely to represent her from the first moment as intrepid and ready to encounter the greatest dangers with more than masculine bravery. But Esther is not presented to us in this light by this history. She comes before us in the usual character of her sex, and of the ordinary attainment in the Divine life. She at first declines the hazardous undertaking for fear of losing her life. Her timidity is overcome by such arguments as ought to influence a believer in the God of Abraham ; and she finally displays resignation and confidence, though not altogether unmixed with fear. Such is the usual conduct, such is the usual confidence, of the people of God.

This book, then, that exhibits the providence of God, is composed in a manner suited to its subject. God is everywhere seen in it, though he is not named. Just so God is every moment manifesting himself in the works of his providence, though he works unseen to all but the eye of faith. He supports and moves the heavenly bodies, while his name is not expressly written on the sun, moon, or stars, and though no herald voice proclaims him in the execution of his office. The Christian also has many ways of acknowledging God, without expressly naming him. The sun, from the time he rises till he sets in silence, preaches the God that made and upholds him : the book of Esther, from the beginning to the end, proclaims the providence of God, though it does not expressly name him.

But not only is the objection invalid, but every one of the same class is utterly unworthy of respect. A book may disprove its divine origin by what it contains, but in no case by what it does not contain. What is to be expressed in any divine communication, is not for man presumptuously to determine by his own wisdom, but lies entirely with a sovereign God. We may as well say that God would not make the sun or moon, without writing his name on it, as that he could not inspire a book that did not contain his name. Vain man will be wise, though he is born as the wild ass's colt. Even in the things of God he must, by his own maxims of wisdom, pronounce on the authenticity of the inspiration of the All-wise!

Another objection alleged to the inspiration of this book is, that it is not quoted in the New Testament. Now, who made this a first principle? What authority establishes the dogma, that a book of the Old Testament cannot be inspired unless it is quoted in the New? Is it a self-evident truth? By no means. Does the New Testament teach this doctrine? No such thing. Where then has it obtained its authority? In the presumption of man. To be quoted in the New Testament is indeed proof of the inspiration of a book of the Old, and may therefore be used very properly as a confirmation; but not to be quoted, is no proof of a want of inspiration. The inspiration of the Old Testament is independent even of the existence of the New. Many books of the Old Testament, indeed, are quoted in the New; but this does not discredit such as are not quoted. To make quotations by the New Testament essential to the recognition of the inspiration of the books of the Old Testament, is as unreasonable as to demand the quotation of every chapter and of every verse. It is perfectly sufficient that there is nothing in the book of Esther that contradicts the New Testament. As far as they teach on the same things, they perfectly agree. To the inspiration of the book of Esther there is not one objection that deserves a minute's consideration; and it bears in every page the impression of the finger of God.

The opinion that the settling of the canon is a matter of criticism, and lies fairly open to discussion, is a wicked and pernicious error. It is the suggestion of Satan to upset the authority of the whole Scriptures. It is impossible to deny the inspiration of one book of Scripture on principles that will not overturn any other. If the book of Esther is to be rejected because it does not express the name of God, then any person is equally at liberty to reject any other book, because it wants something that his wisdom thinks an inspired book ought to contain. That an inspired book must express the name of God, is a principle as arbitrary, and as far from self-evidence, as any other conceit that the human mind may entertain. If, then, its authority is acknowledged, equal indulgence must be granted to every other demand of human wisdom. If the book of Esther is to be rejected, because it is not quoted in the New Testament, then there is not a book in the New Testament that must not be rejected, because there is no inspired authority quoting them; and, by consequence, every book of the Old must also be rejected, because the recognition of it in the New will in that case be of no authority. If the books of the New Testament can on sufficient grounds be received as inspired, although the canon is not settled by the quotations of inspired authority, then may the books of the Old Testament likewise. To reject one book, then, must admit principles that will overturn the inspiration of all. The settling of the canon is not a matter of criticism, but of testimony; and however mortifying it may be to the pride of the learned, they must receive it on the same grounds with the illiterate. The man of literature may indeed go a step or two beyond the unlearned. He may examine the books in which the testimony is contained, and with his own eyes he may read the catalogues of Origen and Melito, with any other accessible evidence. But even here he must rest on testimony. He has not seen the original manuscripts; and though he possessed the very autographs of the apostles, he must depend on testimony that they are really such. The canon of Scripture, then, the critic is not to ascertain by the rules of his art, but he must take it on the authority of testimony, and commence with it as a first principle.

It may appear surprising to some that the Christian public has not been more shocked with the late attempts to shake the authority of the canon, and to displace so great a portion of the word of God from its high rank. But the reason is obvious, from the quarter from which these attempts have proceeded. Had the reasons that some have alleged for rejecting the book of Esther, the two books of Chronicles, and the Song of Solomon, been urged by professed infidels, or noted heretics, they would have been rejected with horror. But when they have been ushered into the world from the pens of reputedly orthodox divines, and, for anything I know to the contrary, men of real godliness, the sinfulness of the attempt, and the danger of the principle on which the opinion is founded, have been concealed from general notice. The very grounds of rejection have a show not only of wisdom, but of concern for the honor of God and his word. Satan appears as an angel of light when he teaches that the book of Esther should be rejected, because it does not express the name of God, and because it is not quoted by the New Testament. What zeal does this manifest for the honor of God! what a high regard for the authority of the New Testament! Baxter says that the Jews were in the habit of casting the book of Esther to the ground before reading it, to express their sense of its deficiency in wanting the name of God; and the thought is quite in the style of Jewish piety, and of the human wisdom of Christians. It is just such a thought as Satan will be likely to suggest to mistaken piety. But Satan conceals from them that by their zeal for the honor of God they rob themselves of all the advantages of that book. They do not see that they give up to him all the treasures of the knowledge of Providence that are contained in that precious record. He gives them a bauble, as the Europeans have done to barbarians, and he takes from them the most valuable diamonds. Satan suggests that the book of Esther cannot be a book of Scripture, because it is not quoted in the New Testament. Who would think that the infernal spirit of darkness has such a respect for the writing of the apostles? Arch deceiver! thy respect is affected for the purpose of overturning the writings for which thou dost profess this respect. Though the dupes who are deceived by thee perceive it not, thy keen eye discerns that this principle will overturn the Bible. When thou deceivest the profane and the ungodly, thou wilt employ a Carlisle or a Taylor; but when the children of God are to be robbed of a part of his word, thou dost prefer an evangelical divine as the deceiver.

It is on this very principle that the grand deceiver has overturned the foundation of all knowledge, through the affected wisdom of the philosopher. Perceiving that false first principles lead to every error, Des Cartes resolved to take nothing for granted but the existence of his thoughts. He did not admit even his own existence as a first principle. This must be proved from his thinking. Here he imagined he had a foundation for all knowledge. But in rejecting his own existence as a first principle, and other first principles equally entitled to respect, he laid the grounds of universal scepticism, on which Mr. Hume afterwards built with such success. If nothing is self-evident but the existence of individual thought, no man has any evidence of the existence of anything but of himself. Some of his followers never advanced farther than this. The Egoists believed in their own individual existence, but, with matchless fortitude, each of them refused to believe that there is any being in creation but himself.

Now, this is just the spirit of the modern efforts to rest the authority of the books of Scripture, not on the canon ascertained by testimony, but on their internal evidence. For the authority of a book of Scripture they seek a surer foundation than testimony, however unexceptionably ascertained. They reject the solid foundation on which God himself has rested the authority of the canon, and have adopted a foundation that sinks from under the whole building. Like Des Cartes, they may themselves adopt many truths, notwithstanding their foundation will not bear them; but others, like the Egoists, may reject almost any part of the Divine word. This wisdom, then, is both impious and foolish. In pretending to add strength to the bulwarks of God, it takes away their foundation. To reject a sound first principle is equally injurious to truth as to admit a false one. Either of them lays a foundation for error.

The book of Esther abounds with valuable instructions. To rob the Christian of the edification and comfort which it affords, is to do him the most serious injury. When critics find themselves at a loss for a field in which to exercise their ingenuity, let them indulge their vanity on the writings of the ancient Greeks and Romans. Here let them gambol with the most frantic movements, and approach as nearly as they choose to the opposite boundaries of credulity and scepticism; but let them cease from the word of God. Let them not dare to put their unhallowed hands on the ark of Jehovah. Let the children of the Most High possess his word in its utmost extent; let them possess it without addition. The curse of God pursues both him that adds and him that diminishes.

One most conspicuous advantage afforded to the Christian by this book is, that it gives him a commentary to all the events recorded in history, with respect to the rise and fall of empires, the prosperity and adversity of nations, the progress and persecution of the Church of Christ, and the exaltation and degradation of individuals. In reading history, people in general look no farther than to the motives, designs, and tendencies of human action. Some are contented even with the knowledge of facts, without attempting to discover their source or to trace the connection of events. But in the book of Esther the Christian may learn to refer every occurrence in the world to the counsels of God, and to behold him ruling with absolute sway, amidst all the confusion of human agency, over all the purposes and actions of men and devils. In the afflictions of virtue, in the oppression of the righteous, in the prosperity of the wicked, in the insolence of power, in the persecution of truth, the philosopher finds it difficult to defend his god, and cannot defend him without making him different from the God of the Scriptures. He excuses his supineness by bringing him forward to reward virtue in another state, by the unavoidable necessity imposed on omnipotency through the establishment of general laws, from which it is impossible to deviate. But the book of Esther teaches the Christian, that the rise, and progress, and triumph of the man of sin, as well as his decline and fall, are according to the purpose of the Almighty—the All-Wise—the eternal. His glory is secured by the exertions of his enemies, as well as by those of his friends. He raises up Haman and Pharaoh, as well as Esther and Moses. Such a God is too wonderful for the discovery or the approbation of human wisdom. This is too dazzling a light in which to view the Divine character, for any who are not taught of God, and who are not accustomed to submit in the most absolute manner to the decisions of his word. It is only the eagle can gaze on the sun. Many of those who, in some measure, are taught of God, are too weak-sighted to look on him in this blaze of light. They prefer to view him through the dark glasses of some human system of theology. My fellow Christians ! I entreat you, as you value the authority of God, as you regard your own edification, study the book of Esther, and see your God ruling even over sin. Behold him in all the wars of conquerors—in all the intrigues of courts—in all the changes of empires—in all the caprices of monarchs—in all the persecutions of truth—as well as in all the progress of the Gospel.

The book of Esther teaches us to see the hand of God, not only in the great events of the world, but in all the transactions of men. It calls on us to see him in every occurrence of every day in our lives ; and to trust in him for provision, protection, health, comfort, peace, and all the blessings of life. Innumerable dangers are around us every moment ; it is only the arm of God can ward them off from us. The most trifling accident might destroy us, as well as an earthquake; it is the watchfulness of Providence must guarantee our safety. How then is this book calculated to nourish our gratitude, increase our dependence on God, and invigorate our confidence! As we need the Almighty protection in all things, even when we see no danger, so even when the most terrible disasters threaten, he can defend. From how many evils has he delivered us in the course of our lives! How many wonders of Providence may we recount in our own escapes! Christians, study the book of Esther, and view God on your right hand, and on your left, all the day long. See his watchful eye upon you, and his guardian hand around you, both night and day. "He will not suffer thy foot to be moved; he that keepeth thee will not slumber. Behold he that keepeth Israel shall neither slumber nor sleep. The Lord is thy keeper; the Lord is thy shade upon thy right hand. The sun shall not smite thee by day, nor the moon by night. The Lord shall preserve thee from all evil: he shall preserve thy soul. The Lord shall preserve thy. going out and thy coming in from this time forth, and even for evermore."

In Esther's success we find encouragement to undertake the most dangerous service to which duty calls us. We are indeed to count the cost, and be willing to serve the cause of God at the expense even of life. But in this example, let us see that God is able to preserve us in doing his will, even when danger is most appalling. There may be safety in the midst of danger, when we go forward in the path of duty ; but death itself is preferable to disobedience. *If I perish, I perish,* is the spirit in which the people of God ought to encounter the most appalling dangers in doing his will. In this spirit we can die in triumph, or live with joy and a good conscience.

If times of trouble are before us—if God is about to call his people to suffer for his sake, let us in the book of Esther alleviate our sorrow with the consideration that God rules in the storm. He can disperse the darkest clouds ; he can preserve us in the midst of the thunderbolts ; so he can give us peace and joy in the most violent death. Is it no consolation that persecution is by his appointment, and that in the end it will turn out for his glory as well as our good ?

Even persecution may be commissioned to benefit the Church of God. It may effect what prosperity has kept far away. It may bring Christians into one body, as they have the one Lord. Their common sufferings will tend to unite them, and the afflictions of the house of God will tend to its purification. The millions who are Christians only in name, and who now by their union with the people of God, defile the temple, and cramp the exertions of believers, may then take their proper place. The interests, the prejudices, and the habits of Christians combine to keep them in ignorance of the nature of Christ's kingdom, and of the laws and institutions with which he has furnished them. When worldly temptations cease to deceive, Christians may become more tractable, and what they did not learn in the time of their peace, they may soon learn in a time of danger. A man may learn at the stake what he could not see in the pulpit.

The consideration that the whole course of affairs on earth is directed by the overruling hand of Providence, as it is kept so conspicuously before our eyes in this book, may be highly useful to Christians in regulating their zeal in the cause of God. The mountains that lie in the way of the Gospel appear so impassable, that any means that promises to facilitate the passage is sometimes eagerly employed, without reference to the authority of divine appointments. The end is made to sanctify the means; evil is done that good may come; means are employed that God hath not ordained—that God hath forbidden. Any means are supposed warrantable, if it appears that the thing cannot otherwise be effected. It is to this baleful principle that the union of the church with the world owes its origin. The nations of the earth, in all their sins, are made a sort of Christians by name, and the enjoyment of the ordinances appointed only for the people of God. In all the worshipping assemblies in Christendom, separate the disciples, and what a poor figure will they make in the eyes of the world! How would they support the Gospel! To act on this principle would, in the opinion of many, be to banish Christianity from the earth. However reluctant some may be to desecrate the ordinances of Christ, they think they must do it, or suffer Satan to triumph over Christ. They complain of the decay of religion—they pray for better times—they strive to breathe life into the dry bones—they warn sinners of their danger; but still they give them the ordinances of Christ, for they cannot work without them. Numbers are necessary for the existence of a sect; and Christ's ordinances must be misapplied in order to promote his system.

Now I entreat Christians who act on this principle, to consider what an affront it casts on the Head of the church. Who is it that governs the world? Has Jesus given up to the devil the power he received from his Father after his resurrection? Does he not still hold all power in heaven and on earth? does not the book of Esther show that his providence extends to all events? May they not learn here, that their Lord directs the actions even of his enemies to fulfil his will? Look here, and behold a few scattered Jews defending themselves, and destroying their enemies in all the provinces of the Persian empire. In the cause of God, then, let them employ no means but such as are sanctioned by the appointment of Jesus. Let the ark of God itself fall, rather than put a hand to it contrary to Divine authority.

It is from the same principle that such an eagerness is always discovered to enlist the authority of kings and rulers in the cause of Christ, although they themselves may give all the weight of their example to the kingdom of Satan. Christians in general seem to think that there is no hope of protection for Christianity from civil rulers, unless they are nominally embodied in the ranks. For the sanction of power they barter the ordinances of Christ. In the book of Esther let them learn that their Lord is the King of kings and Lord of lords —that he rules in the midst of his enemies—and that he can make the most tyrannical princes the protectors of his people, when he pleases. Ahasuerus, who had by an irreversible decree doomed to destruction the whole Jewish people, was, without any conversion to God, without any proselytism to Judaism, made the most zealous friend that ever appeared in favor of the house of Abraham. He not only with the utmost zeal co-operated for their deliverance from the intended destruction, but gave up to them, to the immense injury of his kingdom, all their enemies in his dominions. He gave them unlimited authority to kill their enemies and spoil their substance.   The kings of the earth are the ministers of God ; as such they ought to be honored ; but give them not the throne of the Lord Jesus Christ.   If they are not Christians by being born again through faith in the great propitiation made on the cross, and walk in newness of life, let them not be called Christians —give them not the ordinances of the house of God.

In the book of Esther the conductors of the various religious societies ought to take a lesson.   I am afraid there are few of them that do not need it. The craft, the management, the bartering of the Christian name with Neologians and heretics for co-operation, money, and countenance, that some of them have employed, would induce one to think that they consider the Lord Jesus Christ to be dethroned, and that his friends must work without him till the restoration.   I rejoice in all the good done by any of them.   I wish I could convince them that they will do the more good the more closely they abide by the means afforded by the Head of the Church.   Jesus rules on the earth as well as in heaven, and those who honor him he will honor to do his will.   What have the Samaritans to do in building the temple of God ?   Has Jesus lost command over the treasures of the earth, that we must have recourse to the bounty of Satan ? He will give us his contribution, no doubt ; but he will have a niche in the edifice, in which his statue must be worshipped. It would be more pleasant for me to be bandying compliments with the religious world, than to incur their displeasure by acting as their censor. But wholesome admonition is better than praise. Though the generality may despise it, some Christians may receive benefit. They may be led to see that in the propagation of the gospel, the Lord Jesus has no need of the countenance or co-operation of his enemies. The book of Esther will teach them that he can effect his purposes, even through those ignorant of him, without embodying them among his disciples.

In the Book of Esther the Christian may see the union of two things apparently irreconcilable— the free agency of man, and the over-ruling appointment of God. Philosophers have exhausted their ingenuity in endeavoring to fathom this abyss; but their line has proved too short. Some have erred with respect to both sides of the question. They have held that actions are not free, and that they are necessary in such a sense as to render man inexcusable in guilt. On this foundation some ground the duty of charity. If a man sins under a necessity of this kind, there is no propriety in blaming him for his conduct. In the book of Esther we may see that man's actions are his own, yet that they are, in another point of view, the appointment of God. We see here that man is accountable and blameable when he sins; yet we see that these very sinful actions are the appointment of God to effect his own purposes.

The philosophers who contend for the freedom of human actions, generally deny the eternal decrees of God; because their wisdom cannot reconcile these two things with one another. And must not the penetration of philosophers fathom the deep things of God? Proud worms! can nothing be true of God, but what your minds can penetrate?

In reading the writings of philosophers on this subject, nothing can be more evident, than that one party has proved that men act freely, and that the other proves as clearly that the foreknowledge of God implies the certainty of all actions as they are foreknown. In so far each is right on his own side, but wrong as to the other. They will fight as long as the devil has use for the discussion, for, on their own principle, the dispute never can be settled. The human mind is not able to fathom the subject; they are struggling to grasp infinity; they are both right, and both wrong; truth lies between them; each of them has a hold of its skirt, but neither of them entirely possesses it; it cannot be seized, except it is believed without being comprehended. This removes it altogether out of the road of the philosopher, for he cannot receive anything for which he cannot account. While the philosophers dispute, and, under the specious name of lovers of wisdom, prove themselves fools, let the Christian, from the book of Esther, behold the freedom of human actions in union with divine appointment. Let him not affect to strut in the buskins of the schools, and pretend to explain what on this subject he receives on the authority of God. Let him receive it, because the word of God exhibits it; not because his wisdom can fathom the depth of the Divine counsels. The most illiterate man of God, who receives with meekness what the Scriptures lay before him, is, with respect to the deepest subjects of philosophy, a greater philosopher than any of the mere sons of science. They may seize truth by the garment and tear away a shred, but the Christian, believing the Divine testimony, possesses the substance. I am sorry to be obliged to remark, that Christians too generally affect the philosopher on this subject. They have separated what God has joined together, because they could not comprehend the union; and, from prepossession in favor of one part of truth, have been led to give up or explain away the other. Some, out of zeal for the doctrine of the freedom of the human will, have, in opposition to the clearest testimony of Scripture, denied the decrees of God; while others, from a false zeal for the honor of the Divine counsels, have denied the freedom of human action. Both of them, inconsistently with their character as Christians, act on the same principle of unbelief with the philosopher. They deny what they cannot comprehend. Like infidels, they assume it as a first principle, that nothing is to be received as truth that is not comprehensible to the mind of man.

When will Christians cease from their own wisdom? when will they in all things submit to the testimony of God? when will they practically admit, that God may know, and therefore call upon them to believe, what they cannot comprehend? Will man never cease to make himself equal with God? will the Christian never learn that he is nothing? Disciple of Jesus, go to the book of Esther, and acquaint yourself with the deepest. point of philosophy. There see the solution of the question that has occupied the wise from the very cradle of philosophy, but which philosophy has never solved—which it is not capable of solving, on any other principle than submission to the testimony of God. Degrade not your Master, my fellow Christians, by modelling his doctrines according to the profane speculations of the schools. If any man will be really wise, let him become a fool in the estimation of the world, that he may be wise in the estimation of his God.

Let us read the book of Esther, and in the view of the overruling government of God, let us console ourselves in contemplating the melancholy prospect of this world, in which the counsels of nations in every age are conducted by the enemies of God. We hear much of Christian nations and Christian rulers; but where is the nation in which the counsels of the ungodly do not prevail? where is the government that is conducted strictly on Christian principles? Statesmen, it is true, seek to manage Christianity like every other state engine, and therefore affect to support it. But where is the assembly of legislators, in which it is visible that the Lord God is feared as he ought to be feared? This is a gloomy subject for the contemplation of the man of God. But let him turn his eyes to the book of Esther, and behold the Lord God omnipotent reigning, and working his will by the very instruments employed by Satan to defeat his purposes. God rules even in the counsels of the ungodly. God will glorify himself even by the very empire of Satan.

It is a heart-rending thing to reflect on the sin and misery that prevail in this world. Let us relieve ourselves, in some measure, by this consideration, that God has done all things according to the counsel of his own will. Is the Almighty disappointed in his work of creation? has Satan prevailed over him because of his strength? or will any real dishonor attach to God by the rebellion of men and angels? Impossible; away with the accursed thought! These clouds before my eyes are dark and lowering—I cannot penetrate that gloom—I see nothing but confusion and wretchedness. The very glory of this world is vanity; its highest enjoyments are unsatisfying. But though I cannot see through this dreadful darkness, I will look beyond it by the eye of faith. God reigns; all things therefore must issue in the glory of his name, and the happiness of his people.